Romans and Barbarians

WISCONSIN STUDIES IN CLASSICS
General Editors
BARBARA HUGHES FOWLER *and* WARREN G. MOON

E. A. THOMPSON
Romans and Barbarians: The Decline of the Western Empire

JENNIFER TOLBERT ROBERTS
Accountability in Athenian Government

H. I. MARROU
A History of Education in Antiquity
Histoire de l'Education dans l'Antiquité, translated by George Lamb
(originally published in English by Sheed and Ward, 1956)

ERIKA SIMON
Festivals of Attica: An Archaeological Commentary

G. MICHAEL WOLOCH
Roman Cities: Les villes romaines by Pierre Grimal, translated
and edited by G. Michael Woloch, together with
A Descriptive Catalogue of Roman Cities
by G. Michael Woloch

WARREN G. MOON, *editor*
Ancient Greek Art and Iconography

Romans
and
Barbarians

*The Decline of the
Western Empire*

E. A. Thompson

The University of Wisconsin Press

Published 1982

The University of Wisconsin Press
114 North Murray Street
Madison, Wisconsin 53715

The University of Wisconsin Press, Ltd.
1 Gower Street
London WC1E 6HA, England

First printing

Printed in the United States of America

For LC CIP information see the colophon

ISBN 0-299-08700-X

Contents

List of Maps   vii

Acknowledgments   ix

1: Introduction: Economic Warfare   3

Part I: Gaul

2: The Settlement of the Barbarians in Southern Gaul   23

3: The Visigoths from Fritigern to Euric   38

Part II: Italy

4: A.D. 476 and After   61

5: The Byzantine Conquest of Italy: Military Problems   77

6: The Byzantine Conquest of Italy: Public Opinion   92

Part III: Noricum

7: The End of Noricum   113

Part IV: Spain

8: Hydatius and the Invasion of Spain   137

9: The Suevic Kingdom of Galicia   161

10. The Gothic Kingdom and the Dark Age of Spain   188

11: Spain and Britain   208

12: Barbarian Collaborators and Christians   230

Appendix: The Visigoths in Aquitaine: Why?   251

Abbreviations   257

Notes   263

Index   311

Maps

The Western Provinces of the Roman Empire   4

Gaul   24

Europe c. 526 A.D.   62

Italy c. 600 A.D.   78

Noricum   114

Spain   138

Acknowledgments

The first and last chapters of this book together with those on Italy and Noricum were written in the Institute from which these Acknowledgments are addressed. I can imagine no more lovely place in which to study and write, and would offer my warmest thanks to the Institute's Director for inviting me to spend the academic year 1979–80 in it.

The two chapters on Gaul were first published respectively in the *Journal of Roman Studies*, xlvi (1956), 65–75, and in *Historia*, xii (1963), 105–26. Those on Spain are reprinted from *Nottingham Mediaeval Studies*, xx (1976), 3–28; xxi (1977), 3–31; xxii (1978), 3–22; and xxiii (1979), 1–21. All these papers are republished almost exactly as they first appeared by kind permission of the Council of the Society for the Promotion of Roman Studies and the editors of *Historia* and *Nottingham Mediaeval Studies*.

Three friends, one in the United States and two in England, Professors Frank M. Clover (Madison, Wisconsin), Robert Markus (Nottingham), and Malcolm Todd (Exeter), have helped me by putting me on the track of publications which I should otherwise have missed, by lending me books and above all, by listening to my endless monologues and soliloquies on the subject of barbarism without showing any outward sign of boredom or impatience. For such kindness, such endurance, I am deeply grateful.

Not least, my warm thanks are due to the University of Wisconsin Press for publishing this book and for the skill and accuracy with which they have printed it.

E. A. Thompson

Institute for Research in the Humanities
University of Wisconsin–Madison
June 1980

Romans and Barbarians

1

Introduction: Economic Warfare

In the days of the Western Roman Empire there was a deep division among the northern barbarians. Leaving aside the Celts in the far west and the Slavs in the remote east, the barbarians were divided into two sharply contrasting groups. In central Europe lived the sedentary, agricultural peoples, nearly all of them speaking Germanic languages or dialects. To this group belonged the Ostrogoths, the Visigoths, Vandals, Sueves, Rugians, Franks, Saxons, and many others. And in the steppe lands of southeastern Europe lived the pastoral nomads, who were not Germanic and who knew little or nothing of agriculture: they lived for the most part off their flocks and herds, though they also traded with the settled peoples at the edge of the steppe. To this second group belonged the Alans and the Huns. (It is important to notice that after the death of Attila the Hun in 453, the term "Hun" became a generic term for the steppe nomads in general, irrespective of whether they were true Huns or not.) One thing these two groups shared. To both alike the Roman Empire was a land of unimaginable riches. Both German and nomad looked upon the wealth and high civilization of the Romans with a mixture of amazement and greed. Whenever we can listen to the barbarians speaking about the Roman Empire, we hear words of awe and envy.

I. BARBARIAN IDEAS OF THE EMPIRE

A strange incident took place when the Roman armies were operating in the interior of Germany in A.D. 5 under the command of the prince Tiberius. "When we had encamped on the nearer bank of the Elbe," writes a man who was there, "and the further bank was gleaming with the armed warriors of the enemy, . . . one of the barbarians, elderly, tall, of distinguished rank (as his style of dress showed), embarked in a canoe hollowed out of a tree trunk — that is the custom there — and steering the craft all by

3

The Western Provinces of the Roman Empire

himself advanced into the middle of the river. There he asked permission
to land on the bank which we were holding under arms and to see the
Caesar. Permission was granted. Then, running his canoe ashore and gazing in silence at the Caesar for a long time, he remarked, 'Our warriors are
mad: though they worship your divine power when you are not here,
when you are present they fear your arms rather than win your trust. But
by your kind permission, Caesar, I have today seen the gods of whom previously I used to hear, and I have neither desired nor experienced any hap-
pier day in my life.' Having obtained permission to touch the Caesar's
hand he got into his little boat and, looking back at the Caesar all the
time, he reached his own people's bank."[1] To this old man the Romans
had about them something of the divine. They were more than human.

4

In A.D. 70, when the free Germans looked across the Rhine at the brash new city of Cologne, crowded with Gauls, Ubian Germans, and Roman exsoldiers and their descendants, they are said to have "hated" it for its growing wealth: they would never make peace with Rome unless the Ubian Germans were expelled from it — or, better still, of course, unless it were thrown open to all Germans alike. Some three hundred years later, in 381, the old Visigothic chieftain, Athanaric, a lifelong enemy of the Empire, came at last to Constantinople a couple of weeks before he died. He was astounded at the sight of the busy, bustling city. "Look," he said, "I am seeing what I often heard of, though I did not believe it." He turned his eyes to one side and the other, gazing at the site of the city, the busy throngs of shipping, the vast walls, the people of many nations, the well-drilled soldiers. At last he could contain himself no longer and cried out, "Surely the emperor is a god upon earth, and whoever lifts up his hand against him is committing suicide." His long life's work of battling against the Romans had been lived in vain. For him, too, as for that nameless old chieftain from beyond the Elbe, the Romans, or at any rate their rulers, were something more than human.[2] A hundred and fifty years later still the envoy of a savage nomad khan of the steppe region of southeastern Europe is said to have remarked to the emperor Justinian, "In your empire it happens that there is a superabundance of everything — including, I suppose, even the impossible." The khan had chased his enemies, poor nomads like himself, across the imperial frontier, but at once regretted that he had done so. He saw that so far from injuring them by driving them off the steppe he had done them the greatest of services, for in the Roman provinces they would enjoy a higher standard of living than he himself could ever hope for. While he would drag out his life in an unproductive wilderness, they "will have the power to traffic in grain, and to get drunk in their wine stores, and to live on the fat of the land. Yes, and they will be able to go into the baths, and to wear gold ornaments, the villains, and will not go short of fine embroidered clothes." The Empire was El Dorado. Any vagabond who was accepted into it could dress himself in gold, eat bread, have a hot bath, and get drunk whenever he pleased. That was civilization indeed![3]

This attitude is enough in itself to account for the majority of the minor raids which troubled the Roman frontiers throughout the centuries of imperial history. And this tendency was reinforced by the nature of the Germanic "retinue," a body of warriors which was supported by the chief and which the chief was obliged to supply with a continuous flow of plunder. If once he could get his men across the frontier, the imperial provinces would present him with infinitely more valuable loot than he could ever hope to pick up among the squalid huts of his fellow Germans. And the

5

Roman authorities never had any trouble enlisting barbarian auxiliaries to serve in their armed forces: life in the imperial forces was much superior to that of the forests and marshes beyond the frontier. But the attractions of plunder or of relatively high pay will not account for the massive invasions of the later Roman Empire, when entire peoples with their women, children, and old folks moved across the Rhine and the Danube.

II. SUPERIORITY OF ROMAN MILITARY TECHNOLOGY

Well might the Germans see the Roman Empire as a land of gold, so primitive was their own society. Greco-Roman civilization was essentially urban. Wherever the Greeks and Romans settled between Britain and the northwest of India they founded cities. The Germans did not live in cities. There was no such thing as a German city in Roman times. Although the Romans sometimes refer to the existence of *oppida* in Germany, the word does not so much mean "towns" as "villages" or "hamlets" or simply "native settlements." There were a few fortified points, but the characteristic habitation of the German was neither the village nor the fortified enclosure but the isolated farmstead, whereas the characteristic habitation of the Roman was a city. In the days of the Roman Empire there stood famous cities on the left bank of the Rhine: they were famous Roman cities. On the right bank was a land of lonely farms or tiny clusters of farmhouses. On the left bank was the powerful Roman imperial state. On the right bank a man still depended for his protection and the preservation of his rights, not on the state (which did not exist there at any time or place during the Roman period) but on his kindred; and the same was true of many of the nomads of the southeast. Accordingly, when barbarians joined the Roman army they were sometimes unable to understand the workings of the Roman state power. Thus, when Belisarius was voyaging to Africa in 533 and had reached Abydos three nomad soldiers in his army got drunk together. One of them was teasing the other two, whose sense of humour was limited. They killed him, and Belisarius had the two killers impaled. There was an outburst of anger among the nomads and especially among the kinsmen of the two dead men. They had two complaints: (i) they had not entered into an alliance with the Romans so as to be subject to Roman law, and (ii) in their native customs no such punishment as this was inflicted for homicide. According to Procopius, Belisarius was obliged to make a long speech in order to pacify them.[4]

But the Germans did not always grasp how colossal was the military power of the Romans. They might have been somewhat more diffident about attacking the provinces if they had been able to understand that in comparison with their own resources those of the Empire were all but inexhaustible. Julius Caesar was not the only Roman who was obliged to point out to them that, even if the barbarians won a success here and a victory there, the Romans would and could quickly replace their losses—and replace them with even more powerful forces than before—and could go on replacing them over and over again, indefinitely. It was only at the end of their revolt in A.D. 70 that the Batavians began to see their real position as rebels against Rome. They decided at last that "they must not protract a ruinous struggle any longer. A single nation could not put an end to the enslavement of the whole world. What had they achieved by the slaughter of the legions and the burning of their camp except that other legions, more numerous and more powerful, were summoned to take their place? If they challenged the Roman people in arms, how tiny a part of the human race were the Batavians!" And nearly five hundred years later the same argument was being used.[5] The Germans might indeed score a victory over the Romans: in A.D. 9 they won one of the decisive battles of world history in the Teutoberg Forest in northwestern Germany, expelling the Romans from that part of Germany which lies between the Rhine and the Elbe and destroying in the process more than one-tenth of the legionary strength of the entire Empire. But that was due to Roman mismanagement. The German kindreds could no more have overthrown the Roman Empire of Augustus or Marcus Aurelius or Constantine the Great than the Scottish clansmen of 1745 could have overwhelmed the England of King George II. But later on, the position became different.

Even the great Persian Empire itself, the one power that could meet the Romans on something like equal terms, was no match for it in military techniques. When the emperor Septimius Severus defeated one of his rivals in 193, numbers of troops from the beaten army fled to Persia; and many of these men were technicians. They settled down in Persia and not only taught the Persians how to use weapons which they had not used before but also showed them how to make these weapons for themselves. Presumably the weapons in question were *ballistae* (catapults) of some kind. The result was that the Persians had higher hopes of victory now than formerly when they engaged the solid ranks of a Roman army; and the historian who reports this matter looks upon it with grave concern.[6] A later writer goes out of his way to record at length how a Roman called Busas taught the nomadic Avars how to make a type of siege-engine called an *helepolis,* a "city-taker," which they could not otherwise have made.[7]

The emperor Domitian sent not only money to Decebalus, king of the Dacians in what is now Rumania, but also "craftsmen of all kinds of crafts, both civil and military," and he undertook to keep sending them for an indefinite period in the future; and these craftsmen may have made a substantial contribution to the growth of Dacian power which set in immediately after. For when Trajan defeated the Dacians in 102 and captured a quantity of their arms and siege-engines, he was careful to compel them to hand over not only their personal weapons but also the rest of their artillery *together with the men who had made it.* There can be little doubt that these men included Roman prisoners, deserting Roman soldiers, and the craftsmen whom Domitian had supplied to the Dacians; and indeed the best part of Decebalus's army consisted of men whom he had persuaded to come over to him from the Empire.[8]

In Julius Caesar's day the inhabitants of Gaul were astounded by the military techniques of the Roman army. The Atuatuci were said to be descendants of some of the Cimbri and Teutones who had stayed behind in their old homes when the two peoples as a whole had invaded Gaul and Italy half a century before: and in Caesar's time they lived on the plain of Hesbaye on the northern bank of the Meuse. When Caesar besieged them in one of their fortresses in 57 B.C. and his men began to build a siege-tower at a distance from the wall, the defenders roared with laughter and shouted jeers and taunts at the Romans for building so enormous a structure so far away from the wall: the feeble hands and puny strength of the Roman pygmies would never be able to bring this gigantic contraption into action. But when they saw the great tower in motion and bearing down upon them, crowded with armed men, as high as the wall and higher, their nerve broke: the gods must be fighting for men who could make such huge machines and move them so swiftly. The Atuatuci surrendered to Caesar at once.[9] In their amazement at Roman technical capacity the Atuatuci were not alone. From time to time the mere sight of what the Romans could make, and particularly the speed with which they could build their bridges and enormous siege-engines, would terrify the Celtic armies of Gaul into surrender or would break their will to resist.[10] On every frontier the barbarians sooner or later came to know their inferiority.

The Germans were at a lower stage of material and social development than the Gauls, and they were even more impressed by the equipment of the legionaries. And long familiarity with the Romans on the frontier and even within the frontier did not enable them wholly to overcome their fears of Roman military techniques. The Batavians supplied several regiments of troops to the Roman army in the first century A.D.; and their turbulent, unreliable behaviour together with their high military value were a constant source of anxiety to Roman army officers. Yet as late as A.D. 69, some eighty years after they are first known to have served in the Roman forces, they were taken aback by at least one Roman military device. This was the *tolleno,* a contrivance which was used to defend a besieged city or fort. It consisted of a huge beam set upright on the town wall with a crosspiece swivelling at the top. One arm of the crosspiece was considerably longer than the other, and it had on the end a hideous spike or hook. By manoeuvring a weight on the shorter arm of the *tolleno* the Romans could rapidly swing the longer arm with the hook towards the ground outside the wall, plunge it into the flesh of one (or more than one) of the attackers, and whisk him up to the top of the wall before the astounded gaze of his relatives. Even the Batavians, long accustomed though they were to Roman military methods, were thrown into panic by this strange engine, towering high above them into the sky, its talon poised, ready to swoop like some dreadful bird.[11]

Roman technical superiority was not confined to strictly military matters. In 422 a Romano-Persian war broke out not only because the Persians interfered with Roman merchants but also because they refused to return the skilled gold miners whom they had hired from the Roman Empire. And Roman technicians and industrial products were no more welcome in Persia than they were in distant India, for even there their reputation was exceedingly high.[12] In the reign of Tiberius II (578–82) the Chagan of the nomadic Avars asked the emperor to send him builders so as to build him a bath house. But personal hygiene was not the uppermost thought in the Chagan's mind when he made this request: as soon as the builders arrived in his country he forced them to build, not a bath house, but a bridge over the Danube so that he might be able to cross the river without trouble and plunder the Roman provinces on the other side. On the other hand, cleanliness was of more consequence to Onegesius, Attila's right-hand man, for he did indeed want a bath house, and he forced a war prisoner from Sirmium to construct one for him. No Hun could have built a stone bath house.[13]

Apart from technicians and technical skill the Romans also had at their disposal far greater quantities of the raw materials essential to war than had any of their neighbours. Thus, when the emperor Caracalla about the year 215 made a sham offer to marry the daughter of the king of Persia and to join Rome and Persia into a single empire, he suggested as one of the advantages that would result from this union the circumstance that Persian spices and their widely admired textiles would be freely exchanged for the products of Roman mines and for Roman industrial commodities. Caracalla pointed out that if his offer were accepted the Persians would have an abundance of Roman metals and industrial products which at present reached them only in small quantities, when traders smuggled them across the frontier. Now, Caracalla had no intention of carrying out his alleged plan to marry the Persian king's daughter and to make the two empires into one united empire, as the Persians soon had good reason to know. But his description of what would have resulted from it was true enough and deceived his victims. Again, in 337, when a later Persian king planned to make war on the Romans, he found that, although he had sufficient men in his army, he had not enough iron to equip them. "His power," according to a Roman orator, "was crippled by lack of military machines." So he sent an embassy to Constantine the Great to negotiate the purchase of a quantity of iron. The Persians' own mineral resources, in so far as they had developed them, were unequal to a prolonged and full-scale war; and they therefore turned to the Roman Empire, which they knew would have a surplus of iron for export. Although Constantine was well aware of why the Persian king wanted iron, he nevertheless supplied it. He then died, and his successor saw Romans killed by Roman metal.[14]

The imperial authorities were careful not to allow any knowledge of the *ballistae,* the catapults, of the Roman army to reach the barbarians if this could be avoided. Moreover, of the entire defensive system of the Empire, the legions alone used the *ballistae.* In fact, only a single fort has been identified in which auxiliary troops were allowed to use this form of artillery. It was a British fort. In A.D. 220 the fort at High Rochester (Bremenium) in Northumberland was garrisoned by Vardulli from northern Spain; and they were allowed to use *ballistae,* as inscriptions and excavation have shown. This artillery covered the northern and western approaches to the fort and fired stone balls varying from 100 to 175 pounds in weight. We do not know why the imperial authorities allowed this exception to the rule.[15]

III. RESTRICTED TRADE BETWEEN ROMANS AND BARBARIANS

The limitations of the barbarians' methods of war were well known, of course, to the imperial government. That government reinforced its military superiority with two political measures: (i) they banned the export of strategical materials from the Empire to its enemies, and (ii) they specified the places on the frontier where barbarians might trade with Romans, trade elsewhere being illegal: trade across the frontier must be controlled.

From early in the third century, if not before, it was a capital crime to export armour, weapons, horses, beasts of burden, money, whetstones, iron, grain, salt, or anything that might be of military value (including hostages) to the enemy.[16] Of course, these goods were sometimes smuggled across the frontier, as Caracalla knew (p. 9 above). In the years 370–75 wine and oil and at about the same time gold were added to the list. What is of great interest is that the ban at this date and later was placed upon exports, not to the "enemy," but to the barbarian world in general, whether at war with the Empire or not.[17] In 420 precautions were taken to ensure that the prohibited goods did not reach the barbarians by sea: careful enquiries were made by officials on the spot into each departing ship's destination.[18] In the previous year a remarkable event had taken place. Asclepiades, bishop of the Chersonese (Crimea), had petitioned the emperor to free from prison men who had been convicted of betraying to the barbarians the art of shipbuilding, which had hitherto been unknown to them. The emperor freed them but threatened the death penalty to anyone who acted similarly in the future.[19] The identity of the barbarians in question is obscure, and few will believe that the Hun nomads of South Russia had ambitions to become pirates.[20] In 456 the Eastern emperor Marcian stopped a gap in the regulations. He enacted that it was a capital crime to sell to barbarian envoys, when they came to Constantinople or any other Roman city, or to any barbarian arriving on any pretext, weapons of any sort—breastplates, shields, bows, arrows, swords, or arms of any description whatsoever, or missiles, or iron, wrought or unwrought. Such a sale or gift would be considered dangerous to the security of the Empire and an act of treason. The goods of anyone who perpetrated such a sale would be confiscated and the vendor subject to capital punishment.[21] Procopius speaks of this law a hundred years later and remarks that it was still in force in his day. He observes that as a result of it the peoples of the Red Sea area (whom he is discussing at the relevant part of his book) were unable to purchase iron or any other metal from the Romans. He speaks, too, of the measures taken by Justinian on the Hellespont and the Bosphorus to "search out whether anything of a kind which it is illegal to convey from the land of the Romans to the enemy, was being sent to the barbarians."[22]

The author of the *Expositio Totius Mundi* tells of the merchants of Nisibis and Edessa who were very rich as a result of acting as middlemen between Persia and the Roman Empire: they dealt in all the products of that area "except bronze and iron, because it is not permitted to give bronze and iron to the enemy."[23]

The matter is of greater importance than might appear at first sight. Even the Persian king was unable to arm his forces adequately for a full-scale attack on the Romans in 337 (p. 10 above). Yet his resources were enormous in comparison with those of the northern barbarians. Thus, a minor people called the Buri, during their war with the Emperor Commodus late in the second century, were actually obliged to beg the Romans, not once but many times, to grant them a truce so that they might reequip themselves with weapons before continuing the struggle! In 562 the envoys of the nomadic Avars reached Constantinople and made it their business to buy a supply of weapons there, for they were contemplating an immediate campaign against the Romans. But they were out of luck. The

Romans knew very well what they intended to do; and so they accepted payment for the arms but then arrested the envoys and took the weapons back from them.[24]

Cases of people who were allowed to trade indiscriminately along the frontier and to penetrate freely into the Roman hinterland were very few and were considered worthy of remark by Roman observers. The Hermunduri, a Germanic people whose territory touched the imperial frontier in the neighbourhood of Regensburg on the Danube, were a people of whose "loyalty" the Roman government had assured itself. Therefore, they alone of the Germans in the middle of the first century A.D. were permitted not only to trade on the Roman bank of the Danube but even to cross the river at any point they chose and to travel without surveillance into the interior of the province of Raetia and to sell their wares and to buy goods wherever they pleased. They were free, if they so wished, even to enter Augsburg (Augusta Vindelicorum), a trading city lying on the route which led from Italy over the Brenner Pass to the Rhine armies. They could see the houses and villas of the Romans, an advantage which was of considerable military value to raiding parties, if they should send any out against the provincials. We do not know why the Hermunduri were so privileged, except that they were regarded as "loyal" to the Romans.[25] The other Germanic peoples may have used a different word to describe the attitude of the Hermunduri—treachery.

Traders of other Germanic peoples, if they were given permission to enter the Roman provinces at all, were disarmed at the frontier and travelled under a military escort, and found their activities confined to the fortresses along the frontier. They were not allowed to travel far into the interior; and so, during their visits to the provinces, they would see little more than the military camps and the weapons of the soldiers—a sight that might cause potential raiders to think twice about their raids. Accordingly, the Tencteri complained to the people of Cologne in A.D. 70 of the indignity of being allowed to cross the Rhine only when unarmed, and of moving about under surveillance, and of having to pay a toll to enter Roman territory at all. And the men of Cologne, in spite of their difficult position in the turbulent year 70, agreed to abolish the toll and the payment of customs dues on goods entering or leaving the Empire through their city; but they would not raise the ban on the Germans' crossing the Rhine by night or when carrying arms. In fact, the traders of the Hermunduri enjoyed a unique privilege in the first century A.D. in being allowed to go wherever they pleased and to hawk their goods from town to town, from villa to villa. But it is thought that they did not enjoy their good fortune for very long, though the Marcomanni of Bohemia appear to have had free trading rights late in the second century, and the Visigoths won them by force of arms for a number of years in the middle of the fourth century.[26]

Such restrictions on the right of entry into the Roman provinces are mentioned more than once in our accounts of the Marcomannic wars of Marcus Aurelius late in the second century. In 169–70 Marcus in Pannonia found it politic to make a generous treaty with the Quadi and others; but in spite of his generosity he refused them free access to Roman markets "in case the Marcomanni and Iazyges, whom the Quadi had sworn not to receive or to allow pass through their territory, should mingle with them and pass themselves off as Quadi and so spy on Roman positions and buy what they wanted." Later Marcus Aurelius made a treaty with the Marcomanni and Iazyges themselves; and in the case of the Marcomanni he cancelled their right of trading freely along the frontier—we do not know when they had won this privilege—and he defined "the places and days for mutual trade." He released the Iazyges from all the conditions that had been imposed on them earlier "except those relating to their assembling together and their trading." He did not allow them the use of their boats on the Danube, and he refused them permission to set foot on the islands in that river. Moreover, they could pass through the province of Dacia beyond the Danube to trade with the Roxolani only when the governor of Dacia gave them leave to do so.[27]

Valens was adhering to a well-established Roman practice, then, when in 369 after a victory over the Visigoths he confined Visigothic traders to two cities along the lower Danubian frontier. (It is unfortunate that the names of the two places have not been recorded.) For some years the Visigoths had had free access to the frontier cities indiscriminately, but according to the Roman government they had used these trading facilities to inflict damage on the provincials. Now, the trade had been profitable to both sides alike, both to Romans and to Goths—and there is reason to think that some large Roman landowners had been concerned in the trade—so that Valens's measure brought serious loss to the traders of the cities from which the Visigoths were now debarred, just as Diocletian, when he confined the Persian trade to Nisibis on the Tigris in 298, can have won few thanks in Palmyra and Bostra. The interests of traders, now as often, took second place to the government's strategical policy. This action of Valens was not isolated on the northern frontier in the fourth century. In 371 a Roman officer on the Danube caused his troops to erect a fort (*burgus,* as he calls it) in northern Pannonia "the name of which was Commercium, for which reason also it was built," a phrase that doubtless means that in this region (near Gran) the barbarians from beyond the Danube were permitted to trade only in Commercium. (The fort incidentally was completed in forty-eight days.) We happen to know that the chief import from the barbarians on this part of the frontier, the Sarmatians, was slaves.[28] And archaeology has revealed other places—such as Seligenstadt on the Main—to which barbarian traders resorted.[29]

Similar restrictions were still enforced in the fifth century. On the eastern frontier Roman as well as Persian merchants were confined to Nisibis, Callinicus, and Artaxata: otherwise, military secrets might be given away. Goods merchanted elsewhere were liable to be confiscated, and the traders sent into exile. In the sixth century the trade was still restricted to Nisibis and Daras.[30] Far away, at a place in Africa called Arzugis, the local barbarians swore by their own gods to be well behaved. Their oath was delivered to the decurion in charge of the frontier or to a tribune, who then gave them a written certificate that they had taken the oath. These immigrant workers intended to become porters or harvest-watchers.[31] (Their presence raised agonizing questions for a correspondent of St. Augustine: do not these barbarians pollute the harvest by swearing an oath by false gods? If then the grain is made into flour and if this flour is baked into bread and if the bread is eaten by a Christian, is not that Christian defiled? This man undoubtedly crossed his bridges miles before he came to them.) It has to be admitted that none of the Christian Roman emperors was so Christian as to close the barbarian markets on Sundays, as mediaeval rulers sometimes did.

There were several reasons for this long continued policy of restricting trade so as to make it easy to supervise, and these reasons were based on strategical needs. There is not the slightest hint in any of our authorities that they were designed to protect home-produced commodities. One reason was the need to prevent the export of arms which might strengthen the barbarians. I have already mentioned the Roman fear in 169–70 that if the barbarians were permitted to cross the frontier they might "buy what they wanted" (p. 13 above). One of the barbarians' chief wants was likely to be weapons and armour. Another was the food which might keep a future raiding party in the field when their own meagre food surplus would soon have been exhausted.[32] Again, the traders might well turn out in the end to be not traders only but warriors and plunderers as well; for the Romans had long experience of traders who had been admitted to their frontier towns. And it is true that whenever we catch a glimpse of Germans in the Roman towns their behaviour is seen to be turbulent and lawless.[33] Or again the traders might bring home across the frontier detailed information about Roman defences and troop movements. And they might acquire that precise geographical knowledge which would enable future raiders to strike without loss of time at rich villas or other desirable prizes, when without this knowledge they might be obliged to waste time in looking for sources of booty and food and might perhaps even exhaust their food supply before finding new ones. But Roman traders, if they could hawk their goods beyond the eastern frontier, might also give away military secrets; and so, it was not only Persian traders but Roman ones as well who were confined to Nisibis, Callinicus, and Artaxata (p. 14 above). The Romans themselves had good reason to know the military value of the information which traders might give; and Julius Caesar was not the only Roman commander who turned their reports to good account.

In the year 468–69, years after the fall of the Hun empire, an embassy arrived in Constantinople from the "children of Attila." Its purpose was to negotiate a peace treaty which would reopen the market towns along the Roman frontier to the Huns; but the emperor Leo I saw no reason why the benefits of Roman trade should be given to a people who had done incalculable harm to the Empire, and the embassy was a failure.[34] The demand that the markets should be restored gives us information of importance. At some date before 468 the Eastern government had felt itself strong enough to close the market towns to the Huns, whether on the frontier or anywhere else. This measure is likely to be connected with Marcian's law of 456 reaffirming the ban on the export of weapons (p. 11 above). And it would hardly be too much to say that the Eastern Empire finished off the exhausted strength of the Huns by stopping them from acquiring Roman weapons and from buying and selling in the Roman towns. After 468 the remnants of Attila's Huns are hardly heard of again.

So the Romans defended their frontiers not only with legions and fortresses but also with trade bans and the prohibition of exports of goods of military value. But no armies or defence works, no embargoes or restrictions on trade prevented the terrible series of events which began late in the year 376.

IV. MAJOR INVASIONS OF THE EMPIRE

The major invasions of the imperial provinces occurred in three great waves.

(i) In the autumn of the year 376 alarming rumours began to circulate in the provinces south of the lower Danube. It was said that new and unusually widespread disturbances had begun among the northern barbarians: all the peoples between the Hungarian plains and the Black Sea were on the move. They had been driven abruptly from their homes and were now roving about with their families north of the great river.

The Roman commanders on the southern bank of the Danube were sceptical of these rumours. Their experience told them that nothing unusual could be afoot. Wars among the barbarians in those parts of the world were rarely heard of in the Empire until they were over or until the combatants had patched up a truce. And yet the rumours persisted. Then came envoys from the uprooted peoples, begging that they should be admitted into the provinces. So, after all, the nations *were* on the move. This may have been a surprise to the imperial officers, but it was a pleasant surprise. Here was an unexpected supply of new recruits for the army. The Emperor Valens would now be able to accept gold from his provincials instead of recruits, for rich landowners preferred to part with gold rather than with agricultural labourers, who were in short supply; and so, by enlisting these new barbarians into his forces, the emperor would benefit the treasury and the army alike. It was all very satisfactory, so much so that various officials were sent with carts to transport the expected hordes of refugees from the Danube to wherever they were required. The refugees arrived in ever greater numbers. The Roman officers, with the personal permission of the emperor, ferried company after company of them across the Danube, day after day, night after night, until tens of thousands had crossed. Others of the barbarians made rafts of their own, or hollowed out tree trunks, and so made their own way across. But those who tried to swim across — and they were many — were drowned, for the river was swollen after the recent heavy rains. The officers tried to count the vast numbers of the refugees, but the task was hopeless. The barbarians were beyond counting, though a somewhat later guess — and it seems to have been nothing more than a guess — put the number at not far short of 200,000. The figure is not impossible.

After a time came further news: the enormous commotion had been caused by the arrival in Europe of a people whom no one had ever heard of before. They were called the "Huns." In lightning campaigns these had smashed the huge empire of Ermanaric in what is now the Ukraine. They had gone on to outmanoeuvre the Visigothic leader Athanaric (p. 5 above) in the present Rumania. Riding hard through a moonlit night they suddenly appeared twenty miles from where Athanaric had last heard of them. The Visigoths were stunned by the surprise of the attack. There was no resistance. Athanaric and a few followers made their escape to the foothills of the Transylvanian Alps, but the bulk of the Visigoths fled to the north bank of the Danube. And so it was that in the autumn of 376, in abject fear, they had begged to be admitted into the safety of the imperial provinces. At all costs they must escape from this "race of men which had never been seen before, which had arisen from some secret corner of the earth, and was sweeping away and destroying everything that came in its way." The Huns' attack was "like a whirlwind of snow in the high mountains."[35]

16

So the Roman officers' sceptical attitude towards the rumours had been misplaced. The arrival of the Huns caused the instant destruction of the empire of the Ostrogoths and uprooted the Visigoths from the homes where they had lived relatively peacefully for a century. But no one in those autumn days of 376 could have known that the appearance of the Huns and the arrival of the panic-stricken Goths on the north bank of the lower Danube was also the beginning of the end for the Western Roman Empire itself.

The Visigoths went on to win the battle of Adrianople in 378. Drifting westwards they took Rome itself in 410, exactly 800 years after it had last been captured by a foreign enemy. And in 418 they settled on the western seaboard of Gaul in circumstances which will occupy us at length later on (pp. 23 ff. below). They were the first of the major barbarian invaders whose nobility, instead of wishing merely to loot the Roman villas and to burn them, formed a much better ambition: they would live in them as landowners in the Roman manner. The tendency of the leaders of the barbarian peoples to change sides and to accommodate themselves to Roman interests, political and other, is one of the most remarkable phenomena of the times. Instead of overthrowing the Roman Empire, they would become part of it (pp. 38 ff. below).

(ii) The second great wave of invasion began on the night of 31 December 406, when tens of thousands of Vandals, Alans, and Sueves began to cross the Rhine in the neighbourhood of Mainz. We do not know what had set these peoples in motion. It may have been a westward drive of the Huns into central Europe, though there is no satisfactory evidence for such a movement. At any rate, for three years the invaders turned much of Gaul into a vast "funeral pyre," as a contemporary put it.[36] As they marched towards the English Channel they caused a panic in Britain; but then they turned southwards, crossed the Pyrenees in the autumn of 409, and settled in Spain. After twenty years the Vandals and what was left of the Alans crossed the Straits of Gibraltar and in due course occupied Africa, the most destructive military action of the entire fifth century. But the Sueves remained behind in Spain, and by a stroke of extraordinary good luck we have a chronicle which gives a detailed account of events in the Iberian peninsula from late in the fourth century to the year 469. (If only we had such a chronicle for British affairs!) We shall therefore look in detail at the Sueves as they established a kingdom—a kingdom that was independent of Rome—in the northwest of Spain. There they maintained their freedom for somewhat less than 200 years. The Vandal kingdom in Africa was not so long-lived: after 105 years it was overwhelmed by the armies of Justinian.

(iii) The third massive invasion of the imperial provinces hit the middle

Danubian frontier after the collapse of Attila's empire in 454 and the following years. Throngs of half-starved peoples were let loose on the imperial frontier searching for land on which they could settle and resume the life which their conquest by the Huns had so rudely interrupted. Many of these peoples were fragmented. The Ostrogoths were divided into several groups. Most of the Rugi, whom we shall study later on (pp. 124 ff. below), came eventually to live north of the Danube outside the frontier of the Roman province of Noricum; but a lesser group settled near the towns of Bizye and Arcadiopolis not very far from Constantinople, and we see them going into action in 484.[37] The East Roman government was obliged to protect its frontier, and it did so by setting these starving men at each other's throats. To some they offered land and ready capital with which to stock it. Thus, the Gepids occupied "the whole of Dacia" and wanted nothing more from Constantinople except "peace and annual payments." They received these subsidies with the result that there was usually peace between them and the Romans until the middle of the sixth century. That is why so little is known about such an important people as the fifth-century Gepids: land and regular subsidies from the Roman government were enough to cause them to drop out of history almost entirely.[38] Why the Gepids should have received this favoured treatment, we do not know. Others were not so lucky.

It was useless for any one of these peoples to seize land in the provinces without the consent of the government—even if they had the military strength to do so. In addition to land they had to have seed corn and capital to see themselves through the early years of their settlement; and forcible seizure of land would not provide these. Now, the Ostrogoths were faced with the same problems as confronted all the other shattered peoples who had recently been the "slaves" of Attila: they, too, must have land together with some immediate capital to enable them to resume a peaceful life. In fact, they received land from the Emperor Marcian (450–57) in Pannonia—and there we shall find them when we come to study St. Severinus (p. 124 below)—and he also paid them annual subsidies for a while; but the withdrawal of these "gifts" would compel them to attack other provinces.[39] Their leader then was Walamer, and he frankly admitted that he had attacked the provinces because without the "gifts" his men lacked the very necessities of life (A.D. 459).[40] Indeed, even when the subsidies, which amounted to 300 pounds of gold arrived regularly, the Ostrogoths were still unable to support themselves; and they were reduced to attacking and plundering other barbarians beyond the imperial frontier.[41] Another band of Ostrogoths is actually found c. 467 making common cause with some of their old oppressors, the Huns, in an effort to extort land from the Eastern government. A Roman force, one of whose leaders, Ostrys, was himself an Ostrogoth, eventually starved them into submission.[42] But if the Ostrogoths were sometimes obliged to attack others, others for identical reasons sometimes found occasion to attack them; and their frontiers were crossed more than once by parties of Suevian and Scirian cattle-raiders.[43] (The relationship between these Sueves and those who were now settled in Spain is unknown.) The necessity for unending cattle and plunder raids sometimes led to fairly large-scale wars, like that which culminated in 469 in the battle of the (unidentified) river Bolia, where the Ostrogoths defeated a coalition of Sueves, Gepids, Rugi, and others, all as needy and hungry as themselves.[44] But in the end these activities defeated their own purpose. The slaughter of cattle and the destruction of property reached such proportions that towards the year 470 the entire region of the middle Danube began to starve. Of the Ostrogoths we hear that their supplies not only of food but even of clothing began to fail them, and "peace began to be impossible to men whom war had long provided with means of support." They had been living on plunder and robbery, and they had practically no productive means of their own.[45] And in 473 famine was raging again among at least one group of them.[46] The solution of their problems came only in 489 when with the consent of the emperor Zeno they marched to Italy to overthrow Odoacer, the first barbarian king of Italy, and to take his place. On pp. 77 ff. below we shall see something of what happened to them in Italy.

The invasion of 376, although it began on the lower Danube, robbed the Roman Empire of Gaul south of the Loire. The invasion of 406, although it began on the Rhine, robbed the Empire of part of Spain and the whole of Africa. The invasion of 455 removed Italy itself from the control of the emperors at Constantinople, or at any rate culminated in the work of Odoacer, who had made Italy *de facto,* but not *de jure,* an almost independent kingdom. We shall look first at Gaul, then at Italy and Noricum to the north of it, and finally at Spain.

I. Gaul

2

The Settlement of the Barbarians
in Southern Gaul

In 418 the patrician Constantius recalled the Visigoths from Spain and settled them in the province of Aquitanica Secunda (on the western seaboard
of Gaul between the mouth of the Garonne and that of the Loire) and in
some neighbouring *civitates*.[1] Where these neighbouring cities lay is not
certain. One of them was Toulouse in Narbonensis Prima, and this became
the capital of the Visigothic kings. Salvian writing in 440–41 seems to imply that the Visigoths controlled Novempopulana as well as Aquitanica
II.[2] That is an exaggeration, but it may well be that the additional cities
granted to the Visigoths over and above Aquitanica II lay immediately
south of the Garonne. And this is in some measure confirmed by the fact
that in 439 Orientius, Bishop of Auch, acted as the Visigothic king's ambassador to Litorius and Aëtius.[3] We may conclude that in addition to
Aquitanica the Visigothic kings controlled a strip of land south of the Garonne running from Toulouse to the ocean, but this did not extend to the
Pyrenees. Moreover, they did not control any land north of the Loire.[4]
Whether they allowed themselves to be dispersed uniformly over the
whole of their territory or whether they were concentrated in more or less
dense settlements in restricted parts of their new kingdom is obscure.[5]
When they were defeated and driven from most of their Gallic kingdom in
507 by the Franks of Clovis they retreated to Spain; and in Spain they did
not disperse over all the peninsula. A map of those of their cemeteries
which date from the sixth century or earlier shows that they settled between the upper reaches of the rivers Ebro and Tagus in the triangle between the towns of Palencia, Toledo, and Calatayud, that is to say, in the
province of Segovia and in the surrounding provinces of Madrid, Toledo,
Palencia, Burgos, Soria, and Guadalajara.[6] But this throws little light on
the position in Gaul from 418 to 507.

In 443 the Roman government, of which the effective leader was

Gaul

Aëtius, summoned the remnants of the Burgundians from Upper Germany and settled them in Savoy.[7] Unhappily, there is no evidence to indicate the precise limits of Savoy at this date, and we can only say that it lay between the Lake of Geneva, the Rhone, and the Alps, that it was extensive and that it included a considerable number of cities.[8] In 456 after the fall of the Emperor Avitus the Burgundians with the consent of the Visigoths expanded over a further area of Gaul and divided the land with the Gallic senators who lived in the region in question.[9] There is a late tradition that the Romans of the provinces of Lugdunensis invited the Burgundians to settle among them, and although this is absurdly dated by our authority to the reign of Valentinian I the tradition itself seems genuine.[10] A second extension of Burgundian territory took place in the reign of King Gundobad (c. 480–516), who mentions it in one of his laws.[11] Archaeological traces of the Burgundians in the period before the destruction of their kingdom in 534 have been found at half a dozen places in the Département of Côte d'Or, at one place in Saône-et-Loire, and at one place in Ain.[12]

Finally, two groups of Alans were settled in southern Gaul in the first half of the fifth century. One of these groups under its king, Goar, was given land in the neighbourhood of Orleans by Aëtius, and another led by Sambida was planted in the *agri deserti* around Valence in 440.[13] In all these cases the barbarians were settled on the land as federates: the settlements were designed essentially to serve military purposes. In return for their land the federates were obliged to defend Roman interests from attack. In each case except the last the settlement was based on the principle of *hospitalitas,* i.e. the barbarian *hospes* received two-thirds of the arable on a Roman estate, one-half of the pasture and woodland and so on.[14]

It is of the first importance to understand that the settlement of the barbarians was an act of purely Roman policy. It was not an act of conquest: it was not imposed on the Romans. The case of the Visigothic settlement in Aquitanica II requires some discussion in this connexion. The somewhat surprising fact is that even when the Visigoths had been living in Wallachia and Transylvania in the fourth century they had been so dependent on Roman trade that they could not live without it. In 367–69 Valens fought a war with the Visigoths beyond the lower Danube. In 367 he took the initiative by crossing the river and marching to and fro in Gothia, but he could not bring his enemy to battle: the Visigoths retired before his army into the foothills of the Transylvanian Alps and into the many woods and swamps scattered over their land. In 368 Valens was unable even to enter Gothia; for the Danube was abnormally flooded in that year. In 369, however, the Visigoths did not repeat their successful strategy of 367. They faced the emperor in open battle, and were routed. They begged for peace, and the war was over.[15] What was the reason for this disastrous change of strategy? Our excellent authority for these campaigns, Ammianus Marcellinus, says that Valens had broken off all trading relations between the enemy and the Roman frontier provinces at the beginning of the war, and had maintained the ban throughout the three successive years. Consequently, the Visigoths were reduced to great hardship and distress "owing to their extreme lack of the necessities of life." Ammianus also says that they were unnerved by the emperor's long stay in their country, and their will to continue with the evasive strategy may have been further undermined if the presence of the Romans caused them to lose some of their crops and cattle in 367 and 369, as it certainly must have done. But Ammianus does not imply that either the loss of crops and cattle or the stopping of the payment to them of subsidies by the imperial government was a major factor in bringing about their extreme lack of the necessities of life: this hardship was primarily due to the prohibition of trade with the Romans. An immediate end to the war and an immediate restoration of trading facilities had become essential if many of the Visigoths were not to perish of starvation. As their social life was then organized they could not exist without the goods which they imported from the Roman Empire.[16] Now when the Visigoths were moving about the Roman provinces in the years 376–418 their productive capacity will not have been higher than it was in 369, and it will often have been lower; for at some times during this period they had no land at all which they could cultivate as their own. In other words, their need for trade with the Romans was as imperative in the days of Athaulf and Wallia as it had been in the time of Athanaric and Ulfila. This was a fact of which the Roman government was well aware, and in 414 it suited them to make practical use of their knowledge. Constantius with his headquarters at Arles set up a naval blockade of the coast of Gallia Narbonensis, where the Visigoths then were, and stringently forbade all sea-trade with the Visigoths.[17] Athaulf's settlement in Narbonensis collapsed dramatically and at once. His men fled to Barcelona. The blockade was maintained in Spain, and the Visigoths were reduced to extreme famine conditions.[18] In vain they sought to cross over into Africa, as Alaric had tried to do in 410. Then at last in 416 they capitulated in despair to the Romans.[19] In return for 600,000 measures of grain they undertook to restore Placidia and to fight as federates against the other barbarians in Spain. It was indeed a *pax optima* for the Romans.[20] The great Visigothic invasion, which had begun in 376, had ended in the ignominious collapse of the invaders. When they were fighting in Spain during the following year or two they were presumably still under the control of the Romans. What Constantius had been able to do in 414–16 he could no doubt have done equally well in 417 and 418: he could have starved them into submission in those years as easily as he had done in 416. But in fact he did not do so. Instead he recalled them from Spain in 418, although their work of reducing the Vandals there was not yet complete, and he settled them in Aquitanica II. Our authorities give no hint that the withdrawal from Spain and the settlement in Gaul was a Visigothic move or that the Visigoths had any choice in the matter: they were "recalled" from Spain by Constantius (p. 265, n. 1 below), and although there is no reason to suppose that they resented his orders to them, it was not they who initiated the policy. The settlement in Aquitanica was the considered and voluntary action of the Roman government.

Similarly, the settlement of the Burgundians in Savoy was due to Aëtius, and so far as we can tell the barbarian leaders were not consulted when the decision was being arrived at. The Burgundians had been so crushingly defeated by the Huns in 437 that the downfall of their kingdom centred around Worms was never to be forgotten in Germanic literature.

For the next six years they drop out of history, and Salvian, who wrote in 440–41,[21] and who was intensely interested in the barbarians in Gaul, never once mentions them or even hints at their existence. There is no reason to doubt that during these six years they were considered to be of little interest and of negligible military value by the Roman government. Yet without any obvious reason the imperial authorities suddenly summoned the remnants of them from Germania Prima in 443 and settled them in Savoy as *hospites*. It is impossible to believe that after the catastrophe of 437 the Burgundians were in any position to apply pressure to the Romans or to influence in any way the decision to transfer them to Savoy. This, too, was an act of purely Roman policy.

The settlements, then, were the work of Constantius and Aëtius, and they were in no sense a Roman compromise with the barbarians. What was the reason which led first Constantius and then Aëtius to carry through such curious measures? It could no doubt have been foretold in 418 and 443 that if the settlers should ever go to war with the Romans the imperial treasury would be bound to lose the revenues of the two regions until the settlers should be reconquered. Even as things were, the treasury lost some money, for, although the position of the Burgundian *hospites* is not clear, the lands of the Visigothic *hospites* appear not to have been subject to taxation.[22] Moreover, the conditions of *hospitalitas* meant that the great Roman landowners of the two affected areas lost a very considerable proportion of their rents. Yet we hear of no protest on the part of the landowners of Aquitanica II and of Savoy, although landlords rarely welcome the outright loss of a substantial part of their rents and although the settlements involved the presence of barbarians in many of their homes.[23] It is true that one of the groups of Alans eventually met with resistance from the Roman estate-owners and crushed them by force (p. 266, n. 13 below). But the Alans were a very different people from the Germans. They had been pastoral nomads beyond the river Don until the Huns attacked them about the year 370. It could hardly be expected that they would be willing to settle down as estate-owners with an interest in agriculture, when agriculture was an art almost completely outside the range of their experience. The fact that one group of this primitive people came to blows with their Roman *consortes* by no means proves that disturbances took place between the Romans and their comparatively highly civilized Germanic *hospites*. Where the Germans themselves were concerned we have no record whatever of any serious tension between them and the Roman landlords. The Roman estate-owners made over part of their lands and rents voluntarily and without demur. Had *hospitalitas* been contrary to their interests their champion Aëtius would not have imposed it upon them in 443 — and there is no reason to suppose that Constantius in 418 was any less friendly to them than Aëtius was to be later on.[24] It is difficult to resist the impression that Constantius and Aëtius can only have acted as they did because some serious danger threatened them. They surrendered so much, one might think, only in order to avoid surrendering all. But what was this danger?

Further, the landowners in question were the great Gallo-Roman senators and not the comparatively humble curials. Indeed, we are told explicitly that it was with the "Gallic senators" that the Burgundians divided their lands in 456 (p. 266, n. 9 below). There is no reason to suppose that the smaller landowners' estates were subject to *hospitalitas* at all.[25] Clearly, the smaller an estate was, the less profitable *hospitalitas* would have been for the barbarian guest, and the nearer the Roman host would have come to total expropriation. But to expropriate Roman landowners was by no means the purpose of Aëtius or Constantius or even of Gundobad, the Burgundian king, or Theodoric the Visigoth. A man who owned 25 Roman acres of land could qualify to be a curial, and many curials will have owned little more than this minimum acreage. If such men had been compelled to surrender two-thirds of their arable, one-half of their pasture land, and so on, they would have ceased to be curials. But the curials were so closely associated with the collection of taxes that anything which would have resulted in a considerable fall in their numbers would have caused the groaning machinery of Roman tax-collection to disintegrate altogether. Nothing of this sort would have been considered for a moment by Constantius or Aëtius. Moreover, a Burgundian would scarcely have welcomed very warmly the gift of a fraction of a small estate. For it was a Burgundian custom that a man should divide his property with his sons;[26] and if the original property had been very small this custom, if persisted in, would have quickly resulted in the ruin of the Burgundian *hospites.* Yet Burgundian estate-owners were still dividing their estates with their sons in the early years of the sixth century. Evidently they had been given considerable tracts of land in 443 and 456, and the estates on which they were settled must have been extensive ones. Of course, the largest Roman landowners possessed not one estate only but several estates lying in several parts of the Roman world. Such men as these would not have felt a crippling loss in surrendering two-thirds of any one of their Gallic estates (or of more than one if they owned more than one in Aquitania or Savoy). But the loss of two-thirds of any estate, and especially an estate lying in the rich lands of Aquitanica II, would in normal times have been a sacrifice which they would not have been overjoyed to make. There must have been some compelling reason in 418 and 443 to induce these particular landowners, the most powerful element among the Roman ruling classes

28

in Gaul, actually to welcome *hospitalitas* and to support Aëtius when he carried it through. What was this reason?

The usual practice of the imperial government was to settle the barbarians in positions on the frontier where they could defend exposed regions of the Empire against the onslaughts of other barbarians. Thus, Theodosius I had planted the Visigoths along the Danubian frontier of Moesia in 382 so as to protect that frontier from raids of the Huns beyond the river;[27] and no doubt Honorius planted the Burgundians on the left bank of the Rhine in Germania Prima because he wished to defend Gaul from invasions of the Franks and Alamanni. But how are we to explain settlements of federates deep in the interior of Gaul either in or near some of the richest lands of the West? Why did not Constantius settle the Visigoths, say, near the upper Rhine where they could have helped the Burgundians to keep the Alamanni in check? Why did he not plant them in some region of northcentral Gaul where they could have stopped the encroachments of the Franks? Aquitania was regarded as the very "marrow" of the Gallic provinces. Salvian says that its vineyards, its rich meadows, and its abundant harvests made it an "image of Paradise."[28] In the fourth century its vast surplus of grain was used to supply the troops on the Rhine, and a failure of communications with it would cripple the frontier armies.[29] Barbarians would be given a footing in such a province as Aquitania only if some very acute danger threatened it which could not be met in any other way. What of Savoy? The precise limits of Savoy, as we have said, are a matter of dispute; but it is certain that Savoy was one of the most important strategical areas in the Western Empire at this date. It was the key to some of the major Alpine passes, and whoever controlled it was in a good position to control the essential routes connecting Italy with southern Gaul.[30] It is true that the military forces of the Burgundians had been shattered in 437, but they were by no means annihilated, as subsequent history was to show; and it might have been expected even in 443 that, given time, the Burgundians would recover some of their power. They might then be in a position to sever Italy from Gaul; and even in 443, despite their cruel losses, which cannot have inspired them with any great love for Aëtius and the Western government, they could at least have interfered seriously with the vitally important lines of communication between the valley of the Po and that of the Rhone. A general of Aëtius' calibre would never have made over such a crucially important strategical area to a people who had so recently been his enemies unless a threat of the utmost danger had hung over his head. What was this danger then, which compelled the Western government to take on all the risks involved in settling the Visigoths in Aquitanica II and the Burgundians in Savoy?

It is difficult to believe that any barbarian people, or any group of barbarian peoples, inside or outside the Empire were in a position to reduce the Romans to such extreme measures or to wring such heavy sacrifices from them. That the Franks and Alamanni in northeastern Gaul and beyond the Rhine could not be checked by a force stationed in Aquitanica II goes without saying. The fact that the Visigoths were settled along the seacoast from the mouth of the Garonne to that of the Loire might suggest that Constantius wished them to defend the country from sea-borne raiders. But the suggestion cannot stand. Why should Constantius have undertaken all the risks and inconveniences entailed by the settlement of the Visigoths with a view to repelling Saxon raids when in fact such raids had rarely materialized within living memory and were never to become a serious menace to Aquitania throughout the whole of the fifth century? There remains Spain. We have seen that the Visigoths were under Roman control when they were fighting in Spain late in 416, throughout 417, and during the first part of 418. Wallia and his men had beaten the Siling Vandals in Baetica and had almost annihilated the Alans in Lusitania. If these two peoples were still regarded by Constantius as constituting a threat to Gaul he would presumably have allowed Wallia to complete the task of destroying them. In fact, however, he recalled him when the struggle was not yet entirely over (p. 265, n. 1 below). If Constantius had his own reasons for not allowing the Visigoths to become completely victorious in Spain, why did he not settle them, for example, in the Ebro Valley or in that great triangle between Palencia, Toledo, and Calatayud, where in fact they settled early in the sixth century? This was a far less valuable region to the Roman authorities and probably also to Roman landowners than was Aquitanica II, which supported the Rhine armies and so many of the great Gallo-Roman senators. Or again, if Constantius felt himself obliged for some reason which is unknown to us to settle the Visigoths in Gaul with a view to defending the Garonne valley from attacks by the barbarians in Spain, why did he settle them north of the Garonne? Would it not have been an obvious move to settle them, not in Aquitanica II between the Garonne and the Loire, but in Novempopulana between the Garonne and the Pyrenees? In fact, it is scarcely too much to say that, if the danger which threatened Constantius had its origin in Spain, the settlement of the Visigoths in Aquitanica II is unintelligible.

The conclusion must be that Constantius did not initiate the settlement of the Visigoths because he was afraid of some barbarian enemy. None of the barbarian peoples formed a major threat to that part of Gaul which lay between the Garonne and the Loire, and no military force stationed there was well placed to repel any of the dangerous peoples. As an explanation of the settlement of the Visigoths all the barbarian peoples in Spain, Gaul, and Germany must be ruled out. In that case we may put forward an hypothesis which, it may be suggested, will account immediately and obviously (i) for the place of the Visigothic settlement, (ii) for its curious timing when the wars in Spain were not yet completed, and (iii) for the form which it took — the strange interlocking of the interests of the Roman and the Visigothic *consortes*. The danger which Constantius tried to ward off by settling the Visigoths south of the Loire came from the Armoricans north of the Loire. Constantius was afraid of the Bacaudae.

It is clear that a strong force stationed in Aquitanica II was admirably placed to defend the riches of the Garonne valley against an enemy coming from Armorica. The point hardly requires amplification. The date of the settlement, 418, also takes on a new significance. The great invasion of Gaul by the Vandals, Alans, and Sueves, which began on the last night of the year 406, had given the peasants of Armorica their opportunity, and they had risen in rebellion against the established order. They had expelled the imperial officials, had enslaved the landowners, and had set up an independent state of their own.[31] The revolt was not confined to Armorica;[32] and for ten years the peasants retained their freedom. It was the longest and most successful of all the rebellions of the Bacaudae of which we have knowledge. Even if it was not accompanied by outbreaks in Aquitanica II itself, the very proximity of a social revolution to the great estates of southern Gaul must have been profoundly alarming to the landowners there. Who could tell whether the next revolt might not directly concern the "image of Paradise" itself? But in 417, the year before the settlement of the Visigoths south of the Loire, Exuperantius was in process of reducing the rebels to bondage again.[33] Is it a coincidence that the Visigoths were required to break off their struggle in Spain and to settle down on the doorstep of Armorica in the very next year after Exuperantius had gained the upper hand over the Bacaudae? Clearly, Constantius could not have used the Visigothic federates to fight against the Bacaudae in 416 and 417, although he was able to use them against his barbarian enemies in those years. For the Visigoths' close association with rebellious Roman peasants and soldiers ever since they had crossed the Danube in 376 must have suggested to Constantius that, if he tried to employ them against the Bacaudae of Armorica, there was a distinct possibility that, so far from fighting them, they might join forces with the rebels and make common cause with them or at any rate that they might not offer any effective resistance to them. Before they could be used against the Armoricans they must first be given some stake in the country which they were to defend: their interests must be bound up with those of the estate-owners of Aquitanica. Accordingly, when Exuperantius began to master the Bacaudae in 417 — and presumably he had completed his task by the end of that year or early in 418 — the Visigoths were at once recalled from Spain and were settled in Aquitanica II in conditions in which they could not defend their own interests without at the same time defending those of their Roman *hospites.* In this way we can explain not only the place of settlement but also its date and the strange interweaving which it entailed of Roman and barbarian interests on the estates of Aquitanica II. This hypothesis also shows why the initiative came from the Roman government and why the largest and most influential landlords in Gaul welcomed their *consortes* in spite of the losses of land and the personal inconvenience which their presence there entailed. It shows why so critically important an area as Aquitanica II was chosen for the settlement rather than some frontier region of less economic value — Aquitanica II was chosen precisely because it was important. And it shows why the Visigoths were planted there in 418 rather than in 416 or 417 or for that matter 419 or 420.

Now there is some reason to think that this was not the only occasion on which the Roman authorities settled barbarians in Gaul in order to menace the Bacaudae of Armorica. We have seen that a group of Alans led by their king Goar was settled in the vicinity of Orleans in or before 442. We are fortunate in that on one occasion we catch a glimpse of these Alans taking the field on the instructions of the Roman government. When the Bacaudae under the leadership of Tibatto revolted *c.* 444–45 Aëtius called upon Goar and his men to march against them. Goar and his iron-clad cavalry set out to crush the rebellion when they were interrupted by Germanus, Bishop of Auxerre, in circumstances which need not detain us.[34] Can it be doubted that in this action the Alans were fulfilling the function for which they had been given the lands of Orleans?

As for the Burgundians, it is commonly believed that they were planted in Savoy so as to block the southward expansion of the Alamanni and to protect Arles and Vienne and even Italy itself from their plundering raids.[35] But is this credible? We have seen something of the strategical value of Savoy: would Aëtius have taken the risk of losing Savoy altogether, or even of losing it temporarily, when it would have been far more effective for his purpose to have settled the Burgundians on a line running north or east from Basel, that is to say, either in Alsace or behind the frontier fortifications between Basel and Lake Constance? If it is held that northern Switzerland was already occupied by the Alamanni in and after 406 — and there is no good reason to believe that this was the case[36] — then why did not Aëtius settle his Federates on the vitally important line from the Lake of Geneva to the Lake of Constance, that is, on the Swiss sector of the road which connected Lyon with the Danube? It has been said that "the infiltration of the Alamanni into the wedge of territory between the Rhine and the Danube was dangerous, for it threatened the strip of land through which that road ran, in the area of Lake Constance and in what is now Switzerland; that made it essential for the road to be exceptionally strongly guarded, hence the tremendous fortifications along the Swiss Rhine frontier and on the Swiss sector of the road."[37] Why then were the Burgundians not set to defend the road? But the great Alamannic invasions of the mid-fourth century had shown that their most dangerous thrusts would probably come, not into Switzerland at all, but into Alsace; for in the fourth century they had not merely raided Alsace but had actually proposed to settle in it permanently. And when they did in fact expand in the summer of 455 the affected area would seem to have been around Langres and Besançon, far away from Savoy.[38] It is true that their raids were still sometimes launched in a southerly direction, but the foray carried out by 900 Alamanni in 457 to the neighbourhood of Bellinzona certainly does not prove that eastern or northern Switzerland had been occupied by them or that there was any danger of their sending permanent settlers to the south.[39] We can only conclude that, although it may well have been the expansion of the Alamanni into Alsace in 455 — if indeed they did send permanent settlers into Alsace in 455 — which caused the Roman senators around Lyon to permit the extension of the Burgundians which took place in 456 (n. 9 above), yet Savoy is incomprehensible as a site for the settlement in 443 if that settlement was intended to check Alamannic raids. At no time was Savoy threatened, and at no time did it appear likely to be seriously threatened, by Alamannic raiders. At no time could a military force stationed in Savoy have checked the expansion of the Alamanni or have formed an effective defence of the Rhone valley or of Italy against their raiders.

Furthermore, if Aëtius settled the Burgundians in Savoy solely in order to contain the Alamanni, how shall we solve the chronological problem with which we are then presented? Aëtius and his Huns had smashed the power of the Burgundians in 437. For six years thereafter they drop out of history: no chronicler refers to them, and Salvian, writing in 440–41, in spite of his deep interest in the barbarians living in Gaul, never mentions the Burgundians, the only Germanic people in or near Gaul on whom he is totally silent. Presumably they were of even less significance than the "cowardly" Vandals were thought to be. Aëtius, too, would seem to have ignored them throughout those six years; but then without warning, as it seems, he transferred them to Savoy in 443. He did not do so, we may be sure, without a very good reason. What then had happened in those six

33

years which made him change his attitude towards the Burgundians whom his Huns had so cruelly crushed? Was there any intensification of Alamannic raids on Gaul? If so, our authorities are silent about it. The chroniclers are as silent about the Alamanni in these years as they are about the Burgundians. Even Salvian mentions them only once, and then he does not say that the danger from them had suddenly grown acute. He mentions them only in order to comment on their drunkenness. Their political activities apparently lie beyond his horizon.[40]

Why then after six years did Aëtius see that he could find a use for the remnants of the Burgundians after all? His qualities as a statesman may have been overrated, but it will scarcely be thought that he was inordinately slow to see and to grasp his military opportunities; and yet six years elapsed between the Huns' defeat of the Burgundians and his transference of the Burgundians to Savoy. The answer must be that it was not until towards the year 443 that a situation arose which called for the immediate defence of Savoy. When Aëtius left Gaul in 439 after renewing the treaty of 418 with the Visigothic king Theodoric at Toulouse he may have been tolerably satisfied with the position in Gaul. At any rate the great wars against the Burgundians, the Bacaudae, and the Visigoths had been brought to a successful conclusion.[41] Yet when Salvian wrote in 440–41 there was widespread unrest in Gaul, but it was not due to the Alamanni: it was caused by the deteriorating economic and social condition of the Gallic countryside. It resulted in the flight of many people to the barbarians, especially the Visigoths, and to the Bacaudae. Indeed, Salvian lays so much stress on the part played by the Bacaudae in Gaul that it may have been the case that a new Bacaudic outbreak could already be foreseen at the time when he was writing. Aëtius himself may have been aware that there would soon be trouble; for it may have been in 442 that he settled Goar's Alans in the neighbourhood of Orleans. This move, as we have conjectured, was intended to hold the Armorican Bacaudae in check, and, if the date is correct, it follows that Aëtius was in that year expecting trouble from the poorer classes in Gaul.[42] In 440, however, he settled Sambida's Alans in the vicinity of Valence, where they could control the lower reaches of the Isère valley: they were there defending one of the major egresses from the country in which the Burgundians were to be planted three years later. Does this fact not suggest that at the precise time when Salvian was writing about the dangers of an upheaval in Gaul, the situation in the western foothills of the Alps was causing anxiety to the government? There is reason to think that Savoy was no stranger to the movement of the Bacaudae. In 435, we are told, "nearly all the slaves of the Gallic provinces conspired in a Bacaudic movement" when the first rebellion led by Tibatto broke out.[43] There is no reason to think that Savoy had been exempt from the conspiracy, though there is no explicit evidence for activities by Bacaudae in the highlands in these years. But there is some reason to think that during the great rebellion of the Gallic peasants in 284–85 the region with which we are concerned was not unaffected. It seems that there were disturbances at Reichenstein near Arlesheim and at Champanges and Geneva.[44] Moreover, the evidence is explicit for the year 408. A renegade Visigoth named Sarus was returning from Gaul to Italy in command of a force which had been powerful enough to crush the army of Justinian, a general of the usurper Constantine. But as he crossed the Alps Sarus encountered a force of Bacaudae, and he was obliged to make over to them all the booty which he had taken in Gaul. Now it is interesting to notice what he had been doing in Gaul before he retreated into Italy. He had been besieging Valence itself, where in 440 Aëtius was to settle Sambida's Alans; that is to say, he had fallen back from Gaul towards Italy along the very line which these Alans were intended to watch.[45] We never hear that these mountain Bacaudae were crushed, and it may be that their organization continued in existence. We can at least assume that there were potential Bacaudae in the Alps in the next two or three decades, for, so far as we know, nothing had been done in the meantime to alleviate the lot of the Alpine dwellers and to make them less likely to revolt than they had been in 408. It may seem unlikely that the inhabitants of the mountain region, who had been active as Bacaudae in 408, were tolerably content with their lot in 443 or that they were at any rate more or less resigned to it, for in those 35 years the disorganization of the Western Empire had grown considerably more acute and the conditions of life harsher.[46] There also seem to have been independence movements, which may well have had a Bacaudic character, in Vindelicia and in Noricum. Aëtius was obliged to undertake campaigns in both of these areas in or about the year 430.[47] Is it credible that with Bacaudic movements west of Savoy and with what may have been Bacaudic movements east of it, Savoy, which had had its own Bacaudae in 408, remained unaffected? If then we try to give the reasons for the settlement of Sambida's Alans at Valence in 440 and of the Burgundians in Savoy three years later, our safest course would seem to be to suppose that the description of Gaul in general as given by Salvian in 440–41 was true also of Savoy: and that Aëtius' purpose was to protect the Rhone valley and Savoy itself and the Alpine passes against attacks of rebellious peasants and shepherds in the Alpine region. Both these settlements were designed to solve the same problem as had been in some measure solved by the settlement of the Visigoths in Aquitanica II and of Goar's Alans at Orleans. The whole process of the settlement of the barbarians in Gaul would become more intelligible if it could be assumed that the same remedy was several times applied in order to cure the same disease.

We conclude, then, that the danger which Aëtius sought to counter by settling the Alans at Valence and the Burgundians in Savoy did not originate among the Alamanni far away beyond the Danube. In the first place, if our earlier arguments be accepted, we have the analogous case of the Visigoths and of Goar's Alans, who were admirably placed to seal off Armorica from the rest of Gaul and to isolate the Bacaudae of that region from their possible allies in the rest of the country. Secondly, there is no evidence that the Alamanni ever threatened Savoy or that after being comparatively peaceful in 437 and the following three or four years they suddenly became dangerous in 442–43. Indeed, there is some negative evidence against such a view, for Salvian, apart from his comment on their inebriety, is as silent about the Alamanni in 440–41 as he is about the Burgundians. No reader of his book would gather that the Romans had any reason for fearing the Alamanni more in 440–41 than they had had in 437–40 when Aëtius might equally well have transferred the Burgundians from Germania Prima to Savoy; whereas in the case of the Bacaudae we know that streams of people were deserting to them in 440–41. That is to say, Salvian provides evidence for believing that a crisis arose in Gaul after Aëtius had left the country in 439, but that this crisis was not caused by the Alamanni: it was due to the Bacaudae. There is also perhaps a third reason for our conclusion. The landowners of Savoy would hardly have surrendered a high proportion of their rents unless they had been convinced that the alternative was to lose the whole of their estates permanently. Alamannic raids might well cause great damage, but in a few years the burnt villas could be rebuilt, the lost stock replaced, and the fields sown once more. But such raids would not have deprived the landowners of the ownership of their lands: the ownership of their estates would have remained in the hands of the landlords; and hence the prospect of Alamannic attacks would scarcely have been so alarming as to induce the owners to anticipate trouble by giving away outright a high proportion of their rents and houses. We might argue that the Alamannic danger would only explain the settlement of the Burgundians in Savoy if it could be assumed that the landlords of that region knew in advance that the Alamanni intended not merely to launch raids but to occupy Savoy permanently. But there is no reason to assume that the landowners had such knowledge, and it is scarcely credible that the Alamanni would have chosen to send their people all the way to Savoy when, if they had been looking for land to settle in, northern Switzerland and Alsace lay on their doorstep. Moreover, even if we allow that the Roman landlords had good reason to fear such an extension of the Alamanni in 443, would not their most natural course have been to call on the central government for direct military aid and perhaps for a preventive attack on the Alamanni? In a word, if we believe that the settlement of the Burgundians was due to the Alamannic danger, we must not only suppose (in the total absence of evidence) that Alamannic raids had suddenly become threatening to Savoy or its immediate neighbourhood in 442–43 but also that the Alamanni intended to pass through northern Switzerland and settle permanently in Savoy and that this intention had become known to the large landowners of Savoy. But such hypotheses seem very hazardous, and it may be suggested that a much simpler explanation, which accounts for all the facts, is that the danger which threatened Aëtius and the estate-owners was an internal one: the settlement of the barbarians in Savoy as in Aquitania was due to the rebellious activities of the slaves and their allies in Gaul.

If this explanation is correct, we may well admire the brilliance of the diplomacy of Constantius and Aëtius. At one stroke they converted wandering and hostile masses of barbarians into settled and on the whole contented communities of agriculturalists; they broke the alliance of the invading barbarians with the restless elements of the Roman countryside; and they provided themselves with an effective military force which would defend southern Gaul from the uprisings of the indomitable slaves and their allies who had caused so much damage earlier in the fifth century. It could be further shown, I think (though the point is hardly relevant to the present discussion) that by these settlements the Romans also succeeded in splitting the ranks of their barbarian enemies, for they set the interests of the tribal nobility once and for all in conflict with the interests of the rank and file of the warriors. The nobility were no longer simply the "leading men" of the people. They were now a landed gentry whose manner of life would become increasingly different from that of their followers. Their relationship with them was no longer that of kinsman and kinsman: it had become something like the relationship of landlord and tenant. Few Roman diplomats won so striking and so far-reaching a victory as Constantius and Aëtius won in 418 and 443.

3

The Visigoths from Fritigern to Euric

In 376 the Visigoths were driven out of their homes north of the lower Danube by the Huns, and entered the Roman Empire. On 9 August 378 they won the battle of Adrianople, and on 24 August 410 they occupied Rome itself. These two achievements, in spite of their effect on Roman history, did not bring the victors any land on which they could settle permanently and resume the life which the attack of the Huns had interrupted so abruptly. The Visigoths moved on from Italy to Gaul and from Gaul to Spain, but nowhere could they establish themselves. The great invasion of the Empire which had begun in 376 finally ended in capitulation in 416, when the Patrician Constantius starved the invaders into submission in eastern Spain.[1]

I. FRITIGERN AND FRAVITTAS

In the period 376–418 the position of the Visigothic optimates must have been enormously strengthened over against that of the people at large, and the size and power of their retinues must have grown appreciably. It is difficult to believe, for example, that when the people settled in Moesia in 382 by agreement with the Roman government, the leading men failed to take disproportionately large areas of land for their own private use when the land was being distributed. The actual division of the land in Moesia must have been carried out in the main under the direction of the chiefs and councils, and we may be sure that the optimates thereby obtained executive power which would hardly have been theirs in the normal course of tribal life. Again, the annual subsidies of grain and cash paid over at times during the years 382–418 by the Roman government were delivered in the first instance into the hands of the chiefs and councils,[2] who then proceeded to distribute them, or part of them, to the tribesmen in general. Here, too, their own interests will scarcely have suffered. Again, during the campaign of 394, when Visigothic federates fought under their own leaders for Theodosius against the rebel Eugenius, it is hardly credible that those leaders made no attempt to impose on their followers the rigorous discipline and enforced obedience to orders which prevailed in the rest of Theodosius' army and which was unknown in a tribal levy. But on all these and similar matters specific evidence is lacking; and if we are to understand the essence of the development of Visigothic society in the period 376–418 we must turn to other events.

When the Visigoths stood on the banks of the Danube in 376, driven to desperation by the sufferings which the Romans inflicted on them before admitting them to the provinces, they swore to each other a solemn oath that they would assail the Romans in any and every way and would cause them all the harm in their power, no matter what benefits the Romans should be willing or should be compelled to grant them; and that they would only end their unrelenting struggle when they had gained the mastery of the entire Roman Empire — the Empire which at that moment had brought them to such extremes of starvation that they were forced to sell their children into slavery in return for a crust of bread or the carcass of a dog.[3] It is against the background of this oath that we must view the events of 8 and 9 August 378.

When Valens was trying to decide whether or not to offer battle at Adrianople without waiting for the arrival of the Western army, the Visigothic leader Fritigern sent a private letter to him. In it he hinted to Valens that he would soon be his friend and ally, and he declared that he could not tame the savagery of his fellow Goths and win them over to accept conditions of peace *favourable to the Romans* unless Valens should make a display of his strength in the close proximity of the tribesmen; but if the emperor did this, he would check his men's ruinous enthusiasm for an immediate battle.[4] On the morning of the fateful 9 August Fritigern repeated his offer. He again suggested to Valens that hostages should be exchanged, and he said that he was ready to face fearlessly the threats of his own men which would surely follow the announcement that such an offer had been made and accepted.[5] Were these offers sincere? Valens decided that he could not rely on the sincerity of the first one and refused to accept it. Ammianus Marcellinus, who records the incidents and who was not present, has little doubt that Fritigern had no intention of carrying out his offer if it were accepted and that he made it only in order to lull Valens into a false feeling of security. But when the second message came, Valens changed his mind and with the consent of all his advisers accepted Fritigern's proposal; and on this Ammianus expresses no opinion one way or the other. Clearly, both emperor and historian could only guess at the motives which inspired

Fritigern's proposals; and nothing in our evidence suggests that Valens was guilty of an error of judgement in making his second guess, as a result of which he accepted the offer believing it to be genuine. We are at liberty to conclude that Fritigern sincerely wished to come to terms with the Romans without fighting, that he had in fact a desire to be "the friend and ally" of the Emperor, that he wished to arrange terms of peace which, while securing land for his people, would nevertheless be favourable to the Romans, and that he was well aware that the majority of his fellow Visigoths would angrily oppose any such compromise. The concrete evidence of his two offers to Valens is more persuasive in the circumstances than the mere speculations of Valens and Ammianus on the motives which had inspired them.[6] For if the offers were in fact a sham, then Fritigern was playing with fire: how could he have explained them away to his followers in their present temper if the news that he had made them in secret had leaked out? More than thirty years later another Visigothic leader found himself in much the same frame of mind as Fritigern. He, too, could not hold the "barbarism" of his men in check, and wished in consequence to incorporate them in the disciplined social hierarchy of the Roman Empire. The case of Athaulf and other events which we shall examine presently provide a context to Fritigern's actions which makes it all but certain that in accepting Fritigern's offer Valens was guilty of no error of judgement. As early as 378 the attitude of the Visigothic leader had diverged sharply from that of the Visigoths in general. The chief now negotiated in secret with the hated enemy of his people. He felt that it was his gain now to reach an accommodation with the Imperial government; and he foresaw clearly the anger which such an agreement would arouse among his men. But before any positive action could be taken, two subordinate officers in the Roman army opened the battle of Adrianople on their own initiative, so that the negotiations came to nothing.

After the battle the tensions which existed among the tribesmen were brought out into the open by the emperor Theodosius, and the evidence for them is direct and explicit. After the Roman disaster at Adrianople Theodosius was unable to overthrow the Visigoths by military strength, and so he went vigorously to work to split the enemy's ranks.[7] He began by heaping gifts and honours on "the tribal leaders who were outstanding in rank and birth." He feasted the leaders of each tribe at his own table, he shared his tent with them, and he missed no opportunity of showing them his generosity. It was not long before some of the tribal chieftains began to respond to this treatment: some of them "were puffed up by the imperial honours and saw all power in their own hands." The dissensions which now began to smoulder among them centred on the oath which had been sworn on the Danube banks in 376 and which Fritigern had already disregarded in his secret negotiations with Valens. Some of the tribal chiefs insisted that it was still binding; those who were willing to accept Theodosius' offers held that the oath should now be forgotten and that they should continue to accept and enjoy the comfortable circumstances in which Theodosius had placed them. The leader of the pro-Roman faction, a young man named Fravittas, carried his Roman sympathies so far as to marry a Roman wife (like Athaulf after him) in contravention of Roman law; and he took upon himself the Roman name of Flavius.[8] The other faction, which outnumbered Fravittas' and which included the more influential chiefs in its ranks, was headed by Eriulf, and it held firmly to the terms of the oath. Theodosius punished severely any Roman officers or men — once indeed he punished the whole population of Constantinople — who took up an aggressive attitude towards the Visigoths: it was essential that his subtle tactics should not be foiled by any bludgeoning behaviour on the part of his subordinates.[9] Then, when Athanaric, who had been deserted by his men, left his refuge in the Transylvanian Alps (where he had fled before the Huns in 376), surrendered to the Romans, and came to Constantinople on 11 January 381, Theodosius received him with honour and a show of respect. When Athanaric died in the Eastern capital a fortnight later, the emperor gave him a state funeral and himself led the procession. Many of the Visigoths were deeply impressed.[10] The tension soon came to a climax. The members of both groups, those who wished to come to terms with the Romans and those who were still hostile to them, were invited by Theodosius to a more splendid banquet than ever. The feast broke up in a disorderly brawl. The feasters went outside quarrelling angrily, and Flavius Fravittas drew his sword and ran Eriulf through the side. Eriulf fell mortally wounded, his sympathizers sprang at Fravittas, and the combatants were only separated by the imperial guards.

As a result of Theodosius' policy a number of the Visigothic leaders went over to the Romans. A chief named Modares deserted and showed such fervent loyalty to the Romans that he received a command in the imperial army and proceeded to inflict a sharp defeat on a raiding band of his fellow Visigoths.[11] It was possibly now, too, that one of the optimates named Munderic entered the Roman service: before the end of Theodosius' reign he had become *dux* of the Arabian frontier. It was about this time that Gainas deserted his tribesmen and joined the Roman army as a private soldier: within ten years he had risen to the rank of commander of the Visigothic mercenaries. It was certainly now that Fravittas and some of his supporters changed sides.[12] But these dissensions affected only the leaders and did not spread to any great extent to the mass of the Visigoths.

Those whom Theodosius tried to win over were "the tribal leaders, outstanding in rank and birth."[13] But while some of the chiefs accepted Theodosius' offer of posts in the Roman army,[14] the bulk of the Visigoths remained so hostile to the imperial government that, in spite of their status as federates in Moesia after 382, Theodosius did not call upon them for military help until more than a decade had passed after the treaty of 3 October 382.[15] In a word, the cleavage between the Visigoths as a whole and a section of their leaders has now reached a point where the latter, like Segestes among the Cherusci long ago, were willing to abandon their native society altogether and to enter the service of their people's hereditary enemies.

What we know about the subsequent career of three of these "deserters" (as the Romans frankly called them) shows that the mass of the Visigoths would have gained little by following them. In the year 400 the Visigoth Gainas and his kinsman Tribigild[16] rebelled against the East Roman government, in whose armed forces they were serving as officers, and were thought to have some vague plan to win the mastery of the Roman Empire.[17] But their aim was not to detach themselves from Roman life (with which they had only recently associated themselves) and not to overthrow the Roman state (in which they held high office) but to strengthen their own personal position and to increase their wealth, power, and influence *inside* the Roman world. As soon as Tribigild's rebellion broke out in Asia Minor it was joined by masses of oppressed Romans and by numerous Visigoths whom the Romans had managed to enslave in the preceding years.[18] Although Gainas had secretly instigated the revolt of Tribigild,[19] the government gave him the task of suppressing it. The role assigned to him by the Roman authorities was the same as that which they gave to Fravittas a few months later: he was to destroy his fellow Visigoths and their slave allies. But the purpose of his Visigothic followers was to destroy that very society in which he and Tribigild were trying to establish their personal position more securely. That is why the rebellion was doomed to failure. The interests of the leaders lay in maintaining Roman society and in improving their own position within it, whereas the aim of the rank and file of their followers and of their allies was to overthrow Roman society altogether (p. 31f. above). Hence those aimless and destructive marches and countermarches in Asia Minor and Europe. So far as the leaders' wishes went, they might simply have seized some strong point near Constantinople in order to interrupt the grain supply from Egypt to the capital until the government conceded their demands. But could they have induced their army to accept such a course? Would captive tribesmen, who had been forced to work for years in the fields of wealthy

Roman landowners or of the state, have been content to wait in some seaboard fort until the government promised to pay Tribigild and to promote Gainas? And if the government had agreed to this, would the slaves then have gone quietly back to their bondage comforted by the thought that they had served their leaders well? At all events, when Gainas was at the height of his successes he did no more than demand the overthrow of his chief personal enemies at the court. When he was in control of Constantinople itself, his only request was for the right to use one of the city's churches for Arian services: it was unbecoming for him, a high Roman official, to be obliged to go outside the walls whenever he wished to worship.

The last episode in Gainas' career illuminates the part played by the Visigothic "deserters." He was defeated by Fravittas and the Romans, and he turned at last towards the Danube. Hitherto, he had never considered such a step, for he and Tribigild had left tribal life far behind. They had no wish to return to the poverty and insecurity of Gothia; but now there was no other course open to them. North of the Danube, however, Gainas fell into the hands of the Huns and was killed.[20] But that was not the end of the Romans' troubles. In the confusion caused by the passage of Gainas' force through Thrace runaway slaves and others "who had abandoned their ranks" in Roman society gave out that they were Huns and plundered the countryside until Fravittas marched against them, as he had formerly marched against the brigands of Isauria, and killed off any whom he met.[21] Ever since he had gone over to the Romans, so far as is recorded, Fravittas had been used by the Imperial government for two purposes only — to crush Roman brigands,[22] the potential allies of the invaders, and to suppress rebellious Visigoths. To kill brigands and to kill Goths — that was the role which the barbarians who had deserted their own society were called upon to play.

II. FROM ALARIC TO WALLIA

Although Alaric felt himself at one time to be bound by the terms of the oath sworn on the Danube banks in 376,[23] his election to the leadership of the people in 395 was not a victory for either element among the Visigothic leaders, for he does not seem to have made a clear decision to move in either of the two directions open to him — to destroy Rome or to become part of it. The chief event with which his name is associated, the capture of Rome in 410, was a symbol of one of the great processes of history, the fall of the Western Empire. Yet few would refer to Alaric as a "great man"; and here we have a part of the reason. His policy was a wavering combination of elements of both the rival tendencies in the society in which he had grown to manhood. On the one hand, throughout his entire career as Visigothic leader he seems to have been moving on terms of easy familiarity with members of the official aristocracy of the Empire;[24] and these Roman officials were able to exercise considerable influence over him. They influenced him in matters of such capital importance as the raising of the siege of Ravenna and the deposition of his puppet Emperor Attalus.[25] In the opinion of a later Gothic historian his policy was to bring it about (by what means, is unknown) that Romans and Goths should live together on such amicable terms that both might be considered to be a single people.[26] (The full significance of such a policy will become apparent when we consider the career of Alaric's successor Athaulf and the nature of the Visigothic settlement at Toulouse.) Indeed, the Romans had some reason to think that if Alaric's personal position in the Roman Empire were assured, if he were appointed to a high military office, he would trouble himself less about the position of his men.[27]

On the other hand, although he held scrupulously to the terms of all his engagements with the imperial government, he tried persistently to realize his people's ultimate aim of finding land on which they could settle. And largely because of this, no doubt, his influence over his men was extraordinary. None of his major battles was a complete success, and he lost an unknown number of minor ones which sometimes cost him severe losses —in one recorded case no fewer than 3,000 men.[28] He won striking successes only when there was little or no organized military opposition on the part of the Romans (408–10). He failed to secure permanent homes for his people. Indeed, his followers seem to have survived as an effective fighting force only because of the manoeuvres of Roman internal politics.[29] Yet his influence appears to have been so great that he held in check the dissensions among the Visigoths which Theodosius had fanned into flame. Under his leadership there were few cases of desertion on the part of his men, and in large measure this must be set down to Alaric's ability and prestige. It is true, of course, that a number of his troops abandoned him when they could not endure the hardships of the retreat from Verona in 403. There seem to have been acute disagreements in the Visigothic camp at that time, and it would appear that some of the secret plans of the Goths were made known to Stilicho.[30] Although the dissidents at first were very few, they became numerous later on when the army was tortured by famine and pestilence.[31] But whether those who left Alaric on that occasion lost much time in rejoining him is not recorded.[32] As for the optimates, it may be that one Ulfila, whose name suggests that he was a Visigoth and who had become Master of the Cavalry in 411,[33] and Sarus, the brother of Sigeric (p. 47 below), with a small number of malcontents went over to the Romans during the period of his leadership. We know next to nothing about this Ulfila, and an examination of Sarus' treacherous character would reveal that his loss was a slight one. The fact is that the extensive desertion of optimates which had occurred early in Theodosius' reign is unparalleled in the years 395–410 in spite of Alaric's repeated military and political reverses. "His strange manoeuvres during the next fifteen years [i.e. after 395] may perhaps be explained by this assumption that his interests were not wholly Visigothic (those of his people were limited to subsidies and land), but were concerned with achieving a definite place in the government of the Empire."[34]

After his death in 410 and the accession of his wife's brother[35] Athaulf, the tensions between the Visigothic leaders and their followers revived in an acute form. It is against the background of Fritigern's overtures to Valens on the eve of Adrianople and of Eriulf's murder by Fravittas in the early years of Theodosius that we must read the famous statement made by Athaulf on his change of attitude towards the Roman Empire. Athaulf was associating closely with a number of Romans, who formed part of his entourage,[36] and he made this statement many times in the hearing of a Roman citizen of Narbonne. According to this Roman, Athaulf had often declared that (like Eriulf before him) his original aim was to wipe out the very name of the Romans, to transform the Roman Empire into a Gothic Empire, to substitute Gothia for Romania, and to become himself what Caesar Augustus had long ago been; but later he had changed his plan in order that by means of the military strength of the Visigoths he might win the glory of fully restoring the name of Rome to its former greatness and might be remembered by posterity as "the author of the Roman restoration."[37]

Now, Athaulf did not conceal the reason for his change of plan. "But when he had proved by much experience," he said, "that Goths could in no wise obey laws (leges) because of their unruly barbarism, and that state laws ought not to be prohibited, for without them a state is not a state, he had chosen" to adopt his new plan of restoring Roman power. Like Fritigern (p. 39 above), Athaulf could not control the Visigoths' barbarism. He would restore the Roman state which Fravittas had loyally served and which Fritigern before him had been willing to benefit. Athaulf, however, goes further. He complains that his followers will not obey his laws; and in this he reaches the heart of the matter. In a tribal society there are no "laws." The military leader of a tribal confederacy is only the agent of the confederate council;[38] he is no autocratic ruler who can act as the source of law. A tribal society governs itself in accordance not with laws but with traditional customs, obligations, duties, rights, and responsibilities, and with little coercive power except public opinion. Before they received their first law code the Goths had been governed only by *mores,* "habits," and *consuetudo,* "custom"; and it seems that even in the sixth century a number of old Gothic *belagines,* "precepts," written in the native language, were still known.[39] Athaulf, in fact, was thinking in terms which were wholly alien from those of a loyal leader of a tribal community or even from those of a man willing to acquiesce in the continuance of the old social system. Therefore he wished to transform the society of the Visigoths and incorporate his followers in the very different organization of the Roman Empire, where their barbarism would no longer be unbridled.

Athaulf formed his grandiose plan, then, in order to strengthen his own position over against that of his followers. He saw, as Alaric had failed to see, the direction in which Visigothic society was moving, and what he decided upon was to accelerate the pace of history. He could not impose his personal "laws" upon the Visigoths under the old system of village and confederate councils and of chiefs with influence rather than power. He would therefore incorporate his Goths in a state in which coercive power would be his. He abandoned his hostility towards the Roman government and strove for peace with them because only in this way could he establish personal authority over the mass of his fellow Visigoths and overthrow those free institutions which the wealth of the tribal optimates had already rendered obsolete.[40] He made no secret of his plan. He spoke of it openly and freely, perhaps to some of the optimates, certainly to a Christian Roman of Narbonne. A vivid description survives of his marriage with the Roman princess Placidia whom the Visigoths had captured in Rome in 410. On the advice of a Roman named Candidianus—for in Athaulf's time, as in Alaric's (p. 44 above), individual Romans were able to influence the Visigothic leaders even in essential points of policy—Athaulf clad in Roman dress married the Roman princess in Narbonne according to Roman rites in the house of a Gallo-Roman decurion named Ingenuus; and as he feasted after his wedding he listened to an epithalamium declaimed by a deposed Roman emperor. His marriage delighted the Romans in his train. He could draw upon vast personal wealth when he made his gifts to his bride: he gave her fifty handsome youths dressed in silk clothing, each of them carrying in his hands two platters, one filled with gold and the other with precious stones plundered from Rome in 410. His marriage was intended to make clear to the nations that the Empire had been made one with the Goths. In the course of a single generation the Visigothic leaders had travelled a long way from the simple days of Athanaric.[41]

Athaulf was at Narbonne at the end of 413, and it was presumably then that he finally decided not to destroy Romania after all. In January 414 he married Placidia, and when she gave birth to a child he called it by the imperial name of Theodosius.[42] Thereafter he was more eager than ever for peace with the Roman government. Even when he was driven from Bordeaux and other cities of southern Gaul in 415 by Constantius he was still anxious to reach agreement with the emperor. But because of his change of design, because of his adoption of a plan that would have served the interests of the leaders only at the cost of the freedom of those whom they led, he was murdered by his followers at Barcelona in September 415. Eriulf, it seems, had not fallen in vain.[43]

The struggle between those who wished to incorporate the people in the Roman Empire and those who still clung to their independence did not die with Athaulf. Lying mortally wounded he addressed his dying words to his brother. He advised him to restore Placidia to her imperial relatives and to induce the Visigoths to seek the friendship of the Romans. He advised him, in fact, to carry on the policy which had cost himself his life.[44] Clearly, he expected that he would be succeeded by his brother; but his hope was not realized. One Sigeric seized power irregularly. There was a certain procedure to be observed when a new military leader was to be appointed, and Sigeric brushed this procedure aside. Perhaps he tried to establish a personal hegemony without submitting to the customary election; and the election was not a mere formality which could be dispensed with safely.[45] Moreover, after making the gesture of humiliating Placidia and after securing his own position (as he thought) by the brutal murder of Athaulf's children, Sigeric lost no time in trying to come to terms with the imperial government. The attraction of Romania for the Visigothic nobility seems now to have been intense. The ambitions of Athaulf and the policy followed by Sigeric, whose aims turned out to be essentially the same as his predecessor's, show that the solidarity of the Visigoths had now been shattered. But the independent spirit of the people at large was still as sturdy as ever: Sigeric was killed by his followers on the seventh day of his tyranny not because of his usurpation but because of his attempt to come to terms with the Romans.[46]

With the fate of Athaulf and Sigeric before him a new leader might hesitate to reveal too promptly any desire he may have felt for an agreement with the Imperial government. Wallia was chosen in the autumn of 415 precisely because the bulk of the Visigoths were convinced that he would put an end to such peace as existed with Rome:[47] the old oath sworn on the banks of the Danube may or may not have been forgotten, but the spirit which dictated it was still alive. But the Visigoths did not know their man: Wallia pursued the course which is now familiar to us. It seems to have been impossible to find an optimate who still remained uncompromisingly hostile to the Romans; for Wallia repeated the experience of Athaulf and Sigeric. After the failure of his projected assault on Africa, where like Alaric before him he had hoped to settle his people, Wallia, who had been elected precisely in order to fight the Romans, sought peace from them early in 416.[48] His men evidently did not oppose him at once in this, for they had been reduced to a desperate position by the Patrician Constantius (p. 26 above); and the treaty of 416, which was a surrender to the imperial government, was their only method of ending the famine which Constantius had engineered among them. For the next two years Wallia acted as though it were his ambition, too, to become "the author of the Roman restoration": he fought and defeated the other barbarians in Spain in the interests of the Romans.[49] How long his men would have supported him is unknown, for he died in 418 when they were still at a hopeless military disadvantage to the Romans; and before his death he had been given the land around Toulouse upon which his people settled and lived for ninety years.

The dominating feature of Visigothic history between the time of Athanaric and that of Wallia is the growing conflict between the interests of a minority of the people, the optimates, and those of the rank and file. True, the evidence is sadly fragmentary, but, such as it is, let us summarize it:

(i) The remark of the chieftain reported in the *Passion of St. Sabas* when he was informed that Sabas owned no property — "Such a man can neither help nor harm us" — shows not only that those who had no property were of little account politically before 376 but also the converse, that the property-owners had succeeded in securing a disproportionate amount of influence on political affairs and of control over clan life.[50] In other words, a ruling class was coming into existence inside a social organization which made no provision for it and which it was bound to disrupt.

(ii) Fritigern's ambiguous behaviour in 378 shows that at least one member of this rising class had come to the belief that an accommodation with the imperial government would be more conducive to his interests than would continued hostility; and this in spite of the merciless treatment which that government had given to his people throughout the preceding years.

(iii) After Adrianople Fritigern's attitude was not adopted by all the nobility, as the case of Eriulf and his followers shows; indeed, the followers of Eriulf formed the majority of the optimates. Nevertheless, Theodosius, who presumably knew what he was about, set himself to win over "the tribal leaders, who were outstanding in rank and birth," Eriulf as well as Fravittas. By heaping wealth upon them he tried to widen the gap which already existed between them and their followers. In his opinion the propertied class was more likely to respond to Roman advances than were the rank and file of the warriors. But why should some of the leaders have responded to such overtures? What was the basis for their long continued desire for peace with Rome?

(iv) Athaulf, Sigeric, and Wallia were as susceptible to Roman advances as Fravittas and his adherents had been before them, and Athaulf himself explains the reason: his followers would not obey his "laws" and hence there could be no "State." There were no public means of coercion, no means of adequately protecting the wealth and the social status of the optimates, no means by which the leading men could impose their will on a tribal society. But when Athaulf wished to make peace with the imperial government, he wished to incorporate his men in the social organization of the Roman Empire: that was the only available means of substituting for their egalitarian society a new form of organization which would be consistent with the new social relations existing among them. The corollary of this is that when the Visigothic warriors murdered their leaders sooner than allow them to make peace with Rome they were showing their resistance not only to Rome but also to the overthrow of their old form of society.

(v) It is hardly too bold to conclude that Athaulf's motives were in general identical with those of the optimates as a whole in the years immediately preceding the settlement at Toulouse in 418 and that when he speaks of his own motives he speaks also of theirs. However much they may have quarrelled among themselves on the question of who was to head the new Visigothic state, the optimates in general wished it to be established. A policy which attracted only a minority of them in the early years of Theodosius seems to have won the support of most of them in the second decade of the fifth century, for the Visigoths were unable to find an anti-Roman leader at that time, whereas there is no evidence that many of the optimates in the period 410–18 felt as Eriulf had felt thirty years before and as Athaulf had felt in his earlier period.

What we have seen, then, is the steady and in the end rapid decline of an outworn tribal form of society and a series of attempts to replace that tribal organization by a different form of society. What could the mass of the people oppose to their leaders' policy? By the terms of the oath sworn in 376 they would have continued to fight the Romans until they had won the mastery of the Empire. But such a policy, if they had persisted in it, could only have led in the end to their own annihilation. Even if their leaders had had the will, the Visigoths had not the military strength to crush the Romans. Many a barbarian people during the centuries of Roman history had found themselves in this same dilemma, and at no time down to the year 476 was there any northern people who could have destroyed the

49

Romans singlehanded.[51] Even if they had been able to wrest land from the Romans and had been able to hold it permanently, they could not have resumed the life which they had been leading before 376, for the highly complex social and economic conditions in which they would have found themselves would have made such a return to the past impossible. Such a man as Athaulf would not have been content with the position which Athanaric had held. The rank and file of the Visigoths, in fact, had no practicable policy to oppose to that of their leaders, and it was impossible that they could have had one. Once the Visigoths had entered the Empire, there was no alternative to Athaulf's ambitious plans.

III. THE SETTLEMENT OF 418

After their capitulation to Constantius in 416 the Visigoths fought against the Roman government's barbarian enemies in Spain. But in 418 Constantius recalled them, though their victory in Spain was not yet complete; and he settled them in the province of Aquitanica Secunda on the western seaboard of Gaul between the mouth of the Garonne and that of the Loire. This curious action can be explained, in my opinion, as follows, though it must be emphasized that this explanation has been disputed:

The Western provinces were already smouldering with revolt even before the Visigoths entered them. In 417 the Armoricans were being crushed by the imperial forces. Imitating a similar rebellion in Britain they had expelled the Roman officials, had enslaved the landowners, and were trying to maintain themselves as an independent state outside the Roman Empire. Their revolt was so dangerous that, we may suggest, the Roman authorities preferred to share the riches of Aquitaine with the Visigoths, whom they could control, rather than to risk losing them outright to the Armoricans.[52] The Garonne valley supported some of the richest landowners of the West, and it also supplied the Rhine army with food. From the Roman point of view it was imperative that this region should not pass out of imperial control. But Constantius did not try to use the Visigoths to crush the Armoricans, for if he had done so they might have joined his enemies rather than have fought against them: they had a long tradition of cooperation with oppressed elements in the Roman population, and this tradition dated back as far as the third century. But as soon as the Armoricans had been defeated by other Roman forces, Constantius planted the Visigoths in Aquitaine in conditions in which they could not defend their own interests without at the same time protecting those of the local Roman landowners. Constantius gave each Visigothic optimate a portion (sors) of a Roman senatorial estate—the smaller estates were not affected—and this sors was made up of two-thirds of the arable and one half of the pasture and woodland of the estate, which now supported two *consortes,* "partners," one Roman and the other barbarian, instead of a single Roman owner. In 443 Aëtius settled the Burgundians in Savoy, south of the Lake of Geneva, in similar conditions; and the system was transferred to Spain by the Visigoths when they finally settled there. This method of billeting the barbarians was known as *hospitalitas.*[53]

If Athaulf's statement of policy at Narbonne is any guide, it was no part of the barbarian optimates' plan, when once they had gained control of a Roman province, to set up the poorer tribesmen as independent gentlemen in it. And there are not likely to have been enough senatorial estates in Aquitaine to provide "hospitality" for each and every barbarian family. Now, on each estate there was only one barbarian "partner" (*consors*) of the Roman who had originally owned the estate, and yet it is known that more than one barbarian lived on such an estate.[54] What was the relationship between the barbarian who was *consors* and the other barbarians who, though living on the estate, were not *consortes?* We can hardly doubt that the ownership of the barbarian portion of the estate had been vested by the Roman authorities in the one barbarian *consors* and not collectively in the whole group of barbarians living on the estate.[55] I would suggest, then (though the matter is very obscure) that the rank and file of the barbarians on each estate lived on land which was owned by a barbarian optimate. Now, the Burgundian clans still existed as such at the beginning of the sixth century, and the *faramanni,* as the clan members were called, are assumed in one of the Burgundian laws to be living on the one estate. True, the *faramanni* are only once mentioned by name in the Burgundian law code, but this probably means, not that the kindred was then of little significance, but that the law-makers did not wish to give it recognition. If it had been of little or no significance, it is not easy to see why the legislators should have mentioned it even once.[56] Accordingly, it has been strongly argued that the Burgundian optimates settled their clansmen as tenants on their new estates in Savoy.[57] There is no evidence that the Visigothic kindreds still had much significance in 418, so that the humbler Visigoths, who were settled on the estates of the Visigothic nobles, may have been united by some other bond than that of blood-relationship; but they, too, may have been the tenants of the optimate landowners.[58] It may be, of course, that an optimate would support his "companions" (*comites*) at his own expense, or he might allot to each of them the revenues of some four or five colonus-holdings:[59] he was certainly in a position to present them with land.[60] Moreover, the king would reward his favourite followers by making over to them some of the imperial estates which he now controlled.[61] But in general the rank and file of the barbarians are best as-

51

sumed, in my opinion, to have become the tenants of their own leaders. The Visigothic and Burgundian optimates were now a landed gentry like their Roman partners; and their connexion with their former kinsmen was now an economic one.

In this way Constantius and Aëtius solved four problems at one stroke. They converted wandering and hostile masses of barbarians into settled and on the whole contented communities of agriculturalists. As Roman federates, they lived under their own laws and their own rulers, but they were liable to be called upon to give military service to the emperor. They were not intended to have any powers over the Romans who lived among them. Secondly, the Roman authorities broke the alliance between the invading barbarians and the restless elements of the Roman countryside, for although many Romans still fled to "freedom" in the Visigothic kingdom of Aquitaine[62] it could hardly be expected that Visigothic landowners would have much sympathy with a mass of rebellious peasants. Thirdly, the Roman government provided itself with effective military forces which would defend southern Gaul from the uprisings of the slaves and their allies in Armorica and elsewhere, who had caused so much damage earlier in the fifth century. Finally, if our hypothesis is correct, the ranks of the barbarians themselves were now broken. The interests of the nobility were now once and for all in conflict with those of their followers. The nobles were no longer simply the leading men of the people. They were now a landed gentry whose manner of life would become increasingly different from that of the rank and file of the Visigoths. Their relationship with them was no longer that of kinsman with kinsman or tribesman with tribesman: it had become, we have conjectured, that of landlord and tenant. The settlement of the Visigothic optimates as *consortes* of the Roman landlords of Aquitaine was the form in which Athaulf's ambitions were realized. He had seen that it was necessary for his purpose to reach an accommodation with the Romans. His successors had this same aim; and after 418 the Visigothic rulers were able to enforce their laws in Aquitaine without consulting with their followers, and we may study elsewhere the machinery by which they did so, their state apparatus. But the question which had harassed Visigothic society since 378, the question of their relationship with Rome, was not yet solved, for although the majority of the optimates may have come to terms with the Empire, their followers had not done so.

IV. FROM THEODORIC I TO EURIC

Constantius met with one immediate misfortune in 418. As soon as his treaty with the Visigoths had been signed and the process of distributing the land in Aquitaine had been set in motion, Wallia died. Wallia's later career had suggested that he would be the obedient tool of the Roman authorities, and his death must have been felt as a severe blow by Constantius, who may well have known little or nothing of the character of Wallia's successor. In fact, Theodoric I reigned for no less than thirty-three years (418–51), and the mere fact of his survival for so long a period indicates that he was able to satisfy both factions of his people: he was sufficiently hostile to the Romans to avoid the fate of Athaulf and Sigeric, while at the same time he was able to placate the Visigothic nobility and to secure its position as a landed gentry and a ruling class. What is known of his long career shows that it was one of cautious and selective enmity to the imperial authorities.

In his reign the military strength of the Visigoths was still inferior to that which the Romans even at this date were able to muster. Theodoric never undertook an attack on Roman territory at a time when the Romans could have given him their undivided attention. When they were busy with the usurper John in 425[63] or with the Vandals in the early thirties[64] or with the Burgundians and Bacaudae in 436–39,[65] Theodoric tried to gain a footing in the lower Rhone valley, but never when they were not occupied elsewhere. Moreover, as soon as their hands were free and they could turn their attention to him, they had little difficulty in defeating him and driving him back within the original limits of his kingdom. It is true that after suffering heavy losses he managed to defeat Litorius' Huns in 439, but only to find himself at once confronted with the unimpaired army of Aëtius, to whom he granted terms which were more than favourable to the imperial authorities.[66] Accordingly, throughout most of the reign the treaty of 418, which had established the Visigoths as federates, was still in force. It undoubtedly lapsed during the wars of 425 and 436–39, and it may also have lapsed *c.* 430 when a Visigothic optimate named Anaolsus was active near Arles (though Anaolsus may have been merely a retinue-leader undertaking a raid on his own account without Theodoric's explicit connivance).[67] But throughout the rest of the reign the Visigoths were the federates of the Empire, recognized the overlordship of the emperor, and were liable to be called upon to give military service to the Romans. In fact, they did not send help to them more than three or four times in all those thirty-three years; but that does not mean that the initial policy of settling them in Aquitaine had been a mistake. The Romans never tried to dislodge them from Aquitaine when once they had settled them there;[68] and they never engaged in military operations against them except when the Visigoths had first struck out against the cities of the Rhone valley. True, Litorius went over to the offensive in 439 and pressed on to the walls of Toulouse itself in his anxiety to outshine Aetius. But this was an individual effort of his own, and Aëtius can scarcely have approved of it. There is no reason to think that it was ever official Roman policy to oust the Visigoths from Toulouse or to undo the settlement which they had imposed in 418. Indeed, that they were well pleased with the outcome of the treaty of 418 is suggested by the fact that they went on voluntarily to settle other barbarians in other parts of Gaul on very much the same terms as those on which they had settled the Visigoths in Aquitaine.

The events which followed on the death of Theodoric in 451 are illuminating. No sooner was the old king dead than the question of the Visigoths' relationship with Rome, the question which had vexed them since the days of Fritigern, came to the fore again. Theodoric was succeeded by his eldest son Thorismud. There had been some tension and suspicion between him and his five brothers[69] even before their father's death in 451, for Aëtius knew of their quarrels at the time of the battle against Attila on the Catalaunian Plains, in which Theodoric I was killed: as soon as the battle was won he advised Thorismud to hurry home to Toulouse in case he should be forestalled and replaced as king by his two brothers Theodoric and Frederic.[70] Thorismud went back to Toulouse and established himself, as he thought, on the throne. Then, when Aëtius was busy with the Hunnic invasion of Italy in 452, he went to war with the Alans of Orleans and beat them.[71] This was an anti-Roman move, for these Alans were Roman federates who had been planted at Orleans, as the Visigoths had been planted in Aquitaine, apparently in order to seal off the Armoricans from the rest of Gaul.[72] Thorismud next cast an eye on Arles, which had often been the object of his father's designs.[73] It looked as though he were about to resume the policy which his father had tried to carry out on more than one occasion in the first half of his reign, the policy of trying to annex the wealthy lower Rhone valley, which was still in Roman hands. But after reigning for a year Thorismud was murdered by his brothers Theodoric and Frederic; and the reason why they murdered him was that they felt his policies and activities to be directed against peace between the Romans and the Visigoths. Relations between the two powers had been peaceful, if not friendly, since 439, when Theodoric I had renewed the treaty of 418. But now Thorismud had attacked and beaten the Alans, the federates of the Roman government in central Gaul, and he had then resumed the aggressive moves against Arles. Attempts had been made to deflect him from this policy of enmity with Rome, but he had persevered with it and could not be made to desist. Therefore his brothers killed him.[74]

In a word, Thorismud was assassinated for exactly the opposite reason of that which had led to the assassination of Athaulf and Sigeric. They had fallen because of their desire to reach an accommodation with the imperial government, whereas Thorismud fell because of his hostility to it. Although the result was different in 453 from what it had been in 415, the issue at stake had not changed. The struggles within Visigothic society still centred around the same question in 453 as they had done forty years earlier, the question of the people's relations with Rome. But this question itself concealed a deeper and more vital problem. Athaulf and Sigeric had been killed because the ultimate aim of their pro-Roman policy was the establishment of a coercive power over their followers (pp. 45 ff. above). But in 453 this power was in existence: the Visigothic rulers had now attained to the social and political status of the Roman landowners and they had inherited the Roman apparatus of state in western Gaul. Accordingly, the aim of Thorismud's murderers was to preserve the *status quo* and to maintain themselves in their new position. But something of the old hatred of the Romans still survived among the Visigoths at large, and this was expressed in the policies of Thorismud. Yet it is difficult to avoid the impression that Thorismud had diverted their wrath into a course of action which would scarcely have satisfied the murderers of Athaulf and Sigeric. These two had fallen because of the people's resistance to their own leaders' attempt to impose their "laws" on Visigothic society. But the basis for such opposition had now gone. The coercive state power now existed, and in the conditions of the settlement in Aquitaine it could hardly be done away with. The official revival of an anti-Roman policy by Thorismud, then, was not altogether a revival of the ideas of those who had killed Athaulf. The outward form (the opposition to Rome) of the old policy still existed in 453, but the inner content (maintenance of the old liberties) had disappeared. And it is not easy to see how the position could have been different. Continued hostility to Rome would have achieved little. As in the days of Fritigern and Athaulf (p. 49 f. above), it was hardly possible for the rank and file to have a satisfactory policy to oppose to that of their leaders.

Thorismud was succeeded by one of his assassins, his brother Theodoric, the second son of Theodoric I; and the opening years of his reign were no less remarkable than the reign of his predecessor. Theodoric I had never been called upon, or at any rate had never been willing, to aid the Roman landowners by crushing an uprising of the Bacaudae (though the Roman policy of *hospitalitas* had been successful to the extent that no peasant uprising had troubled Aquitaine during his reign). Indeed, when a Bacaudic revolt broke out in Gaul in 435 Theodoric had taken advantage of it to attack the lower Rhone valley; and Aëtius had used other allies to crush it. It would, of course, have been politically impossible to call upon the anti-Roman Thorismud to undertake a campaign against Bacaudae beyond his frontiers. But now at last in 453 came the Roman government's opportunity. Theodoric II and his brother Frederic were solidly on the Roman side. What, then, is the first recorded action of the new reign? Before the murder of Aëtius on 21 September 454 the Bacaudae in the province of Tarraconensis in Spain were attacked and defeated by a Visigothic force operating under the command of Frederic, who had helped to assassinate Thorismud; and this Visigothic force had entered Spain and had attacked the Bacaudae there on the authority of the Roman government.[75] Now and only now could the Roman government have called on a Visigothic king to act in such a way as this; and as soon as the opportunity came, they grasped it.

In 462 the Visigoths of Theodoric II fought for the new Emperor Libius Severus against some rebellious Roman forces. They took possession of Narbonne and hence probably of most of the province of Narbonensis Prima.[76] The king's brother Frederic forced the rebels out of southern Gaul, pursued them to the Loire, but was killed in a battle at Orleans in 463.[77] Theodoric had gone a step further than either he or his predecessors had ever dared to go before: since the foundation of the kingdom in 418 we never hear elsewhere of the Visigoths taking part in the civil wars of the Romans (apart from their interference against the Bacaudae in Spain). This Theodoric had received the elements of a Roman education from Avitus before the latter became Western emperor. He had learned something of Roman law and of Virgil; and his instructor did not fail to implant in him a desire for peace with Rome.[78] And in the last period of his reign, sometime in the years 462–66, a Gallic landlord refers to Theodoric as "superior to his mighty father, glory of the Goths, pillar and salvation of the Roman race."[79] In the end, it seems, he was the champion not of the Visigothic nobility only but of the Gallo-Roman aristocracy as well, and he was prepared to make their wars his wars. He was a worthy successor to Athaulf and Sigeric, and he met the same fate as they. He was murdered by his brother Euric, who put an end forever to the treaty of 418. He proclaimed the full independence of the Visigothic kingdom in 475, a year before the disappearance of Romulus Augustulus and the Western Empire itself.[80] From then until the destruction of the kingdom of Toulouse by the Franks in 507 the Roman landowners in the kingdom lived in comparative harmony with their barbarian rulers and indeed played a considerable part in the royal administration, even though Romans and Visigoths had not wholly fused even in 711 when the Muslims destroyed the last remnants of the Goths.

Among the frontier peoples of the first century A.D. the dominating political question had often been that of their relations with Rome. Whether the same was the case among the Visigoths before 376 we cannot say owing to the paucity of the evidence for their political life in that period. But as soon as our sources become fuller, that very question comes to the fore; and it remains the leading aspect of Visigothic political history until the disappearance of the Western Empire. We have suggested that in the fifth century a struggle was fought out between the rank and file of the barbarians, on the one hand, and, on the other, an increasing proportion of the Visigothic nobility acting in conjunction with the Roman government, and that this struggle concerned not only the question of the people's relations with Rome but also that of the form of government under which they were to live at home.

II. Italy

4

A.D. 476 and After

In the summer of 449 a party of Romans and others crossed the imperial frontier on the lower Danube north of Naissus (Nish) into barbarian country and made their way on horseback over the plains of Wallachia.[1] The party was composed of a Roman ambassador on his way to interview Attila the Hun. With him went his advisers and servants together with some representatives of the Huns. These Hun representatives had gone to Constantinople in the spring on a diplomatic mission and were now on their way back to their master. They included two of Attila's most trusted lieutenants. One of the two, oddly enough, was a Roman. He came from Pannonia, and by serving as Attila's secretary — the paper work of the Hun empire, such as it was, was in the hands of Latin secretaries — he had risen to a position of importance in the barbarian empire. His name was Orestes. The other, who at that date was much more influential, was a native-born Hun. His name was Edeco, one of the most powerful men under Attila, a famous warrior, commander of part of the Hun army.

By a strange turn of fate the sons of these two fellow-travellers, Orestes and Edeco, were to play a spectacular role in the history of Europe. Some years after this journey of the ambassador, Orestes fathered a son whom he called Romulus after his father-in-law; and the child became known to history as Romulus "the little Augustus," Romulus Augustulus, the last of the Western Roman emperors. The man who was to dethrone him in August 476 and to become *de facto* the first barbarian ruler of Italy was the son of Orestes' travelling companion, Edeco.[2] This was Odoacer, who was a sixteen-year-old youth when Edeco and Orestes rode across the scorching plains of Wallachia.[3]

After Attila's death in 453 and the collapse of his empire a year or two later (p. 115 f. below) Orestes did not become a vagabond or a homeless brigand on the Danubian frontier of the Roman Empire like so many of

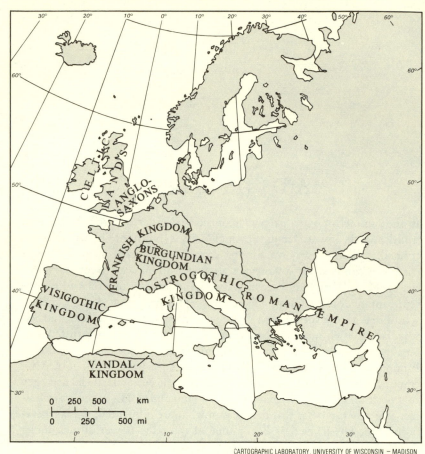

Europe c. 526 A.D.

Attila's former henchmen and like Attila's sons. He must have returned to the West and served with outstanding distinction in some military capacity, for in little more than twenty years (in 475) the Western emperor Julius Nepos appointed him as patrician with the supreme command of his army. But in that very same year the new patrician rebelled at Ravenna and elevated his son Romulus to the throne in Julius Nepos' place. Thus, Romulus, though we call him the last of the Western emperors, was in fact a usurper; and the man who was truly the last Western emperor was Julius Nepos. As Bury remarked, these names in the pages of the chroniclers —Julius, Augustulus, Romulus—meet us like ghosts rearisen from past days of Roman history.[4]

Edeco was not so lucky as Orestes. With the fall of Hun power in 453–

54 a throng of hungry and shattered peoples were released on to the middle Danubian frontier of the Roman Empire (p. 18 above). The Huns had destroyed the normal way of life of these peoples and had shifted some of them from their old habitations. Thus, when the Huns first appeared in Europe *c.* 370 they overran the Ostrogoths in the Ukraine, but when their empire fell the Ostrogoths appear on the middle Danube: they had been shifted halfway across Europe. The Huns' old subjects were now fragmented, divided, and subdivided. They owned few cattle and no land; and they spent their lives in cattle-raiding, marauding, and in ambushing and even fighting pitched battles against men as rootless and hungry as themselves. In the tumultuous confusion of the years following the destruction of the Hun empire we catch a glimpse of Edeco. In 469 at the battle of the unidentified river Bolia in Pannonia we see him and his son Hunoulf, but not Odoacer, at the head of the Sciri for a moment, as they and their allies attack the Ostrogoths. But the Ostrogoths defeated them, and Edeco is never heard of again.[5] Hunoulf wandered off to Constantinople, where he very quickly rose to become Master of the Soldiers in Illyricum; but Odoacer and a band of other uprooted and ruined men, who had taken no part in these events, had made their way to Italy to try their luck as soldiers of fortune in the West Roman service. On the journey to Italy *c.* 461 (p. 117 below) Odoacer visited St. Severinus in his cell at Favianis in the province of Noricum; and Arian Christian though he was, he impressed the holy man, who was a Catholic. Now somewhat under thirty years of age, he was poorly dressed, very tall—he had to remain stooping as he spoke to Severinus in case he should knock his head against the cell roof—and evidently impressive. "Go to Italy," said the man of God as the barbarian was taking his leave, "go, and although you are now dressed in the shabbiest hides, you will soon bestow many gifts on multitudes of people." It is clear that the barbarian had made a deep impression on him, and Odoacer never forgot Severinus. Years afterwards, when he was acting as *de facto* king of Italy, he wrote to him offering to grant him any wish that he might name. The holy man asked only that a certain Ambrosius should be recalled from exile; and Odoacer gladly recalled him. We cannot reasonably doubt the high regard in which Odoacer is said to have held Severinus: Eugippius, our source of information for these events, was writing in 511 when Odoacer and Severinus were alike long since dead and no longer to be feared or flattered.

In the summer of 476, then, the legitimate Western emperor, Julius Nepos, was in exile in Dalmatia, the usurper Romulus Augustulus was seated on the throne of the West, his father Orestes was the effective ruler of Italy, Odoacer was a rising soldier in his army, and Edeco was forgotten or dead. The youthful emperor sat like a voiceless shadow upon the throne for ten months. But then the troops under Odoacer rebelled. Orestes was killed at Pavia. The rioting in the town and the fires caused by it were fierce; and Odoacer was afterwards obliged to remit the taxes of the place for a period of five years: the destruction must have been enormous.[6] The young emperor was then pensioned off, a pretty and ineffectual boy, to live in the castle of Lucullus (the consul of 74 B.C.) in Campania, not far from Naples, in which the Emperor Tiberius had died centuries ago. He was given a handsome pension of 6,000 *solidi* a year and is never heard of again.[7] When we next hear of the castle of Lucullus in the time of Pope Gelasius (492–96), it appears to have been owned by a lady of the highest ("illustrious") rank called Barbaria, who turned it or part of it into a monastery. What had become of Romulus Augustulus nobody knows.

I. *HOSPITES* ("GUESTS") IN ITALY

Why was the last of the Western Roman emperors dethroned? Only one ancient authority discusses the reason for his downfall, and there is no reason to doubt his explanation so far as it goes.[8] The "Roman" army in Italy at this date was mostly, perhaps wholly, composed not of Romans but of a mixed group of barbarians. Indeed, there is no reference at all to Roman soldiers in Italy in 476. The troops were Turcilingi (of whom we never hear in any other connexion and who were presumably speakers of some Turkic language),[9] Germanic Sciri, Heruls, and others.[10] These troops had evidently observed that the barbarian armies in Gaul had been settled on the land as *hospites* in Aquitanica Secunda, Savoy, and elsewhere and were now relatively prosperous peasant-soldiers; and they aspired to be settled on the land in Italy on similar terms. They demanded that Orestes should impose *hospitalitas* upon Italy, and this Orestes refused to do. It is not clear why he refused. Few, I think, will be satisfied with the sentimental suggestion of Bury — that Orestes "was sufficiently Roman to be determined to keep the soil of Italy inviolate."[11] The system of billeting known as *hospitalitas* had been imposed in Gaul not by the barbarians but by the imperial government. Its purpose was to satisfy Roman interests, not barbarian ones. It appears to have been welcomed generally by the great Roman landowners of Gaul: at any rate, we hear of no resistance on their part. Why then did the Patrician Orestes now risk and lose his life in order to avoid imposing it on northern Italy? Procopius does not tell us, and we have no means of guessing with any certainty. In my opinion, this form of billeting was accepted by the Gallic landowners because their estates were menaced by internal enemies, by rebellious peasants: they preferred tame barbarians to untamed and hostile peasants (pp. 31 ff. above). But so far as we know, there was no hint of such a threat to the landed estates of Italy.

Hence, the settlement of the barbarians on the soil of Italy had to be forced upon the Italian landowners. Theodoric stresses that by sacrificing part of the land the Romans had obtained a defence force; and he hints that by surrendering part of the estates they assured the security of the whole property.[12] The only probable enemy in Italy, it seems, was not a hostile peasantry (though there is no proof that that was not the case): it was rather the barbarian troops themselves. So the terms of the settlement in Italy were less favourable to the "guests," the *hospites,* than they had been in Gaul. In Gaul each barbarian settler received two-thirds of the arable land of the estate on which he was planted, whereas in Italy he received only one-third. Thus, the word *tertia* when used in this connexion in Gaul refers to the part of the estate which was left in the hands of the original owner, whereas in Italy a *tertia* was the part that was made over to the barbarian. Perhaps this variation of the terms of the plantation was a sop to the resentful Roman landowners of Italy, though that is no more than a guess.

At all events, Orestes refused the request of the barbarian troops in 476, and the troops rebelled. Odoacer, who had evidently become very prominent among them, undertook to satisfy their demand if they would accept him as their leader. The troops agreed. They killed Orestes at Pavia on August 28 and sent Romulus off to live on his pension on the bay of Naples. Thereupon, Odoacer imposed the system of *hospitalitas* on Italy.

II. ZENO AND ODOACER

What was his constitutional position now that Romulus had fallen and Orestes was dead? The question is a vexed one. At one extreme is Mommsen, who held the view that Odoacer was not only king of the barbarians but also had been appointed as Master of the Soldiers by the Eastern Emperor Zeno: he was an official of Zeno, governing Italy in Zeno's name, as Orestes had governed it in the name of Romulus or as Aetius had ruled it in the name of Valentinian III. At the other extreme, A. H. M. Jones held that Odoacer was a completely independent king: he was as free as Geiseric in Africa, owing no allegiance to Constantinople. Italy was no longer part of the Roman Empire. Jones undoubtedly showed that Mommsen's theory is hardly tenable as it stands: in particular there is no valid evidence that Odoacer or Theoderic held the office of Master of the Soldiers. And yet I think that Mommsen is nearer to the truth than Jones in his thesis on the independence of Italy from the power of East Rome. Italy was still part of the Roman Empire, and no one at that date would have considered it as an independent state.[13]

I believe that Odoacer's position was not as clear-cut or as sharply defined as either of these two theses would suggest. In the winter of 476–77, as soon as he had established himself in Italy, Odoacer obliged the Roman senate to send an embassy to Zeno in Constantinople.[14] The ambassadors handed over the imperial insignia which Romulus Augustulus had worn and declared that they no longer needed an emperor in the West: Zeno would reign over both halves of the Empire. Those words are of capital importance: the envoys, in fact, openly admitted Zeno's claim to be the ruler of Italy. So far from asserting that Italy was no longer part of the Empire, they explicitly declared that it was indeed part of it. The view that Italy was part of the Empire was not in dispute. They went on to say that Odoacer would be adequate to protect Italy, for he was a skillful politician and an experienced soldier. They made two requests of Zeno—that he should appoint Odoacer as patrician, and that he should make over to him the administration of Italy. But the title of patrician by itself would be a mere mark of status. It carried no powers in itself, either civil or military. Such a title would not put Odoacer on a par with the great patricians of the last years of the Western Empire, Aëtius, Ricimer, Gundobad, and Orestes; for these men had also occupied a high military office, and it was not the patriciate but their military post that had given them their power. Since the ambassadors did not ask for a specific military office by virtue of which Odoacer could govern Italy, their intention was presumably to leave it to the emperor to decide what post Odoacer should hold. No doubt they expected that Zeno would appoint him as Master of the Soldiers, for if this officer were granted the status of patrician he would thereby be recognized as the supreme commander.

The envoys did not remind Zeno that there was in existence a legitimate Western emperor, Julius Nepos, whom Orestes had dethroned in favour of his son Romulus and who was still living in Dalmatia. Zeno needed no reminder. Nepos himself had an embassy in Constantinople at the very time when Odoacer's envoys were there. But, sympathetic though he was with Nepos, Zeno was fundamentally uninterested in foreign affairs: he had too much to occupy him at home, and he was certainly not strong enough to intervene in Italy. He therefore took a middle course in his reply to the two groups of envoys. To those of the legitimate Western emperor, Nepos, he said that he would supply neither men nor money to restore him to Italy. To those of Odoacer he gave a reply of considerable ambiguity. He instructed them to accept Nepos back to Italy as their rightful ruler. If Odoacer wished to become a Patrician he must apply to Nepos for the appointment—though if Nepos had not anticipated him by granting the title of his own accord he would himself confer it upon him! Nepos was the legitimate ruler of the West, and Odoacer was to restore him to his throne and—one way or the other—was to become a Patrician: he was presumably to be Nepos' right-hand man and his military commander-in-chief, though that was not stated explicitly.

So far, so good. If Zeno had stopped there his intentions would have been clear. But Zeno did not stop there. Although he had formally refused to appoint Odoacer as patrician, he went on to address him as "Patrician" in a letter which he now wrote to him, apparently before Nepos had a chance of even considering the matter. Thus, the emperor addressed Odoacer as a patrician when in fact he was not formally a patrician. Odoacer may well have been puzzled. Indeed, he seems to have drawn the inference that he was *not* a patrician, for in his surviving documents he never refers to himself as such. Of the envoys' second request — that Zeno should appoint Odoacer to govern Italy — the emperor said not a word. And yet he went on to praise the good start that Odoacer had made in governing Italy. He even seems to say that Nepos also approved of Odoacer's start in controlling Italy. It is not easy to see how his answer to the envoys of Odoacer could have been less specific or more ambiguous. We are assured that his aim was to help Nepos, but of that emperor's exact relationship to Odoacer, if the latter accepted Nepos back to Italy, he said not a syllable.[15]

What is of the first importance is that Zeno is never reported to have resumed these inconclusive negotiations of 476–77. So far as we know, he never explained or unravelled these cryptic utterances, and Odoacer's constitutional position was never made any clearer. While Julius Nepos lived, of course, there was on paper no constitutional problem whatever: Nepos was Western emperor with full control in theory over Italy. And we are told that the numismatic evidence puts it beyond doubt that Odoacer recognized him as Western emperor and minted coins for him in Italy until his murder in 480. True, he will not have had much — or indeed any — power in Italy, but he was still nominally and beyond all cavil the emperor of the West.[16] Odoacer's recognition of him contradicted his original statement to Zeno that the West did not need an emperor of its own. But that was a nicety that will hardly have troubled the barbarian; and presumably Nepos had not returned to Italy before 480 because he feared that if he did so his life-expectancy would be short.

The question is, what happened after Nepos had been murdered? He was assassinated in the early summer of 480, and, so far as we know, neither Zeno nor Odoacer saw fit to raise the question of what the position was now. Odoacer's envoys had explicitly recognized Zeno as ruler of both parts of the Empire, and Zeno had certainly given not the slightest hint that he regarded Italy as in any way an independent country — any such thought (in my opinion) would have been inconceivable at this date. But that is all that was clear and agreed upon.

There was a Western consul for 480 and the following years; but, although chroniclers might use the names of these consuls for the purpose of dating the events which they were recording, it is not at all certain that the Eastern government recognized them.[17] Basilius, the consul for 480, was certainly recognized, but he was beyond a doubt the nominee of Julius Nepos. If Zeno had recognized consuls appointed by Odoacer he would thereby have admitted publicly that Odoacer was on an equal footing with himself; and this, naturally, he would not do. The attitude of Odoacer towards appointing Masters of the Soldiers is a matter to which we shall return (p. 71 below).

How did Odoacer regard himself? In a document in which he makes a grant of land to a powerful Roman nobleman called Pierius he calls himself "King Odoacer." At a synod of Italian bishops which met at Rome in 483 the chairman, the Praetorian Prefect and Patrician Basilius, the consul of 480, is described as "vicegerent of the outstanding king Odoacer." On the other hand, Symmachus, consul of 485, on a bronze tablet speaks of "our lord Zeno and the lord Odoacer"; he did not know how exactly to distinguish them, and so he put the pair of them on an equal footing while avoiding niceties.[18] On a public inscription which Odoacer himself set up in the Colosseum at Rome, where all the world could read it, he does not refer to himself as "king" at all, but simply as "the most excellent" (or the like) "Odoacer." (The adjective has been lost from the inscription, but enough of the wording survives to prove that there was no reference to royalty.) That is to say, on this official and public document Odoacer is a private citizen and does not claim to be anything else.[19] We are told that he has left practically no mark on the numismatic history of the time. It used to be held that on the silver and copper coins which he was alleged to have minted at Ravenna he referred to himself simply as "Fl(avius) Odova(cer)," but it has now been discovered that all the coins bearing his name and likeness are forgeries![20] So when Cassiodorus tells us that "Odoacer assumed the name of king, though he did not wear the royal insignia," he exaggerates: there were occasions when Odoacer did *not* use the title "king."[21] And finally, like Theoderic after him but unlike the independent Visigothic kings of Spain, he never dated his official documents by the year of his reign, nor did any other ruler in Italy.[22] Documents were usually dated by the name of the Western consul.

The fact that Odoacer's power was never defined explains why those contemporary and later writers who had occasion to speak of him found themselves in a quandary: how were they to describe him? They describe him sometimes as "king" of one or other of the barbarian peoples who supplied troops to his army. He can be "king of the Goths and Romans." He is also "king of the Turcilingi" or "king of the Turcilingi and Rugi."[23] But usually he is simply "king" without further qualification.[24] If he himself did not know precisely what his position was, historians could hardly decide the point for him.

It would not be an exaggeration, then, to say that from 476 until Theoderic's invasion of Italy in 489 Odoacer had no constitutional position in Italy that could be juridically defined. He was a patrician and yet not a patrician. He had no warrant from the emperor to govern Italy, and yet the emperor had congratulated him for maintaining proper law and order among the Romans. Moreover, the emperor had acquiesced in the following thirteen years of his government. Odoacer often, though not always, referred to himself as "king." In practice, though he never wore the purple, he usurped the powers of the Western emperor. Without reference to Zeno he made appointments, preserved the old Roman offices and institutions, and directed the government in both civil and military matters. But these activities, I would suggest, had no constitutional justification. Was he subordinate to Zeno, or was he on a par with him, or was he independent of him? There can be no doubt about the last of these questions: he did not claim to be independent of Constantinople, and certainly Zeno did not recognize him as such. The other questions were never officially asked and never officially answered. In fact, he had no official existence at all. If we suppose that Odoacer was an official of Zeno's, what office did he hold? There is no answer: he was certainly not Master of the Soldiers. Was he on a par with Zeno? But that would be to suppose that he was an Augustus, and Odoacer himself never claimed to be that. Nor was he in any sense a constitutional king of the Italians as well as of the barbarians who lived in Italy: there was no such person as "king of the Italians." And the leader of the barbarian federates, though he might well call himself king of the barbarians who followed him, was never recognized by the emperors as king. Although we may reject the general position taken up by A. H. M. Jones, we cannot disagree with his remark that "there is in fact no evidence that Zeno ever gave any kind of official recognition to Odoacer."[25] The one point on which Odoacer and Zeno agreed explicitly and formally was that Italy was still part of the Roman Empire (p. 66 above). Odoacer admitted that publicly in his negotiations in 476–77; and Theoderic the Ostrogoth was to admit it some years later.

Odoacer gave Italy thirteen years of domestic and foreign peace. He carried through the measures which settled the barbarian soldiers on the soil of parts of Italy in the normal manner of federates. After the fall of Orestes we hear no hint of Roman discontent or resistance to his actions in this respect. One Roman panicked when he found Italy under the unrestricted control of a barbarian: an Italian priest and nobleman, who had been closely associated with Orestes and whose name was Primenius, fled to the remote province of Noricum Ripense "fearing the assassins of Orestes." He was not afraid of barbarian rule as such. He was afraid that his association with Orestes would bring him down with these particular barbarians.[26] (His flight to Noricum Ripense shows that that province lay outside Odoacer's dominions.) But in fact Odoacer turned out to be, more than any Roman emperor, the champion of the liberties of the Roman senate. "The freedom of the Roman nobility," wrote Ernst Stein, "that freedom for which long ago Brutus and Cassius had died at Philippi, was never so fully re-established as by the first barbarian king to rule over Italy. . . . In his concessions to the Roman nobility he went even further than his predecessors, Aëtius and Ricimer, since there was no longer any representative of the imperial traditions in Italy to stop him."[27] We might have expected that the position of the Catholic Church would have been difficult under the rule of an heretical monarch—Odoacer was an Arian. In fact, so far as he was concerned its life could hardly have been simpler. On the whole, life in general in Italy went on much as before. The aristocracy had little reason to complain: they could influence a relatively civilized barbarian king in Italy very much more easily than a bureaucratic emperor far away in Constantinople. The Church was not persecuted. The peasantry tilled the fields and paid their rents and taxes as they had always done. The decay of the cities was probably not accelerated to any appreciable extent.

But if no Roman senator had to fear the public executioner in the reign of Odoacer, the same was not true of his Germanic followers. Whether because they disapproved of his attitude towards the Roman nobility or for some other reason, there was dissatisfaction among some of the king's influential followers in his early days. On July 11, 477, a count called Brachila was put to death at Ravenna, and Jordanes remarks curiously that this was done so as to strike terror into the Romans! In 478 another Germanic noble, whose name was Ardaric, rebelled against Odoacer and was executed with his mother and brother on November 19.[28] It is lamentable that nothing is known about these rebels and their aims.

In Italy, then, the "fall" of the Western Empire—in the sense of the deposition of Romulus Augustulus—could hardly have gone more smoothly. As Mommsen pointed out, the Germanic Italy of the earlier sixth century, which we tend to regard as the creation of Theoderic the Ostrogoth, was in fact brought into being by Odoacer. It was not Theoderic who introduced religious toleration or who first refrained from passing new laws or who began to preserve the old Roman institutions, achievements of which

70

the Goths make so much in the pages of Procopius. All these matters were due to Odoacer, and the arrival of the Ostrogoths meant only a change of personnel.[29]

III. ODOACER'S POSITION IN THE EMPIRE

By a curious coincidence neither Mommsen nor Jones considered the actions of Odoacer when he understood that Zeno had sent Theoderic and the Ostrogoths to Italy to overthrow him. He was now a usurper, and it is unfortunate that this important episode in his career is known only from a single fragment of John of Antioch.[30] It appears that in the years 489–93, when the outlawed Odoacer was fighting Theoderic, he began to mint silver and bronze coins which discarded the name and likeness of Zeno and replaced them with personifications of Rome and Ravenna.[31] In all other ways, too, Odoacer threw off the pretence of allegiance to Zeno; but he did not declare himself an independent king. What he did was to declare his son, Thela (whose name is also given as Ocla) as Caesar: he was to be the new Western emperor.[32] Odoacer evidently intended to do what none of the other great barbarian commanders of the West had ever achieved — to seat a barbarian's son on the throne. He also appointed a certain Tufa as Master of the Soldiers on 1 April 489, and after him a man called Livila to the same post. Now, an appointment to the post of Master of the Soldiers was one that only the emperor was entitled to make. Odoacer had never presumed to fill it before (and Theoderic never filled it throughout his long reign later on). The implication is that Odoacer was now taking over imperial powers, presumably in the name of Thela.[33] So it looks as though he was trying to restore the position as it had existed in 476. There was to be a new Western emperor, Thela, with unrestricted power to establish even Masters of the Soldiers. The two "parts" of the Roman Empire were to be in existence once again, and he himself was to be the patrician to Thela as Orestes had once been the patrician of Romulus. He was thinking exclusively in Roman terms. The idea of a kingdom that would be independent of the Roman Empire does not seem to have entered his head. Thela was Caesar, not *rex*.

But it is far from clear why it was Tufa rather than Odoacer who took the field against Theoderic. Odoacer was not an old man — he was sixty when Theoderic murdered him in 493. Nor is it clear what his military post was to be. But the essential fact is that he did not declare himself an independent monarch. From the time when he joined the Roman army, perhaps about the year 461 (p. 117 below), until the day of his death in 493, he was part of the Roman Empire and never thought of himself as anything else. He was no Geiseric, no Euric.

IV. THEODERIC *REX*

Theoderic, now a Patrician, set out for Italy in 489 on the understanding that, if he should overthrow Odoacer, "he should rule in his place only until Zeno arrived there."[34] That is the statement of a well informed contemporary writer, and it deserves belief. Theoderic was to take over the *de facto* position of Odoacer, even if that position had never been defined in law or in a formal treaty. But there is no definition of what that position was to be: when a modern scholar tells us that Theoderic was provisionally to be "king,"[35] we reply that the word "king" is neither used nor implied. The position had not been defined in Odoacer's time, and it was not defined now.[36] But Odoacer had ruled Italy for over a dozen years, and custom had no doubt established his powers. Yet there is a clear implication that Italy was to remain part of the Roman Empire and that Zeno was its rightful ruler: he had the right to go there, and one day he would arrive. But in the meantime Theoderic, after suppressing the "revolt" of Odoacer, would look after Italy for Zeno and would govern it for him. That is to say, Zeno had never recognized the independence of Italy, and he did not do so now. Nor did he appoint Theoderic as Master of the Soldiers, as Jones showed, though for several years the leader of the Ostrogoths had been a patrician.

Zeno died in 491 and was succeeded by Anastasius (491–518). Shortly after his accession to the throne, "the Goths confirmed Theoderic as their king without waiting for the new emperor's command."[37] Hitherto there had been two barbarian rulers in Italy, Odoacer and Theoderic, each with his own followers. Now Odoacer had been eliminated. Evidently Theoderic ought to have awaited the new emperor's recognition as leader of both barbarian factions in Italy, both the men of Odoacer (in so far as they had survived) and the Ostrogoths. But his men were impatient. They anticipated the emperor. The words do not say that Theoderic was now *appointed* as king of the barbarians: he had been king of at least the Ostrogoths for many years. He was now *confirmed* as king, presumably not of the Ostrogoths alone but also of the remnants of Odoacer's Heruls, Rugi, and the others.[38] What we can be sure of is that Theoderic did not become king over the Italians as well as the barbarians. There was never in this period a "king" of the Italians. Henceforth in his official documents his sole title is that of "king," but he never defines of whom or of what he is the king. He is not "king of the Goths" (though in fact he may well have been that); but if he had taken this title he would seem to have excluded his power over the Italians.[39] Nor is he "king of the Romans" nor "king of Italy." He is simply "king" without qualification.

There were limits to his powers. Certain Gothic representatives, whose words are reported by Procopius,[40] point out that Theoderic never passed a law, whether written or unwritten. He could and did issue "edicts" within the framework of Roman law, though he interpreted this limitation liberally.[41] The envoys also pointed out that Theoderic always allowed the Eastern emperors to nominate the Western consuls. He could not confer Roman citizenship on a Goth or appoint a Goth to a Roman civilian office or to the senate. In this last matter he may seem to have stretched a point when, if some words of Cassiodorus can be pressed, a Goth called Arigern entered the Roman senate—though in fact Theoderic describes Arigern as "almost" a Roman citizen.[42] (A Goth called Tuluin certainly became a senator and a patrician in the exceptional circumstances that followed Theoderic's death when the new king was a child—and for all we know, Tuluin's admission to the senate may have been sanctioned by the Emperor Justin.)[43] Theoderic could confer the title *vir illustris* upon Goths, a title that in Roman times had carried with it admission to the senate. But the Visigothic kings of Spain also conferred this title upon Goths, and in Spain there was no senate for them to enter. So if Theoderic gave the title *illustris* to Goths, it does not follow that they were necessarily enrolled in the senate.

Whatever his precise office may have been, it took Theoderic no less than five years (492–97) of patient negotiation before he persuaded the Emperor Anastasius to recognize it; and from this time forward he discarded the title patrician which he had used hitherto. When Athalaric, Theoderic's grandson and successor, announced to the Emperor Justin (518–27) his succession to his grandfather's throne in 526, he expressed the hope that Justin would grant him his friendship "on the same terms, on the same conditions" (*illis pactis, illis condicionibus*) as he and his predecessor had granted it to Theoderic. But he made not the slightest attempt to explain the nature of these "terms" and these "conditions."[44] I believe that the terms and the conditions could not be defined now because they had never been defined in the past. Indeed, Anastasius may have recognized Theoderic's position no more than Zeno had recognized that of Odoacer. There are many occasions in our sources when we would think that a specific reference to the constitutional position of the ruler of Italy must inevitably be made, and yet no such reference appears in our authorities. Perhaps the most noteworthy of these occasions is the dialogue between Belisarius and the Ostrogoths at Rome in 537–38 when "if the Goths . . . could have cited a formal treaty or grant authorizing Theoderic's rule over Italy, they surely would have done so."[45] I conclude that the constitutional position of Theoderic, like that of Odoacer before him, was never defined.

It is interesting to see how Procopius in his exceedingly detailed narrative handles this point. He does not seem to know any precise title by which he could call the Gothic leaders. He says that Theoderic overthrew Odoacer and that he himself held the "power" (*kratos*) over the Goths and Italians: he did not assume the dress or name of "emperor" (*basileus*) of the Romans but continued to be called *rex,* a term used of barbarian rulers.[46] In another passage he repeats that Theoderic had *kratos* over the Goths, though he makes no reference to the Italians.[47] He ascribes to Belisarius the remark that Zeno "did not send Theoderic to fight Odoacer so that Theoderic should rule Italy. Why should the emperor exchange one tyrant (usurper) for another? His aim was that Italy should be free and subject to the emperor."[48] Athalaric, too, according to the historian, had *kratos* over the Goths and Italians. When Amalasuntha decided to sell out her people to Justinian, she proposed to make over to him the *kratos* over the Goths and Italians.[49] And that is exactly what Theodahad also wished to do.[50] On the other hand, in a remarkable passage he gives us his personal opinion that Theoderic was "in name a usurper (*tyrannos*) but in fact a true emperor (*basileus*), second to none of those who have won glory from the beginning in this office."[51] And he goes on to stress the vast popularity of Theoderic among Italians as well as among Goths. But this is a value judgement, not a constitutional description of the barbarian.

When the great war began in 535 the usage changes somewhat. Wittigis is simply the "leader" (*hegoumenos*) of the Goths; but his envoys to the King of Persia make a very much higher claim for him. They refer to him by no less a term than that which was used to describe the emperor: he was *basileus* of the Goths and Italians.[52] In 536 the Goths chose him as *basileus* of themselves and the Italians. And in 540 they clad Ildibad in the purple and proclaimed him *basileus* of the Goths without reference to the Italians.[53] It looks as though Procopius wishes to indicate some change in the terminology used by the Goths, though he may not have been very clear about the precise significance of the change—and indeed the Goths themselves, if they wished to suggest an innovation in the titles of their leaders, may not have been wholly clear in their own minds about its significance. At all events, it will hardly be thought that the Goths intended to call their leaders "emperors." There is no question of a barbarian "emperor." But the language of the Ostrogoths' offer to Belisarius in 540 is beyond dispute: Belisarius was certainly to be *basileus* of the West, and (in another passage) *basileus* of Italians and Goths.[54] The words can only mean Western emperor, and they can scarcely have expected to win Belisarius over by any lesser title. That is why Belisarius felt that if he accepted the offer without Justinian's permission, he would be a usurper. In their second offer to Belisarius the Goths undertook that Ildibad would lay his purple robes at Belisarius' feet and would do obeisance to him as *basileus* of Goths and Romans, that is to say, as Western emperor.[55] The offers to Belisarius prove beyond question, I believe, that the Ostrogoths wished to remain in the Roman Empire and had no plans to form an independent kingdom. They wished to re-create the position as it had been before 476. But quite apart from the offers to Belisarius, what is also conclusive in this connexion is the Goths' repeated statements of their war aims. Both Theodahad and Totila made it clear that what they wanted was to be recognized as federates with the duty of supplying the Eastern emperor with troops—up to 3,000 men, according to Theodahad—whenever he requested them to do so. In addition, they would pay him an annual tribute which Theodahad specified at 21,000 *solidi* per annum, though Totila is not reported to have mentioned a precise figure. Both kings offered to withdraw from Sicily, and Totila in addition offered to evacuate Dalmatia. They were willing to make other concessions, too, which would put it beyond all doubt that they were Justinian's subjects. In every case Justinian rejected their proposals firmly and explicitly.[56]

At the very end of his reign (541–52) Totila minted silver and bronze coins at Rome which bore on the obverse his own name and his bust wearing the Imperial diadem; but we can hardly infer from that that he proposed to regard himself as emperor of the West.[57] He himself might not have found it easy to discover a single Latin word which would define precisely an office that the emperors themselves had never been able to define. On practically the last page of his *History* Procopius tells us that when the last Gothic king, Teias, had been killed in the battle on Mons Lactarius the Romans cut off his head and hoisted it on a pole so as to show the warriors that he was dead. The historian remarks that the Ostrogoths fought on although they knew that their *basileus* was dead.[58] Is it a slip of the pen? Or does he mean to imply that that is what he was in their eyes—their "emperor"?

V. ITALIAN INDEPENDENCE QUESTION

I infer that the Eastern emperors never reconciled themselves wholly to the position in Italy after the deposition of Romulus Augustulus in 476, or rather after the murder of Julius Nepos in 480. The question of independence for Italy never arose: the question of its constitutional position could not be defined. Zeno was far too weak to displace Odoacer with his own resources. To send Theoderic and the Ostrogoths to displace him solved some of the problems of the Eastern Empire—it got rid of the Ostrogoths —but Theoderic's victory left the position of Italy unchanged. To abandon the Roman claim to Italy was unthinkable. To reconquer it was impossible —until Justinian came to the throne. After the great war began in 536, the

Gothic rulers of Italy simply became usurpers from the Roman government's point of view. The individual who set up an inscription in which he referred to Theoderic not only as "king" but actually as "Augustus" may well have regretted his indiscretion: he had gone beyond anything that Theoderic himself had ever claimed.[59] A certain Valerius Florus was wiser when he began his inscription by calling Anastasius "Augustus" and Theoderic simply "most glorious and triumphal" Theoderic.[60] That was flattering, vague, and safe.

5

The Byzantine Conquest of Italy: Military Problems

On 9 or 10 December 536 Belisarius entered Rome. On 21 February 537 the Ostrogothic King Wittigis, marching south from his capital at Ravenna to besiege him, reached the Salarian bridge over the river Anio.[1] Belisarius had fortified the bridge and had left a garrison on it; but during the night following the king's arrival Belisarius' garrison panicked and took to their heels. Next morning, accompanied by 1,000 horsemen, Belisarius rode out towards the bridge to reconnoitre the land, unaware that his men had disappeared and that the Goths were already across the river. He was at once surprised and vigorously attacked by a force of Gothic cavalry. Deserters pointed him out, and the Goths directed their main assault at him personally. The fighting, while it lasted, was fierce, and only by a near miracle was Belisarius able to escape unhurt and to gallop back to Rome with the Goths on his heels.

I. BELISARIUS' ANALYSIS OF GOTHIC WARFARE

This was his first contact with the enemy, and in spite of the excitement and the tumultuous confusion of the battle, and the speed of the events (which are brilliantly described by Procopius), he was cool enough to observe something that interested him deeply. When he got into Rome he made an announcement to the people of the city that he was now confident that he would win the war. The announcement was greeted with loud laughter by the Romans: they thought that a man who had barely escaped with his life in his first brush with the Goths had little claim to ask them to treat the enemy with contempt.[2] But they were wrong.

What he had noticed was that there was a point of difference—and he believed it to be of fundamental difference—between the Byzantine and the Ostrogothic forces that had taken part in the skirmish. He had known already, of course, that practically all the Byzantine cavalry and the cavalry

Italy c. 600 A.D.

of the allies—who were recruited from among the nomads of the steppe lands of southeastern Europe—were mounted archers. But now he saw that the Gothic cavalrymen were equipped, not with bows and arrows, but with spears and swords: they were mounted spearmen, while their archers were footmen and only went into battle under cover of their cavalry. It occurred to him at once that the Gothic cavalry, unless they managed to get to close quarters, could not defend themselves against the Byzantines' arrows.[3] Provided the Byzantines were properly handled, the Ostrogoths would have no answer to mounted archers and might be killed without ever getting close enough to make use of their spears, still less to draw their swords. As for the Gothic infantry, they could never charge a force of heavily armed mounted archers.

Now, in all this there is a question which I cannot answer. Indeed, I have rarely seen it even raised.[4] It is this. How was it possible for Belisarius to reach Rome itself before he discovered this elementary fact about his opponents? Is it conceivable that he should have done no research on the matter before he left Constantinople? The narrative of Procopius puts the matter beyond all doubt: Belisarius knew little or nothing of the Goths' methods of warfare until that day when they surprised him outside Rome.

And that was not the first time that such a thing had happened to him. In 533, when he was on his way to attack the Vandals in Africa, his great armada touched in at an uninhabited part of Sicily near the foot of Mount Etna; and Procopius watched him on shore, perplexed and worried by the thought that he did not know what sort of men these Vandals were against whom he was proceeding, what their fighting methods were, what kind of warfare confronted him, or—more understandably perhaps—where he should establish his base.[5] And yet there was no shortage of travellers between Vandal Africa and the outside world at this date. Indeed, a number of Eastern traders present in Carthage were imprisoned by the Vandals on suspicion of having incited Justinian to begin the war; and there were other foreign and Carthaginian traders in the city who had not been molested by the Vandals.[6] Yet it was only when he had reached Sicily that Belisarius took steps to find out such basic facts as where he ought to anchor in Africa and where he should establish his base. Presumably the inadequate character of ancient maps explains his difficulties in this respect. To obtain the information he sent Procopius ahead to Syracuse to see what he could learn; but even then, if we may press Procopius's words, he did not ask him to find out the Vandals' methods of fighting.[7] (Procopius was also to discover whether any enemy fleet was likely to be lying in wait to intercept the Byzantine fleet; but that, of course, was a matter on which Belisarius could not have found out information earlier.) Even more strange, perhaps, is the fact that when Belisarius and his vast armada had reached Sicily, the Vandal king had not yet learned that the fleet was on its way.[8] And yet the armada had left Constantinople in June, had made many halts on the way, and only reached the coast of Africa at the beginning of September.[9] Indeed, the king had actually chosen this unfortunate moment to send an expedition to Sardinia, which was in revolt against him. The chief rebel in Sardinia had appealed to Justinian for help;[10] and so the Vandal king thought that if a force were to arrive from Constantinople, it would be directed against Sardinia.[11] He did not know that it had already arrived, and that it was not directed against Sardinia. The king's ignorance of the movements of a fleet of no fewer than 500 transport ships escorted by ninety-two warships, is almost inexplicable; but Procopius is quite clear on this, and the king's action in sending a powerful force to Sardinia, and his own departure to Hermione, a place in Africa four days' journey from the sea,[12] puts the matter beyond question: he knew nothing of Belisarius' movements. To make it even more unaccountable, it seems that the. Moors, or some of them, who lived to the west of the Vandals in Africa, *were* aware of the fleet's approach before it reached Africa.[13] Now, Procopius gives his readers minute details about the Vandals' methods of warfare: he expects his readers to know nothing whatever about them.[14] That is reasonable enough, but that Belisarius should know equally little is difficult to understand. There seem to have been strange discrepancies in the news that circulated and that failed to circulate in the sixth-century Mediterranean.

II. BELISARIUS' MILITARY TACTICS

To resume, Belisarius lost no time in putting his new knowledge to the test. He was defending Rome with an army perhaps of 5,000 men against a Gothic force which has been estimated at some 20,000 warriors.[15] He had been defending himself with his usual aggressive energy. He now sent 200 of his cavalry to seize a hill a short way outside the Salarian Gate of the city with strict instructions to fight with bows and arrows alone, when the enemy came out to engage them. They were on no account to touch their spears or swords, and, when their arrows were exhausted, they were to gallop back to Rome at full speed. On no account whatever were they to come to close quarters with the Goths.

In due course, the horsemen occupied the hill. A strong force of Goths rushed out of their camps and charged up the hillside to dislodge the Byzantine cavalry; but the horsemen poured flights of arrows into the densely packed attackers, and, when they had no arrows left, they galloped back to the city, as Belisarius had instructed them. A throng of Goths pursued them, only to come within range of the arrow-firing catapults mounted on the city walls. A few days later Belisarius repeated the performance with perhaps heavier losses to the Goths. A third sally brought the total of Gothic casualties, in Procopius' reckoning, up to about 4,000 men—though Procopius's estimates of enemy casualties are often suspiciously high.[16]

What is most remarkable is that Wittigis, who was not wholly incompetent, at any rate at this date, is explicitly stated to have failed to see the significance of this lesson, which had cost him so high a price. He drew the quite mistaken conclusion that what Belisarius' cavalry had been able to do his own horsemen could do equally well: they, too, could win such a victory as those which Belisarius had just scored. So, he sent 500 horsemen to seize a hill outside the range of the Roman catapults. Having occupied the hill they stood there waiting for the Byzantines to come and try to dislodge them. Belisarius accepted the challenge. A thousand of his horsemen charged out of the city, galloped round and round the hill on which the Goths were helplessly standing, and decimated them with clouds of arrows.[17]

III. TOTILA'S MILITARY SUCCESSES

Our next question is: how could the Goths overcome this handicap? After all, the war lasted for another fifteen years, so that some solution, or at least some partial solution, must have been found. During the reign of Wittigis no solution made its appearance. Since we are explicitly told that Wittigis did not notice the existence of the problem, his chances of solving it were slight.[18] And so it is no surprise that by 540, when he was deposed, the Goths had lost the whole of Italy south of the Po, including their capital at Ravenna. To be sure, no one could change an army of spearmen into an army of mounted archers overnight. Archery, I believe, is work for the expert, work that requires a long training if it is to be done well. You cannot be a spearman one moment and an archer the next, especially if you are acting on horseback. But events underwent a dramatic change in 540–41. Wittigis was deposed, Belisarius was transferred to the eastern frontier of the Roman Empire, and his successors were divided and incompetent. And furthermore, the Goths chose as their king the greatest of all their kings after Theoderic the Great. His name was Totila, though he was also known as Baduila.

He became king in September or October 541, and for over five years his successes were uninterrupted. Towards the end of his life he began to mint coins which showed his own head wearing the imperial crown, but the significance of this is unknown.[19] He won his battles, and he captured the cities of Italy. How was it done? The problem was even harder than I have suggested, for there is some reason to think that the Ostrogoths were deficient in defensive armour. It is true that the old Roman arms factories appear to have continued to function under the Ostrogothic kings, though with what efficiency we cannot tell.[20] But it is ominous that Procopius turns aside from time to time to remark that this or that Ostrogoth was armed with a helmet and breastplate. If this had been the norm he would hardly have felt obliged to mention it. And the men of whom he makes the comment are without exception leaders or influential warriors.[21] The mere fact that the historian occasionally finds this worthy of mention suggests that an Ostrogoth with a breastplate and a helmet was exceptional, and hence that it was the Ostrogothic nobility alone who possessed these: the rank and file did not have any defensive armour other than a shield. On

81

the other hand, the regular Roman mounted archers were protected by breastplates and greaves, and some of them had a small shield slung round their necks so as to protect their faces. In case they should be forced to fight hand to hand they also had a sword hanging from their belts at their lefthand side, and they might even carry a spear into the bargain.[22] The skill of Totila, then, and the courage of his followers are impressive. Their chances of being shot down by the Byzantine cavalry without ever thrusting with a spear or drawing a sword were high. How then did they survive? I think that it was the strategical ability of the king which brought them victory after victory. What he did was to manoeuvre his men into positions where they could surprise, ambush, and route the armies of Justinian.

It must be admitted that his victories were not vital ones, but their cumulative effect was very great. He soon defeated an enemy army at Faventia in 542, and another outside Rome in 546, and a third outside Portus in that same year. In all three cases he won his success by ambushing his opponents rather than by meeting them in a face-to-face encounter.[23] In 541 at a place called Mucellium (modern Mugello) outside Florence he defeated three Byzantine generals, but he won because the Byzantine troops panicked.[24] In 547 he scattered an enemy army in Lucania, but he did so by attacking them while they were still asleep. Immediately after, he annihilated a Roman cavalry force at Ruscianum (modern Rossano) in Bruttium: he surprised them when they were dispersed.[25] We know no details about the Gothic victory near Salona in 549, but their victory in Sardinia in 551 was due to surprise.[26] They hardly ever defeated a Roman force in a pitched battle.

IV. WAR WITH WITTIGIS

The war in Italy became one of sieges. The Byzantines rapidly occupied the cities, and it became the task of the Ostrogoths to dislodge them. How did they set about besieging walled cities? Throughout the whole period of the Roman Empire the Germanic peoples were notoriously incompetent at siege warfare, and Wittigis was the only Gothic commander of the sixth century who tried to storm enemy-held cities by means of some of the siege-engines which the Byzantines were accustomed to use as a matter of course. In 537, when about to assail the walls of Rome, Wittigis constructed wooden towers of the same height as the walls, with a wheel at each of the four corners of each tower. These towers were drawn forward by oxen, and they were intended to enable the men and the battering rams inside them to approach the wall in safety. In order to get the engines across the ditch outside the wall the Goths collected bundles of sticks and reeds in enormous numbers: they would throw these into the ditch, fill it up to ground level, and so their towers would cross smoothly to the base of the wall. That, at any rate, was the plan.[27]

Belisarius burst out laughing when he saw these contraptions lumbering towards the wall, though his men felt some dismay. As soon as the towers came near the ditch, he took his bow and shot and killed two of the approaching Goths who were not concealed inside the tower. His whole army, as it stood watching from the wall, raised a shout of delight and sent a shower of arrows into the oxen which were pulling the towers forward. The oxen promptly fell dead, and the towers came to a halt.[28]

In the following year Wittigis made another attempt to use siege-engines in his assault on Rimini. Once again he constructed a high wooden tower resting on four wheels, but this time he did not propose to have it drawn forward by oxen: in this respect at least he had learned his lesson at Rome. The men inside the tower were to push it forward, and when they reached the wall of Rimini they were to swarm up a very wide ladder inside the tower and so emerge out on to the top of the wall, where they would engage the defenders on equal terms. But when the tower was set in motion and was now approaching the wall, the men inside it observed that it was growing dark and that night was about to fall. (We might have thought that they could have predicted that sooner or later this was bound to happen.) The warriors left a few guards at the tower and went away for the night. During the night the Romans came out of Rimini and dug a deep trench in front of the tower, a task in which they were not handicapped by the fact that the guards had fallen asleep. Next morning Wittigis was not unreasonably annoyed with his guards, some of whom he put to death. But he did not abandon hope of using his tower. As at Rome in the previous year, his men gathered great bundles of sticks, and with them they filled up the ditch which the Romans had dug during the night. But the king forgot that at Rome the towers had not actually crossed the ditch and its sticks and reeds. When the tower was now drawn forward the sticks subsided under its weight, and the tower stuck fast. In fact, the Goths eventually succeeded in pulling it back to their camp, but only at the cost of severe casualties.[29]

The efficiency and know-how of Wittigis were not impressive, and in fact this was the last attempt that the Ostrogoths made to build and use siege-engines of this type. As for the catapults with which the Romans hurled arrows and rocks with devastating results, the Goths rarely tried to use them. At the siege of Rome in 537 Wittigis set up some *ballistae*: Belisarius' men set them on fire and it is not clear whether they ever went into action.[30] They certainly had some in 552, but it is perhaps significant that they never went into action.[31] On other occasions they used a different tactic. Some of their number would fire a sustained storm of arrows at the battlements of a besieged city so as to oblige the defenders to keep under cover for a considerable time; and while the defenders were pinned down by this barrage, others of the Ostrogothic warriors would rush forward carrying ladders. They would hope to put the ladders in position and climb the wall before the defence was free of the covering fire. In fact, this tactic never enabled the Goths to capture a Byzantine-held city, though once or twice it very nearly did so.[32]

For all such activities Totila had no taste. True, he tried to storm Rome in 547, but was sharply repulsed by Belisarius himself, the king's first reverse.[33] He took Perugia by storm in 549, but we have no details about the nature of his final attack upon it; and since the city had been under constant siege for four years, the defenders may have had little strength to withstand an attack of any kind.[34] We do not know how he took Caesena, Petra, and Beneventum at the beginning of his career.[35] But his normal procedure was to disregard frontal attacks altogether—presumably he was aware of his men's technical limitations—and simply to invest the Italian cities and wait until the garrisons were forced by starvation to surrender. Since the Byzantine opposition in the interval between Belisarius's two commands (540–44) was so feeble—and indeed continued to be so even during Belisarius's second spell of duty in Italy—Totila could well afford to wait until hunger did its work or until some of the citizens or of the garrison, already in the agony of starvation, opened the gates to him. That is how he took, or tried to take, city after city throughout the length of Italy; and Placentia was not the only place where cases of cannibalism were reported.[36]

V. OSTROGOTHIC DESTRUCTION OF CITY FORTIFICATIONS

It was a practice of Totila, when once an Italian town had fallen into his hands, to slight or even level the walls with the ground. Wittigis had already reduced by half their height the walls of Pisaurum (Pesaro) and Fanus (Fano) on the Adriatic coast, and he destroyed those of Milan; but he spared the walls of Rome and the other cities.[37] Totila took the practice more seriously. He planned to level the walls of Naples to the ground, but in fact after destroying a large part of them he left the remainder standing.[38] He completely destroyed the walls of Spoleto and Beneventum.[39] He dismantled the fortifications of Tibur (Tivoli) but found himself obliged to build them up again later on.[40] The great question was what he should do at Rome when he took it on 17 December 546. At first he decided to raze the city to the ground (a task which he might have found difficult.) In fact, he set about pulling down the fortifications. He destroyed them in several places so that about one-third (so we are told) of the entire circuit disappeared—it will be remembered that the walls of Aurelian extended for twelve miles around the city. He burned down some parts of Rome and then withdrew from it.[41] It was on this occasion that the Eternal City was left empty of inhabitants for some forty days or more. There was nobody there—only the wild beasts; it was the only time it has lain desolate, I suppose, since Romulus and Remus had founded it thirteen-hundred years before.[42]

There were two reasons for the Ostrogoths' policy of destroying the fortifications of the cities that fell into their hands. In the first place, they knew very well that if the fortifications were left intact and if the cities were then reoccupied by the Byzantine forces, the prolonged siege warfare would have to be started all over again, whereas the case of Pisaurum and Fanus, where Wittigis had destroyed the fortifications, showed that from such cities no danger was to be feared.[43] So Totila pulled down the walls of Beneventum "in order that an army coming from Byzantium might not use it as a strong base and cause trouble to the Goths."[44] But the very thing that the Goths feared took place at Rome. They had not completely destroyed the fortifications, as we have seen, and now Belisarius was inside the walls again. Procopius ascribes a speech to Totila in which he makes the king discuss the matter, for some Gothic nobles had gone to him and had criticized him bitterly for not having destroyed the city when he had the power to do so.[45]

But the Ostrogoths had a second reason for their policy of destroying the fortifications of the cities that they captured, and that second reason is something of a surprise. Again and again Procopius stresses the ardent desire of the Goths to have done with siege warfare and to force the Byzantines to meet them in pitched battles in the open. He makes Totila say, in the speech which I have just mentioned, that "when we took Beneventum we pulled down the walls and immediately got control of the other towns whose circuit-walls we decided to pull down in the same way, in order that the enemy's army might not have any strong base from which he could carry on the war by stratagem but might be immediately compelled to descend into the plain and come to grips with us." When Totila took Naples, "he set about pulling the wall of Naples down to the ground in order that the Byzantines might not seize it again and, using it as a powerful base, cause trouble to the Goths: for he wanted to reach an outright decision in a battle against them on the plain rather than fight a long struggle with a variety of devices and tricks." This is as early as 543. Again, in 550 he appeared outside Centumcellae (Civita Vecchia) on his way to reconquer Sicily. There was a strong Byzantine garrison in the city, and the king challenged it to come out quickly and reach a decision in a pitched battle.[46] Throughout his reign, then, his ambition was not merely to grapple with subordinate or secondary Byzantine forces in open combat —these he often encountered and, as we have seen, defeated by means of ambush or surprise—but the king wanted to engage and destroy the main bulk of the invading army.

I cannot understand this attitude of Totila's unless he, like Wittigis before him, had failed to grasp the superiority of the mounted archer over the mounted spearman. It is hardly possible to believe that the matter had completely escaped him throughout the eleven years of his reign. Yet there is no reason to think that he introduced any tactical reforms into his army, still less that he had taught his cavalry to fight with bow and arrow.[47] It is true that Totila's strategical ideas were audacious. It was no timid strategist who invaded and overran Sicily in 550, when both sides of the Straits of Messina (to say nothing of other fortresses) were still in Byzantine hands. The man who sent a fleet of 300 vessels to Corfu and the Dalmatian coast in the autumn of 551 and who invaded and subjugated Corsica and Sardinia in that same year was not obsessed by defensive ideas. And his diplomatic offensives were equally daring. He may have negotiated with the Slavs. He certainly negotiated with the Franks.[48] But so far as we know, in the equipment and tactics of his main military arm, his cavalry, he made no change. What Belisarius had noticed in that first furious skirmish outside the walls of Rome—the superiority of the mounted archer over the mounted spearman—Totila either did not notice at all, or, if he did notice it, he underestimated its importance, or else he saw that there was nothing that he could do about it.

VI. FIGHTING AT SEA

But one of the great puzzles of his career is, why did he try his luck at sea? The sea was an element of which the Goths had little experience or knowledge. It is true that Theoderic the Great in the last years of his life had planned to create an Ostrogothic navy of 1,000 *dromones* so as to carry supplies at sea and to engage the enemy fleet.[49] But evidently his plan was not carried out completely. Occasionally during the war the Goths would fit out some ships. We hear that Wittigis was able to send out "many" warships against Salona.[50] More than once we hear of *dromones* at the disposal of Totila.[51] But in the summer of 551 no fewer than 300 Ostrogothic ships sailed across the Adriatic, plundered Corfu and some neighbouring islands, and crossed to the mainland of Greece, where they ravaged three cities and interfered with Roman shipping. But then came a crucial event.

A sea fight took place off Sena Gallica (modern Sinigaglia), some seventeen miles north of Ancona, between another Gothic fleet of forty-seven ships and a Byzantine force of fifty ships; and it is difficult not to admire the extraordinarily vivid and satisfactory description which Procopius gives of it. This battle had a significance which I do not find it easy to understand. Procopius represents the Roman commanders as telling their men before battle was joined, that this engagement would be decisive for the outcome of the whole war;[52] but the commanders seem to be thinking, not of the sea battle in itself, but of the strategical importance of the defence of Ancona. But their judgement, for whatever reason, was not wholly wrong. The result of the battle was a crushing Gothic defeat, and Procopius makes a surprising comment on it: "this battle to an exceeding great degree smashed the self-confidence and the power of Totila and the Goths."[53] He is confirmed by the fact that a little later the four fortresses in Sicily which the Goths still held were starved into submission: the men in them had been gravely disheartened by the news of the sea fight, and indeed even before then morale had been low.[54] It is not easy to understand why events at sea should have had these far-reaching results. Surely the sea was a side issue for the Goths? The only explanation that suggests itself is to be found in Procopius' statement that the ships were manned by Gothic "notables" (*logimoi*).[55] It may be that a disproportionately high number of the Gothic leadership was wiped out at Sinigaglia. Otherwise, the reason for the decisive nature of this engagement is not easy to find.

At the end of the summer of 551, before the battle off Sinigaglia, Totila decided to occupy Corsica and Sardinia. Procopius cannot tell us his motives. Was this audacious action intended to boost his men's morale? Or was it a plain error judgement? In any event it divided his forces at what turned out to be the greatest crisis of his life. When the Byzantines unexpectedly managed to break the Ostrogothic siege of Croton, the morale of the Goths sank far deeper than ever before; and indeed the besieging Ostrogothic forces at Croton panicked.[56] As a result of the surrender of the fortresses in Sicily and the disaster of the sea fight, according to Procopius, the Goths "were in a state of deep alarm and were beginning to despair of the war, being now wholly without hope."[57] But an immediate result of the breaking of the siege of Croton was that the Gothic garrisons at Tarentum and Acherontia began negotiations for surrender, their morale being broken.[58]

As his doom closed in upon him, Totila tried desperately, as he had several times done before, to reach an accommodation with Justinian (p. 75 above). Justinian dismissed the envoys who offered his terms. The emperor's aim, we are told, was to wipe out the very name of the Goths from the Roman Empire.[59]

VII. OSTROGOTHIC SUCCESSES

Not many months after his troops had sailed off for the conquest of Corsica and Sardinia, Totila was given at last the opportunity for which he had waited so many years. The great bulk of the reinforced Byzantine army marched south from Ravenna, struck inland somewhat west of Ariminum (which was still in Gothic hands), and made in the direction of Rome down the Flaminian Way. When the news reached Totila he grasped the chance that he had so often prayed for. He set out for the north along the name road, and the two armies made contact in the Appennines at a place which Procopius calls Tadinum (though the topography of the ensuing battle is a matter of considerable obscurity—Procopius was not an eyewitness.)[60] In the vicinity lay some monuments called *Busta Gallorum,* the "Tombs of the Gauls," a name that commemorated a long forgotten victory which the old Romans of the Republic had won over the Celts nearly a thousand years before. The morale of the Byzantines had recovered from the effects of the plague of 542–43 and of Totila's earlier victories. And on his arrival at Busta Gallorum Totila will not have been encouraged to see that—perhaps for the first time during the war—the army facing him was decidedly larger than his own. It is thought that some 15,000 to 20,000 Goths and Roman deserters fought against at least 25,000 or 30,000 Byzantines.[61] He probably did not know the significance of the fact that the Byzantine army was commanded by an aged Armenian eunuch. That eunuch was Narses, a commander whom history was to reveal as hardly less brilliant than Belisarius himself.[62]

Just before battle was joined at "the Tombs of the Gauls," Totila gave his men the order to fight with their spears only and on no account to use bows or any other weapon.[63] Procopius found this order unaccountable, and I do not know that any satisfactory explanation of it has ever been discovered. Totila's tactical disposition of his army was atrocious. At the supreme moment of his life his abilities deserted him. The talent that had brought him countless victories over the Byzantines throughout eleven years vanished when he needed it most. His cavalry was decimated by the Byzantine archers, and in their flight they swept away the Gothic infantry with them in a headlong, uncontrollable route, "as frightened as if ghosts had fallen upon them or as if heaven were fighting against them."[64] Six-thousand warriors fell, and many others surrendered: all the prisoners were remorselessly put to death. The Roman deserters fought on to the end and were all but annihilated.[65] Totila either fell in the battle or was killed in the flight after it.

What estimate are we to make of Totila? Notice that during the five years of Belisarius's second command in Italy (544–49), the great man was a failure.[66] He was short of troops, thanks to Justinian's overstraining the resources of the empire and to the great plague of 542–43, which carried off many a potential Roman soldier. Even his admiring secretary Procopius is obliged to admit that in 549 "Belisarius went back to Byzantium with no glory: throughout five years he had not disembarked anywhere on the Italian countryside nor had he been strong enough to march there on land. During this whole time he had hidden himself in flight, sailing continuously from one fortress on the sea-coast to another maritime fort without a break." In his *Secret History* he repeats this judgement and adds that "Totila was burning to catch him outside a walled town, but he did not find him, for Belisarius himself and the whole Roman army were gripped by a deep fear."[67] Totila was no ordinary commander if he could keep Belisarius at bay for five years on end, skulking helplessly off the shores of Italy. We can say of Totila that he succeeded in holding up the onward march of history for eleven years. He stands in the line of those noble but doomed heroes, like Vercingetorix and Caratacus and many another, who have fought bravely to maintain the independence of a lower culture against the aggression of a higher. It is not easy to see what Italy would have gained if Totila had managed to defeat Justinian's dreams of conquest.[68] Two incidents in particular throw light on the matter. In 539 the Goths took Milan: the city was starved into submission. By agreement with the garrison the Goths allowed the troops in the city to depart. They then massacred in cold blood the entire male population of the city and presented the womenfolk to the Burgundians to be their slaves.[69] At the same time when this outrage took place, according to Procopius, Milan was after Rome the second city of Italy in size and population.[70] Therefore, it may have been the second city of western Europe when it came to so gruesome an end. On this event Bury remarks,[71] "In the long series of deliberate inhumanities recorded in the annals of mankind, the colossal massacre of Milan is one of the most flagrant. . . . the career of Attila offers no act of war so savage as this. . . . It gives us the true measure of the instincts of the Ostrogoths, claimed by some to have been the most promising of the German invaders of Europe." That is one event which the Italians will have found instructive.

The second event is this. When the Ostrogoths took Tibur (Tivoli) in 544, they put the inhabitants to death (including the bishop of the town); and they did so with such hideous cruelty that Procopius refuses to describe so odious a scene: he will not leave to posterity a record of such inhumanity.[72] We do not know what Justinian thought of these two incidents. He must certainly have thought about Milan, because a brother of the pope of that day, who was in Milan and managed to escape, made his way to Constantinople and told the emperor personally what had happened. Belisarius, too, sent the emperor a special report on the matter.[73] But we have no knowledge of the emperor's private thoughts on these matters.

VIII. MILITARY PUZZLES

So even in the study of the military aspect of the Byzantine conquest of Italy there is no shortage of problems and puzzles. For example, the extraordinarily late date at which Belisarius set out to discover even elementary facts about the warfare of his enemies. Why had he and his staff taken so few steps, before the campaigning began, to find out every possible detail about his opponents? And how was it possible for Wittigis to remain unaware throughout his whole reign of the problem of the mounted archer? Those traders and other travellers, who could have informed Belisarius about the Vandals and the Ostrogoths, could equally well have informed the Vandals and Ostrogoths about the Byzantines. Surely a prudent Ostrogothic ruler would have taken steps to inform himself about Byzantine warfare, even if there had been little or no reason to expect a Byzantine invasion of Italy? And doubly so if Theoderic expected that any attack on his realm would come from the east: that is thought to be suggested by the geographical position of his followers' settlements in Italy.[74] During the years between the fall of Attila's empire and the departure of Theoderic for Italy in 489 the Ostrogoths had endless opportunities for observing Byzantine armies in action: is it the case, then, that the role of the mounted archer was strengthened and developed in the period 489–536? But even so, we might have expected the Gothic commanders to have taken some notice of the development.

The Ostrogoths were equally surprised by the Frankish footmen and those axes which they threw with murderous effect. At all events, the lack of foresight on the part of sixth-century commanders on all sides is hard to imagine in Julius Caesar and many another.

I have suggested that Totila met the threat of the mounted archer by using the weapon of surprise. That is certainly part of the story: is it the whole story? It is not easy to see from what Procopius tells us what else he was able to do. But then, why did he consistently try to meet the Byzantines in a pitched battle? And what are we to say of his rather passive method of taking the walled cities—by simply starving them out? It is easy to forget, of course, how difficult it was in the ancient world for anyone, even the Romans at the peak of their power, to take a well-walled city. Again, why did Totila plunge off into the remote west with his conquest of Corsica and Sardinia in 551? What possible relevance had Corsica and Sardinia to his great enemy, the Byzantines? And finally, sea power. Something happened in the naval battle off Sinigaglia which we have not discovered. Procopius himself seems to have been aware of the significance of the battle; but I am not sure that he knew *why* it was significant. And he certainly had not the whole story about the battle of Busta Gallorum.

There is still plenty of work to be done on the subject of the Byzantine military conquest of Italy. Few of those who carry it out will feel distress at the destruction of those who assassinated Tivoli and Milan.

6

The Byzantine Conquest of Italy: Public Opinion

In 493 the Ostrogoths under their king Theoderic took over the government of Italy with the consent of the East Roman emperor in Constantinople. In these new conditions the standard of living of most of them must have become very much higher than it had been in the first half of the century, when the Ostrogoths were lost in the darkness of Attila's empire, and the Huns came down on their food supplies "like wolves," as we are told.[1] In Italy the Goths were settled on the great estates of the Po valley and elsewhere,[2] and in addition to the income which the individual Gothic soldier derived, directly or indirectly, from these estates, he also received an annual donative of perhaps as much as five *solidi* a year from the king. When the Gothic soldier was on active service, whether in the field or on garrison duty, he also received "rations" (*annonae*) either in kind or in the equivalent cash.[3] So, with the income from the land, his donative, and his rations when on service, and perhaps a salary from an official administrative post if he held one, to say nothing of the plunder which he might collect on his campaigns, his position was very different indeed from that of his father or grandfather who had starved under the Huns.

But even a sharp increase in prosperity does not in itself put an end to racial tensions and hatreds. What Theoderic stresses as much as anything else in his letters is that the Goths must not be oppressive to the Italians, must not plunder their goods or ravage their fields, and must try to live amicably with them. He makes endless, high-minded appeals to the warriors to behave themselves. In fact, the animosity of the Gothic rank and file against the Italians is made clear over and over again; and no plea that might hold it in check is left unused by the king. No concept lay closer to his heart than *civilitas*. He never misses an opportunity of propagating it and of recommending it to others. *Civilitas* means the maintenance of peace and order, of racial harmony, and the outlawing of oppression and violence. In a word, it means civilized life, civilization.[4]

But the need for exhortation never disappeared. In one of his letters Theoderic writes to "all the Goths settled in Picenum and Samnium" ordering them to come to his presence on June 6 of one of his last years so as to receive their donative, and he warns them not to commit any outrages on the way, not to lay waste the crops and meadows of the Italian landowners as they passed by.[5] Woe betide the Roman farms if they lay in the path of a Gothic army! When Gothic troops marched through the Cottian Alps in 509 on their way from Italy to Gaul the damage and loss that they caused to the Roman landowners through whose property they passed was so severe that Theoderic was obliged to remit the taxes of the affected area: the countryside looked as though a river in full flood had swept over it. In 508 he found himself obliged to send 1,500 *solidi* to a bishop to distribute to the provincials who had suffered loss "as our army was passing through their midst."[6] His wish to impose racial harmony upon his kingdom was the dominating feature of his internal rule.[7] From the beginning of his reign to the day of his death in 526 he struggled to achieve this noble aim. His insistence on harmony between the two nationalities, an insistence which he expressed year after year, decade after decade throughout his reign, makes him uniquely great not only in the sixth century but for long after it. But he was like a man trying to turn back the wind and the tide, and the wonder is that he succeeded for so long. This is one factor in the background of the Byzantine conquest of Italy of which the importance could hardly be overstressed, the hostility of Goth and Italian even in peacetime. We must never forget that they differed in language, religion, tradition, in customs, and even in law.

When Theoderic died in 526 his daughter Amalasuntha became regent for her son, Athalaric, who was a minor. One of her first acts was to issue a proclamation stressing (in the spirit of her father) the virtues of racial harmony and promising that she would introduce no change in the treatment of Goths and Romans.[8] But in two ways she fell foul of a number of her own followers. In the first place, she could not lead their army in war, and in many Gothic eyes a Gothic ruler must be a brave and famous warrior. Was not war still the favourite occupation of the barbarians ? Had not Theoderic himself said that "it is the delight of a warlike race to put itself to the test"?[9] Secondly, the mass of the Ostrogoths in spite of the long years of Theoderic's conciliatory government were still very hostile to the Italian population, very turbulent and unruly; and Amalasuntha "did not give way to their passionate desire to wrong them." The Goths resented her romanized ways, and above all they objected to the manner in which she was bringing up her son, Athalaric, the king. They would have no romanized Goth to rule over them; and when she began to provide a Roman education for Athalaric, many Goths protested openly. They wanted as their king a man, a man who would be "audacious in action and of great renown." They wished to be governed in a more "barbarian" way. They quoted Theoderic as saying "that one who had feared the schoolmaster's rod would never face the sword and the spear with disdain." In fact, as Gibbon puts it, the prince must be "educated, like a valiant Goth, in the society of his equals and the glorious ignorance of his ancestors." There was uproar one day when Amalasuntha, finding the boy up to some mischief in his room, chastized him, and he went to the men's apartments of the palace in a flood of tears. Resentment against the queen was widespread, though not universal, among the Goths and was shared by some of the Gothic nobility.[10]

I. GOTHIC LEADERS NEGOTIATE

The queen's position was eventually so threatened that she opened secret negotiations with Justinian with a view to taking refuge in the Eastern Empire should she be driven out of Italy altogether. She proposed to take the staggering sum of 2,880,000 *solidi* with her![11] Even before Athalaric died on 2 October 534, his mother took the astonishing step of offering to hand Italy over to Justinian. She made her offer explicitly and specifically.[12] Her personal safety had become more important than the very existence of her people's independence. Her offer to the emperor could be justified, of course, on constitutional grounds, for she was merely proposing to give Justinian what was in law his own property. Yet beyond a doubt, as Bury describes it, the offer was "an act of gross treachery towards her own people."[13] When her son died she tried to secure herself further by appointing to the throne her cousin Theodahad, the son of Theoderic's sister. It is not easy to see how she could have made a worse choice. He owned vast estates in Tuscany, which he expanded by unpopular and violent means. He had no interest in the warlike pursuits of the Goths, and, when he was not busy grabbing land, he devoted himself to the study of Latin literature and the philosophy of Plato. It is no accident that to him alone of the Ostrogothic kings of Italy did a Latin poet address poems.[14] In fact, he was precisely the sort of man, an almost wholly romanized Goth, whom the Goths in general did *not* wish to have as their king. And although she did not know it, he was the queen's bitter enemy—she had tried to curb his land-grabbing. And he was even more eager than Amalasuntha to do a deal with Justinian. Even before the death of Amalasuntha he, too, had opened secret negotiations with the emperor, offering to hand over Tuscany to the East Roman government on condition that he might live the rest of his days at Byzantium as a member of the senate there with a substantial income.[15]

There is no need to retell the story of how Theodahad had Amalasuntha murdered and how Justinian used this murder as his pretext for attacking Italy. In June 535 the great war began, which ended with the ruin of Italy and the destruction of the Ostrogoths eighteen years later. In the first year of the war Theodahad made his second offer to Justinian: if the Emperor would supply him with estates that produced an income of 86,400 *solidi* he would hand over the entire Italian kingdom to the Eastern emperor.[16] Nor did his son-in-law do much to reassure the Goths, for no sooner had Belisarius landed in Rhegium than this man, Ebremud or Evermud or Ebrimus, together with his dependents, whom Theodahad had sent to defend the Straits of Messina, joined the Byzantines. The renegade was instantly sent to Constantinople, where he received rich gifts and the rank of patrician. At one stroke he had achieved what Theodahad, seated on his tottering throne, would have been glad to possess.[17]

At the end of 536 when he had lost Dalmatia, Sicily, and even Naples, Theodahad was deposed and killed by his followers, and in his place they elevated Wittigis. When Cassiodorus praises Wittigis he mentions his military qualities only: he cannot point to any cultural attainments.[18] Evidently, this was no romanized Goth, given over to Plato and poetry. His reign ended in the spring of 540 after a series of shattering defeats by Belisarius. The Goths were chafing under Wittigis's rule because of his unbroken and disastrous ill-fortune. The extent to which their morale had cracked is illustrated by the action of their garrisons in Tudera and Clusium in Tuscany in the middle of 538. When these learned that Belisarius had set out from Rome and was making in their direction, they did not await his arrival. They surrendered the two towns, stipulating only that they themselves should remain unharmed.[19] Nothing remotely resembling this capitulation had happened before and was not to happen again until the closing months of the war when it was clear that all was lost.[20] In 540 the Goths were suffering appallingly from a famine. They therefore made the astonishing proposal to Belisarius that they were willing to put Wittigis aside and to declare Belisarius himself as nothing less than Western emperor and king of the Goths. (Notice that they intended to stay inside the Empire: they had no ambition to set up an independent kingdom: p. 66 above). This amazing suggestion was put to Belisarius by the leading Goths supported by Wittigis himself.[21] Their fear was that if the colossal defeats should continue, they were in the end likely to be transported from Italy and would be forced to settle in the vicinity of Byzantium—the very fate which would have been so welcome to Theodahad and Amalasuntha and others.[22]

Belisarius gave them to understand that he was willing to accept the offer, entered Ravenna (which would otherwise have been all but impregnable), and then went off to Constantinople taking Wittigis and a number of Gothic nobles with him. Wittigis was given the rank of patrician and an estate near Persia, where he survived for two years.[23] During his calamitous reign he had never been tempted to surrender Italy to the enemy; and in this respect he differed fundamentally from Amalasuntha and Theodahad. Yet in the end that is precisely what he did. And he received the reward for which they had been willing to pay so high a price. Further, since Justinian gave him the rank of patrician, it looks as though he even abandoned his Arianism for the doctrines of Nicaea. Having once capitulated, Wittigis capitulated wholly.[24]

But that was by no means the end of the war. After Wittigis's surrender there remained about a thousand men who refused to submit. They were holding out at Pavia and Verona, and they quickly won control of Liguria and Venetia, but for reasons which are not clear they found themselves obliged to accept as their leader one of the Germanic people known as the Rugi (p. 124 below) whose name was Eraric. They accepted him for no more than five months, but during the five months of his reign Eraric followed the course which is now familiar to us. He opened secret negotiations with Justinian: he offered to retire from the kingship of the Ostrogoths and their allies and to hand over all that part of Italy which he controlled in return for a substantial sum of money and the rank of patrician.[25]

So, in the course of some half a dozen years one Gothic monarch after another offered to subject Italy to Justinian in return for a secure and respected position in East Roman society with a substantial income. One ruler, Wittigis, actually carried out this project, though paradoxically he was very much more reluctant to do so than any of the others would have been, had they had the opportunity. To their Gothic followers, of course, they could have argued (though they are not known to have argued) that they were doing nothing illegitimate. Italy had always been the possession of the Roman emperors, as Odoacer and Theoderic had frankly recognized. These later rulers were merely offering to the emperor what was agreed to be his own property. He would now (if he accepted their offers) rule it directly and no longer through barbarian kings. Of Eraric's attitude we know little, but Amalasuntha and Theodahad (and doubtless Matasuntha, too, whom I have omitted for brevity's sake) were repelled by the warlike and brutish tastes of their followers and wished to become absorbed into civilized Roman society. This argument might not have impressed their followers, but the attraction of Roman civilization for several members of the Gothic nobility, perhaps for most of them, as well as for Eraric, was overwhelming. Latin literature and the philosophy of Plato were more to their taste than the spear and the sword. The fact was that in the process of entering the Roman Empire and of settling on the Roman estates and of living not wholly unlike Roman landowners, the Ostrogothic nobility to a considerable extent had become romanized.

On the eve of the Byzantine invasion of Italy, then, and in its early years we find in Italy an Ostrogothic people of whom the rank and file were uncultured, warlike, and aggressive barbarians, hostile to the Italians in whose midst they lived, always ready to wrong and plunder them, for the most part showing little culture of their own but clinging fanatically to their independence. Roman civilization and the delights and achievements of Roman society had no attractions for them. On the other hand, many of their leaders were well able to appreciate the joys and comforts of Roman civilization and would have been glad at any cost to leave Italy altogether and to obtain a position in Byzantine society near Constantinople. But one of the factors which prevented the Ostrogoths in general from capitulating to Belisarius in 540 was this very fear, that, if they did so, they would be forced to do precisely that — to migrate from Italy and settle near Byzantium.[26] In fact, the Ostrogoths entered the struggle a deeply divided people. The nobility were only too willing to compromise and even to sell out their people in return for being accepted into high East Roman society — with an income, to be sure, and not a small income.

II. GOTHIC SOLDIERS AND SETTLERS

It is no surprise, then, to find that in Procopius' long and detailed history of the Gothic war we rarely hear of desertions by the common Gothic warriors to the forces of Justinian. The Goths in the Cottian Alps surrendered in 540 when they heard that their womenfolk and their children had fallen into the hands of the Byzantines, though, curiously, Belisarius had received a report earlier that they wanted to come over to him even before the capture of their families.[27] But that was exceptional. Although outgeneralled for many years on end, and always outclassed in equipment and tactics (although not until the end in numbers),[28] the rank and file fought with a consistent and unyielding determination and with a resolution that lasted almost to the end of the war. The defence of Auximum (Osimo) in 549, for example, was an astonishing example of courage and tenacity.[29] They were indeed true to those barbarous ideals which had so distressed Amalasuntha. In two cases we hear of desertion by Gothic settlers in outlying parts of the kingdom — in Dalmatia and Liburnia in 536 (though the troops in the field there withdrew to Ravenna) and in Samnium in that same year, where Pitzas and the Goths who were planted on the land there surrendered the maritime part of Samnium to Belisarius. It is no surprise to learn that Pitzas was a large landowner there.[30] The first major act of treachery by a Goth—Procopius does not tell us his name or his status— dates from the last few weeks of the Ostrogothic kingdom's existence, when the commander of the Gothic fleet off the west coast of Italy handed his ships over to the Byzantines.[31]

At the end of five months the Goths killed Eraric, and in September or October 541 they appointed Totila in his place. (His name appears as Baduila on his coins.) They might have been somewhat hesitant about appointing him if they had known that at the very moment when he was elevated he was in the act of negotiating the surrender of Tarvisium (Treviso, north of Venice), where he was commanding, together with its Gothic garrison, to the local Byzantine commander at Ravenna. He had even agreed on the date of the surrender.[32] It was his first and last act of treachery to his people. From the day when he became king until the hour of his death he fought the Byzantines with an unequalled resolution and skill. At last the Goths had found a member of their nobility who was not prepared to betray them.

III. BYZANTINE DESERTERS

Let us turn to the invaders. In sharp contrast with the loyalty of the Gothic rank and file is the attitude of the Byzantine troops. Among them we hear endlessly of desertions to the Ostrogoths. Indeed, in no other war of ancient history, so far as I know, do we hear of anything like so many desertions. This was true even of Belisarius's first tenure of the high command in Italy (535–40), the period when he won his most spectacular successes. Even before the first siege of Rome began in 536 twenty-two barbarian cavalrymen serving in the Byzantine army went over to Wittigis and actively helped him.[33] And it is ominous that during the first siege of Rome in 536–37 Belisarius was so alarmed by the possibility of treachery among the guards of the city gates that he changed all the keys of the gates twice a month. He moved the sentries from one guard-post to another a considerable distance away and gave them different officers every night. He was afraid that Gothic emissaries might come up to the wall and tamper with the sentries' loyalty, and so he sent Moorish troops with dogs outside the walls every night so as to intercept such persons if they should come.[34] These are the actions of an officer who has a limited confidence in his men. And in the early days of the siege his plans to fight a pitched battle against the Goths were constantly betrayed by deserters.[35] It is not without significance that when a drunken Hun approached the Gothic camp so as to attack it and win the war single-handed, the Goths took it for granted that the solitary figure who was approaching them was a deserter, an assumption that they would not have made unless deserters had been a common phenomenon.[36] When the Goths in 537 despaired of ever being able to take Rome, they sent some envoys to Belisarius, and one of these envoys was a Roman of high standing among the barbarians. Unfortunately, Procopius does not give his name or any details about him or his motives for throwing in his lot with the enemy.[37] It is more than a little surprising that in the year 540 itself the thousand men who held out at Pavia and Verona (p. 96 above) and determined to continue the war after Wittigis had capitulated were composed not of Goths only but also of "as many of the Roman soldiers as wished for a revolution."[38] We do not know what the proportion of Romans to Goths may have been in this crucially important force, but Procopius certainly speaks of it as though it were significant. The inference is that Belisarius with all his vast abilities was unable to prevent a substantial stream of deserters from going over to the enemy.

But with the departure of Belisarius from Italy in 540 and the arrival there of Alexander the logothete (discussor, "auditor") and his harsh financial policies the position deteriorated much further. From the military point of view it was his withholding of the pay of the troops that was so catastrophic. Over and over again we hear that the troops had not been paid, that accordingly they would not fight, and that they survived by plundering the countryside which they were supposed to be defending.[39] When Belisarius sailed for Constantinople in 540 total victory had been within the grasp of the Byzantines, but the activities of Alexander together with the petty squabbles of Belisarius' military successors, their incompetence, and their reverses in the field caused the Byzantine position to crumble.

In 542 Totila's kindly treatment of his prisoners "succeeded in winning them over and thenceforth most of them campaigned with him against the Romans."[40] In 545 when Belisarius had now returned to Italy, he wrote to the emperor, according to Procopius, that "the majority" of the imperial soldiers had now deserted to the enemy.[41] He complained that he had returned to Italy "without men, horses, arms, and money."[42] We subsequently hear again and again of deserters from the Byzantine army. When Belisarius returned to Ravenna in 544 he made a spirited appeal to the Goths and Romans serving with Totila to change sides: not a man came over.[43] In that same year all the Illyrican troops stationed at Bologna packed up without warning and went home: their reason was that they had not been paid for so long.[44] At Auximum in that year two Byzantine generals planned a secret withdrawal by night: one of their soldiers instantly deserted, informed Totila of the plan, and caused the death of 200 of the thousand men involved.[45] What was to have been a surprise attack on Totila outside Portus in 545 was reported to him by a deserter with disastrous results to the Byzantines.[46] In 546 Spoletium was garrisoned by a mixed force of Goths and Roman deserters.[47] In that year, too, a Byzantine general routed a force of Moors, Byzantine deserters, and Goths, led by a Gothic commander called Recimund: it is remarkable that most of the Moors and Byzantines fought to the death, whereas the Goths eventually surrendered.[48] In 547, as a result of a Byzantine victory in Campania, "no less than seventy Byzantine soldiers of those who had previously deserted to the Goths" decided to return to their allegiance to Justinian.[49] In 548 a Roman force at Rome declared that if Justinian did not pay them their arrears of pay within a fixed time they would go over to Totila without delay. Justinian paid up.[50] A barbarian who had served in Belisarius's own bodyguard deserted without warning or excuse in 548. Totila at once gave him a command.[51] At the battle of Busta Gallorum in 552 (p. 88 above) large numbers of Roman deserters fought for Totila. Indeed, the first casualty in that battle was a Roman deserter named Coccas who was fighting for the Goths.[52] In the reign of Totila's successor, Teias, the Gothic garrison of Perugia was commanded by two Byzantine deserters.[53] Most astonishing of all perhaps: it was the treachery of some Isaurian troops which, not only in 546 (in conditions of severe famine) but also a second time in 549, handed over to Totila the greatest prize of all, the city of Rome itself. The Isaurians who betrayed the city on the second occasion had not been paid for years, but they saw that those who betrayed the city on the first occasion had been richly rewarded.[54] Towards the end of the war Narses came to Italy with a special fund earmarked for bribing deserters to return to the imperial service.[55] There can be no doubt that throughout the war substantial numbers of Byzantine troops, demoralized at the sight of their hard-won victories being undone through the incompetence of Belisarius's successors and above all because they were unpaid for years on end, believed that they would enjoy a brighter future under Gothic rule than in the restored Roman Empire of Justinian. It must be stressed, however, that these considerations apply almost exclusively to soldiers.

IV. ITALIAN CIVILIAN LOYALTIES

What was the attitude of the Italians? Let us consider the cities first. It is concerning Naples that we have most information. When at the very beginning of the war Belisarius addressed the Neapolitans, according to the historian, he made it clear that he had come in order to "free" Italy:[56] the present position of Italy under Ostrogothic rule was "slavery,"[57] like that of Sicily and Africa before the Byzantines had reoccupied those places. He

presented the choice between imperial rule and Gothic rule as a choice between "freedom" and "slavery."[58] But Procopius nowhere implies that this
was the attitude of the Neapolitans. The historian mentions four of the
citizens by name. The first Neapolitan to negotiate with Belisarius was
called Stephanus. In his speech as reported by the historian he is by no
means pro-Byzantine: his sole aim was to prevent an attack on his city.[59]
Belisarius did not rule out the possibility that the Neapolitans would combine with the Gothic garrison in the city to defend it.[60] But he proceeded
to bribe Stephanus to induce him to try to win over the citizens; and
thereupon Stephanus advised the Neapolitans not to resist the invaders.[61]
It is important to notice that Stephanus only took up this attitude because
he had been bribed to do so. The only convinced pro-Byzantine was not a
Neapolitan at all but a Syrian merchant called Antiochus, an overseas
trader, whose commerical interests would certainly be served by an extension of Byzantine power to his adopted city.[62] On the other hand, two Neapolitans called Pastor and Asclepiodotus were warmly in support of the
Goths and wished to see no change in the city's position. When they addressed the populace, their argument was one of expediency alone. It
would be more expedient to support the Goths, because if the Goths
should win—and the citizens evidently expected that they would win—
they would punish the Neapolitans severely.[63] Finally, the Jewish inhabitants of Naples were on the side of the Goths; and when the city was attacked they defended the part of the wall that had been entrusted to them
with fierce tenacity. The Ostrogothic kings, like most of the Arian kings,
had treated the Jews well.[64]

Even so skilful a writer as Procopius cannot conceal the fact that with
the exception of a foreign trader not a single inhabitant of Naples at first
supported the Byzantines. And he gives not the slightest hint that the citizens were overjoyed at the thought of returning to the Roman Empire.
The historian and Belisarius knew that they were restoring the old Roman
Empire of Augustus and Constantine. Whether the Italians were equally
knowledgeable is not clear; and, if they were, it is far from certain that
they welcomed the prospect. What weighed very much with them was
the question of what punishments the Goths would inflict on them if they
sided with Belisarius, and Belisarius then lost the war.[65] Indeed, after the
siege began, the Neapolitans sent a message to King Theodahad in Rome
begging for immediate help.[66] For the sake of an antithesis Procopius says
that on the day when Belisarius stormed Naples the citizens "became prisoners and regained their freedom."[67] It may be doubted if the Neapolitans
drew this conclusion, for as soon as the city fell to the Byzantines it became the scene of a horrifying massacre. The Huns in Belisarius's army

outdid all the other troops in cruelty. They did not even spare the churches, and they killed many who had taken refuge in them. Procopius does his best to understate the magnitude of the disaster that befell Naples; but in this respect there is no hint of support for him in our other authorities.[68]

When we turn to the minor sources of information for the fall of Naples we see how clever is Procopius' narrative. By telling at length of debates and discussions and doubts about whether or not to admit the invading army, he blurs the issues (though he is never downright dishonest). Our lesser sources make it plain that the Neapolitans refused Belisarius admission to their city.[69] In the end Gothic garrison and Italian citizens were impartially cut down. The attackers made a speciality of murdering husbands before the eyes of their wives. They spared no one, neither priests nor monks nor nuns. There was no pity.[70] But this gruesome policy paid off. The Romans admitted Belisarius to their city "because they feared lest what had befallen the Neapolitans might happen to them."[71]

Before the first siege of Rome began in 536 Wittigis thought it not impossible that the inhabitants of the great city would support the Goths rather than the invaders.[72] But the citizens, or some of them, aiming above all to avoid the fate of Naples, admitted Belisarius without opposition. The leaders of this policy were Pope Silverius (who, rather quaintly, was deposed by Belisarius later on) and Fidelius, who had been Athalaric's quaestor. Whether the general populace was enthusiastic for such a policy is not wholly clear: they certainly allowed the Gothic garrison to leave the city unhindered, though Procopius seems to imply that they might have done them some injury if they had so wished.[73] The historian only mentions the attitude of the people at large when he comes to tell of the preparations for the siege: when the people saw Belisarius making the city ready to stand siege their attitude was one of dismay.[74] When the siege began, even the senators were highly critical of Belisarius, though Belisarius shortly afterwards described the Romans as well disposed to the Byzantines.[75] And after Wittigis' massacre of his senatorial hostages at Ravenna, we find the Romans in general enthusiastic against the Goths.[76] Tradesmen and craftsmen, who had no military experience and had no armour, voluntarily took up arms in the cause of Byzantium (though we have already been told that they were "forced" to guard the walls).[77] They were joined by sailors and even by slaves, and flocked to help Belisarius, though in view of their total inexperience their help was not an unmixed blessing to the general. Their help may have been due less to idealogical support for Byzantium than to the fact that there was no work to be had in the beleaguered city, and if Belisarius had not paid them a daily wage to serve in his forces, their loyal support of the Roman Empire might have been somewhat cooler.[78]

Cities which came over to Belisarius "not unwillingly" or "with no trouble" were Narnia, Spoletium, Perugia, and others. It is not clear whether they did so because they supported the Byzantine cause, or because they feared such treatment as Naples had received, or simply because they wished to avoid becoming a battleground. At any rate, Procopius gives no hint at general enthusiasm for the East Roman cause.[79] In 538 the inhabitants of Rimini invited the Byzantines into their city. Indeed, the hostility of the Italians of that whole region obliged the Goths to withdraw from Rimini as soon as a force of Byzantines approached.[80] In 538 the archbishop of Milan and some other notables of that city begged Belisarius to send them a small force with which they undertook to deliver Milan and the whole of Liguria into his hands.[81] The case of Verona in 542 is hard to understand. The fortunes of the Goths were then at their lowest; yet it is clear that the citizens did not wish to join the Byzantines, perhaps because there was a Gothic garrison within their walls. But a rich citizen, by means of efficient bribery, almost succeeded in making over the city to the local imperial general.[82]

These were the sentiments of city-dwellers. What of the countryfolk? No sooner had Belisarius set foot in Rhegium than "the men of that area kept coming over to him." Their reason was that "their farms were unfortified, and because of their enmity to the Goths, especially to the present government," that is, the government of Theodahad.[83] Procopius reports that the Calabrians and Apulians went over, "there being no Goths present in their country."[84] There are two noteworthy points here. Some southern Italians are opposed to the Goths and especially to the government of Theodahad, who was equally unpopular with the Goths themselves. But Amalasuntha had been exceedingly popular with both nationalities: would the southern Italians have joined Belisarius so readily if she had still been their ruler?[85] And there is also the fact that the southern Italian countryfolk had neither fortifications nor a Gothic garrison: what would have been their attitude if they had had both? Perhaps it is significant that in 542 Bruttium and Lucania, Apulia and Calabria all alike went over to Totila without resistance or hesitation.[86] Yet in spite of ill-treatment at the hands of the Byzantines the inhabitants of Bruttium and Lucania declared in 546 "that it was not of their own free will that they had gone over to men who were barbarians and Arians": they had been obliged to do so by the superior force of the Goths and by the injustices that had been inflicted on them by the imperial troops. Once they obtained a guarantee of fair treatment in the future they rejoined the Byzantines.[87] It is not easy to resist the impression that the excuses and explanations which Procopius reports were adapted by the Italians to their audience: they told the Byzantines what the Byzantines wanted to hear.

Whether the peasants of the countryside were very devoted to the Byzantine cause may be doubted. Procopius watched the arrival of the Byzantine forces in Picenum. As soon as they appeared, the local people were thrown into panic, and those of the womenfolk who could do so took to flight: those who could not get away were carried off by anyone who chanced upon them—that is to say, apparently, they were kidnapped by any chance Italian. After a considerable time the inhabitants were told that the imperial army had come there to damage the Goths and that the Roman population would suffer no harm. Only then did they return to their homes.[88] Clearly, their ignorance of the imperial forces and what they stood for could hardly have been more complete. Again, in 546, when an influential Roman of Lucania raised a force of rustics to keep the enemy out of his neighbourhood, Totila raised a similar force of peasants to oppose them; and the two groups of Italian peasantry engaged in a stubborn battle against one another, the Gothic side being routed. But when the landowners directed the peasants of the victorious force to go back to their fields, they did so apparently without question.[89] It would seem that the poorer elements of the country population did very much as their masters ordered them. It probably mattered little to them whether it was Goths or Italians or Byzantines who extorted their rents and their crushing taxes. What Totila wanted them to do was to till the fields as usual and to pay their rents and taxes to himself. On these terms he did them no injury throughout the length of Italy.[90] Certainly, the Goths will have won few friends in the Italian countryside if they made a practice of plundering the Italians in order to obtain supplies for their troops, as they did at Auximum in 549.[91]

As for the slaves, a number of these deserted to Totila; and in 546 the king swore that he would never negotiate on their return to their owners. In this he was merely defending volunteers who had fought for him: he had no grandiose plan to free the slaves of Italy, and he is not said to have freed these men.[92]

Thus, both sides in the war were sharply divided, the Goths between their nobility and their rank and file, the Byzantines between soldier and civilian.

V. GOTHIC TREATMENT OF ITALIANS

The Ostrogoths described the attitude of the Italian gentry and city-dwellers as "treachery." They were at a loss to account for it, and Procopius gives a remarkable amount of space to setting out their point of view. They repeatedly criticized these two categories of Italians for their actions. At the very beginning of the war, when the first siege of Rome was about to begin, according to Procopius, King Wittigis remarked: "We should be glad to ask the Romans here what complaints they have against us, seeing that up to this day they have enjoyed our kindness and now have also had experience of your [i.e., the Byzantines'] 'assistance.'"[93] He had already sent a man to the Salarian Gate of Rome to abuse the defenders on the Roman city wall for their "treachery" to the Goths. He chided them for the treason which he said that they had been guilty of towards their country and themselves, "for they had exchanged the power of the Goths for mere Greeklings who could not protect them and of whom they had never previously seen any come to Italy except tragedians and actors of mimes and cut-purse sailors."[94] Had not Theoderic nurtured them in a life of luxury and in freedom besides?[95] When the siege of Rome was still in progress Procopius depicts a Gothic envoy as saying that the Romans had continued to appoint the Western consuls. The Goths had permitted absolute freedom of worship to their Gothic subjects: they had obliged no Italian to go over to Arianism, and if a Goth had been converted to Catholicism the kings had taken no notice of it. The right of asylum of the Catholic churches had been carefully preserved.[96]

It is a formidable case, so far as it goes. But it omits that barbarous attitude of the Gothic rank and file towards the Romans which Theoderic had so much deplored and which must have caused untold damage to the Italians. Indeed, before many months had passed it was to cause the colossal and inexcusable massacre of the civilian population of no less a city than Milan. But the same case was put forward before the battle of Faventia in 541 by Totila himself (who was silent about the recent events at Milan.) He was able to add, however, that the abominable behaviour of Belisarius's successors in Italy had left the Italians in no further need of punishment for their "treachery" to the Goths: every evil had been inflicted on them by those whom they had once welcomed to their country.[97]

To the very end, it seems, the "ingratitude" of the Italians remained an inexplicable mystery to the Ostrogoths. They had themselves occupied Italy and overthrown Odoacer on the instructions of the Emperor Zeno himself: it could never be said that they had wrested the country from the emperor by force. They had preserved the laws and the constitution as scrupulously as the emperors themselves. They had issued no legislation of their own, written or unwritten, knowing well that the enactment of laws was the prerogative of the emperor.[98]

Totila did his utmost to change this attitude of the people of Italy. He severely punished outrages perpetrated by his men on the civilian population. When he captured the wives of some Roman senators at Cumae he treated them with scrupulous courtesy and set them free, an action which deeply impressed the Romans. When he captured Rusticiana, the widow of Boethius, in Rome in 546 his men were eager to put her to death, for she had destroyed the statues of Theoderic in vengeance for the murder of her father and her husband. But Totila saw to it that neither she nor any other Roman woman came to harm, and once again his action made a profound impression on his enemies.[99] Sometimes, when enemy troops surrendered to him, he gave them a choice: *either* they could leave behind their horses and weapons, and after swearing an oath never again to fight against the Ostrogoths return unharmed to Byzantium, *or* they could keep their possessions, join the Gothic army, and enjoy complete equality with the Goths.[100] When the starving inhabitants of Naples capitulated to him in 546 he was anxious that, when food was at last available to them, they should not gorge themselves with it and "choke themselves to death." Accordingly, he gave them a small supply at first, but gradually increased the ration until they had built up their strength: only then did he allow them to leave the city and go where they wished. At least one Byzantine thought that it was an action "that could be expected neither from an enemy nor from a barbarian."[101] To the great bulk of his prisoners he was gentle and kind; and yet, although his behaviour in this respect was appreciated by the enemy, it failed to shake the loyalty of the Italians to the Byzantines. As late as 549 Pope Vigilius and the inhabitants of Rome, among whom were many men of note, were still bombarding Justinian with requests that he should reconquer Italy. In spite of all that Totila could do, the loyalty of Italy to Byzantium never seriously faltered.[102]

In 547–48 he admitted that in previous times the Goths had paid less respect than any other people to justice and that they acted impiously towards each other and towards the Romans; and we have seen something of the attitude of Theoderic the Great on this very matter. Totila still thought it necessary to warn his followers to change this attitude.[103] In fact, Wittigis had been guilty of an atrocious act of savagery during the great siege of Rome in the spring of 537. He had sent a number of Roman senators to Ravenna as hostages, and after the repulse of his heaviest attack on the capital he had had them vindictively done to death (p. 102 above).[104] There is no need to linger over the hideous massacre of the male population of Milan by the Gothic commander Uraias in 539 (p. 89 above).[105] When Rome fell to Totila on 17 December 546 his troops massacred twenty-six soldiers and sixty civilians; but this was done without the king's knowledge, and as soon as he heard of it he stopped the slaughter immediately. It was on this occasion that he won "great glory" from his protection of the Roman womenfolk, especially the widow of Boethius.[106] But it cannot be denied that he was himself guilty from time to time of horrifying outrages. In addition to the senseless brutality at Tibur (Tivoli) in 544 (p. 89 above) was an incident that took place in the following year. In 545 Pope Vigilius sent some ships loaded with food to the starving inhabitants of Rome; but in Portus the Goths intercepted these ships and captured the Romans sailing on board them. Totila massacred them all with one exception, a bishop called Valentinus, whose see lay at Silva Candida.[107] He then questioned Valentinus, accused him of giving false information, and cut off both his hands.[108] This and other instances seem senseless cruelty, but we have no clue to Totila's motives. What we can be sure of is that they must have made a disastrous impression on Italian public opinion.

What were the chief reasons for the fall of the Ostrogoths and the establishment of Byzantine Italy? Procopius gives us Belisarius' explanation of the defeat of the Goths. They were not beaten, said the great man, by lack of courage or inferiority in numbers: they were beaten, he said without undue modesty, because they were outgeneralled! And on another occasion his envoys explained that it was the emperor's resources in manpower that enabled him to overcome the enemy.[109] The brilliance of Belisarius certainly contrasts sharply with the uninspired, mediocre leadership of Wittigis. In normal days that king might well have been found competent, as Bury says, and in times of war he would have served capably under the lead of another.[110] Indeed, during the last year of his reign, although he was active diplomatically and even opened negotiations with the Great King of Persia to initiate joint action against the Eastern Roman Empire, yet in the military sphere his nerve seems to have cracked, and in the end he was unable to make any move at all. But Totila was a different proposition. He was more than a match for Belisarius' incompetent, divided successors; and he had little difficulty in recovering practically the whole of Italy and Sicily apart from Ravenna and a handful of other fortresses. His real test came when Belisarius was reappointed to the high command in Italy in the summer of 544, and he passed that test triumphantly. Belisarius did indeed score some local victories, and he reoccupied Rome for a while thanks to a blunder on Totila's part, a blunder which Belisarius exploited with all his old initiative and brilliance. But on the whole, during the five years 544–49 it was Totila who gained the upper hand, and the great man returned to Byzantium a failure, as Procopius candidly admits. We cannot explain the fall of the Ostrogoths in terms of the inadequacy of their leadership.

There were not unimportant factors such as the Byzantine control of the sea, which enabled them to provision maritime cities when these were under siege, to transport troops from one theatre of war to another, and to blockade enemy-held ports.[111] There was the highly important matter of the superiority of the mounted archer over the mounted spearman (p. 77 f. above). And, of course, the financial resources and the reserves of manpower of the Byzantines (as Belisarius' envoys pointed out) were far beyond anything that Wittigis or Totila could even have dreamed of. But I believe that another fundamental matter was that after their initial hesitation the bulk of the Ostrogoths' subjects opposed, or at any rate did not actively support, the Goths. It is true that shortly before Belisarius' return to Italy in 544, when the Byzantine troops, unpaid and out of hand, were ruthlessly plundering the Italian countryside, they caused the Italians to yearn for the barbarians to come.[112] But this did not remain the case. The Italians were basically pro-Byzantine. As soon as a Byzantine army appeared before the walls of an Italian city, the gates were opened to them (sometimes even when there was an Ostrogothic garrison inside the walls). The inhabitants were prepared to suffer hardship, though not without loud complaints, when the Goths laid siege to them. The citizens of Rome, for example, held out against the Ostrogoths in conditions of indescribable difficulty sooner than submit to Wittigis. The Goths, in fact, received none of those aids and services which a civilian population can render to a friendly army. Byzantine troops might desert in substantial numbers, but the Italian population made no diversions to distract the attention of the invaders and rarely passed on information about the Byzantines' whereabouts or their numbers or their plans (though deserting soldiers often did so). It was as though the Goths were themselves the invaders, fighting a hostile population in an alien land.

Why was this the Italian attitude? Procopius describes a scene which took place near the end of the war and which, in my opinion, throws light upon the question. Totila wished to delay the start of the battle of Busta Gallorum so as to allow 2,000 men, who had not yet joined him, to come up to his help; and an extraordinary scene followed. The king rode forward into the no-man's-land between the two opposing lines. He was dressed in gold-plated armour, adorned with gold and purple ornaments, and he rode an enormous horse. Before the eyes of the watching armies he began with the utmost skill to dance a Gothic war-dance. He wheeled his horse in a circle, throwing it from side to side. As he rode he hurled his spear high into the air and caught it as it came spinning down. From hand to hand he hurled it with masterly skill. He would lie far on his back or lean steeply down to one side or the other. His ability, in the opinion of Procopius, was as that of a dancer who had been trained from childhood.[113]

What a contrast between the Emperor Justinian in his palace, diplomat, jurist, and theologian, and this dancing dervish of Busta Gallorum! It is hardly a problem to see why educated Italians rejected Ostrogothic rule in spite of all the generosity of Theoderic and his successors. The war was fought between barbarians on the one side and civilized men on the other. The Italians chose civilization, and no one followed them more heartily than some sections of the Ostrogothic nobility. Totila's successor, Teias, fought at the battle of Mons Lactarius with tactics which showed little improvement on those of Agamemnon and Achilles and Hector, the tamer of horses.[114] And Aligern, the last of the Ostrogothic rulers, more wisely decided to surrender Cumae and all the Gothic treasures, to take on Roman citizenship, and to abandon the barbarian way of life: if the Goths could not take possession of Italy, he argued, it was better for its old inhabitants and its ancestral rulers to have it back. He was wise, even though some Franks called him a traitor to his race.[115]

III. Noricum

7

The End of Noricum

No literary work of the later fifth century A.D. is more valuable to the historian than Eugippius' *Life of Severinus*. In a few dozen pages it gives us a wealth of specific information about the riverside towns of Noricum Ripense (between Passau, say, and Vienna). It narrates the events of the final years of these towns and their ultimate fate to an extent that must arouse the envy of students of fifth-century Britain. There we have nothing but a few vague generalizations of Gildas, and we do not know the specific fate of a single city. Eugippius, though he by no means avoids the miracles that were thought necessary to the *genre* in which he was writing, composed his work in a style of such lively and convincing vividness that one might have thought it impossible for any scholar to deny its general truth.

And yet what Austrian scholars tell us nowadays about St. Severinus often resembles what Irish writers used to tell us long ago about St. Patrick: they report those things that we should very much like to know but for which there is no evidence whatever. Now, when Bury published his epoch-making book on Patrick in 1905 he proved that in fact we know very much less than nineteenth-century scholars knew — or thought they knew — about him. And when Binchy and Hanson published their works about Patrick in the 1960s they made it clear that we know far less about the saint than Bury knew — or thought he knew. That is to say, as the present century has progressed, our knowledge of St. Patrick has diminished in proportion as our attitude to the sources of our information has become more critical.[1] Severinus has attracted the attention of no Bury and no Binchy or Hanson.

In the case of the saint of Noricum the whole process has taken the opposite direction. Our knowledge of Severinus has increased so enormously in recent years that Eugippius, our sole source of information about him, is shown to have been a pitiful ignoramus. About most of his subject's life

Noricum

his ignorance could hardly have been more complete. In fact, Professor F. Lotter's knowledge of Severinus is an iceberg of which Eugippius knew only the tip—and even with the tip he had only a nodding acquaintance: is not his narrative bedevilled with doublets, traditional topics, and plain misunderstandings? Worse still, he thought that he was beginning his story with the events of 453–54 soon after Attila's death: that is what he says in his opening sentence. Of course, he was utterly mistaken: his narrative, we are told, does not begin until 467.[2] But what is worst of all is that the misguided biographer did not know such blatant, elementary facts as that Severinus had enjoyed a powerful and famous career in high politics before Eugippius' narrative opens. The saint had been a public figure of the utmost distinction. He had reached the consulate itself in 461. As the man who gave his name to the year, he could not have been more widely known. All the literate persons in the West had heard of him—all, with one exception. The one exception was his biographer, who had not the faintest idea of the political eminence of his subject. Before opening his career as a saint, Severinus had wielded vast powers on the Danubian frontier. He had rubbed shoulders with emperors and patricians. But he fell from power when the Emperor Majorian fell. By an unfortunate oversight his biographer never heard of any such facts and so—not surprisingly—is not able to mention them in his biography.[3]

An attempt will be made in the following pages to begin the task of restoring some confidence in the magnificent biography which Eugippius wrote and to bring to these studies a quality which has recently been in short supply—common sense.

I. SEVERINUS: ESTABLISHING DATES

In the opening words of the book we must accept the text as it is given by the Class II manuscripts: among other reasons it is confirmed by a partial quotation in the Chronicle of Prosper of Aquitaine, 1370 (*Chron. Min.*, i, 483). The words which I have italicized in the following lines are omitted in the manuscripts of Class I: "tempore quo Attila rex Hunnorum defunctus est, utraque Pannonia ceteraque confinia Danuvii rebus turbabantur ambiguis *ac primum inter filios eius de optinendo regno magna sunt exorta certamina. qui morbo dominationis inflati materiam sui sceleris aestimarunt patris interitum.* tunc itaque . . . Severinus de partibus Orientis adveniens . . . parvo quod Asturis dicitur oppido morabatur."[4] Some believe that Prosper composed the additional (italicized) words.[5] But in the interests of brevity Prosper would be more likely to omit those words than to compose them and insert them gratuitously into his work. And in fact he has shortened the passage: he omits the words *qui morbo . . . patris interitum.* On this theory we would have to suppose that Prosper expanded the words of his source, and that a copyist not only included Prosper's words in the text of Eugippius but also "improved" them by adding *qui morbo . . . patris interitum* on his own account. We must suppose further that Prosper's refinement of Eugippius and the copyist's refinement of Prosper made their way, not into a single freak manuscript, but into the whole of the Class II manuscripts of Eugippius. Few will deny that it is simpler to suppose that Eugippius wrote the longer version and that some of his words were omitted from the manuscripts of Class I. For a translation see p. 286 below.

This text is of the utmost importance as it gives us a precise date for the opening of Severinus' career, in so far as Eugippius knew it. Attila died in the spring of 453, and his sons at once began quarrelling. But the struggles of the sons were quickly ended by a general revolt of their subjects, which culminated in a battle at the unidentified river Nedao in the summer of 455 at latest.[6] There the sons were overwhelmed and virtually disappear from history. But Eugippius says nothing of the rebellion of the subject peoples or of the battle or of the liberation of the subjects from the rule of the Huns. He does *not* say, "When Attila died and his sons were overthrown." He does *not* say, "When Attila died and his subjects regained

their freedom." He makes no reference to the outcome of the quarrels of
the sons. All he says is that when Attila died and his sons first began to
quarrel Severinus made his appearance. No one in his senses would deny—
though it has been denied—that the date is after the spring of 453 and
before the battle of the river Nedao, which may have been fought in 453,
or in 454, or at the latest in the summer of 455.[7] So at some time between
the summer of 453 and that of 455 Severinus was found to be living in
Asturis. That, then, is the date of the beginning of Eugippius's narrative.
Let us call it "454." That cannot be wrong by more than a few months in
either direction.

Severinus had not been long in Asturis in 454. He had not imposed his
authority on the inhabitants of the little place. The clergy and citizens disregarded his words when he warned them of a coming barbarian attack.
Indeed, the old man who lodged him, the sacristan of the church there,
did not even know his name when the attack took place (i. 5).[8] It follows
that Severinus moved from Asturis to Comagenis *c.* 454–55. There is no
means of saying how long he had been in Comagenis before the destruction of the garrison there, which we shall examine in a moment; but the
narrative of Eugippius does not suggest a long interval. It is not out of the
question that the earthquake which caused such uproar in Comagenis may
be identical, as has often been suggested, with the earthquake which overthrew Sabaria seven days before the Ides of September, 455.[9] The famine at
Favianis (cap. iii) is said to have happened "at the same time," *eodem tempore,* as the destruction of the federates at Comagenis. And cap. iv begins
with the words *per idem tempus* and narrates the victory of the tribune
Mamertinus over the barbarian marauders as well as the construction of
the monastery at Favianis. Of course, Eugippius was writing some half-
century afterwards when it would have been difficult, perhaps even impossible, to find out the exact dates of these early events. And an exact chronology is not a matter that greatly interested him. He believed that no vast
intervals separated these happenings; and so we may suppose that they followed fairly quickly one after another. There seems no reason why they
should not all have occurred before *c.* 460.

But there is another indication of date. The author tells us in cap. vi
how Severinus cured a Rugian boy of an illness. When the boy was later
seen hale and hearty in the barbarians' market, everyone was amazed; and
from that time "the whole race of the Rugi" used to visit the holy man to
pay their respects to him and to ask him to cure their illnesses, too. Men of
other nations also wanted to see him: and even *before* the cure of the Rugian boy a party of barbarians on their way to Italy turned aside to see the
saint and to obtain his blessing (vi. 6). One member of this earlier party

which was travelling to Italy was Odoacer, still a *iuvenis,* according to Eugippius' narrative (cap. vii). But in the chapter headings (*capitula*) prefixed to his narrative Eugippius calls him, not *iuvenis,* but *adulescentulus.* According to Isidore of Seville, the time of life known as *adulescentia* extended from fifteen years of age to twenty-eight.[10] Let us say, then, that Odoacer was at most twenty-eight years of age at the time of his visit to Severinus. We know that he was born in 433, for he was aged sixty when Theoderic the Ostrogoth murdered him in 493.[11] It would seem then that the visit is to be dated to approximately 461. We cannot make Odoacer much younger than twenty-eight, for in that case there would not have been enough time before the meeting with the saint for Severinus to have won his reputation in Noricum (assuming that he arrived in Asturis in 454). Nor can we make Odoacer much older, for in that case we would make nonsense of Eugippius' use of the word *adulescentulus.* So the cure of the Rugian boy, which led to "the whole race of the Rugians" visiting Severinus, took place *later* than *c.* 461, the probable date of Odoacer's visit. There is yet another indication of date in cap. xvii. 4, where we hear of a Gothic attack on Tiburnia, the capital of the province of Noricum Mediterraneum. It seems to be agreed that the Ostrogoths moved away from Pannonia *c.* 472, out of range of Tiburnia,[12] so that the events of this chapter would appear to have taken place before that year. If that is granted, then the whole narrative of capp. viii–xvii took place before 472, for it is conceded on all sides that Eugippius tells the various events in chronological order.

It is unfortunate that he is not a little more explicit in cap. xx. 1. He says there that when state pay stopped reaching them the military units of the frontier garrison and the frontier itself went out of existence. But he does not make it clear when, in his opinion, the pay ceased to arrive. Nothing whatever indicates that he is thinking of the year 476 and the fall of Romulus Augustulus.[13] It may well be that the author himself, writing in 511, did not know exactly when the frontier had disappeared or when the last pay-packets had reached the troops. The process will have happened fairly gradually, and it is not the sort of thing that would have been recorded in the history books or the chronicles of the time. The fact that two small, understrength units still survived in the province when Severinus arrived there (those at Favianis and at Batavis) by no means proves that their pay was still reaching the men at that time.

Thereafter there seems to be no indication of date in the *Life* until cap. xxxii, which must refer to the period following 476, for Odoacer is now "king" (*rex*). It had taken him about fifteen years to win the confidence of the troops in Italy and to put himself at their head.

I conclude that Severinus appeared in Asturis in 453–54, that he met

Odoacer *c.* 461, that the events of chapters viii–xvii took place before 472, and that the events of chapter xxxii happened later than 476. But if these earlier dates are accepted, and especially 453–54 as the time of Severinus's arrival in Asturis, it follows that those great theories of Lotter about Severinus's official career and his consulate of 461, must fall to the ground. Lotter's whole edifice was a house of cards, and the removal of a single card brings the entire structure tumbling down in ruins.

Eugippius tells us the date of Severinus' death: it was January 8. We wait eagerly for him to add the year; but he is silent. He is not interested. He thinks it important to record the saint's day. The year is beside the point. He is writing the life of a saint. He does not wish to write history. Perhaps we are lucky to have as many indications of date in the narrative as in fact we have.

II. DISAPPEARANCE OF IMPERIAL POWER IN THE FIFTH CENTURY

The entire book contains not a single reference to the governor (*praeses*) of Noricum Ripense or to any member of his staff, or to the military commander (*dux*) of Pannonia Prima and Noricum Ripense (for both provinces were under the command of the one military commander). Although the writer has so much to say about Comagenis and Favianis and Lauriacum[14] in wartime, he never implies that these towns were each protected by a fleet of warships; and yet the *Notitia Dignitatum* had assigned fleets to them earlier in the century. In the first few lines of his book Eugippius tells how the barbarians took the little town of Asturis. He tells us that the inhabitants of Asturis were made up of "priests, clergy, and citizens" (i. 2) or "townspeople," *oppidanei* (i. 5). They are all civilians. He distinctly implies the absence of any military garrison. Yet, according to the *Notitia,* the place had contained an infantry unit commanded by a tribune. The inhabitants of Noricum Ripense had much to complain of in Severinus' time, but the payment of taxes was not among their burdens, or, if it was, they did not talk of it to the saint. It is hard to think of any other province of the entire empire where the taxes were not a crushing burden.

The explanation of these facts is simple: throughout the whole period of Severinus' activity there was no imperial civil administration and nothing but a couple of fragments of the imperial army in the province of Noricum Ripense. Roman power had already disappeared from this part of the frontier when Severinus arrived there *c.* 454.[15] This assertion can be proved.

In fact, proof is given in the very first chapter of the book. In the town of Comagenis, says the author, there was living a band of barbarians, *barbarorum intrinsecus consistentium,* i. 4; *barbari intrinsecus habitantes,* ii. 1. They were living there as the result of a treaty, *foedus inierant,* i. 4. That is to say, these barbarians were in the technical sense *foederati,* "federates"; but they were federates of a kind to which only one exact parallel is known from Western Europe (p. 120 below).[16]

These federates were not billeted on the estates of the countryside, as were the federates whom Constantius and Aëtius had planted in Gaul in 418 and 440–43 respectively. These men were stationed in the town of Comagenis, just as Roman soldiers used to be billeted in the towns.[17] But a much more important difference between the barbarians in Comagenis and, on the other hand, the Visigoths of Aquitanica Secunda and the Burgundians of Savoy is that the former made their treaty, their *foedus,* not with the emperor or his representatives, but with the *Romani,* i. 4. A little later in the story this word *Romani* reappears, and it is paraphrased by *habitatores oppidi* (ii. 1), the citizens of Comagenis. That is to say, the barbarians made their treaty, not with the imperial authorities, but with the townsfolk of a single town.[18] The importance of this fact could hardly be exaggerated. In earlier times it would have been treason of the highest degree for townsfolk on their own initiative to open the frontier and to admit barbarians to the soil of the empire: it would have been unthinkable.[19] In the fifth century the central government might plant barbarians (who had already forced their way into the provinces and could not be forced out again) in an entire province or in an ill-defined but extensive area like Savoy (Sapaudia), but they would not have settled federate troops in a single city. The chief purpose of such settlements was to provide the government with a sizeable force of soldiers. The relatively few who could have been billeted in a minor town like Comagenis would have been of negligible military value to the government of the Empire as a whole. At any rate, no case is known where the Roman authorities admitted federates to one town and to one town only. What would they have gained by doing so?

The clear implication of these facts is that, if such a treaty could be struck by the townsmen of a single city and the frontier opened to a group of barbarians, the imperial administration had completely disappeared from the province. No such agreement could possibly have been arranged if the provincial governor had still been in existence in Noricum Ripense. The governor would have been quick to take fierce action against any town that dared to admit barbarians within the frontier or to treat with them on their own initiative. It is clear that the provincial governor and all his staff have disappeared. Noricum Ripense is no longer a part of the emperor's dominions. Evidently, each town now can — or must — fend for itself, just as in Britain the towns had to fend for themselves in and after 410.

The identity of these federates is unknown. Across the river from Comagenis lived the people known as the Rugi.[20] Presumably, then, the federates who had been admitted to the town were invited in the first place so
as to defend Comagenis from the Rugi and from bands of Rugian marauders: but we do not know who they were. The only probability is that they
were not Rugi.

In spite of the presence of federates inside their walls, the citizens were
despairing of their own safety when Severinus arrived there (i. 4). Why?
Who were the enemy who so terrified them? The answer is not obscure.
The citizens dreaded their own federates, that is to say, the barbarians
whom they had themselves settled inside their own walls. There is no
other enemy in the picture of whom they could have been frightened. It is
clear that the relations between the townsfolk and those whom they had
hired to defend them had deteriorated and were now very bad. But then
came a fortunate event (from the citizens' point of view): one night an
earthquake occurred. The barbarians panicked, rushed out of the town,
and fled in different directions, fearing that they were beset by "their hostile neighbours," *vicinorum hostium obsidione,* ii. 2. There have been gross
misunderstandings of the phrase. It means their Roman neighbours, the
citizens who had been living side by side with them in the town.[21] In the
confusion of the darkness the barbarians proceeded to massacre one another (ii. 2).

The incident throws light on conditions inside the town. The citizens
had admitted federates to defend them but then began to despair of their
own safety because of the presence of these very federates. And the federates on their side also feared surprise attacks by the citizens who had hired
them. The atmosphere of the town was evidently electric. Anything
might have caused an explosion. In fact, it was the earthquake which set
events in motion.

A remarkable parallel to the general situation can be found in British
history at a time when the Roman administration had long been gone
from that island. According to Gildas, a "proud tyrant" some years after
446 (when Aetius had been consul for the third time) invited Saxon warriors into his part of Britain and settled them there as "federates." Not
long after, he was on even worse terms with them than the citizens of Comagenis were on with "their" federates. Unfortunately for the proud tyrant, earthquakes were unusual in his part of the world, and none occurred
to rescue him from his difficulties.[22]

So from this first chapter of the *Life* we infer that before the beginning
of Severinus' career in Noricum Ripense the imperial civil power had already disappeared from the province. It had vanished utterly. But if the cit-

izens of one town were reduced to inviting barbarians to come inside their walls so as to provide them with some protection and if no retributive action had been taken against them, we may be sure that little or nothing of the Imperial garrison survived. A tribune called Mamertinus (who afterwards became a bishop) still commanded some troops in Favianis soon after the start of Severinus' career; but his men were so few and so ill-armed that he felt unable to attack a band of barbarian robbers outside the town. In fact, although his unit was inside the town, the raiders were able to carry off any people or cattle who happened to be outside the walls. And when the troops eventually did attack them, they were operating only two miles outside Favianis (iv. 1–4). There is not the slightest hint in the narrative that Mamertinus had any colleagues in the vicinity to whom he could appeal for reinforcements. He clearly had none. He was on his own. The morale of the citizens on this occasion is noteworthy: when the raiders made their appearance, the citizens did not assume that the tribune would defend them. They did not even run to Mamertinus and urge him to attack the marauders. Still less did they arm themselves and try to drive off the enemy on their own initiative. Instead, they went in tears to Severinus and bleated to him about their woes, but (if we can press Eugippius' words) they had no constructive proposals to put before him (iv. 1). They were helpless.

A little later the Rugian queen, Giso, was in the next village to Favianis and ordered a number of free Romans to be carried off north of the Danube. No mention is made in this case of the presence of any troops whatever in Favianis—whether the troops of Mamertinus or of anyone else—who might have protected these unfortunate men (viii. 2). A little later still the robbers known as the Scamarae were operating only two miles from the town; and again there is no reference to any imperial troops there (x. 1–2). Although the author speaks of Favianis several times later on, there is not the slightest indication of the presence of any military unit in it —indeed, in xxxi. 1 we find that the town is paying tribute to the Rugi. It can hardly be denied that soon after Mamertinus' victory over the robbers, the tribune became a bishop, and his company of men disbanded. Thenceforth, the town had no military defenders.

But the unit at Batavis lasted longer. In cap. xx the author tells how this unit sent some of its number to Italy to fetch their "last pay," *extremum stipendium.* What is the meaning of the epithet? How did they know that it was to be their "last" pay? They certainly could not have predicted that the authorities in Italy had decided not to pay them again. These men were soldiers, not prophets or clairvoyants. Only one answer appears to be acceptable. It was the men themselves who proposed to make it their last pay-packet. Once they had got it, they proposed to disband and to scatter to their homes or to take to another way of life. At all events, we can hardly doubt that when their envoys to Rome or Ravenna were intercepted and killed by the barbarians, the men of this unit dispersed. They knew now that they would never be paid again. Moreover, it would be a mistake to infer the existence of numerous military units from the fact that several *castella* were still occupied by the Romans. In xl. 1 we hear that practically no *castellum* was escaping military attack; but the inhabitants of the *castella* who appealed to Severinus for help are described in terms which beyond a doubt indicate civilians—*accolae, cives eiusdem loci, pars plebis, plebem* (xi. 1–2). And this is true also, no doubt, of the *castella* of Noricum Mediterraneum, which are mentioned in chapter xxv. 2. The dwellers in all the *castella* are civilians, not soldiers.

The last soldier of whom we hear on the Norican frontier is Avitianus, evidently a private soldier rather than an officer—he is described simply as *miles*. He makes his appearance after the death of Severinus in 482. He was forced by the Rugian Ferderuchus to steal articles from the altar of Severinus' monastery church (xliv. 2). He was a solitary figure. He had not even one comrade whom he could ask for help. In this part of the world he had the strange distinction of being the last soldier of the Roman army. For how long he had been a unique figure and when he had last been paid, we have no means of knowing. But since the date of the episode in which he makes his none too glorious appearance is so late—after 482—he may well have been a solitary figure for years, something little better than an aged and lonely ghost.[23]

That the frontier existed no longer is also shown by the considerable traffic which Eugippius reports between the Rugian territory north of the Danube and the old Roman province south of it. Early in the saint's career, as we have seen (p. 116 above), the son of a Rugian woman was brought to Severinus to be cured of an illness. As a result of the cure of this boy "the whole race of the Rugi" flocked to Severinus to pay him their respects and to ask aid for their illnesses. Other non-Rugian barbarians also came, among them Odoacer. Severinus spent much effort in ransoming the Roman prisoners of the barbarians. He told one of those who had been ransomed along with his wife and children to go back north of the Danube and find a certain man in the market of the barbarians, *in nundinis barbarorum* (ix. 1 f.), a weekly market, if the word *nundinae* is used strictly. Evidently, there was nothing remarkable in the sight of a Roman at the market. And yet apparently Romans were not free to trade there, for the citizens of Boiotro begged Severinus later on to go to King Feva and obtain permission for them to trade in the market (xxii. 2). (It would be of interest to know

(i) why the citizens of Boiotro were so anxious to trade in the country north of the Danube, (ii) what goods they proposed to offer for sale, (iii) what they hoped to import in exchange for their exports, (iv) why there was no local market inside the old Roman frontier which could have satisfied their needs. Unhappily, on all these points Eugippius is silent.) Severinus himself crossed the river in his early days, but not into the land of the Rugi: he went into the country of the Scamarae (x. 2).[24] In xlii. 1 Eugippius tells how Ferderuchus, Feva's brother, came to greet Severinus near Favianis. He came *ex more,* that is to say, he was in the habit of coming. The clear inference is that even in the saint's earliest days in the province there was no longer any Roman frontier on this stretch of the Danube. Anyone who wished to do so could cross from north to south of the river, though—a sad change from earlier days—it may have been somewhat more difficult to cross from south to north. At a much later period of Severinus' career he went to the northern bank of the river, but he went no further than the river bank: he did not journey into the interior (xxiii. 1). Among those who travelled from the land north of the river to the country south of it in the saint's early days was the Rugian queen Giso. She is reported to have been in the village nearest to Favianis (p. 121 above). She was south of the Danube again a little later, when she thanked Severinus for rescuing her son from his kidnappers, and yet again at a much later time, when she and her husband visited Severinus on his deathbed in 482 (xl. 1). (It is hard to imagine some fourth-century Giso crossing the Rhine or the Danube in the teeth of Valentinian I!) So throughout the whole of Severinus' career in Noricum the imperial frontier on this part of the Danube had disappeared, and there was no check on travellers who wished to cross the river. A man could travel into the Empire or out of it, as he wished. We have seen that the imperial administration had also vanished, and that there was no imperial armed force there apart from a couple of fragments of units which perhaps had not been paid for years. We know from various passages in Procopius that when a situation arose in which the army was left unpaid for a considerable period of time, the desertion rate would be high, and yet some units would continue to serve for years, though with considerable ill-will. They would "earn" their keep by plundering the Roman provincials whom they were supposed to be guarding, though we hear of no such practices in Noricum.

Finally, when the Patrician Orestes was murdered in 476 by Odoacer and his supporters, a noble Italian priest called Primenius, who had been closely associated with Orestes, took to flight in fear of the assassins. He fled for safety to Noricum Ripense. Now, it would have been senseless to fly from one part of Odoacer's dominions to another for security. The inference is that Noricum Ripense was no longer part of the Italian Empire.[25]

The view that the imperial frontier was still in existence in the time of St. Severinus is untenable. Unfortunately, we have no means of saying when exactly or even when approximately the power of the emperors had disappeared from Noricum Ripense. We hear of a very remarkable event which took place in Noricum in 430–31: the provincials there rebelled and were crushed—apparently in two successive years—by Aëtius in person.[26] It is rare to find a revolt of the provincials (as distinct from military or even civilian officials) in the Western Empire in the fifth century. The only revolts of the civilian population in that period would seem to be those of the general population of Armorica and Britain, revolts which, according to the historian Zosimus, had a social character and were indeed aimed at secession from the Roman Empire altogether.[27] Whether that was also true of the Norican rebellion or rebellions in 430–31 we do not know. Nor do we know for how long thereafter Aëtius was able to hold Noricum down. When Priscus visited the camp of Attila the Hun in 449 he met there a certain Promotus, whom he describes as "governor" (archon) of Noricum, but unfortunately he does not say whether Promotus was governor of Ripense or Mediterraneum: there is some very slight reason for thinking that Mediterraneum is intended.[28] If that was in fact the case, then imperial control of Noricum Ripense may not have survived for very long after the uprising of 430–31. The rebellions of those years must have been extensive, for they required two campaigns, each conducted by Aëtius in person.

III. THE RUGI

Who were these Rugi who figure so prominently in the Life?[29] They lived opposite Favianis (viii. 2, xxxi. 1) and were one of the minor Germanic peoples living outside the northern Roman frontier. They were akin to the Goths,[30] but they were far weaker than the Ostrogoths who lived in Pannonia Inferior at the time when the Life opens—or not long thereafter. The Rugi asked these Ostrogoths for permission to travel through Noricum Mediterraneum to Italy; and when the Goths refused this permission the Rugian king, Flaccitheus, inferred from this refusal that the Goths would kill him.[31] The Rugi are the only barbarians known to us outside the northern imperial frontier who were the victims of Roman brigands. Roman robbers actually raided them from south of the Danube (v. 3). Some brigands, turba latrocinantium, carried off some Rugi.[32] Severinus advised the Rugian king, Flaccitheus, not to cross the Danube in pursuit of them: "if you do," he said, "you will be killed." Three ambushes had been laid for the pursuers. This advice of the saint's means, "do not cross to the south of the river," for, of course, the Rugi lived north of it. The clear implication is that the brigands lived south of it: these were Roman brigands who raided the country of the barbarians and carried off barbarian prisoners, whom they presumably intended to sell as slaves further south.

So weak were the Rugi in comparison with the other barbarians in this region that we can best explain their request for permission to emigrate to Italy as an attempt at flight: they were in danger of being overwhelmed by wilder and more powerful barbarian peoples if they stayed where they were.[33] No doubt they hoped to collect some loot, too, in Italy and land to settle on; but their main objective may well have been safety. When they eventually did reach Italy many years later, they managed to supply a king, Eraric, to the barbarians (including the Ostrogoths) who were settled in Italy at that time. This Eraric had served in the Gothic army and had won great power there; but it is not at all clear why the Goths accepted his rule. It was the Rugians in Italy who proclaimed him king in 541, and the Goths endured him for five months before getting rid of him.[34] In his narrative of the incident Procopius gives us the interesting information that it was contrary to the Rugian people's customs for a Rugian to marry a non-Rugian.[35] Otherwise, we only know of their internal affairs that the kings could impose their will on their followers with difficulty.[36]

In addition to being raided from the south, the Rugians were unique in a more important respect. They were at this time the only Germanic people living outside the northern frontier of the Roman Empire who were Christian. In circumstances of which we know nothing they had been converted to Arian Christianity.[37] Ludwig Schmidt supposes, probably rightly, that they had been converted soon after being liberated from the Hun empire.[38] But by whom? It is tempting to think that the Ostrogoths had had a hand in it, for it was Gothic rather than Roman priests who spread the Gospel among the Germanic barbarians. And Roman priests at this date would hardly have spread Arianism. If the conversion of the Rugi was due to the Goths, it was their one success outside the frontier. But we know very little about the origins of Christianity on the middle Danube.[39] It is tempting to think that the barbarian brigands, *praedones barbari*, of chapter iv. 1–4, were Christians, because Severinus uses Christian arguments to dissuade them from their brigandage. Indeed, he appears to assume that they were Christians. The Rugian kings, with that tolerance which was characteristic of the Arian monarchs in general, were on remarkably friendly terms with Severinus although he was an uncompromising Catholic. Their attitude was very different from that which a Catholic king would have shown to an heretical holy man.[40] Yet Severinus is never said to have made any attempt to convert them from their Arian-

ism to the Catholic faith, great though his influence was. (He did not need
to proselytise the native population of Noricum, for in spite of the pagan
practice reported in one passage of the *Life* (cap. xi) the native population
was apparently already Christian when he first arrived in the province.)
One of the Rugians who visited him was an optimate of King Feletheus:
the saint cured his son but did not use the occasion to convert the optimate
to his own brand of Christianity (xxxiii. 1). In conversation with King
Flaccitheus, Severinus referred candidly to the difference of religion which
separated them, "si nos una Catholica fides annecteret. . . ." (v. 2); but he
did nothing to alter this state of affairs. The king made many approaches
to the holy man. Flaccitheus at the beginning of his reign consulted
Severinus on his difficulties with the Ostrogoths of Pannonia (v. 1) and
also on the kidnappers of some of his people by Roman brigands (v. 3:
note especially xlii. 2.). Flaccitheus's son and successor, Feletheus (also
known as Feva) copied his father in this respect from the very beginning of
his reign (viii. 1). Even the strongly Arian Queen Giso appealed to Severinus to rescue her son when he was held hostage (viii. 4). But sometimes
the approaches came from the Roman side. The saint sent to Queen Giso
asking her to release some Romans whom she had carried off as slaves. The
queen refused the request (viii. 2). The inhabitants of Boiotro asked Severinus to approach Feva and obtain from him permission for the Romans to
trade in the market of the barbarians north of the Danube. The saint on
this occasion refused the request on the grounds that Boiotro would soon
be destroyed (xxii. 2). When Feva wished to remove the inhabitants of
some of the frontier towns forcibly and transport them to other dwellings,
the holy man went out and met the king and reached some sort of compromise with him (xxxi. 2). And when Severinus lay on his deathbed, he
urged (*commonuit*) Feva and Giso to come to his bedside, where he admonished them sternly (xl. 2); he urged them not to oppress the innocent. Later he admonished Ferderuchus (xlii. 1). Nothing was said on any occasion
about converting them to Catholicism.[41]

Incidentally, it is remarkable that at none of these interviews do we hear
of the presence of an interpreter. Could the Rugian royal family speak
Latin? If they could, it would be interesting to know where and when
they had learned it and who their teachers may have been.

Even more striking than his relations with the Rugian leaders is his influence over the Alamannic king (*rex*) Gibuldus, for Gibuldus was neither
an Arian nor a Catholic nor a Christian of any sort: he was a pagan.[42] Yet
he is reported to have gone towards Batavis to meet the saint, being most
eager to see him. He said after their meeting that he had never been struck
with such trembling either in war or anywhere else as he had been afflicted

by in the saint's presence (xix. 2). He undertook to release his Roman prisoners, though in fact he did not do so with much alacrity. And yet we hear
of extensive and numerous Alamannic raids later on (xxv. 3; xxvii. 1–2; cf.
xxxi. 4), and Gibuldus is never heard of again. Did the saint lose his influence over the king, or did the king die, or were the raids carried out by
other *pagi* of the Alamanni, *pagi* which Gibuldus did not control? We have
no means of telling.[43]

But even with the Rugian royal family the relationship was not always
an amicable one. Queen Giso tried to rebaptize some Catholics, that is, to
accept them into the Arian church (viii. 1). It is important to notice what
exactly the queen is said to have done. She is *not* said to have tried forcibly
to convert them.[44] Evidently, they were themselves ready to become
Arians, and the queen simply wished to receive them into her church in
what to an Arian was the normal way, that is, by rebaptizing them. The
Arians did not recognize Catholic baptism, so that in their eyes rebaptism
was a necessity. If she had been trying forcibly to convert them to her religion, it is certain that Eugippius would not have neglected to tell us of
such an enormity. Who were these Catholics who wished to lapse? One
scholar refers to them as "some of her Catholic subjects." Another goes so
far as to suggest that she wished to rebaptize *all* her Catholic subjects.[45]
But Eugippius does not refer to them as her subjects. The only possible explanation, in my opinion, is that some Romans thought it expedient to accept the religion of the neighbouring barbarians, the Rugians; presumably
they proposed to enter the service of the Rugians. There is no parallel to
this in the rest of the *Life,* but it would be a painful subject to a Catholic
writer and one which he would not wish to linger over. Certainly, the
queen is not said to have proposed to convert to Arianism all those Romans who fell into her power. For example, she ordered some free Romans to be carried off from a village (*vicus*) near Favianis to serve as slaves
north of the Danube. They were to serve in the lowest type of slavery,
though it is not clear what type of slavery that was (viii. 2). But the narrative gives no hint that the slaves were the persons whom the queen wished
to baptize, nor was there any reason why she should wish to do so—the
Arians were never great proselytisers. It would be of interest to know the
scale of the defection (if there was defection) to the Rugians and what exactly the motives of the defectors were. At any rate, this phenomenon is
not known anywhere else along the northern frontier—and for a very
good reason: nowhere else at this date was there a Christian barbarian people living beyond that frontier.

When Giso wished to rebaptize these persons, she was doing nothing
wrong by the tenets of her faith. The only sacriligious action recorded in

the *Life* is that of Ferderuchus, who plundered the clothing that was to have been given to the poor, and also looted the silver chalice and other altar vessels from Severinus's monastery church at Favianis. In fact, he did not leave the church until he had completely stripped it of its contents.[46] Arians in various countries may have confiscated Catholic churches so as to use them for their own services, but they rarely plundered them merely so as to obtain loot.[47]

There is only one reference to pagan practices in the province. When Severinus came across a band of persons who still offered pagan sacrifices at Cucullis, a *castellum* inhabited by civilians (*cives*), the saint was able miraculously to identify the guilty. These then openly admitted their guilt, and Eugippius implies that they returned to the fold of the righteous. He does not go on to say that the saint smashed any cult objects that they may have possessed.[48] So when Severinus arrived in Noricum *c.* 454, paganism was already dead, and the province was virtually Christian.

IV. BARBARIAN MILITARY ACTIVITIES

Of military activities we hear most about the barbarians' assaults on the Norican cities. As we have seen, Comagenis was defended by its barbarian federates who were so obliging as to massacre one another. The town is not known to have fallen to the invaders, nor did the enemy ever storm Favianis, though they raided right up to its walls (iv, 1 f., x). Tiburnia, the capital of Noricum Mediterraneum, was attacked by the Ostrogoths but did not fall to them (xvii. 4). In Ripense, Lauriacum, too, was not stormed, though its inhabitants eventually vacated it (xxxi. 6). Eugippius speaks of the *excidium* of the towns on the upper Danube, but he means the emigration of the inhabitants, not the military destruction of the *oppida* in question (xxviii. 1). But a number of the towns did fall. Asturis was surprised by an unidentified band of barbarians (i. 2 *insidias*), who devastated the little place and wiped out all its inhabitants except one. Eugippius may not have been able to find out which barbarians took Asturis. This is the earliest event in Noricum which he records, and it happened over fifty years before he was writing. Besides, the solitary survivor may never have learned the identity of the attackers. It was certainly through surprise that Batavis fell. The Alamanni had constantly raided it (xix. 1 f.), but they never captured it. As late as the date of the events narrated in chapter xx there were still troops in the place. But although the Alamanni did not take Batavis, they did carry off a number of the inhabitants as slaves. Eventually the town was surprised by a certain Hunumund leading only a few barbarians (xxii. 4) at a time when the population at large was busy with the harvest and only forty men had been left to guard the place.[49] Presumably there were no troops there at this time. But this disaster was not the end of Batavis. Life continued to go on there, and indeed the people of Quintanis retreated to it later on (xxvii. 1). The town had been worn out by the incessant raids of the Alamanni; and when the majority of the townsfolk migrated to Batavis, the remaining minority were surprised by the Thuringians, who killed some of them and took others prisoner (xxvii. 3 *Thoringis irruentibus*). But when the town had its complete population the barbarians had not been able to take it. Finally, Ioviaco was rushed by the Heruls, who laid it waste, took many prisoners, and murdered a priest (xxiv. 3).

At one stage we are told that a very large force of Alamanni "laid everything waste, but the forts felt no danger," thanks to the Christian attitude of their inmates (xxv. 3). It is clear that the storming of a Norican city was a rare event and indeed only took place when the number of the defenders had been reduced by emigration or by harvest work. The one great weapon of the barbarian was surprise, and it was by surprise that all those cities were taken which we know to have fallen. Night was a favourite time for surprise (xxx. 2 f.): then the raiders might turn up with scaling ladders (xxx. 4). To anticipate a barbarian attack the citizens, if they followed Severinus's advice, would carry all foodstuffs from the countryside to within the city walls (xxx. 1).[50] It was because of the possibility of surprise that the citizens of Lauriacum had scouts out watching for the invaders (xxx. 1 f.) Since a continuous, organized, systematic watch on the frontier had disappeared with the frontier itself, it was the task of each town to organize its own watch; and so it is perhaps curious that we do not hear more often of scouts watching for potential enemies, though at one time there were sentries watching from the walls of Lauriacum *ex more* (xxx. 2). It may be that this precaution was so obvious that Eugippius does not trouble to mention it, though on the other hand the labour of such scouts could perhaps not be spared indefinitely from the day-to-day work of the town. Yet the result of *not* having scouts was, for some of these towns, a disaster.

On the two occasions when we are given figures, these figures are small. We have seen that when the harvesters went out of Batavis they left only forty men behind to keep watch over the town (xxii. 4). Again, the raids of the Alamanni led to a number of the inhabitants of Batavis being carried off as slaves. An emissary of Severinus managed to restore seventy of them to freedom; and a later envoy recovered a "great crowd" of prisoners (xix. 5 *magnam . . . copiam*). The total number of those involved may not have been more than a couple of hundred. It would seem to follow that the invading bands, too, were small. When the Visigoths crossed the

Danube into the Roman Empire in 376, and the Vandals, Alans, and Sueves crossed the Rhine in 406, their numbers in both cases, it seems, amounted to scores of thousands of persons. But in the frontier raids on Noricum the raiding bands probably did not number more than a few hundred warriors at most. Their aim was plunder, not settlement, which was the purpose of the Visigoths, the Vandals, and the others.[51] So it was by no means impossible for the inhabitants to hold their own against individual bands of invaders. When the Ostrogoths besieged Tiburnia in Noricum Mediterraneum, the citizens fought them with varying results and eventually signed a treaty with them and paid them the alms which they had collected to give to Severinus (xvii. 4). This can hardly have amounted to a large sacrifice on the part of the citizens. (Why the Ostrogoths should have wanted to have bundles of used clothing is not clear.) What the citizens lacked was a spirit of aggression. They might fight the barbarians when a fight was forced upon them. They did not take the initiative and attack the enemy, or take him off his guard, or throw him back into the Danube when he was crossing the river so as to plunder the countryside or the cities.

Pitched battles are rarely recorded, and there is no case where the townsfolk were defeated. On the contrary, more than once the barbarians were beaten by the townsmen. This happened at Batavis when the citizens fought a pitched battle against the Alamanni and defeated them (xxvii. 2). Yet most of the citizens withdrew from the town and went to live in Lauriacum. But even after the victory at Batavis we never hear that the townsmen armed themselves on their own initiative and went out aggressively hunting for groups of raiders, still less that they crossed to the north of the Danube so as to bring the war into the barbarians' homeland. We never hear that the citizens of several cities combined to form one united force. Each city acted on its own, if it acted at all. It was left to the barefooted "soldier of Christ," as Eugippius likes to call him, to organize the unsoldierly citizens of Noricum, to advise them, to raise their courage, to plan their strategy. No doubt Eugippius has exaggerated the importance of his hero, but he can hardly have invented it.

What really seems to have destroyed the Danubian towns was the persistency of the barbarians' raids. The citizens could not sow or harvest their crops, and so were obliged to move away and live somewhere else.[52] It is surprising how rarely we hear of outright starvation. The worst case that Eugippius reports (cap. iii) was due to bad weather and had nothing to do with the barbarians.

Late in Severinus's career Feletheus, king of the Rugi, came with his army to take away all the peoples who had (in chapter xxvii) taken refuge in Lauriacum, and to settle them in towns that were tributary to him and were, from his point of view, near at hand. One of these towns was Favianis, where there had been Roman troops in Severinus's early days. The king gave out as his motive his desire to prevent the people in question from being laid waste by the Alamanni and the Thuringians, who would otherwise plunder, kill, or enslave them (xxxi. 4): they ought to be settled in neighbouring tributary towns. But was he really acting in such a selfless way? Was he thinking solely of the good of the people in Lauriacum? If so, why did he come with his army? He can only have come with an army because he proposed to remove the people by force, if necessary — and he thought that it would be necessary. Now, since his plan involved adding to the population of the towns that were tributary to himself, his motive may not have been so high-minded as he claimed. His aim may simply have been to increase his own revenues. We may think that he was merely collecting protection-money. The citizens certainly did not think that Feletheus's motives were generous. They begged Severinus to go and meet the king and persuade him to change his plan. Severinus clearly thought that the citizens would fight rather than accept the plan; and if they fought, they would be devastated.[53]

The episode ended by being the greatest failure on the part of the saint which Eugippius records. The citizens were in fact obliged to leave Lauriacum and to live in the tributary towns after all. It must not be thought, of course, that the Rugi coexisted with them in the towns. There is no likelihood that the Rugi lived in towns at all, and Eugippius records no case where they did so. Indeed, he provides no evidence that *any* barbarians (except the federates in Comagenis) were living permanently south of the Danube in the old imperial province of Noricum Ripense. The only barbarian (apart from the federates) whom he describes as permanently resident in Noricum is a Catholic monk, a barbarian who had taken the baptismal name of Bonosus (cap. xxxv). (There is no hint that Severinus had converted him.) Whatever the aims of the Rugians may have been, there is no evidence that at this date they planned settlement south of the river apart from their ambition to reach Italy. And their plan to migrate to Italy was presumably abandoned for the time being when the Ostrogoths left Pannonia *c.* 472. Eugippius finds it tactful to omit all reference to the tribute which the citizens must now have been obliged to pay to Feletheus (xxxi. 6). Even so good a writer as he is cannot conceal the fact that Severinus was unsuccessful on this occasion. The most that can be claimed for him is that, by giving away the citizens' case, he saved them from being defeated in a battle.

This is the first time in history that we find a Roman town being subject to the payment of tribute to a Germanic ruler. According to Procopius, the barbarians on the Danube were not accustomed in his day to exact tribute; and when the Heruls exacted it from the Lombards and others, the historian turns aside to remark on the unusual character of this action. Evidently, Procopius had not heard that the Heruls had been anticipated in this respect by the Rugi. By a coincidence the Heruls were then living where the Rugi had lived in St. Severinus' time, the Rugi having in the meantime moved off to join their old enemies, the Ostrogoths, in Italy.[54] Another innovation in Germanic history is this. We never before hear that a Germanic king—in this case Feletheus-Feva—could give a Roman city away. We are told that Ferderuchus "received" Favianis from his brother, the king (xlii. 1). And the king seems to have had the absolute and unfettered right to dispose of the town as he pleased (though this is not what Ennodius would have led us to expect: p. 288 n. 36 below). In earlier times we hear of Germanic kings giving their followers money and horses. He might even give them estates to live on. But no Germanic king before Feva is known to have given away a town. The expression can hardly mean anything other than that Ferderuchus received the revenue from the town. Presumably, what was left of the curial order levied the tribute; but how they levied it, how much they levied, and exactly from whom they levied it, we do not know. (It may be that the lady called Procula, whom Eugippius describes as *nobilissimis orta natalibus* [iii. 2], was the wife or widow of a decurion, for when he wants to describe a member of the high nobility he knows the correct term to use, *illustris,* xlvi. 1.) The king's action certainly does not mean that Ferderuchus was appointed administrator of the town (xlii. 1): that task would have been far beyond him. And why he should appear somewhat later as a poor man (*pauper*) is also far from clear (xliv. 1). Yet so impoverished was he that he stole the charity goods, the silver chalice, and other church property.

What did the barbarians achieve militarily? They failed to take Comagenis, Favianis, and (in Noricum Mediterraneum) Tiburnia. They did not take Lauriacum or Quintanis, though the inhabitants evacuated both these places. Of the towns which they did capture, Asturis and Ioviaco and perhaps Quintanis were tiny places of minimal importance. Their only significant achievement was the capture of Batavis. Considering that the narrative of Eugippius covers the years from 454 to 482, the achievement is hardly impressive.

The enemies who threatened Noricum were the Rugi, Alamanni, Ostrogoths, Thuringians, and Heruls. It is noteworthy that the one barbarian people of whom Eugippius has nothing to say (apart from the chronological note in his first sentence) is the Huns. The destruction of their empire at the battle of the river Nedao must have been total. In the 460s a few Huns lurked as squalid brigands on the lower Danube; but it is hard to see how their disappearance from the neighbourhood of Noricum could have been more complete.

V. ST. SEVERINUS

Severinus is the only cleric of whom we know from the northern frontier provinces who regularly hobnobbed with the barbarian leaders, advised them, influenced them, and occasionally roused opposition to them. He is absolutely unique. Germanus of Auxerre is sometimes quoted as a parallel; but apart from his inciting the Britons to fight a single battle against the invaders, the parallel does not exist.

Severinus wrote nothing, and, although the biography by Eugippius is successful as an historical document, we cannot learn much about the saint personally. Indeed, it is not certain that Eugippius knew him very well. He was one of those prodigious, if unsavory, ascetics about whom mediaeval man loved to read. Unsavory? He owned only one cloak, and this he never removed from his body, night or day (xxxix. 2). Ascetic? He possessed no shoes and walked barefoot through the Austrian winter. Although he rarely broke his fast before sundown, and during Lent satisfied himself with one meal a week, yet his face shone with a cheerfulness which we may suspect of being unprepossessing. The world is not always grateful even to saints, and it did not always appreciate Severinus's holy works. When he required others to mortify the flesh as he himself was doing, there were rebuffs. "Go, holy man, I beg you," said a priest of Passau, "go, and go quickly. With your departure we may have a little rest from fasts and vigils." The man of God burst into tears at the vanity of the speaker but was soon able to comfort himself: is not scurrility clear evidence of hidden sins (xxii. 3)? But worse was that when he raised a man from the dead, the ungrateful corpse asked the saint to return him to the eternal peace from which he ought never to have awakened him (xvi. 5). There were misunderstandings, too. When he told a Rugian woman to give alms to the poor, she instantly tore off her clothes and began to distribute them to the poor of the immediate neighbourhood. The saint had to tell her (in some haste, I imagine) that that was not exactly what he had meant (vi. 2).

But what even Severinus could not resurrect was the Roman province of Noricum Ripense. That was dead and buried when he began his career in the little town of Asturis in 454.

IV. Spain

8

Hydatius and the Invasion of Spain

If there were no Chronicle of Hydatius there would be no history of Spain in the fifth century. Were it not for Hydatius we would know of a mere half-handful of disconnected events which happened there. The chroniclers of Gaul had little interest in what was going on south of the Pyrenees, and they rarely mention that part of the tormented world. In 456–57 the Visigoths of the Kingdom of Toulouse fought a murderous campaign in western Spain, and this we would in some sense know of, even without Hydatius: for a hundred years later a Gothic historian describes it, though with gross and patriotic distortions of the truth. We could draw inferences of more or less consequence from a few ecclesiastical documents which still survive; but in fact, if we had lost the Chronicle of Hydatius and a few letters addressed to and from the Popes of the day, we would know little more of fifth-century Spain than we know of Britain in that same dark period of history. That is to say, we would know practically nothing at all.

Happily, there before us stands the slender figure of the Bishop Hydatius. I call him "slender" because in Mommsen's marvellous edition of the Late Roman Chronicles the whole corpus of his life's work fills less than two dozen pages; but he is not quite the enigmatic writer who used to puzzle us a quarter of a century ago. In a masterly article published in 1951 the late Christian Courtois fell upon wide tracts of his Chronicle, tore them ruthlessly from the main body, and pitchforked them into a limbo of *spuria vel dubia*. No longer is Hydatius allowed to believe that Theophilus, Patriarch of Alexandria, was the Pope of Rome, or that St. Augustine lived on for half-a-dozen years after he had died, or that the eclipse of the sun of 28 May 458 took place in 457.[1] No longer is he so far-sighted as to be able to tell us of a few events which possibly took place a year or two after he was in his grave. Since Courtois completed his surgery the Chronicle has taken on a new and more acceptable aspect; but a more or

137

Spain

less complete text of the more or less uninterpolated Chronicle has been preserved only in a single manuscript, a ninth-century work now in Berlin, which is known as B, and even B contains Hydatius' text in a condition which Courtois describes as "disastrous." For all our hopes that it might be otherwise, we cannot but believe him.

Yet in spite of the woeful state of its manuscript tradition Hydatius' Chronicle is one which would be welcome to the student of any period of ancient or early mediaeval history. It throws light on Spain, and especially on northwestern Spain, that is to say, on Galicia, or Gallaecia, as the Romans used to call it; and the light continues to shine, though not uniformly over the whole Iberian peninsula, throughout the fifth century until the year 469 (not 468, for Courtois will not even allow us to believe in the traditional date of the end of the Chronicler's work). In 469, then, the Chronicle stops, the light goes out, and night swallows up Spanish history for the best part of a century—night, but even then not quite the Tartarean blackness that engulfs late fifth-century Britain. True, the landscape is dark and mysterious, but there are a few stars shining—the inscription of 483, some nontheological references in the papal letters addressed to Spain—and so

138

we catch glimpses now and then (but only, as it were, by starlight) of men who write and move, and seem to have some purpose in their movements.[2]

I. HYDATIUS

Some 40 kilometres due south of Orense ("Auria" in Roman times) lies the small town of Ginzo de Limia or Lima (*civitas Limicorum* or *Lemicorum*) just outside the northern Portuguese border. By the modern road if you care to brave it, the place is situated about 120 rugged kilometres from Braga (*Bracara Augusta*), away to the southwest inside the Republic of Portugal. In those days Braga was a fairly considerable place, the capital of the Roman province of Galicia, but Ginzo de Limia was as remote and unheard of in Roman times as it is now. The little town has only one claim on the attention of the outside world, and that not a very dramatic one. It was there, in or about the year 394, that Hydatius was born.[3]

It is not the case that the *civitas Limicorum* was an out-of-the-way spot in an otherwise famous and frequented province. The entire province was out-of-the-way. In 561 its own metropolitan bishop frankly described his dioceses as situated on the edge of the world; and he was only echoing words which the Pope himself had uttered a few years earlier, "the extreme parts of the earth." The old Greeks centuries ago had regarded all of northern Spain as mountainous, cold, inhospitable, hard to reach, a very wretched place to live in, and the inhabitants as wild, intractable, and brutish, for in pre-Roman times, in spite of its mineral wealth and its cattle, the place had a vile reputation for brigandage and for unbroken ruinous warfare between the native tribes, the warfare of poor mountaineers against hardly less poor valley-dwellers.[4] Galicia was in truth the very verge of the world, the Finisterre, the land's end.

In 407, at the age of twelve or thirteen or so, for reasons which he does not choose to record, Hydatius travelled from his backwoods province to some of the famous centres of the East. He or his family must have been of some substance to allow him to visit Alexandria, Cyprus, Caesarea in Palestine, Jerusalem, and—most important of all, as it turned out—Bethlehem, for at Bethlehem he had the good fortune to see St. Jerome.[5] In later life his memory of the Orient was blurred: he thought that the Syrian city of Antioch, which he had not visited, lay in Isauria and not in Syria at all. But forgive him. Does not Gregory of Tours, a far greater man than he, stray even further afield in this matter of the elusive site of Antioch? For Gregory held the unusual opinion that the fourth city of the world lay neither in Syria nor in Isauria, but in Egypt.[6]

Back in Galicia Hydatius was ordained in 416 and was consecrated as Bishop in 427. Mommsen guessed that he may have been Bishop of the see of Aquae Flaviae, the modern Chaves on the River Tamega, 100 kilometres as the crow flies to the east of Braga. Homer nodded: Aquae Flaviae is not known ever to have been a bishopric, and the truth is that we do not know our Chronicler's see. He was certainly an eminent churchman. He cooperated in 445 with Turribius, Bishop of Astorga, a prominent Priscillianist-baiter, in examining some Manichaeans who had been discovered in Astorga; and Pope Leo the Great, in his letter on Priscillianism dated to 21 July 447, spoke of Hydatius as a suitable man to help organize a Spanish, or at any rate a Galician, synod to consider the question of Priscillianism.[7]

Hydatius' one and only direct contact with the great ones of his day came a few years after his consecration. In 431 he journeyed to Gaul to meet the most famous Roman statesman and general of the century, Aëtius, "the last of the Romans," though not yet a patrician. The Spanish bishop was allowed to negotiate with him, hoping that he might be able to take some steps which would check the endless, heartless, murderous raids of the Sueves in Galicia; and it is more than ordinarily unfortunate that Hydatius felt no need, or had no inclination (p. 142 below), to draw any pen-picture, however slight, of that eminent man as he struggled to shore up his collapsing world.[8] Historians have often pointed to the fact that when the provincial bishop needed the help of the imperial government he made his way not to the emperor in Italy but to Aëtius in Gaul. Later on, in 460, Hydatius was obliged to keep decidedly less distinguished company, for in that year he was kidnapped in the town of Aquae Flaviae and was held prisoner for over three months on end by the Sueves.[9] It cannot have been an enlivening experience, though perhaps it taught him something of the barbarians.

That is all that we know of the external events of his life, but it is enough to show that the Chronicler, though not at all widely travelled in his later years, was a man who had seen a little of the world and much of its uncertainties. From time to time he had ventured outside his scholar's study and his episcopal palace and had entered the turmoil and chaos into which the Western Empire was dissolving.

The meeting with the formidable saint at Bethlehem must have impressed him deeply, but he could hardly have forecast, when he was a young lad in 407, that one day he would himself write a continuation of the great man's epoch-making chronicle. We do not know in what year he decided to compose his own chronicle or in what year he actually began to write. In his preface he says that he wrote in extreme old age; but the phrase doubtless refers only to the composition of the preface itself and to the completion of the entire work. What we want to know is, when did he start? Was it in 427, the year with which he certainly had to abandon all written sources and gather his information laboriously by word of mouth? Perhaps so; but every answer to the question must be subjective, for he himself is silent. It would profoundly affect our view of the value of his work if we could be sure that he began in 427, or in 450, or in 469, or whatever the year may have been.[10] At all events, whenever he may have reached his decision to begin compiling, he started his entries with the year 379 where St. Jerome had stopped. For the period 379–427 he used earlier writers as well as oral sources of information; but for the period 428–69 he was an eye-witness — and that is the period which especially concerns the study of the heyday of the first of all the barbarian kingdoms as well as the study of how Roman Spain sank to its dismal end. It is true that on a few occasions he cites written authorities — though only for overseas events — even in the period after 427. He cites letters of Cyril of Alexandria, of Flavian of Constantinople, of Euphronius of Autun;[11] but the overwhelming bulk of his information came not from them but from what he heard.

His chronicle is agreed on all sides to be a work of good judgement, careful, methodical, reliable, "auctor pro aetate diligens et fidei optimae," as Mommsen put it,[12] well worth studying even 1,500 years after it was written. True, it is hard to believe in those 50,000 slain at the Battle of Otricoli in 413,[13] harder still to credit the 300,000 men who allegedly fell at the Battle of the Catalaunian Plains in 451[14] — and indeed Hydatius himself blenches somewhat at that last stunning figure — but there are few faults of this kind, and considering how he had suffered at the hands of barbarians he is surprisingly detached in his political outlook. Naturally, he often blames the Sueves for their faithlessness;[15] but he is not antibarbarian as such. He never criticizes the Visigoths in general. To be sure, he does not like the anti-Roman King Thorismud (451–53).[16] He disapproves of the Goths for not sending help to the Emperor Avitus just before his fall in 456.[17] He deplores the horrors of the sack of Braga, Astorga, and Palencia by the normally pro-Roman Visigothic King Theoderic II.[18] (The region of Palencia had already been cruelly devastated by barbarian federates in or before 409.)[19] These, however, are individual cases: he has nothing to say in principle. He hates no man and no people merely because they were non-Roman. On the other hand, he does not usually praise his characters, whether Roman or barbarian; yet he does turn aside to write a special word of commendation for Aegidius, an admirer and supporter of the tragic Emperor Majorian.[20] He even speaks with something like fervour when he comes to mention Merobaudes the poet, the panegyrist of Aëtius. He stresses the poet's noble birth and his eminence in his art — he is "comparable to the ancients" — as well as his military skill.[21] Merobaudes was a fellow Spaniard, but he came from distant Baetica in the extreme south of the Iberian peninsula, and his Spanish birth is unlikely to have been the reason for the Galician Hydatius' enthusiasm for him. There was little love lost between Majorian and Aëtius,[22] and although the chronicler admired

Aëtius' panegyrist it does not necessarily follow that he admired Aëtius himself. I have already mentioned his omission of any description of him. In fact, he had small cause to eulogize him, for Aëtius had done little or nothing to rescue remote Galicia from devastation; and after his visit in 431 Hydatius never again asked the patrician for assistance, although the patrician governed the West for another twenty-three years. With the periphery of the Western Empire—Britain, Spain, the all-important Africa —Aëtius rarely bothered. He never visited those luckless lands. He did little or nothing to save them from their invaders, though Hydatius and the thrice-groaning Britons begged him for his help. The "last of the Romans" was interested in the landlords of southern Gaul and Italy: the rest of the world could fend for itself.

At first glance it looks as if Hydatius wrote for Spaniards, perhaps even for Galicians, alone. Why else record the eclipse of the sun of 11 November 402 which was total in northern Spain, where he lived, but was scarcely visible at all in Constantinople?[23] The entry of the barbarians into Spain in 409 was an event which made an impact, but not a resounding impact, on the chroniclers of the outside world. Most of them speak of it, but they do so briefly—only in a few words; and the Eastern chronicler, Count Marcellinus, passes over it in silence. For Hydatius, on the other hand, it was a calamity which deserved as much space as the fall of Rome itself in 410, a disaster which dumbfounded the civilized world.[24] If the amount of space which he devotes to any one event reveals his opinion of its significance, then the most important occurrence of the fifth century down to 469, when his chronicle stops, was the Visigothic invasion of Galicia and other parts of western Spain in 456–57, a judgement which was not shared by non-Spanish chroniclers. So he looks like a true provincial, interested only in that far-off and miserable part of the world where he himself chanced to live out his life. However, we shall see evidence (p. 147 below) which suggests, though by no means conclusively, that this was hardly the case, that he did his utmost to write a world chronicle, that he tried to overcome the daunting limits of his knowledge of the outside world, and that he wanted to include in his work every scrap of information which he could find out about the Roman Empire in the East.

Throughout his whole period he is familiar with events in Gaul and Italy, and indeed he gives us several pieces of information about both countries which none of the native authorities mentions. As for Gaul, he alone tells us of Aëtius' campaign of 431, in which he crushed a rebellion of the province of Noricum. He alone gives us the figure of 20,000 Burgundians slain when the Huns destroyed the never to be forgotten Burgundian Kingdom of Worms in 437,[25] (yet such is his authority and status that historians have rarely called in question this improbable figure). It is from him alone that we hear about a Visigothic optimate called Anaolsus who was taken prisoner, and his followers massacred, by Aëtius near Arles in 430.[26] He is well informed about Gaul because there was plenty of coming and going by diplomats and churchmen between Spain and Gaul, as we shall see. Oddly enough, there may not have been as much unofficial, social intercourse between the aristocrats of the two countries as we might have expected, for in the interminable collection of the letters of Sidonius Apollinaris only one or two are addressed to Spaniards.[27] On the other hand, there is evidence for substantial sea-borne trade between Gaul and Galicia in the later years of the sixth century, and we shall find some facts easier to account for if we assume that this trade was already flourishing in the fifth century, when Hydatius was alive. It is important to remember that if a traveller tried to journey from Gaul to Galicia by the western end of the Pyrenees in the fifth and the following centuries he would have to brave the wild and pagan Basques in their impenetrable mountains; and that even if he took an enormous detour through the province of Tarraconensis and came up the Ebro valley the route westwards from Leon would expose him to the attention of uncontrollable mountaineers; yet it is certain that Gaul and Galicia were in contact during Hydatius' lifetime, and it is likely that contact was made across the open sea rather than across those vast and ambush-laden mountains.

As for Italy, the chronicler happens to mention a native of Rome called Pascentius who was residing in Astorga in 448. Whether Pascentius had come there in connexion with his Manichaeism — for he was a Manichee — or for some other reason, we do not know;[28] but there is no indication in Hydatius' words that his journey from Italy was anything very extraordinary. Nor apparently was it a surprise to find an Italian immigrant in Galicia. In 447 Turribius, Bishop of the Galician see of Astorga, was able to send his deacon to Rome; and Pervincus returned again to Galicia without mishap. Again, Hydatius knows of the accession and death of the various Western emperors, of the lynching of the Patrician Felix at Ravenna in 430, of the rivalry of Boniface and Sebastian with Aëtius.[29] He knows well of Attila's devastating campaign in Italy in 452 (pp. 151 below), of the murder of Aëtius in 454, and so on. Not only that: alone of all the writers of his time he tells of Palladius Caesar, son of the Emperor Petronius Maximus, and his marriage to the daughter of Valentinian III.[30] In fact, he was familiar with at least the outstanding political events which took place in Italy during the period of his own bishopric.

That is not the whole story. When Turribius and Pope Leo I corresponded on the subject of Priscillianism in 447 their letters seem to have travelled to their destinations without hindrance; but that was not the case a few years later, when Suevic power was at its height. When the Pope wished to distribute throughout the Western provinces certain writings of Flavian, Patriarch of Constantinople, and of Cyril of Alexandria on the heresy of Eutyches, and in particular his own famous *Tome* addressed to Flavian, he was apparently unable to send the documents directly to Spain, or at any rate to Galicia; for the documents went first to Gaul, and it was from Gaul that they came to the knowledge of Hydatius in 450.[31] Again, the Council of Chalcedon met in October 451, and on 27 January in the following year Leo wished to report to the West the satisfactory conclusions of this great ecumenical Council. He wrote to the bishops of Gaul, but he was obliged to ask them to see to it that the good news got through to Spain.[32] Apparently, even in a matter which the Pope considered to be of critical importance, he could not be sure that a letter addressed directly to Spain would reach its destination. What he felt reasonably certain of was that communication between Gaul and Spain was still open. It seems once again to follow that after about 450 Sueves and Basques and, as we shall see, Bacaudae had interrupted communications between Tarraconensis and Galicia, and that the sea-route from Gaul was the only one which remained possible. Presumably, then, Hydatius' knowledge of events in Italy in the early fifties of the century had mainly reached him across the Bay of Biscay. It was certainly from Gaul that he heard of the death of the Western Emperor Libius Severus in 465, for he tells us himself that a report of this event was brought back from Gaul by Suevic ambassadors who happened to be there at the appropriate time.[33] The news did not travel direct from Italy to Spain—or rather (as perhaps we should say) from Italy to Galicia: for who knows that it did not reach Tarragona or Cartagena direct from Italy?

As it turned out, Hydatius did indeed receive the documents sent from Gaul in 450, but there is no evidence that he ever heard of the contents of Leo's jubilant letter of January 452. Even more surprising, there is no evidence that he ever heard of the Council of Chalcedon itself. True, Chalcedon made curiously little impact on the West outside the Holy See. The issues which were vital in the East were not issues at all in the West; and if the West heard of the Council of the Easterners—for hardly any representatives of the West attended it—it did so in the main with incomprehension and indifference.[34] Yet if Hydatius had heard of it, would he not have spared it a passing mention, as Prosper of Aquitaine did in his chronicle? The importance of Chalcedon was certainly clear to Martin of Braga and the Galician bishops a century later; but of Hydatius it is easier to believe that he never heard of it than that he dismissed it as of minor consequence, a trifling affair not worthy even of one single line in the record of the events of his time. As for Leo's letter of January 452 its failure to reach Hydatius may have been due more to the negligence of the Gallic bishops, who did not see its significance and omitted to forward it, than to any breakdown of communications.

Of Africa after the death of St. Augustine in 430, the fateful surprise of Carthage by the Vandals on 19 October 439 and Geiseric's measures against the clergy of Carthage in that same year,[35] Hydatius' knowledge is small, even negligible. Naturally, he knows of Geiseric's activities abroad—in Sicily in 440, for example, or at Rome in 455—and is willing to record them; but of events inside Africa itself his ignorance is almost total. Vandal ambassadors reached Galicia in 458, but they did not come in order to interview a country clergyman: Hydatius had no opportunity of conversing with them, or, if he had—and we can scarcely believe it—they told him little or nothing. Why should they discuss matters of high diplomacy with any Roman? For some reason the chronicler is aware of the murder of Sebastian in Africa in 450, but that event is not easy to parallel in the rest of his chronicle.[36] Evidently, news did not readily travel outwards from the interior of the grim kingdom of the Vandals.

His note on Geiseric's capture of Rome in 455 includes a curious detail. Geiseric entered the city, he says, because he was incited to do so by no less a personage than Eudoxia, the widow of the Emperor Valentinian III. Now, Hydatius is the first writer to record this report, but it was to become known later on to Count Marcellinus in the Eastern Empire and to nearly half-a-dozen other writers at the far end of the world.[37] Hydatius describes it as "a wicked rumour," one of the two occasions on which he admits that he is recording a rumour.[38] (The other rumour which he reports —and he emphasizes that it is no more than a rumour—is the unlikely tale that Geiseric was a Catholic originally and was only at a later stage of his life converted to Arianism.)[39] By this phrase "a wicked rumour" he does not apparently intend to discredit the report that the empress had instigated the Vandal: he deplores it. Why then, if he believes the tale to be true, does he use such a disparaging phrase, a phrase which throws doubt on its truth? Why record the matter at all? Whatever the answer may be, he will have obtained this information from Italy, where Eudoxia was living at the time of her alleged invitation. It is not likely to have reached him from inside Geiseric's Africa.

He knows nothing, then, of the Council of Chalcedon. What are we to say of his knowledge of the Eastern Roman Empire? In the very year in which he was ordained, in 416,[40] a priest of Braga who chanced to be living in Jerusalem, Avitus by name, wrote to Balconius, Metropolitan of

Braga, and to all the clergy and people of that see, and mentioned how often he wished to return home to his native city. He had left Spain before the massive invasion by the Vandals, Alans, and Sueves in 409, and at the time when he was writing his letter he was daunted in his desire to go back there by the fact that "the enemy was now scattered throughout the whole of the Spanish provinces." Avitus was an old man and, although he did not venture to make the journey himself, he expected his young friend, Orosius, the future historian, to take home to Spain for him some relics of St. Stephen the Protomartyr, whose remains had been discovered in December 415.[41] Even Orosius failed to complete the journey. He travelled as far as the town of Magona in the island of Minorca, stayed there for a short while in 417, and saw that he could not hope to reach Galicia: so he left Stephen's relics in Magona and went on to Africa.[42] Now, if the voyage from Minorca to Africa was safe and easy, there can be little doubt that the voyage from Minorca to Tarragona was equally so. There was little difficulty, we may suppose, in travelling across the western Mediterranean Sea in 416–17. Why should there be difficulty? The trouble started when the traveller reached the Spanish coast and tried to journey up-country to the far northwest. From the coast onwards the difficulties might well be thought insurmountable. In 417, an exceptionally turbulent time in the interior of Spain, when Wallia the Goth was campaigning against the other barbarians there, when marauding armies were marching this way and that, and entire peoples were being decimated or even exterminated, at such a time Orosius thought it pointless even to cross from the Balearics to the mainland.

Hydatius makes no secret of the fact that he was unable to find out information about Eastern events which he would have been glad to record. He can tell us that after the expulsion of Nestorius from Constantinople Flavian (447–49) became patriarch there;[43] but he does not appear to know that two other patriarchs, Maximian (431–34) and Proclus (434–47), intervened between Nestorius and Flavian—a very remarkable gap in his information. Again, although Hydatius spoke to some clerics who had travelled from the East to Spain, they were not able to tell him—astonishing though it seems—the date of the death of John of Jerusalem (in 415–16) or even—is it credible?—of Jerome himself (in 420) and others. They could not say who it was that succeeded John at Jerusalem before Juvenal became bishop there—for Hydatius had managed to find out that "an elderly man" did occupy the see for a short while.[44] In fact, John's successor was Praylius, and he occupied the bishopric from 415–16 until 421, no fewer than five or six years. The chronicler also admits candidly (in §. 40) his difficulty in finding out which bishops preceded John in Jerusalem, and (in §. 61) in discovering who was Patriarch of Alexandria after Theophilus, who died in October 412. In fact, Theophilus' successor was none other than Cyril of Alexandria, of whose existence Hydatius knew well;[45] but he evidently thought that someone had intervened between Theophilus and Cyril, though in fact nobody had done so.

Hydatius is able to record the accessions and deaths of the Eastern Emperors, but this information need not have come directly from the East to Spain. Thus, a Suevic embassy, which set out from Galicia in 467 to meet the Western Emperor Anthemius and returned two years later, brought news of the preparation of the catastrophic expedition of the Emperor Leo I against Vandal Africa, which sailed in 468.[46] That news, then, did not make its way from Constantinople direct to Spain. It arrived in Italy, and was there picked up by men who carried it on to Spain; and these men were not ordinary travellers, but official representatives of the Suevic king, who were present in Italy by coincidence—the news did not travel from Italy to Spain in the ordinary way of trade or whatever normally brought men from the one country to the other. So, too, Hydatius' knowledge of the imperial family of the East probably reached him from Italy or Gaul.

In the Chronicle there are two explicit references, and only two, to Eastern travellers who arrived in Spain.

In 435 Germanus, a priest of Arabia, and some other "Greeks" arrived in Galicia and were able to give Hydatius information about the measures taken in Constantinople to crush the heresy of Nestorius.[47] They also gave news of the Council of Ephesus which had met in 431; and yet it was they who were unable to give Hydatius the information about the sees of Jerusalem and Alexandria which he wanted to know.[48]

In 456 the chronicler records the arrival of Oriental ships at Seville with the news (apparently) that the Emperor Marcian's army had inflicted a defeat on a people called the Lazi, who lived at the eastern end of the Black Sea.[49] If Mommsen has restored the text correctly—and his restoration is adventurous—this entry in the Chronicle is of fundamental importance. The defeat of the remote people of the Lazi in the Caucasus at the far end of the Black Sea could hardly have been of less consequence to Spain. It is not easy to think of any event of the fifth century which was less relevant to Spaniards. Even the conversion of Irishmen by St. Patrick might have been of more immediate interest by far. The defeat of the Lazi was of such minimal importance to Spaniards that, if Hydatius was prepared to record this, we must believe that he would record any and every piece of news, however trivial, however shadowy, which reached him from the East. This entry, if we may trust Mommsen's reconstruction of it, suggests strongly that the chronicler is reporting, not a selection, but rather the whole, of what he knew about the Orient in the time of his manhood.

Throughout the period 427–69, then, there is evidence for only two direct contacts between Spain and the East—the arrival of the ill-informed Greek clerics who reached an unstated part of Spain in 435 and then went on to Galicia, and those Oriental ships which touched in at Seville twenty-one years later, in 456. It is possible that documents and news may also have arrived directly from the East in 436,[50] but if this had been the case Hydatius would perhaps have said so. Everything else that the chronicler knows about the Roman Empire in the East he could have learned, and in some cases is known to have learned, from travellers arriving from Gaul or Italy.

The result is that in his account of the last twenty-five years which his chronicle covers (444–69) he can tell us only of the death of Theodosius II and the accession of Marcian, of the death of Marcian and the accession of Leo I, of the death of the Empress Pulcheria, and of some events connected with the great African expedition of Basiliscus in 468.[51] Otherwise he mentions only a single Eastern event throughout this quarter-century. This is the earthquake which damaged Antioch in 461, a report for which he does not cite his authority and which contains one or two puzzling chronological problems.[52] Of other major Eastern events which took place in this period he appears to know nothing whatever. He does not mention Attila's devastating onslaught on the European provinces of the Eastern Empire in 447, and, most remarkably, as we have seen, he makes no reference to the Council of Chalcedon, which met in 451.

Apart from those Eastern ships which tied up in Seville in 456 Hydatius never refers to the reports of traders among his sources of information; and in no case at all does he refer to news brought back by Spanish merchants who had ventured to sail over the intervening seas. Does this mean that few merchants left or reached Spain in his day? Not necessarily: another explanation is possible. It may be that, if merchants sailed to the Mediterranean ports of Spain, their news failed to reach Galicia. Why should an overseas merchant, arriving on the Mediterranean coast, make his way far off to the northwest, beyond the Suevic battlefields to the plundered towns? Why not trade his wares instead in the relatively rich ports of the east coast and leave the hinterland to the marauders and their victims? Was the humble trader of the middle of the century likely to be more venturesome than Orosius had been or Avitus of Braga in 416–17? And who in Galicia had money to spend on luxuries imported from the Near East? If there was little inducement for traders to come up-country to Galicia from the eastern seaports of Spain, it is not surprising that the gaps in Hydatius' knowledge of East Rome are substantial. The wonder is, indeed, that he knows so much. On the other hand, the Atlantic sea-route to northwestern Spain and on as far as Ireland was used often enough in this period, and may even have been sailed by Eastern ships: and yet Hydatius gives not the least hint that he had learned anything at all from such seamen as braved the Ocean.[53] The world is disintegrating, and he who would chronicle the events of the world can do little more in practice than chronicle the events of his own province.

There is a contrast between Hydatius' meagre knowledge of what went on in the Mediterranean world in general and some information that has reached us from somewhat later sources. It would appear to have been the case that the rest of Spain was not so cut off from the Orient; and when we recall what Strabo had said long ago (p. 139 above) about the inaccessibility of northern Spain this is no surprise. The disturbing fact is that at a date in the period 468–83, the decade and a half after his chronicle had ended, when the times were no less tumultuous than they had been in the years of his life, communication between Rome and Seville or Merida is known to have been frequent. Pope Simplicius (468–83) begins his letter to Zeno, a bishop in southern Spain, with the words, "We have learned by the report of many" about Zeno's excellent administration of his see.[54] That is to say, not one but many travellers had reported to the pope on certain ecclesiastical conditions in southern Spain. The pope has it in mind to appoint a papal vicar in that part of the world, and he gives no hint that he anticipates any difficulty in sending his letters or his instructions or his representatives to that distant land. Again, we hear incidentally that a man named Vincentius travelled from Tarraconensis to Rome and came back again, and there is no indication whatever that his journey was thought to be exceptional or adventurous.[55] Several letters were exchanged between Tarragona and Rome in the years 463–65, and in not one of them is there a single hint at any difficulties of communication.[56] Even as late as 483, perhaps later, we hear of a member of the nobility, a *vir clarissimus*, called Terentianus, who had travelled to Italy and was on the point of going back again with a letter from Pope Felix II, without any indication that the feat was unusual.[57] Later on we shall see something of the journeys of Pervincus and others. It is beyond question that for several years after Hydatius' death and for some years before it communication between Italy and eastern and southern Spain was easy.

What inference must we draw from these facts? If news about Constantinople were to reach one of the east-coast cities of Spain, it by no means followed that Hydatius would necessarily have heard of it. When we speak of communication between the outside world and Spain we must draw a distinction. Communication between Italy and even Constantinople with the east-coast ports of Spain or even Seville was one thing, but communication with Galicia *via* one or other of the east-coast ports was something very different. It would be more difficult, therefore, for a chronicler living in Galicia to gather information about the eastern Mediterranean than it would have been had he lived in Tarragona, or Cartagena, or Malaga, or even Seville. It seems to be the case that, although Vandal fleets swept the western Mediterranean after 429, it was not these which broke communications with Galicia. The real obstacles lay on the Spanish mainland itself. The Basques, the Bacaudae, and the Sueves formed a barrier around Galicia which at times could only be penetrated by a brave and determined traveller, and sometimes could not be penetrated at all.

From this conclusion there follows a further inference which is of much importance for students of Hydatius. The papal letters certainly suggest that contacts of the outside world with the eastern seaboard cities were relatively frequent, but Hydatius' knowledge of what was going on in his own day on the eastern seaboard of Spain itself is limited. He has hardly anything at all to tell us. In fact, he is not able to record a single event there after the tragic defeat of the Emperor Majorian in 460. For the nine following years he is silent. Indeed, apart from events in the province of Tarraconensis he cannot speak of anything which happened at any date after 427 in eastern Spain. Galicia was cut off not only from Constantinople but even from a large section of Spain itself. This is another reason for thinking that if ships from the East had touched in at, say, Tarragona or Cartagena, it was by no means inevitable that Hydatius would have heard of their arrival or of the news which their crews were able to report in their chatter on the quayside. The fact that he records the arrival of ships at Seville bringing news of stupefying tedium about the infinitely remote Lazi (if Mommsen's text is correct) suggests that he would have recorded the arrival of other ships, too, if he had known of any, however trivial the information about Eastern politics which their crews were able to report in the harbour bars. Although very little direct evidence seems to exist for overseas trade between Spain and either Italy or Africa or the East in the mid-fifth century, yet there is no reason to doubt that it was relatively abundant: it was Galicia rather than Spain as a whole that was so nearly completely cut off from the bustling cities of the eastern Mediterranean.[58] The only really free outlet from Galicia may have been the sea-route to Gaul.

There is one entry in Hydatius' Chronicle which is so strange and of such importance that it deserves special consideration, though I cannot explain it. It is his unique and convincing account of the reasons which led

Attila the Hun to call off his campaign on the plains of northern Italy in 452 without ever setting foot south of the Appennines. Hydatius says nothing of the famous meeting, which other writers report, of Pope Leo the Great with the Hun leader. Now, that astonishing interview is not likely to have achieved much. As Bury remarks, "It is unreasonable to suppose that this heathen king would have cared for the thunders or persuasions of the Church."[59] But that is not the point which concerns us at present. Even if it was not necessarily of the faintest interest to Attila or to the Huns at large, the interview was of deep interest to Christians in general. Yet Hydatius says of it not one syllable. Did he ever hear of it? If he did, why did he exclude it from his Chronicle? Did he think, unlike the rest of the Christian world, that it was of small historical interest? The truth more probably is that he had never heard of what is perhaps the most dramatic and dangerous journey on which a pope has ever travelled. If this is surprising, what follows is astounding.

According to his account of what happened, it was not the words of a pope which caused Attila's retreat. It was not alone the famine and the plague (though these he does mention) which were beginning to rage in northern Italy, striking impartially at invaders and invaded alike. According to Hydatius' unparalleled account, it was also and chiefly the fact that the Eastern Emperor Marcian (450–57) had sent an army under an East Roman officer called Aëtius (a different Aëtius from the Western patrician) beyond the Danube to the north lands, into the Hun kingdom itself, where it defeated the Hun garrison in its own homeland.[60] There was an immediate danger that the Germanic subjects of the Huns would rebel; and, if the bulk of the Hun forces were to linger in Italy, and most of all if they were to become victims of famine and plague there, the outcome of such a revolt could not fail to be of the utmost peril to the nomads. A rebellion in these circumstances would threaten the very existence of their power.

This explanation of Attila's decision to retreat from Italy is absolutely convincing, and it is confirmed by the fact that the Aëtius in question was rewarded with the Eastern consulship for the year 454;[61] yet no other authority either of the East or of the West refers to his audacious march into the Hun dominions or to his victory there, which had such salutary consequences for the cities of peninsular Italy. In this matter the chronicler of northwestern Spain, far away at the edge of the world, knows what the surviving writers of East Rome themselves do not know or have forgotten to tell us. Of his authority he says not a word. We cannot even begin to guess at his identity.

II. THE SETTLEMENT OF THE SUEVES IN SPAIN

We do not know much about the history of the Sueves before they crossed the frozen Rhine on the night of 31 December 406 and entered the Roman Empire. Their relations with those Sueves whom Roman writers mention in earlier centuries have not been elucidated. The most widely held opinion is that the Sueves of Spain are identical with the Quadi of whom many authors had spoken in earlier times and who lived north of the middle Danube in what are now lower Austria and western Slovakia. The evidence, or what passes for evidence, is a passage in one of St. Jerome's letters, his letter to Ageruchia, in which he lists the invaders of Gaul in 406.[62] The Quadi are in his catalogue: the Sueves are not. Nothing is heard later of the Quadi in Gaul, whereas all the world knew that the Sueves were active in the ranks of the invaders. It follows, according to this improbable argument, that the Sueves *are* the Quadi, and the Quadi are the Sueves. That is to say, because we hear no more of the Quadi in Gaul, the Quadi were somebody other than themselves, somebody of whom we *do* hear. In other words, they were the Sueves.[63] We have only to state the argument to see how ill-founded it is.

We also hear of Sueves who battled on the middle Danube against the Ostrogoths in 469.[64] Later on, Vacho the Lombard attacked and defeated them and in 568 the Lombards brought with them to Italy the remnants of many peoples, one of whom was these Sueves.[65] We do not know what was the relationship of the Spanish Sueves with the enemies of the Ostrogoths who were finally engulfed in Lombardic Italy. That a relationship existed need hardly be doubted: the identity of their names at this date will scarcely have been a coincidence. Not one of the great Germanic peoples who fled away to the west and the south in the early years of the fifth century failed to leave some of their number behind in their old homeland. Vandals, Visigoths, Ostrogoths, Burgundians and others could all be found in their previous homes outside the Roman frontier when the bulk of these peoples had travelled far away to the Western provinces, just as there were Saxons still remaining on the continent of Europe long after other Saxons had crossed the narrow seas to Britain. Is it not likely, then, that the same was true of the Sueves, and that the Sueves of Spain had once lived on the middle Danube along with those enemies of the Ostrogoths, indeed as part and parcel of them? But who were these Danubian Sueves? Who were their forebears? And what was their earlier history? And again, what of the Sueves or *Swaefe* who, coming from west Schleswig, it is said, invaded Britain with many other peoples in the fifth century and left their name in places which are nowadays called Swaffham and perhaps Swavesey in eastern England? Happily, an enquiry into these elusive groups of Sueves who appear fleetingly in Roman authors and lurk behind a couple of familiar English place-names would doubtless be inconclusive and would certainly distract us from the problem of how Roman power came to an end in Spain and how the first barbarian kingdom was founded.[66]

Be all that as it may, the barbarians—Vandals, Alans, and Sueves, whether the Sueves were the Quadi or simply themselves—crossed over the Pyrenees from Gaul into Spain either on 28 September or on 13 October 409. Hydatius gives us both dates without deciding between them and without explaining how he had come to have two chronologies instead of one. He says that the crossing took place on a Tuesday, and while 28 September 409 was indeed a Tuesday, 13 October was a Wednesday. Some scholars take the two dates to mark the beginning and the end of the crossing of the mountain range, for so many people—scores of thousands of them (p. 159 below)—cannot have made the crossing of that formidable barrier in a mere twenty-four hours.[67] This may be right, but it is not what Hydatius says. At all events, the barbarians had devastated Gaul in three successive years, 407, 408, and 409. The harvest of 409 cannot have been an abundant one after the massacres and the burnings of Gaul, which the writers of the time lament loudly and bitterly. In the late autumn of 409 it was some weeks since the feeble harvest had been gathered in, and the invaders must now look to the future and try to assure their dwindling food-supply. There across the mountains lay Spain within their grasp, not so fertile as Aquitaine, but nonetheless intact and unravaged.[68] It was not without good reason that Spain had spent those three years "trembling," already aware that she was doomed.[69]

It is often thought that the Sueves were settled in Spain—the term *Suavia* or *Suevia* is never used of Galicia—as federates by the Roman government on similar terms to those on which the Visigoths were to receive Aquitaine in 418 and on which the Burgundians were to be planted in Savoy in 443, and other peoples elsewhere at different dates. We are never told which enemies the Sueves, if they were intended to act as federates, were supposed to watch and ward off, or which emperor or which usurper signed the treaty (*foedus*) which made them federates; yet even Mommsen describes the Sueves in Galicia as Federates.[70] Bury remarks that "the Asdings and the Suevians appear to have been successful in obtaining the recognition of Honorius as federates," but his footnote stresses that this is only an inference "from what actually happened." What actually happened suggests all but explicitly that the Sueves were by no means recognized as federates and were far indeed from acting as such.[71] Ernst Stein thinks that the usurper Maximus c. 410–11 made an arrangement with the barbarians whereby they took over the western half of the Iberian peninsula. Ludwig

Schmidt suggests that a treaty was struck between Honorius and Hermeric the Sueve in 411.[72] And so on, and on. The very variety of the opinions expressed by these eminent historians shows a radical fault in the train of reasoning.

In fact, there is no convincing evidence for any "treaty" with the Sueves. Such conjectures are not supported by the actions of the Sueves themselves, for there is no hint in any of our fifth-century sources that the Sueves had any military obligations to any of the emperors at any date or to any of the many usurpers of that dreadful time. The Suevic leaders acted with absolute independence over against the Empire. If the Romans settled the Sueves in Galicia as federates they had miscalculated. Never once, not even during the wars of 416–18, when Wallia's Visigoths came from Gaul and fought for Rome against the barbarians in Spain—never once did the Sueves intervene in favour of Rome.[73] These barbarians, once Wallia's Visigoths had returned to Gaul in 418 and had ceased to menace them, and the Vandals left for Africa in 429, were chronic and incurable raiders and plunderers. They ravaged right and left. They plundered friend and foe. Take the period 457–69, the last years covered by the Chronicle of Hydatius. These were years in which Suevic power had been reduced as a result of their crushing defeat by the Visigoths in 456; and yet Galicia, the very province in which they were themselves living, suffered a Suevic raid in every one of these dozen years except 465 and 466—and 465 was not an exception if the unidentified *Aunonenses* are to be located in Galicia, as they almost certainly must be.[74] If the Sueves settled in Galicia as a result of a treaty, that treaty was void and meaningless from the day on which it was signed. It is safer by far to believe that the Sueves had seized Galicia without Roman consent, that they had never been in alliance with emperors or usurpers, that no "treaty" was ever signed, and that they behaved accordingly.

What in fact the chronicler says—and the contemporary Spanish historian, Orosius,[75] supports him—is that in 411, two years after they had first entered Spain, the barbarians decided upon peace and divided up the Spanish provinces among themselves "by lot," *sorte.* He says nothing of any treaty. Many scholars think that the reference in "lot" may be to the "allotments," *sortes,* which barbarian federates received when they were settled by the Roman government on Roman farms and landed estates. Such federates shared the estates with their Roman owners and were known euphemistically as "guests," *hospites,* or "partners," *consortes.*[76] Here are the Latin words of Hydatius when he speaks of the settlement of Spain (§. 49): "barbari ad pacem ineundam domino miserante conversi sorte ad inhabitandum sibi provinciarum dividunt regiones." There is no reference to federates or to a treaty. The barbarians turned to peace, not because of Roman diplomatic approaches to them as a result of which a *foedus,* a "treaty," could have been drawn up and signed, but simply because the Lord took pity, *domino miserante.* The words *ad inhabitandum* throw no light on the question of whether or not the Sueves were federates. The phrase is not a technical term, used of planting federates in the provinces, though some would have us believe that it is.[77] They simply divided Spain up in order to settle in it.

Hydatius is describing an action taken by the barbarians alone, an action on which the Romans were not consulted and in which they played no part.[78] There is no implication of a treaty in his words, nor could such an inference be fairly extracted from his Latin. Indeed, any such inference as that the Sueves were federates would positively contradict his Latin. He says simply that the barbarians cast lots for the provinces of Spain so as to decide where each of them should live—and this is a way in which no Roman government would have proceeded. We have no reason at all for disbelieving Hydatius. The suggestion that the word *sorte* refers somehow to the allotments of land which the Roman government handed over to federates in its provinces is far-fetched, even fantastic, and must be rejected out of hand.

There is one strong and positive reason for believing the chronicler, apart from the corroboration of Orosius, which is itself positive and strong. This reason is that, not surprisingly, the lot turned out to be arbitrary and wholly unfair. The Asding Vandals, all 80,000 of them, and the Sueves were alike crowded into the poor and remote province of Galicia at the edge of the world, where the provincial capital, Braga, fell to the lot of the Sueves.[79] The Asdings, who were the most powerful and populous people of all the fifth-century invaders of Spain, were thrust away into the mountainous western parts of that barren province. (How could we possibly believe that the Asdings had become federates of Rome and had put their arms at the service of the emperors in return for the prize of being banished to the narrow western boundary of the earth?) On the other hand, the Alans received not only the rich Lusitania but also the largest of all the provinces of Spain, Carthaginiensis, a wholly disproportionate share of the Iberian peninsula. Finally, the Siling Vandals were allotted Baetica, the most Romanized of the Spanish provinces. (Notice that Tarraconensis was left wholly in Roman hands.) If the distribution of the provinces had been carried through on any rational basis—whether in proportion to the number of persons in each people, or to the military strength of each, or the like—we may be sure that the result would not have turned out at all like this. On any reckoning the share of the Alans was far too generous, and the share of the Asding Vandals was far too miserably small and poor. Now, if we were to suppose that the four peoples divided up Spain on the basis of the population of each, or if we supposed that the Roman authorities divided it for them on any such basis, consider an inference that we should have to draw. The Alans received at least six or eight times as much land as the Asdings, and it would therefore follow on this hypothesis that they were six or eight times more numerous than the Asdings; but since the Asdings numbered about 80,000 persons (as they are known to have done), it would follow that the total number of the nomadic Alans in Spain was in the region of half a million persons, a figure that will hardly commend itself to students of this period of history. The very oddity of the outcome of the casting of lots confirms Hydatius' statement that lots were cast and that the simple barbarians assigned the provinces to themselves by lot and hazard; and we must note furthermore that, if these arrangements were made in agreement with the Romans, then all four of these discrete peoples must have been federates of the Empire in 411 (or whatever the date may have been). There would have been four separate series of negotiations with Rome. All four peoples struck treaties (we are asked to believe), and all four treaties were left unmentioned by Hydatius and Orosius.[80] Is it credible?

If the lot was so unfair, why did the four barbarian peoples acquiesce in it? The Alans, of course, had every reason to welcome it, for it had treated them more than generously. (It would be interesting, by the way, to know what would have happened had the lot tried to fob off the brutish, nomadic Alans with the western mountains of Galicia, which were all that fell to the Asding Vandals.) The Siling Vandals had little cause to complain at receiving the rich province of Baetica. It was the Asding Vandals and the Sueves who had every reason to protest, crowded as they were into the wet, overcast, mountainous province of Galicia; but they were precisely the peoples who dared not make any move when the ferocious Alans were still intact, just across their frontier, in Lusitania, overawing and dominating them.[81] It is not a surprise to find that it was in the very moment after the Alans had been destroyed, and after the Visigoths, who destroyed them, had withdrawn from Spain in 418, that the Asdings and the Sueves flew at one another's throats.[82]

Whatever the nature of the settlement of 411, there followed a period of peace in Spain, a peace that was hardly ever broken except when the imperial government itself broke it or persuaded others to shatter it for them. It was the Romans who drove the Visigothic leader Athaulf into Spain in 415 and who loosed Wallia and his warriors like a tempest upon the Siling Vandals (whom they exterminated) and the Alans (whom they decimated) in 416–18. Even so, Orosius truthfully implies that before the fighting of 416 and 417 there had been a period of peace in Spain.[83] After the time when Orosius wrote (in 417), it was the imperial government which sent Castinus to Spain in 422,[84] and we shall notice later on his dismal failure there. Before 425 the barbarians disturbed the peace only when the Asdings besieged the Sueves in the Nervasian Mountains in 419–20,[85] though after that time the Asdings began plundering on an extensive scale, inside and even outside Spain.[86] The most surprising and the crowning event of this period of relative peace was the conversion of the Vandals from paganism to Arian Christianity, though the Sueves were left unscathed, so far as we know, by this unlikely and yet undeniable occurrence.[87]

The struggle between the Asdings and the Sueves in the Nervasian Mountains in 419 was no doubt intended to decide who would possess the whole of Galicia.[88] (It is a somewhat unexpected struggle, as we never hear otherwise of the invaders of 406 fighting among themselves during their three years of ravaging in Gaul and their first decade of life in Spain.) These Nervasian Mountains, where the Asdings beleaguered the Sueves, have never been identified;[89] but under Roman pressure the Vandals soon abandoned the siege, and, after killing some Sueves in Braga, made their way southwards to Baetica, to take over the lands of the slaughtered Silings.[90] Henceforth, the Sueves had the whole of Galicia to themselves, and for 174 years (411–585) they maintained themselves there as a free, autonomous people, more or less forgotten by the outside world. Although foreign statesmen often enough sent embassies to negotiate with them, yet the writers of the provinces outside Spain, and even the writers of Visigothic Spain itself, found no need to say a syllable about them for decades on end.[91] We might almost think that in the late fifth and throughout most of the sixth century theirs was a forgotten realm, a ghost kingdom; and yet it was the first in time of the barbarian kingdoms of the West, the first of all the independent successor states to the Roman Empire, the first and the least.

The Sueves did not distribute themselves evenly throughout the entire province of Galicia. We are told explicitly by St. Isidore of Seville that part of Galicia remained independent, and in this matter there is little reason to doubt his word,[92] especially as we often find at a later date that these barbarians were raiding and devastating cities and rural districts within their own province. There were parts of Galicia itself, then, where the writ of the Suevic king did not run throughout the early sixth century.

Those few localities in Galicia which they did not plunder were presumably the areas where they lived themselves. There are only three such places. Braga in the north of Portugal, the old Roman Bracara Augusta, is one of them. It was the provincial capital in imperial times; and it was no doubt the Suevic capital, too, for it was Theoderic's first objective after his defeat of the Suevic army in 456, and it was certainly the Suevic capital in the late sixth century—and we have just seen that there were Sueves in the city, for the Vandals were able to kill them there in 419.[93] Secondly, there were Sueves living in the city of Astorga; and so, although Sueves ravaged places in the territory of this city in 469, they did not attack the city itself.[94] Thirdly, there were Sueves living in Lugo, the second city of the province.[95] Here they dwelt alongside the Roman inhabitants, and in 460, we are told, they attacked and killed some of the Romans there.[96] The incident throws a sad light on conditions in a city where Sueves and Romans lived side by side; for the Sueves fell upon the Romans and massacred a number of them when they were off their guard at Eastertide, trusting in the holiness of the day. Presumably during other times of the year they were on the watch and never off their guard.

There is no evidence that the Sueves lived in any other city of Galicia besides these three, Braga, Astorga, and Lugo. Now, we can hardly assume that the entire people of the Sueves had been urbanized and that since 409 they had one and all become city-dwellers. Nor can we readily suppose that they were able to live exclusively off the plunder which they collected in their raids, continuous though these raids may have been; for the more frequently a region was ravaged the harder it became to live off it. The majority of the Sueves, then, must have been settled on the land *somewhere:* and since they devastated the country districts outside all the lesser Galician cities, including two of those in which they were themselves living (Lugo and Astorga), it looks as if the bulk of them lived in the territory of Braga itself, the one and only rural area which they are never recorded to have raided.

If the majority of the Sueves lived in the territory of a single Hispano-Roman city, even though that city was the provincial capital, it is difficult to believe that they were very numerous. It would be hard to disprove the view—or even to throw much doubt upon it—that they amounted in all to no more than 20,000 or 25,000 persons, with a fighting force of some 6,000 or 7,000 warriors. Salvian holds the Vandals for one of the weakest barbarian peoples at the time of their entry into Spain, indeed for the weakest of them all;[97] but he has rhetorical reasons for writing them down, and it can hardly be doubted that the Vandals, weak though they may have been in comparison with the Goths, were very much stronger than the Sueves, whom Salvian never thought worthy of mention at all in any connexion.[98] The Sueves, always feeble in numbers, appear to have been weakened further still by the fact that some of them enlisted in the

Roman army as *gentiles* and are found early in the fifth century serving in the Gallic provinces of Lugdunensis II and Aquitanica I. Others of them went off to Africa with Geiseric and the Vandals, and there was found at Hippo Regius the tombstone of a Suevic woman (*Suaba*) called Ermengon, the wife of Ingomar, who died there in 474.[99] In point of numbers, then, perhaps we can compare the Sueves with one section of a people called the Heruls. In Justinian's reign some of the Heruls lived in or near Denmark, and these sent raiders by sea to Spain in the fifth century; but other Heruls inhabited the countryside around Belgrade south of the Danube. The latter group could muster no more than 4,500 warriors, and yet the part which they played in the history of the mid-sixth century was by no means negligible.[100] These southern Heruls may have been little less than the Sueves in point of numbers.

We are now in a position to assess, though very roughly and with an enormous margin of possible error, the scale of the invasion which burst upon Gaul in 406 and affected Spain in and after the autumn of 409. Let us assume that the Siling Vandals, who were annihilated by the Visigoths, were decidedly weaker than the Asdings; and let us assume further that the Alans, who were nomads, owed their military power more to the efficiency of their cavalry than to their numbers. We might then conjecture that the Silings would have amounted to some 50,000 persons and the Alans to some 30,000 or 40,000 persons. Add these to the 80,000 Asdings (the one figure that is certain) and the 25,000 Sueves; and it would follow that the invaders of 31 December 406 amounted in all to rather less than 200,000 persons. Since the Siling Vandals may not by any means have been so few, this figure should perhaps be regarded as a minimum. It is not out of the question, then, that no fewer than a fifth of a million people entered Gaul at the beginning of 407. Although they cannot all have crossed the Rhine on that one night of 31 December 406, we do not know how many crossing places they used: and it is worth remembering that in the year 357 no fewer than 35,000 Alamanni (though without women, children, or old folk) crossed the Rhine in seventy-two hours.[101] The crossings early in 407, then, need not have been spread over many weeks.

The Elder Pliny, writing 400 years before the date of the events which interest us, gives figures for the population of northwestern Spain.[102] The Asturians, he says, numbered 240,000 free persons, the *conventus* of Lugo had a free population of 166,000, and the tribes around Braga contained 285,000 people. The total population of what long after Pliny's day became the greater part of the Suevic kingdom amounted to little less than 700,000 persons, exclusive of slaves. Many scholars believe that the population of the Roman Empire declined substantially between the time of

Pliny and that of Aëtius; but even if the population of Galicia had been drastically reduced in the interval, it is still clear that the Sueves formed only a fraction of the total population of their own kingdom.

A memorial of the invasion of northern Spain by the barbarians has been discovered at a place called Cueva de Chapipi near Coalla, south of Grado in Asturias. (Grado is some sixteen miles by road due west of Oviedo). Someone buried a hoard of nine *solidi* and two *trientes* there, and he never came back to recover his treasure. The eleven coins in the hoard were minted between 385 and 408, but eight of the eleven were issued between 402 and 408. One of them is a *solidus* of Constantine III issued at Lyons in the second half of 407 or the first half of the following year: so their owner may have buried them in the first chaotic months of the settlement of Galicia in 411, when the Sueves and the Asding Vandals moved hungrily into that already desolate province.[103]

The Sueves, then, seized Galicia by force. They were never the federates of Rome, never received Roman subsidies, and certainly never fought in the interests of the emperors, far away in Rome or Ravenna. They fought frequently, and they fought for themselves always, for the emperors not at all. They never spared the provincials of Galicia, in whose midst they had settled and by whom they were outnumbered on a vast scale. They had arrived there in 411 as a result of the casting of lots, and when the Asding Vandals left the province in 419 they had Galicia and the Galicians to themselves. They lived within the city walls of Braga, Lugo, and Astorga, and in the countryside around Braga; but of their relations with the Hispano-Romans of the province we know nothing more than that the Sueves acted like persistent and professional brigands and plunderers, while the Romans lived in a condition that Hydatius is able to call "slavery."[104] The minority tyrannized over the majority, not for the last time in Spanish history. The devastation caused by the Sueves was so implacable, so unremitting, that it is something of a wonder that they and the Galicians managed to survive the fifth century at all. In these dark and desperate conditions was founded the first independent kingdom of western Europe, as sombre, cruel, and suffocating as Spanish history itself.

9

The Suevic Kingdom of Galicia

I. THE SUEVIC ASCENDANCY

It would be tedious to list all the campaigns, raids, battles, negotiations, all the broken treaties, all the sacked cities, the lamentable columns of prisoners, which Hydatius one by one laboriously and sadly records. If we looked at them all, the trees would swallow up the wood: we would see the individual calamities of the time but not the general direction in which history was moving. However, it is not as easy to be selective as we might think at first sight, for, like the entire tribe of chroniclers, Hydatius shows a tendency to set down his facts as if they were all equally important. True, he may give four lines to one event, two to another, and six to a third; but these microscopic distinctions hardly alter the case. Nothing is easier than to follow him in this respect — merely to copy him out or to copy most of him and, like him, to regard all that he reports as being on the one level of significance or insignificance. Let us, then, throw his method aside and try to find out what was the position in Spain in the year 456.

At the beginning of that fateful year there was only one barbarian people remaining in the peninsula: the Sueves. The Siling Vandals had long ago (in 416–18) been practically exterminated by Wallia's Visigoths, who had themselves gone back to southwestern Gaul in 418. The Asding Vandals had crossed to Africa in 429, taking the remnants of the Alans with them, for the Alans, too, had been decimated, all but obliterated, by Wallia's warriors. A few years before their voyage to Africa the Vandals had made a couple of preliminary expeditions by sea — one to the Balearics, and then on to Mauretania — so that the decisive expedition to Africa in 429 was not their first taste of the salt water.[1] Now, over a quarter of a century later, in 456, the Sueves, alone of the invaders, remained between the Pyrenean range and the Pillars of Hercules.

In that year it must have seemed that the Sueves were on the brink of subjugating the entire peninsula. Indeed, most of it had already fallen feebly into their hands. By the year 439 they are reported to have occupied Merida.[2] Two years later they took Seville and went on, we are told, to conquer the provinces of Baetica and Carthaginiensis.[3] This alleged conquest of Carthaginiensis may be an exaggeration due to Hydatius' defective knowledge of events in eastern Spain, particularly in the coastal areas. We can infer from several facts that the Sueves, though they may have overrun the interior, are not likely to have seized the Mediterranean coast of this huge province. We do not ever hear of Cartagena falling to them; and yet when the Vandals had occupied that city in 425 Hydatius did not omit to mention so grave a misfortune.[4] We never hear that the Romans later on were obliged to reconquer the maritime region; nor is it reported that in 460 the Emperor Majorian had to fight his way southwards from Saragossa in order to get there;[5] yet the barbarians had doubtless occupied part, presumably the western part and the centre, of Carthaginiensis, for Hydatius is not likely to have been wholly in the wrong.

At all events, the Sueves had taken Merida in 439 and Seville in 441—one of their kings died in Merida later on.[6] Now Merida and Seville were the capital cities of the provinces of Lusitania and Baetica respectively; but if the capital cities were in the hands of the Sueves we may be sure that the barbarians also controlled the Roman administration of the two provinces —and there can be no questioning the statement that the whole of Baetica had fallen.[7] It follows that in the early 440s the Sueves had won control of the entire south, west, and centre of the Iberian peninsula in addition to their own Galicia in the far northwest. We may believe that eastern Carthaginiensis was free of them; but the only province which had entirely escaped their presence was the northeastern province of Tarraconensis, directly south of the Pyrenees and including the valley of the River Ebro. This region and most of the Mediterranean coast, we may think, were still in Roman hands. Were these to fall, the entire Iberian peninsula would lie under the barbarians.

So in 449 the Sueves turned against the Ebro valley, and it is recorded that their aim was to complete their conquest of the whole peninsula by overrunning Tarraconensis.[8] They attacked the region of Saragossa and even entered Lerida, where they took a number of prisoners, though they do not appear to have held this region for long.[9] They withdrew without approaching the provincial capital, Tarragona, a city which like so many other cities of the West lay in decay and ruin;[10] but in 455, according to Jordanes, King Rechiarius "presumed" on his relationship with Theoderic II, the Visigothic King of Toulouse—he was his brother-in-law—and determined to occupy practically the whole of Spain. He invaded Tarraconensis, which his men had not molested since the raid on Saragossa and Lerida in 449.[11] No moment could have been more favourable. Both the Patrician Aëtius and the Emperor Valentinian III as well as the new Emperor Petronius Maximus had all three been murdered. Geiseric and the Vandals had entered Rome in June, 455, and had plundered it for two weeks on end. The latest emperor, Avitus, had practically no power of his own. The Western Empire had never in all the centuries of its history been so disorganized, so helpless. It was very close to its end.

This assault on Tarraconensis, which was intended to complete the conquest of the Iberian peninsula, in fact led to the downfall of the assailants. The Emperor Avitus may have had little military power, but he had power of another sort. He could influence the Visigothic court at Toulouse. He was able to persuade the Visigothic king to attack the barbarians in Spain. Rechiarius' confidence in his brother-in-law had been misplaced. The Goths acted as their protégé, Avitus, wished them to act; and a Gothic army entered Spain.

For Hydatius the campaign which followed deserved more space in his chronicle than any other event of the century (p. 142 above). What were the Sueves to do? They could not easily have marched far to the east to engage the invaders, for Tarraconensis was the province which they had never controlled, and, had they now advanced deep into it, they would have found themselves in unfamiliar territory, subject to ambush by the Hispano-Romans or by the Basques, whom Rechiarius had needlessly provoked in 449. On the other hand, there was no need to allow Theoderic to penetrate into their own country and cause damage there. They would therefore meet him just beyond their frontier on the edge of Tarraconensis. That was the plan, and reasonable enough it seemed to be; but it turned out that, like the Alans and the Siling Vandals before them, the Sueves were no match for the warriors of the Goths. On Friday, 5 October 456, they engaged the invaders in a battle at the Campus Paramus, 12 miles from Astorga, on the banks of the River Orbigo (Urbicus). This is a tributary of the River Esla, a river which itself flows into the Douro and which formed, or at any rate lay close to, the eastern boundary of the province of Galicia. The "Gothic" army was in fact made up of men of various nationalities, Burgundians and Franks as well as Visigoths.[12] Indeed, we are told that Theoderic had with him the Burgundian Kings Gundioc and Chilperic. In the subsequent Gothic campaigns in Baetica in 458 and 459 at least one Roman—Sidonius' friend Trygetius—appears to have been present; and so he and other Romans may well have fought side by side with Goths and Burgundians and Franks at the Campus Paramus in 456.[13] At any rate, in the course of the battle the Sueves were routed, and Rechiarius, who was wounded,[14] managed with difficulty to make his escape to Oporto in the remoter parts of Galicia. In due course he was taken prisoner and was put to an unlamented death in December.[15] On 28 October Braga fell and was sacked,[16] and the Goths went on to "liberate" southern Spain from its Suevic overlords. What horrified Hydatius in this campaign was the brutality with which the Goths sacked Braga, defiled the churches, broke up the altars, carried off nuns, though without raping them, and stripped the clergy naked. Why the Visigoths behaved so uncharacteristically we do not know.

That was the end of the period of Suevic domination in the Iberian peninsula. Their empire had been a house of cards, and a single Gothic campaign was enough to scatter it to the winds. These barbarians appear to have used the entire time of their ascendancy for plundering only. They made no attempt, so far as we know, to settle in the provinces outside Galicia or even to station permanent garrisons in them. They collected no taxes and no tribute, though they may have used the Roman administrative machine to collect taxes on their behalf (p. 169 below). They were marauders, nothing else. There was no effort to reconcile the Hispano-Romans to their rule, still less to convince them that Suevic domination was preferable to rule by Ravenna, though late in the period covered by Hydatius' Chronicle some Romans were beginning to throw in their lot with them. The simplest explanation of their failure to take over the whole of the Iberian peninsula is probably to be found not only in their uncultured barbarism but also in their small numbers.[17] They were not too weak after 456 to launch further raids on Lusitania. Indeed, they are recorded to have plundered that province on no fewer than four occasions in the years 457–69: in 457 itself, in 459, in 467, and in 469.[18] We do not know all the regions of Lusitania which they attacked; but it is clear that they learned nothing from their defeat on the Campus Paramus. Life in future as in the past would consist of plunder and marauding. There is no reason to think that they managed in this period to hold any city outside Galicia for years on end as they had held Seville and Merida in the years before Theoderic's campaign in Spain put an end to their great days of marauding. However, we shall see that after the time with which Hydatius deals they did indeed expand permanently and hold much of northwestern Lusitania for nearly two hundred years. Their strength had not been wholly drained away by the Campus Paramus.

The rise and fall of the Suevic power showed that the days of the Roman Empire in Spain were numbered, and that the future of the peninsula lay with neither Romans nor Sueves but with the Visigoths. On later pages we shall see that when the armies clashed on the River Orbigo there had for many years been no Roman military presence in Spain and that the Visigothic domination, so far from ending when Theoderic returned to Toulouse, continued without a break until 711.

What of the internal life of these barbarians? In Hydatius' day a monarchy had developed among them. Indeed, on one of his coins Rechiarius (448–56) explicitly describes himself as a "king"; for two or three specimens of a *siliqua* of his survive, bearing the legend *ivssv rechiari reges.*[19] This monarchy was hereditary, or at any rate the kings at this date had won so much power that they could often designate their sons as their successors. The first of them who is known to us is Hermeric. The Vandals had penned him in, and his followers with him, on the Nervasian Mountains in 419, and it was only because of Roman intervention that he had been released from their grip.[20] When the Vandals were in his neighbourhood he was a peace-lover, no man of the sword; but in 429 the Vandals sailed from Spain to Africa, and then he had no one to fear in Spain. So in 430 he disclosed his true tastes. In that year began his persistent and remorseless raiding of Galicia, which caused Hydatius to travel to Aëtius in 431 and beg him to help stop the barbarians' forays (p. 140 above). We need not doubt that Hermeric continued his raids until sickness made him retire from the leadership of his people in 438.[21] He then appointed his son, Rechila, as king; and this Rechila was succeeded in turn by *his* son, the Catholic Christian Rechiarius, in 448 — the man whose coins we have just mentioned. In this last case there was secret opposition to the new King's accession, but it came to nothing, and the grounds on which it had been based have not been recorded.[22]

In not one of these cases do we hear of an election or even of discussion among the Sueves at large or among their elders or among their leading men or among any section of them whatever. It seems that the Suevic people had no rights at all when a new ruler was to be selected, at any rate in those cases where the old ruler was survived by a son; nor do we hear of that division into pro-Roman and anti-Roman policies and factions, or of pro-Roman and anti-Roman kings, which caused so much damage and internal strife in Visigothic society throughout most of the fifth century. It may well have been the case that the Sueves, unlike the Visigoths, were more or less united in their enmity to the Romans; and, again unlike the Visigoths, their nobility was probably too poor, too undifferentiated from the rank-and-file warriors, to have much interest in combining with the Roman rulers over against their own followers.[23] So far as we know, the people had no voice in declaring war or peace; but no doubt the continuous forays and campaigns will have been almost universally welcome among these wild tribesmen. Nearly all the raids were successful, and therefore few of the warriors will have had any fault to find with the policy of unceasing plunder. Whether the rank and file of the Sueves could in any sense control or depose their kings is unknown: we never hear of them murdering their kings, though it may have been his followers who strangled Maldras in 460 (p. 167 below).

The monarchy, then, had been strengthened since the days when Tacitus was writing about the Germans as a whole. It was now in effect hereditary, which it had not been in Tacitus' day; or at any rate the king now had the power to nominate his son, if he had one, as his successor, a right which had not been his in the first century A.D.

Although the king was the chief military leader, he was not necessarily the only one. In 429 a man named Heremigarius was plundering Lusitania — the first but by no means the last Suevic foray against that province — and he was now in the neighbourhood of the provincial capital, Merida. Hermeric was king at the time, and Heremigarius seems to have been acting independently of him.[24] Heremigarius was so powerful that Geiseric the Vandal, who was on the point of crossing from Spain to Africa, thought fit to turn back into the hinterland and lead an expedition against him in person.[25] A Gothic parallel to Heremigarius can possibly be found in that Gallic Anaolsus, a Goth of whom Hydatius alone tells us (p. 143 above). In the year 430 Aëtius defeated a Gothic force in the neighbourhood of Arles and killed its leader, Anaolsus. This force of Goths appears to have been operating independently of the Visigothic King, Theoderic I. Perhaps Anaolsus, who is described as an optimate, was leading his "retinue" (comitatus, as Tacitus would have called it) in a personal plundering expedition when Aëtius caught and killed him; and Heremigarius may have been a Spanish equivalent, the sort of man who was the leader of a "retinue" and who was operating with or without the connivance of his king. This can be no more than a guess; but there is certainly no reason to think that the Sueves had partitioned themselves as early as 429, or that they lived in two independent sections as they were to do later on, in 457.

When the Visigoths put Rechiarius to death in 456 the royal line of Hermeric became extinct; and now we hear of some matters which point in a new direction. In 456, Hydatius tells us, "the Sueves set up Maldras as their king"; and the phrase seems to imply that the people at large had a voice in the matter.[26] This Maldras, the son of Massilia, is not said to have been related to Hermeric;[27] but not all the warriors were prepared to accept him as their leader, and in the following year, 457, the people divided, and, while part of them continued to recognize Maldras, part "called" Framtane king.[28] Evidently, then, the Sueves in general could exercise some rights when a dynasty came to an end and a new king, unrelated to the previous ones, came to be appointed; but the institutions whereby they made their choice are wholly unknown.

At any rate, in 457 the two groups went on to act independently of one another for Maldras and his son are alone recorded to have plundered Lusitania and to have taken Lisbon in that year, while Framtane is not said to have taken any part in the raid. When Framtane died after a few months the two parties did not coalesce;[29] while Maldras and his section of the people continued to ravage western Lusitania the former followers of Framtane back in Galicia appear now under the leadership of Rechimund. They are not said to have established Rechimund as king.[30] It had happened frequently in former times that a Germanic people would elect two war-leaders simultaneously; and Jordanes describes the Sueves of the middle Danube (opposite Dalmatia) as headed by two leaders, Hunimund and Alaric, when they fought at the Battle of the River Bolia in 469.[31] It was an event of great rarity, at any rate in earlier centuries, for the people to partition themselves, to divide into two distinct parts, and for the two parts to act independently the one of the other. That is what happened now; and so far as Rechimund's group was concerned the kingship appears to have lapsed altogether.

This curious state of affairs lasted for a year, until Maldras, who murdered his otherwise unknown brother, was himself strangled by unknown assassins for unrecorded reasons in February 460.[32] (Presumably Hydatius was badly informed on such matters: as a Roman, he would have been unfamiliar with the internal intrigues of the Sueves.) After these displays of fraternal affection we might have expected that Rechimund would become king with the consent of both groups. Not at all. A new and equally unpleasant figure appeared on the scene. This was Frumarius, whose claim to ill-fame is that he and those who followed him kidnapped the chronicler Hydatius at Aquae Flaviae in 460 (p. 140 above). They ravaged the town and held the luckless historian prisoner for over three months.[33] Frumarius, too, was apparently a war-leader rather than a king.

Both these ruffians, Frumarius and Rechimund, competed for the throne, but neither was successful;[34] and for four or five years (460–64) the Sueves appear to have recognized no king at all. In the end, as it turned out, an ambassador who travelled to and fro several times between Galicia and Gaul at this time eventually managed to have himself recognized as king by all the Suevic people. This was Remismund, whose earlier history has not been recorded in any detail.[35] We are told that he brought all the Sueves under his sway "when Frumarius was dead"; but the significance of that last remark is obscure. At any rate, Rechimund is not heard of again, and Remismund was recognized by the Goths. Theoderic II sent him weapons and gifts together with a wife.[36] The kingship had been reestablished, the line of squalid kinglets was to continue, and the Visigoths had accepted the situation.

After the extinction of Hermeric's line, then, we hear in succession of the dual kingship, the partition of the people between two kings, and between a king and some other kind of leader. We hear of the disappearance of the kingship altogether, and finally of the restoration of the monarchy. Something of a partial parallel may perhaps be found in the events of West Saxon history after the death of Cenwahl in 672, when, according to Bede, *subreguli* took over the rule of the people, and held separate sway for some ten years; but then Caedwalla took over the kingship, and the monarchy was restored.[37]

A curious incident had taken place in 456 when Theoderic II was in Spain with his army of "various nations" (p. 163 above). After his victory on the Campus Paramus and the sack of Braga the King marched southwards to Lusitania; but a man called Aioulf, "deserting the Goths," remained behind in Galicia and, while he hoped to make himself king of the Sueves, died at Oporto in June 457. That is how Hydatius narrates the incident,[38] and it might seem impossible to doubt the general truth of what he says. He was on the spot, he was well informed, and he had no axe to grind; but when we turn to Jordanes' version of the same incident we find a more complicated tale. According to Jordanes, Theoderic after his victory over the Sueves appointed one of his retainers (*cliens*) called Agriwulf to govern the Sueves. Agriwulf did not "desert" the Goths, according to this version: he was Theoderic's deputy, but urged on by the Sueves themselves he aimed without loss of time to make himself the independent ruler of Galicia. Naturally, according to the patriotic Jordanes, so villainous a character could not have been a noble Goth: no noble Goth would have stooped to such foul treachery. No, he was a member of the people called the Warni. That is why he had no thought for liberty or for loyalty to his patron. The Gothic king at once sent a force against him which beat him in the very first engagement, took him prisoner, and put him to death. The Sueves therefore sent their clergy to Theoderic in supplication, and he received them "with the reverence due to episcopal rank" (*pontificali reverentia*) and allowed the Sueves to choose a king of their own—Rimismund, as Jordanes calls Remismund.[39]

Jordanes lived a century after the event, he lived at the other end of the world, and he is well known to be muddle-headed, befogged, and jumbled at each and every turn.[40] It can hardly be doubted that the trappings of this story, as Jordanes tells it, are a fabrication designed to explain away a disgraceful incident in Gothic history and to flatter Theoderic and his followers. In fact, there is no reason whatever for preferring Jordanes' view, that

Theoderic appointed Aioulf as governor, to Hydatius' view that Aioulf deserted the Goths; and there is every reason for preferring Hydatius' account. There is no reason for thinking that Aioulf was one of the Warni rather than one of the Goths themselves. The truth no doubt is that Jordanes or his source had heard of how a Goth had acted treacherously in Galicia in the rear of the Gothic army, in that sensitive area between the army and its distant homeland; and the historian tried to save the fair name of his people by asserting that Aioulf was not a Goth after all; but in making his apologia he introduced into his narrative the obvious anachronism — though it may not have been obvious where Jordanes was writing — of the Christian bishop or bishops of the Sueves, a people who were still pagan and would remain pagan for nearly a decade to come.

It is of interest that a foreigner, whether Aioulf was Gothic or Warnic, should have thought it likely that the Sueves would tolerate him as their leader. It was a characteristic of the early Germanic peoples that they were not always averse to putting themselves voluntarily under the leadership of foreigners; and to this practice the Sueves seem not to have been alien, if we may judge by the incident of Aioulf.[41]

We hear nothing explicitly about the finances of the kings except that they possessed a "treasure"; and when the Visigothic King Leovigild (568–86) finally overran the Suevic kingdom in 585 he captured this "treasure."[42] Now, the Visigothic kings also had a "treasure" in the middle of the sixth century; and they seem to have carried it about with them when they went on their campaigns, for when King Agila was defeated by the rebellious citizens of Cordoba in 550 he lost not only his army and his son but also his "treasure."[43] It would be interesting to know if Hermeric and Rechiarius and the others transported the *thesaurus* with them on each and all of their interminable campaigns, and also what became of it in those periods when the kingship had lapsed. Who looked after it then and guarded it?[44]

There is a slight piece of evidence which suggests that the kings continued to maintain the Roman civil administration of Galicia or at any rate that they did not suppress it. In 460 the Sueves killed some Romans in Lugo "along with their *rector*, a man of honourable birth."[45] Now, the word *rector* is one of the normal terms for a Roman provincial governor, and the implication of Hydatius' use of the word here is that even in 460 the Roman provincial governor still continued to function in the province of Galicia. That is to say, Roman law was still in some measure administered, and the Roman taxes were still collected there. No doubt it was not only their plunder but also these taxes, or part of them, which replenished the "treasure" of the savage kings.

The old judicial districts of the Romans were also in existence, though we know little about them in Roman times and nothing at all beyond the fact of their existence in the days of the Sueves. They were called *conventus,* and St. Isidore of Seville informs us that "'regions' are parts of provinces, which are commonly called *conventus,* as Cantabria in Galicia."[46] Hydatius refers to these *conventus,* though neither he nor anyone else except Isidore mentions that of Cantabria. Hydatius speaks of the *conventus* of Lugo,[47] of Braga,[48] of Aquae Flaviae,[49] and of Astorga,[50] so that with Cantabria there were at least five of them in the kingdom in Suevic times. They had once existed in the other Spanish provinces, too, but in the fifth century we hear of them in Galicia alone.

These were Roman juridical districts. Of Suevic law and its administration we know nothing. There is no reference in any of our sources to a written Suevic code of laws. Is this lack wholly unconnected with the fact that the Sueves had never been federates, that they had never had to share the landed estates with the Roman landlords, as federates would have been obliged to do, and hence that they had never had to regulate land relationships with Roman estate-owners? As for their marriage customs, it is remarkable that on all four occasions when we have any information at all we find Sueves marrying foreigners. Kings Rechiarius and Remismund married Visigothic women. The notorious Patrician Ricimer, who had such a sinister influence on the closing years of the Western Empire, was a Sueve on his father's side, a Visigoth on his mother's; and an inscription tell us of a case of intermarriage between a Roman and a Suevic woman.[51] Evidently, then, there was no ban on marriage with foreigners as there was, for example, among the contemporary Rugi in lower Austria and among the Visigoths.[52]

No Suevic cemetery has yet been discovered in Galicia. The stray finds are unrevealing. Reinhart illustrates a few of them,[53] but in fact three of the four objects which he pictures can hardly be ascribed to the Sueves at all. No doubt, like the other Mediterranean Germans, they liked gold jewelry inset with garnets and other precious and semiprecious stones, if they could get them, but of their material culture we know nothing.

There is a tiny piece of evidence which may perhaps show — at any rate, the inference has been drawn — that the Sueves anticipated the Visigothic King Leovigild in founding a new town. Leovigild founded his city of Recopolis in Celtiberia in the year 578.[54] The *Parochiale* of Suevic Galicia, which we shall discuss later on, mentions a *Portucale castrum antiquum* at the mouth of the River Douro on its left bank. At the time when the *Parochiale* was written — a few years before Leovigild built Recopolis — this Portucale was a parish in the diocese of Coimbra. However, one text of this document speaks of Portucale "in the new camp of the Sueves," *in cas-*

tro novo Suevorum, on the right bank of the river; and the phrase appears to point to a new foundation, though the evidence is frail enough.[55]

Although Suevic history in this period is little more than a record of raiding and warfare, practically nothing is known about the Sueves' methods of fighting. Jordanes mentions that those Sueves who were active on the middle Danube in the mid-fifth century were infantrymen rather than cavalry;[56] and perhaps this is true also of the Sueves who had ventured far away to Spain, at any rate in the fifth century.

They captured and plundered many cities of the Hispano-Romans. In some cases (Astorga, Coimbra, Lisbon) they took the one city on more than one occasion. We might ask, then, whether they had at last overcome the age-old incapacity of the Germanic peoples to storm walled cities? There is no evidence that they had, and it is in the walled cities that the Romans are explicitly said to have taken refuge in the early days of the invasion of Spain.[57] In 449 Rechiarius broke into Lerida "by a trick." The Goths took Astorga in 457 "by tricks and perjuries." Barbarian plunderers had already got into that city by pretending to the citizens that they were acting on the orders of the Roman authorities.[58] In 457, too, the Sueves of Maldras entered Lisbon by pretending that they came in peace, and, when admitted by the citizens in good faith, they plundered the place.[59] In 465 the Sueves entered Coimbra "treacherously,"[60] and—since the citizens of these cities appear to have been unusually gullible—they did so again by the same means in 468, when they destroyed the houses and part of the walls.

There was also the matter of Roman treachery. Lisbon was betrayed to the Sueves in 469 because a citizen called Lusidius handed it over to them.[61] Treachery on the part of two Romans named Ospinio and Ascanius also led to the fall of Aquae Flaviae to Frumarius in 460. Lusidius, Ospinio, and Ascanius betrayed the Romans at a time when Roman military power had disappeared from the Iberian peninsula, and it looks as if some Hispano-Romans were becoming reconciled to Suevic power by 460, and were prepared to throw in their lot with the invaders.

There is only one recorded case of a successful siege in Suevic history: Mertola was reduced by siege in 440.[62] Indeed, the only other siege in the entire Chronicle of Hydatius is the unsuccessful siege by the Asding Vandals of the Sueves on those mysterious Nervasian Mountains, where German beleaguered German (p. 157 above). Otherwise, the Roman cities fell because of ruses or treachery. They were never stormed or, apart from Mertola, starved into submission.

In certain cases the barbarians did not even try to take the cities. They are explicitly said on some occasions to have ravaged the "region" of a city, not the city itself. This happened at Saragossa in 449, in Orense and at Lugo in 460, and at Astorga in 469.[63] In yet other cases we have no information. We do not know how Rechila managed to enter Merida in 439 or Seville in 441,[64] and yet these were remarkable feats since the two cities were provincial capitals. We do not know how the Goths took Palencia in 457 and Scallabis in 460,[65] or how the Vandals captured Seville twice in four years (425 and 428),[66] and took Cartagena into the bargain[67] — for Cartagena, like Seville and Merida, was a provincial capital. There is no reason to think that the Sueves or the Goths or the Vandals or any other barbarians in Spain at this time were able to use the deadly siege engines of the Romans either for attack or for defence, engines that the barbarians always longed to use and were hardly ever able to master.

In the first part of this study we found that several facts could be best explained if we supposed that one of the chief lines of communication between Galicia and the outside world was the sea route to western Gaul. It is true that in Hydatius' Chronicle there is only one reference to this route: in 465 some envoys of Aegidius on their way to Vandal Africa began their journey by sailing from Gaul to Galicia in May, and returned by the same way in September; but there is impressive evidence from the sixth and seventh centuries. About 560, according to Gregory of Tours, communications between Tours and Galicia were commonplace. In 585 the Visigothic King Leovigild overran Galicia and destroyed the kingdom of the Sueves. While doing so he intercepted the merchant ships which were plying between Galicia and Gaul, plundered their cargoes, and killed or imprisoned their crews. About the year 650, according to one version of the *Life of St. Fructuosus of Braga,* the Saint wished to visit the Orient and proposed first to sail to Gaul and thence to make his way to the East. This passage of the *Life* also shows that Gaulish merchants could be found in Galicia at that date.[68] In view of the voyage of Aegidius' envoys it is not unreasonable to suppose that similar conditions existed in the fifth century.

II. THE END OF THE ROMAN GARRISON

The years 429 to 456, then, were the period of Suevic ascendancy in Spain: and a bleak, dismal time it was. No wonder that there was no Prudentius, no Orosius in those tormented years, no Isidore or Braulio. All the more honour to Hydatius for persisting, in spite of the horrors around him, in writing up the entries in his chronicle, year by disastrous year.

What of the Roman military forces in the peninsula during those tumultuous times? Why was there so little organized opposition to the unremitting barbarian forays? It has been calculated that a little earlier in the fifth century the Roman forces in Spain amounted to some 10,000 or

11,000 men, whose Commander-in-Chief was known as the "Count of the Spanish Provinces," *Comes Hispaniarum*. We first hear of this office in connexion with the year 420, when Asterius, Count of the Spanish Provinces, forced the Vandals to raise the siege of the Nervasian Mountains and to set free the beleaguered Sueves.[69] That was the Roman government's last successful military intervention against the barbarians in Spain. Whenever the Romans moved against them in later years their effort ended in calamity. In 422 the imperial authorities sent to Spain a Master of the Soldiers (*Magister militum*), Castinus by name. This officer took with him a large army of his own together with Gothic auxiliaries, and suffered a devastating defeat at the hands of the Asding Vandals, the first of endless defeats inflicted by the Vandals on Rome. Castinus is said (though not by Hydatius) to have lost no fewer than 20,000 men in the encounter.[70] We do not know what percentage of the Spanish garrison fought and fell with Castinus' routed army, but it is not out of the question that the disaster—for disaster it was, whether or not we believe in those "approximately 20,000" slain—reduced drastically the number of troops in the country at a time when fresh forces were hard to find.

In 438 a certain Andevotus appears to have been Count of the Spanish Provinces; at any rate, Isidore of Seville describes him as commander of the Roman troops, and it is not easy to see exactly what other office he can have held.[71] He was heavily defeated by the Sueves in that year on the River Jenil (Singillio), a tributary of the Guadalquivir, in Baetica. In the years 441–46 the position in Spain was so desperate that the central government actually sent out no fewer than three "Masters of Both Services" (*Magistri utriusque militiae*) in succession, an unprecedented step in any Western province in the fifth century.[72] These three men, Asturius, Merobaudes the poet, and Vitus, presumably brought their own troops with them to Spain. Indeed, Vitus is explicitly said to have done so,[73] and no doubt the three also drew on the Spanish garrison to serve with them, to the extent that any Spanish garrison still survived. Asturius in 441 and Merobaudes in 443 won victories over enemies whom we shall discuss later on. It was only in 446 that Vitus at last turned upon the Sueves, having expended his main energies in harassing the provincials of Baetica and Carthaginiensis whom he was supposed to be defending from the harassment of others; but he did not turn upon the Sueves with much success. On the contrary, he was utterly beaten by them, proving himself thereby to be a fitting successor to Castinus and Andevotus. No Roman officer in fifth-century Spain, whether leading throngs of soldiers or only a few, was capable of beating the barbarians or even of himself avoiding catastrophic defeat at their hands if he engaged them.

That is as far as we can carry the inglorious story of imperial military resistance to the barbarian invaders of Spain. The remarkable fact is that, leaving aside the visit of the Emperor Majorian to the peninsula in 460, we never again after the rout of Vitus in 446 hear of Roman forces south of the Pyrenees. Indeed, if the three Masters, Asturius, Merobaudes, and Vitus, fought exclusively with the troops whom they brought with them from Italy or Gaul, or wherever they came from, we may say that the Roman garrison in Spain is never heard of after the defeat of Andevotus in Baetica in 438. It is true that a Count of the Spanish Provinces reappears in the year 452, when a man named Mansuetus held the post; but he is not said to have had any troops under his command. The count is now simply a diplomat; and along with a colleague, a count called Fronto, he managed to negotiate a treaty with the Sueves in that year. Of armed forces he had none.[74]

It is remarkable how little the garrison of 10,000 or 11,000 men managed to achieve in the period which ended with Andevotus' defeat in 438. This force should have been adequate, at any rate in point of numbers, to take the offensive and at least to pin the Sueves down in Galicia; and yet there was never at any time in this period an organized Roman assault on Galicia. Even more surprising, there was no spoiling attack, no reprisal, not even an ambush by the state forces of a single raiding party of the Sueves. Not once were the barbarians cut down when crossing a river, or ambushed in a mountain pass, or surprised when exhausted or drunk after a day's plundering, or massacred in their tents after dark. Although the civilian population might take steps now and then to defend itself, the official forces of the emperor never once took the offensive. Earlier in the century, according to the historian Zosimus, the Spanish troops liked to defend Spain themselves without the help of non-Spanish forces;[75] but that was years ago. What had happened in the meantime? Had the loyalty of the imperial forces evaporated? Was their morale so low as to make them unmanageable? Or did the garrison of 10,000 or 11,000 men guard Spain on paper only? Did they exist at all?

Be that as it may, Vitus' losses were heavy, and they were never replaced. With his defeat effective Roman military control over any part of Spain outside Tarraconensis came to an end, except for one momentary occasion in 460, when Roman troops under the emperor himself paid a fleeting and tragic visit to Cartagena; but there is no need to tell once again of the unfortunate Majorian, the last Western emperor to deserve the august title. He brought a powerful army and a fleet of 300 ships to Spain in May 460 with a view to attacking Vandal Africa, and the Vandals burned his fleet as it lay at anchor in the Bay of Alicante.[76] When Majorian ignominiously led his army back across the Pyrenees to Gaul he was taking away the last regular Roman fighting force that ever set foot in the Iberian peninsula. After that lamentable event any troops who remained in Spain took their orders not from Rome but from elsewhere (see p. 176 below). After 460 no further Masters went out from Italy to Spain, and the Count of the Spanish Provinces never reappears.

Ahead of his marching column and his fleet Majorian had sent to Spain his Master of the Soldiers, whose name was Nepotian; and one or two points in the career of this Nepotian are of the deepest interest. His first duty in 460 was to attack and reduce the Sueves of Galicia. It may be that Majorian's aim in sending Nepotian against the Sueves was to eliminate all possible threats to his right flank as he marched southwards from the Pyrenees through Saragossa to Cartagena.[77] Now, this is the one and only time that we ever hear of a Roman officer who was given the task of entering Galicia. He had no Roman troops under his control with whom to attack the barbarians there; and so we find him going to Galicia with a *Gothic* force of which he shared the command with a Goth called Sunieric. Together they harassed the Sueves at Lugo and elsewhere.[78] Throughout the whole of the fifth century no other Roman officer is recorded to have set foot in Galicia. Why did not Nepotian take Roman soldiers with him to Lugo? Presumably because there were no Roman forces in Spain which he could have taken: they had all vanished years ago.

More striking still is the fact that in 461 this Nepotian was replaced in his office by a man named Arborius; and it is of the utmost interest to find that Arborius was appointed to the highest "Roman" military command in Spain, not by the Roman government, but by the Visigothic king, Theoderic II, in southwestern Gaul. It was the king who recalled Nepotian and substituted Arborius in his place. The Roman office continued in existence. It continued to be held by a Roman; but the Roman officer accepted his appointment and took his instructions, not from any Roman government, but from the Gothic King of Toulouse.[79]

At a somewhat later date we find another strange phenomenon. The bishops of Tarraconensis, writing to Pope Hilary (461–68), mention a man named Vincentius, and they describe him as "military commander (*dux*) of our province",[80] but "Duke of the Province of Tarraconensis" is a title which is wholly unknown to the Roman military service. A Gallic chronicler describes Vincentius as "Duke of the Spanish Provinces," another title which had never been used in Roman times. Later on, that same Gallic chronicler, not knowing what on earth to call him, despairingly refers to Vincentius as "a sort of Master of the Soldiers." The careers of Nepotian and Arborius together with the new titles of Vincentius show beyond doubt, I believe, that after Majorian's defeat in 460 the imperial authorities in Italy lost control, or at any rate effective military control, of the Spanish peninsula. Even Tarraconensis was lost, for after the death of the Western emperor, Anthemius, in 472 King Euric's armies took Pamplona, Saragossa, and the neighbouring cities, and a little later this Vincentius, who was in Euric's service, helped to capture the maritime towns.[81] After Majorian's disaster in Spain and his withdrawal to Gaul the Goths of Toulouse set up and controlled a new High Command, for the Roman Command had disappeared. The Goths continued to employ Romans; but in this new order of things the officers' titles were fluid. They were not what they had been under the rule of the emperors, and they were not what they were to become later on under the Visigothic kings of Spain. Civilians were puzzled to know what exactly to call these officers; and perhaps the officers — maybe even Theoderic II himself — would have been hard put to it to say how they ought to be formally addressed.

The Romans kept some sort of administrative system functioning even in the darkest times. Indeed, there is no reason to think that the provincial administration ever went out of existence in the fifth century, for it still survived under the Visigothic kings of the sixth century. Our only specific piece of information relates to the year 460, and we have already mentioned the death of the Roman *rector,* the provincial governor, at Lugo in that year (p. 169 above). We do not know, and can hardly even guess, how the governor of Galicia was appointed and how he was paid in the last four decades of the fifth century; but it would be rash to deny that he existed in that period.[82] We also find that "a part of the plebs of Galicia," whom the Sueves were fighting, were able to make peace with the barbarians in 438.[83] The plebs of Aunona (p. 154 above) were able to negotiate with the Sueves in 466, and a few years later they succeeded in making peace with the Suevic king, who went on to ravage neighbouring places.[84] Are we to conclude that part of the population of Galicia, without the nobility, were sufficiently organized to reach agreement with the barbarians? It appears so; but how did *part* of the populace, or the citizens of one *civitas,* organize to negotiate? Who were their representatives? How were these representatives selected and instructed? What powers did they have? On these matters we know nothing at all. On other occasions — in 431 and 433 — we seem to hear of peace being made, not with only a part of the population of Galicia, but with the Galicians as a whole.[85] Presumably in these last cases the *rector,* the provincial governor of the day — at those dates his existence can hardly be called in question — was the person who acted for the provincials as a whole and with whom the Sueves struck their readily broken treaties.

In a letter dated 30 October 465 Pope Hilary mentions that he had received a communication from the large landowners (*honorati* and *possessores*) of a number of cities (*civitates*) in the province of Tarraconensis.[86] He fortunately gives us the names of these *civitates*, seven of them in all. They are Tarazona, Cascantum (modern Cascante, a short way southwest of Tudela), Calahorra, Varega (presumably an error for Vareia the modern Varea, on the south bank of the upper Ebro, east of Logroño),[87] Tritium (now Tricio, near Najera, which itself lies some seventeen miles southwest of Logroño),[88] Leon, Virovesca (modern Briviesca, some twenty-five miles northeast of Burgos). Such a meeting resembles nothing so much as one of the old provincial councils, which had been so widespread in the earlier centuries of Roman power. It would be of much interest to know how the landowners of Tarraconensis met together and combined and discussed and formulated a letter. In this case their communication was addressed to the pope: did they also on occasion address their letters to the emperor? They will hardly have done so after *c.*473, when Euric's army overran the province. The fact that the pope's letter includes mention of places situated so far to the west as Briviesca and especially Leon, which lay close to the border of Galicia, shows that Tarraconensis was still a unit and still intact: the provincial boundaries still had a meaning, for no town of Carthaginiensis or Galicia was represented at the gathering. The continued existence of Tarraconensis gives rise to a small problem. In a letter written sometime in the years 463–64, a year or two before Pope Hilary addressed his letter to Tarraconensis, the bishops of that province speak of the see of Calahorra as being in the "furthest part of our province",[89] but in fact Calahorra is about half way between Leon and the Mediterranean Sea; and Leon, though so far away to the west, nonetheless lay in the province of Tarraconensis. How then is it possible to speak of Calahorra as situated "in the furthest part of our province"? It is hardly a slip of the pen. I suppose that it would be facile to guess that in 463–64 the Sueves or the Basques or some other enemy had overrun the westernmost parts of the province of Tarraconensis and had removed from Roman control most of the area of the province that lay west of Calahorra, so that that city now lay at the extreme edge of the province and that by October, 465, when Hilary wrote, these enemies had withdrawn or had been driven out of Tarraconensis. The true explanation of the discrepancy may well be less complex and cataclysmic, though it does not seem easy to think of any other sequence of events which would account for the strange expression which the bishops use. At all events, the province was still in some sense an organized and coherent unit late in the year 465, but of the nature of its organization we know little. We cannot tell whether the civilian officials took their orders from

Italy or from Toulouse, or whether at times they were independent of Italian and Goth alike. Perhaps the safest hypothesis would be that they were at least nominally dependent on the emperors until the conquest by Euric's generals in 473–74.

Be that as it may, with the departure of Majorian in 460 the Roman Empire in Spain had come to its military end. We cannot speak of a "fall": Roman power simply faded away or was gently transformed into Gothic power. It was an administrative alteration, an organizational change. There was no sharp break. There was an adjustment at the top, nothing more.

III. ROMAN ATTITUDES

The large landowners and the higher clergy still looked upon the barbarians in much the same inhuman way as the devout poet and hymn-writer, Prudentius, their fellow countryman, had regarded them at the beginning of the century, that is, as subhuman. We rarely hear that they resisted these subhumans in arms. In 409 some kinsmen of the Emperor Honorius—for Honorius' father, Theodosius the Great, had been born at Coca (*Cauca* in Roman times) in the modern province of Segovia—tried to defend Spain against usurpers and barbarians alike in the name of the emperor.[90] They assembled "rustics" and the slaves from their landed estates, and tried to hold the Pyrenean passes with their "private garrison" against the invaders; but a "Roman" regiment known as the *Honoriaci*, which was in fact composed of barbarians, opened the Pyrenees to the barbarians coming from Gaul, the Sueves, Alans, and Vandals, and threw in their lot with them.[91] They went on to devastate the neighbourhood of Palencia;[92] but these Roman landowners had fought to the end, and their action is one of the few cases of resistance to the invaders that we know to have been organized by the Roman aristocracy in the West on their own initiative.

A handful of cases is recorded from Spain where the civilian population in general, apart from the great landowners, put up some resistance. The Westerners were not wholly abject before the barbarians. The Galician *plebs* (to use Hydatius' phrase) who held the stronger forts of the province were able to beat off Hermeric and his Sueves in 430, and they forced the Sueves to surrender the families whom they had taken prisoner. They achieved this by means of the heavy casualties which they inflicted on the barbarians and by the number of prisoners whom they took; and yet, since the Suevic king himself was present with this band of marauders, it cannot have been a negligible one. Again, when seven ships of the Heruls landed near Lugo in 455 a "multitude" of the Galicians assembled and put the pirates to flight. In 457, after the Visigoths had ruthlessly ravaged Astorga and Palencia, the defenders of the *Coviacense castrum*—it lay thirty Roman miles from Astorga, but we do not know its exact site—resisted and slew a number of the Goths, though it must be admitted that the brave resistance of this fort is said explicitly to have been unique.[93]

In general it is true that we find in Spain that same degree of apathy on the part of the civilians, that inability to combine, plan, and attack, which is all too obvious in other regions, too, of the falling Empire. Eugippius in his *Life of St. Severinus* relates the events which took place in Noricum Ripense around the year 480. The Noricans were helpless before the raids of the barbarous Rugi: they did not know what to do. It was left to the holy man himself, Severinus, to organize the unsoldierly citizens, to advise them, to negotiate on their behalf with the Rugian leaders, to raise their fainting courage, to plan their feeble strategy—and even then they never once attacked aggressively their tormentors. We do not hear that the Roman population of Galicia had any such holy and militant man as Severinus to inspire them. Hydatius himself, for example, negotiated with Aëtius on behalf of the Galicians; but we never hear that he negotiated with Rechila or Rechiarius in the way in which Severinus negotiated with the savage leaders of the Rugi. The Galician bishops in general were almost entirely inactive and apparently indifferent. To hunt down a Manichaean was more important than to save their flocks from Suevic raiders. True, Hermeric made peace with the Galicians in 453 "on episcopal intervention"—a bishop, or a number of bishops, intervened to negotiate the peace;[94] but on one occasion a bishop acted on the other side. The same king in the very same year used the Catholic Symphosius to negotiate with the Western court, just as the Visigoth, Theoderic I, once negotiated through Orientius, Bishop of Auch.[95] No doubt the king in both cases believed that a Catholic Roman bishop would carry more weight with the imperial authorities than a pagan barbarian could possibly carry, and also that the educated bishop would present the king's case more persuasively than any fur-clad barbarian could hope to do in his uncouth and stumbling Latin. Neither Hydatius nor any other man of God organized the population to resist the Sueves in the field as St. Severinus was ineffectually to do a little later or as St. Germanus of Auxerre was successfully doing almost at this very moment in Britain.

Churchmen like Orosius, who were in Spain in 409 when the invasion began, fled overseas, abandoning their congregations to the full savagery of the invaders. Churchmen like Avitus of Braga, who were already overseas when the barbarians crossed the Pyrenees, did not feel it their duty to come back, though they had no hesitation in sending their best wishes and kindest regards for the future to the embattled clergy and the brethren at home.[96] St. Augustine speaks of this distasteful matter. Some holy bishops of Spain, he says, fled because their congregations had already melted away in flight, and there was no point in the shepherd's staying where there was no flock for him to tend. Others fled because their congregations had been massacred or were shut up in besieged cities or were scattered in captivity. (He omits to explain to us how the churchmen had escaped in these cases when otherwise the entire congregation had fallen victim to massacre, siege, or captivity.) Still others, according to St. Augustine—and there is no reason to doubt him—braved all the dangers in company with their flocks. Unhappily, that was not the whole story. The Saint is obliged to add a painful fact. There were some clergy—is it possible?—who took to their heels helter-skelter and left their flocks to fend for themselves to the best of their ability—and he might have added, had he been so indelicate as to cite a specific example, that his young friend, the future historian Orosius, only made his escape from Spain under a shower of barbarian stones and spears without any thought of his congregation to impede his wild rush through the surf to the waiting ship. We hear further of a Jew who fled before the invaders and took refuge in the island of Minorca. He will hardly have been the only Spaniard to find it expedient to beat a rapid retreat overseas.[97]

The Atlantic coast of the Spanish peninsula was comparatively free from the attentions of barbarian pirates and sea-raiders throughout that part of the fifth century with which Hydatius' Chronicle deals. When sea-raiders did make their appearance there is no trace of any official Roman coast-guards to repel them, and the attitude of the civilian population varied from occasion to occasion. In 445 Vandal pirates sailed through the Straits of Gibraltar and up the Atlantic coast. They made a landfall at Turonium on the shores of Galicia and carried off numerous Spanish families.[98] We hear nothing of any Spanish resistance. (Incidentally, whether raiding or negotiating—we never hear of them trading with Spain—the Vandals showed no interest in returning to their old homes there, or in controlling the country from a distance, or in colonizing it, or in exacting taxes from it or tribute. Africa was to be their home, and there was no going back westwards into the past.) On the other hand, seven ships of a Germanic people called the Heruls, who lived in Denmark, it seems,[99] were suddenly sighted off the shores of the territory of Lugo in the year 455. The seven ships carried approximately 400 lightly armed warriors. A Spanish crowd collected in order to deal with them, but the pirates escaped with the loss of only two men. On their way home to the far north they mercilessly pillaged the maritime parts of Vardullia and Cantabria. (The Vardulli lived between the Basques and Cantabria with their chief settlement at the modern Bilbao.)[100] We do not hear of opposition from the local inhabitants.

Four years later, in 459, another band of Heruls cruelly raided some places on the coast near Lugo, but they then put out to sea and made for Baetica, where Hydatius lost sight of them.[101] Again there was no resistance. The arrival of Herul ships off the Spanish coast raises the question whether they had completely bypassed Britain on their voyages to the far southwest, or whether there were Heruls, too, among the invaders of that desolated island. There is no place-name evidence for Herulian settlement in Britain, as there is for Suevic settlement there; but since all the other peoples in the neighbourhood of the Jutish peninsula seem to have taken part in the conquest of Britain it may be thought on the face of it unlikely that the Heruls contented themselves with sending a few ships to distant Spain and none at all to not-so-distant England. Be that as it may, no Roman troops repelled pirates from the west coast of Spain.

There were Romans who did not think of resisting the barbarians or of taking to flight before them: the only thought of flight which entered their heads was flight *to* the barbarians and *away* from the Roman administration. Orosius speaks of Romans who had run to the barbarians because they preferred freedom and poverty among them to the payment of the grinding taxes which were still (in 417, when Orosius was writing) exacted in the Roman-controlled areas.[102] These men believed that their social and economic position was improved under barbarian rule: bad though the invaders may have been, they were less remorselessly oppressive than the remote and indifferent government and its corrupt tax-collectors. In 440 or 441 Salvian wrote his *Government of God,* and in it he, too, remarks that the difficulties of life in the Roman-controlled parts of Spain were such that even men who had not fled to the barbarians were nonetheless compelled *to be barbarians themselves.* "A great part of the Spaniards," he writes, had become "barbarians."[103] This was true not only of poor men but even of noblemen; and in an obscure passage Hydatius tells us of two Romans called Ospinio and Ascanius who, acting in the interests of the Sueves, caused the retreat of a Gothic army as it harassed the Sueves in 460. These two Hispano-Romans went on to facilitate the kidnapping of the Bishop Hydatius in 460 (p. 140 above) and the capture of the town of Aquae Flaviae by Frumarius; and the chronicler was only freed against their explicit wish.[104] We have seen, too, the anti-Roman activities of Lusidius. Worst of all, it was the actions of "traitors" (*proditores*) which caused the disaster to Majorian's fleet in the Bay of Alicante in 460 — and these men must have been Romans, for barbarians could hardly be called "traitors" in this connexion.

It would be dangerous to generalize. Some Romans may indeed have welcomed the invaders, but it is hard to believe that the peasants of western Spain were attracted or favourably impressed by all those raids which the Sueves launched on so many parts of the countryside of Galicia and Lusitania in so many summers. The remarks of Orosius and Salvian were written in 417 and 440–41 respectively; and perhaps these writers would have had less reason to use such generalizations if they had been composing their works in 460 or 469. We may doubt, too, whether many Galician peasants or townsfolk, clergy or lay, would have had reason to use such language at *any* date. It is true that the years following on the barbarians' division of Spain in 411 were years of relative peace (p. 156 above), and it was in those years of tranquillity, according to Orosius, that many a Roman ran off to join the newcomers; but was this the case in Galicia? Even in 430 the "plebs" in the central parts of Galicia occupied the more secure forts and compelled the plundering Sueves to restore peace, handing back the families whom they had carried off (p. 178 above). Such men did not prefer the poverty and freedom of life among the Sueves to their old life as Hispano-Roman taxpayers: they differed from the fugitives of whom Orosius speaks; and when the holocaust of Suevic raiding began after the Vandals set sail for Africa in 429 there was little room for collaboration between plundered Roman and pitiless barbarian.

In addition to all these phenomena there was yet another—massive and organized revolt by Romans against Roman rule. Let us recollect what happened. In 438 Andevotus had been defeated by King Rechila, and the provinces of Baetica and Carthaginiensis were subjugated by the Sueves (though there does not seem to be conclusive reason for supposing that the eastern, coastal parts of the latter province had in fact been won by them). The Romans no longer controlled Lusitania, for the Sueves had taken Merida, the provincial capital, and were to hold it for years.[105] That was the position in 441, and in that same year, at this desperate crisis, the Roman government felt itself obliged, as well it might, to send out the "Master of Both Services" from Gaul or Italy. We might have expected, therefore, that the first action of the Master, when he set foot in Spain in these catastrophic circumstances, would have been to stop the barbarian advance at any cost as soon as he possibly could do so, and try to regain the lost provinces or some of them. Surely, we might think, he must at the earliest moment search out and engage the barbarian marauders. This was vital. Why else had he been sent so promptly to Spain?

Not at all. He did nothing of the kind. What in fact happened was quite different. The first of these Masters, Asturius, was in Spain in the critical year 441, the year in which Seville fell: but it was only *five years later,* in 446, that Vitus, the third Master to go to Spain in this decade, occupied himself with the Sueves, at whose hands he suffered his annihilating defeat

(p. 173 above). The first and second Masters, Asturius and Merobaudes, remained in Tarraconensis, the one province where there were no Sueves at all: it was not even threatened by the Sueves at this date. If we knew no more, their behaviour would be amazing, even inexplicable; but by good luck we are told what they were up to. They were by no means inactive. In the outwardly peaceful province of Tarraconensis they were fighting a bitter war. They were attacking the peasants, the rebellious countryfolk, the Bacaudae.

At times during the period 409–440, as we have seen (p. 181 above), many Hispano-Romans went off and joined the barbarians, though not perhaps in Galicia or northern Lusitania; and many others, though they did not throw in their lot with the Vandals and the Sueves, imitated them by plundering the countryside on their own account, independently of the barbarians. These last had reached that degree of organization which earned them the title of "Bacaudae" in Hydatius' Chronicle. They were not mere companies of brigands: they were much more. These were organized bands of peasants and slaves and others who had thrown off Roman rule altogether and had been known in Gaul under that name since the late third century.[106] We do not know when they first made their appearance in Spain; but in 441 Asturius ignored the Sueves and killed a "multitude" of the Bacaudae, whom he fought for a couple of campaigning seasons. In 443 came his successor, the poet Flavius Merobaudes, himself a Spaniard of Baetica. Hydatius says of him that "in the short time of his command he broke the insolence of the Bacaudae of Aracelli," an unidentified place not very far from Saragossa.[107]

At that crucial time, then, two successive Commanders-in-Chief in Spain, men who had been sent from overseas specifically to deal with the calamitous state of the peninsula, interpreted the crisis very differently from the way in which a modern student of the period would assess it at first sight. They both allowed themselves to be pinned down—or they willingly pinned themselves down—in the one and only province where there were no barbarians at all; and this happened at a time when all the other four provinces in the Iberian peninsula had been lost by the imperial government. These Roman commanders believed the Bacaudae to form an even more serious and more immediate threat than the triumphant barbarians. At the very least it would seem to be true that the menace of the Bacaudae was so acute that the Roman officers on the spot dared not hunt out and engage the Sueves without first removing the peasant and slave menace in their rear. The Roman rear was so restless and insecure that an offensive against the barbarians could not be contemplated immediately— and could not be contemplated at all with the forces which remained in the country in 440. Reinforcements were a necessity, and with their help the campaigns of 441–43 crushed the Bacaudae for the time being, to an extent that made it possible for the next Master to turn at last in 446 against the Sueves. Asturius and Merobaudes consolidated the Roman rear and so enabled Vitus to launch his ill-starred offensive.

The Sueves kept very quiet and are not reported to have made any offensive move as long as Asturius and Merobaudes were in Spain. They made no effort, for example, to come to the help of the Bacaudae; nor did they strike out on their own account at Cartagena or Malaga or the like when the Masters were busy far away in the Ebro valley. That does not mean that they were paralysed and incapable of an offensive action. They were not immediately threatened. They had no interest in joining the Bacaudae, and so they remained quietly on the watch; but when the third Master, Vitus, took the field against them they did not wait to be attacked. They were far from leaving the initiative wholly to the Romans. They marched down to Baetica or Carthaginiensis, where Vitus was wasting time in plundering the provincials, wrested the initiative from him, and routed him.[108]

Before commenting on these perplexing events let us complete the history of the Bacaudae in Spain. The utter defeat of Vitus in 446 left the Roman forces in the peninsula so weak as probably to be all but nonexistent. So in 449 a man named Basilius assembled the Bacaudae once more—for the victories of Asturius and Merobaudes had not been so crushing as to drive the organization of the Bacaudae out of existence for more than a few years, if at all. Basilius and his followers, like their predecessors in 441 and 443, were active in Tarraconensis. They managed to massacre federate troops in a church in the city of Tarazona; and the local bishop, Leo, died of wounds inflicted by them there. The nationality of these federates is not stated, but they can hardly have been other than Visigoths from southwestern Gaul. Presumably Tarazona as a whole had fallen into the insurgents' hands for the moment, but there is no reason to suppose that the capture and permanent occupation of the Spanish cities was part of the programme of these Bacaudae any more than it was the aim of the Gallic Bacaudae to occupy the cities of Gaul permanently, though they more than once attacked them.[109]

A more sinister event from the Roman authorities' point of view occurred in the same year as the outrage—or the "success," if you look at it from another direction—at Tarazona. The Suevic King Rechiarius went so far as to join forces with the Bacaudae of Basilius in 449 and to plunder the region of Saragossa, though apparently without taking the city itself; but Lerida (Ilerda) fell, and many prisoners were taken there.[110] Clearly, if the barbarians and the Bacaudae were to cooperate in this area over a

period of years the imperial authorities would almost certainly lose Tarraconensis, their last remaining province in Spain. Such a combination of
barbarian and peasant might well have been an overwhelming one; but in
fact throughout the entire history of the later Roman Empire cases where
barbarian and Bacauda are reported to have joined forces in the field are ex-
cessively rare; and the example of Rechiarius and Basilius in 449 would
not be easy to parallel at any date in any province in the West. Even the
collaboration of Basilius and Rechiarius did not last beyond a single campaigning season, nor was it ever repeated, so far as we know. Barbarian
landowners will have had as much distaste as Roman landowners for rebellious agricultural workers; and in addition the Sueves were never able to
maintain themselves in the Ebro valley for any length of time, whereas the
Bacaudae, so far as we know, never operated in Spain outside the province
of Tarraconensis. So even if both parties had had the will to cooperate,
which they had not, geography would have made cooperation difficult.
We are still left, of course, with the puzzling question of why the Bacaudae existed only in the province of Tarraconensis. Why not in Baetica or
Lusitania or Carthaginiensis? Was it easier for them to take the field under
the rule, such as it was, of the Romans than under that of the barbarians?
If so, why? Or was there some difference between the social relations in
Tarraconensis (which the barbarians had never occupied) and those in the
other provinces of Spain, which the barbarians had occupied? At present
there seems no means of unravelling these enigmas.

The Bacaudae did not go out of existence after their successes at Tarazona, Saragossa, and Lerida, for they were still active enough in Tarraconensis in 453–54 to bring about a surprising event: they made it imperative for the Roman government to intervene once again and to do so in an
unexpected way. That government had no military force in Spain at this
time and no force of their own anywhere else which they could send to
Spain, so they authorized an army of their Visigothic federates to move
south of the Pyrenees and to operate in the valley of the River Ebro. It was
not the only occasion on which the imperial government instructed its
federates to attack the Roman countryfolk: did not Aetius order Goar and
his Alan federates to attack the Armorican Bacaudae in 448? At all events,
Frederic, the brother of King Theoderic II, led a Gothic army from Toulouse into Tarraconensis at Roman instigation and succeeded in massa-
cring the Bacaudae.[111] So far as we know, that was the end of organized revolt by the countryfolk of Spain for more than a hundred years. We never
again hear of a rebellion of the "rustics" until the years 572 and 577, when
the Visigothic king of that time, Leovigild, crushed rebellious country
people, though the revolt of neither of those years can be safely located in

the Ebro valley.[112] Why was a single Visigothic campaign sufficient to destroy the Bacaudae as completely as the Siling Vandals and the Spanish Alans of a somewhat earlier day? It is possible to exterminate a group of barbarian invaders: but how was it possible to destroy the organization of the peasantry of the Ebro valley? Or did economic circumstances change after 454 in some way which was advantageous to the labourers and caused them to lose their taste for warfare? We cannot tell. Whatever the reason, it is sad that no Spanish authority gives us any details about the aims and the organization of the fifth-century Bacaudae in the Iberian peninsula. Since they were called by the same name and were active about the same time as the Bacaudae of Gaul, they presumably had much the same kind of organization and approximately the same ambitions as their Gallic brothers-in-arms, that is, to overthrow the landlords, to expel the imperial officials, to administer justice in their own courts under their own laws, and to set up a new and more equitable state of their own that would be independent of the Roman Empire.[113]

Their activities were confined to a very limited area of Spain. They are never mentioned outside the province of Tarraconensis. Their actions were almost restricted to the valley of the Ebro. They are unknown in the other regions of the peninsula, and we have no means of telling why Tarraconensis should have been more explosive than the provinces to its west and south. The history of the Spanish Bacaudae is also very limited in time. Outside the period 441–54 we never hear of them by name. Some fifteen years saw the beginning and the end of the history of the Bacaudae in Spain. True, 454 did not bring the end of large-scale brigandage. When the Visigoths smashed the Suevic forces in 456 brigands ravaged part of the territory of Braga itself; and they did so on such a scale as to earn an entry in the chronicle of Hydatius,[114] but the chronicler does not call them "Bacaudae" now. Presumably the brigands of 456 had not the same organization (if they had any extensive organization at all) or precisely the same aims as the true Bacaudae of the Ebro valley. Their purpose, no doubt, was simply to do nothing more constructive than to loot, plunder, rape, and burn. After 456 there is no evidence even for this kind of activity. The papal letters which have survived from the 460s include no reference to Bacaudae or to any kind of unrest on the countryside, although they deal with Tarraconensis itself, the very area in which the Bacaudae had so recently made their mark.

What comment are we to make, then, on the short and restricted history of the Bacaudae in Spain? In spite of the limitation in time and space of their actions it is not out of the question that they played an indirect, and yet an important, perhaps even a vital, part in the collapse of Roman power in the Iberian peninsula. We have seen that after 438 the imperial government may have had no military forces left in Spain; and consequently when they wished to conduct military operations there they were obliged either to send out forces from Italy or Gaul, as in 441–46, or else to persuade the Visigoths of Toulouse to act on their behalf, as in 454. We have wondered why they did not recruit fresh forces in the peninsula itself; but if we observe that the scene of the activities of the Bacaudae was the valley of the Ebro we shall be obliged to ask *where* exactly the government could have raised fresh forces. In the early forties of the century the barbarians had won complete military control of Galicia, Lusitania, Baetica, and at least western Carthaginiensis. The one area, therefore, where the Romans might have called for recruits was Tarraconensis; but that was precisely the place where the Bacaudae were most active, organized and aggressive. It is not illegitimate to suppose that the existence of an organized army of Bacaudae had been preceded in Spain — as it certainly had been preceded in Gaul, as the evidence of Salvian proves — by mass flights of peasants from the land to the outlaws in the hills or the forests. The farm workers, the very persons in whom the imperial recruiting officers were most interested, must have flocked to join the outlaws. Only so can we explain the extent and success of their movement in Gaul and probably in Spain, too.

This is not to say, of course, that the rebellious peasants caused the downfall of Roman Spain; but it would be unsafe to ignore the part they may well have played. It is true that a major difficulty which prevented late Roman governments from raising troops was their chronic financial weakness. The barbarians, too, had removed the main recruiting grounds in that they had detached most of the Spanish provinces from the control of the central government. The last chance of forming a new Spanish garrison, of fighting back against the invaders, disappeared when Tarraconensis was torn from the government's grasp. No doubt the countryside in that province was still restless and turbulent in 460, when Majorian visited it, too turbulent and dangerous to supply troops in his brief reign, too chaotic for the authorities to compel the landowners to supply recruits. The Bacaudae may well have destroyed any hope that there may once have been.

187

10

The Gothic Kingdom
and the Dark Age of Spain

I. THE VISIGOTHIC CONQUEST

We have been looking at the fifth century in Spain from the point of view, first, of the Sueves, and then of the Hispano-Romans, the sheep that were slaughtered. We must now look at the same period of Spanish history from the direction of Toulouse and study the policies of the Visigoths of south-western Gaul, for the immediate political future lay with them rather than with the Sueves or the Romans. It was by them, not by the Sueves or the Romans, that most of Spain was to be governed throughout the sixth and seventh centuries and for the first few years of the eighth.

We must be careful, of course, to avoid the mistake into which Isidore of Seville tumbled when he wrote of Kings Theoderic I and Theoderic II of Toulouse: he thought that they were one and the same person.[1] In fact, they were two very different persons: they differed in many matters and not least in their attitude towards Spain. The long-lived Theoderic I, who reigned from 418 to 451, looked upon the Suevic kingdom with an eye of benign neutrality and even indulgence. To be sure, as a federate of Rome he was obliged to send auxiliaries to help Roman commanders whenever the imperial government called upon him to do so. That is why we find Gothic auxiliaries accompanying Castinus in Spain in 422; but it would have been well for Castinus if they had stayed at home, for they betrayed him in his engagement with the Vandals in Baetica. There was also a large band of Gothic auxiliaries with the Master Vitus in 446 when he, too, like Castinus, was catastrophically defeated.[2] Hydatius gives no hint that the Goths betrayed him to the Sueves, as their predecessors had betrayed Castinus to the Vandals; but the main interest of the Gothic federate soldiers was not so much opposition to the Sueves as the plundering of the Hispano-Romans. It is remarkable that the Sueves on this occasion actually managed to defeat the Visigoths, the one and only occasion in their history when they were able to do so, for the Visigoths were the scourge in turn of the Siling Vandals, the Alans, and the Bacaudae. Three years later, in 449, there were federates in Tarazona (p. 184 above); but in that year the aged Theoderic I showed his good will towards the Sueves by marrying his daughter to King Rechiarius. He is not known to have regretted his action when later on in 449 Rechiarius visited him in Gaul and then went on to plunder Saragossa and Lerida on his way home to Galicia.[3]

But in 451 Theoderic I was killed fighting against Attila and the Huns in the Battle of the Catalaunian Plains. His eldest son, Thorismud, who was bitterly anti-Roman, did not survive long enough to reveal any attitude towards Spain and its problems. But as soon as the Romanophile Theoderic II came to the throne of Toulouse in 453 he quickly made it clear that he had formed decided views on Spain. He was the enemy of Rome's enemies. In 454 a Gothic army marched to Spain at the instigation of the Roman government and crushed the Bacaudae of the Ebro valley (p. 56 above). In 456 Theoderic invaded Spain in force, and on 5 October of that year he routed the Sueves at the Battle of the Campus Paramus and put an end to their plans for the conquest of the whole of Spain.

The victorious Gothic king then took a remarkable step. He sent an army to Baetica in 458 under the command of one Cyrila;[4] and this action can well be described as marking an epoch in the history of Spain. It is recorded without comment by Hydatius in his matter-of-fact way: he could not have foreseen its significance. But in fact the Goths are never reported to have withdrawn this force from the south. From now until the arrival of the Moors in 711, some two and a half centuries later, the Visigoths occupied Baetica, the southernmost province of the peninsula. Bury makes the attractive suggestion that, although Theoderic went to Spain "in the name of Avitus and the Roman Republic, we cannot doubt that he was deliberately preparing for the eventual fulfilment of the ambition of the Goths to possess Spain themselves, by weakening Suevic power."[5] Whatever the motives of the king, Baetica was paradoxically the first Spanish province to receive a Visigothic garrison, though of all the provinces of Spain it lay furthest from Toulouse; and there is evidence that it was the province where fewest Visigoths were ever to settle down and live permanently.[6]

In the following year, 459, Thederic reinforced his army in Baetica, appointed Sunieric to command it, and recalled Cyrila to Gaul.[7] This southern force was active against the Sueves in 460, the year in which it took Scallabis, and, although Sunieric returned to Gaul in 461, his men still remained in southern Spain.[8] There for a moment we shall leave them.

In the time of Theoderic II, then, Gothic military action against the

Sueves was severe. There was also much diplomatic activity. Here is what Hydatius reports.[9] Twice in the year 460 Theoderic sent embassies to the Sueves.[10] In 461 two more Gothic embassies reached them, and in 465 three more did so.[11] The years 466 and 467 saw yet another pair of embassies sent off by Theoderic and his successor.[12] Nothing is recorded about the purpose of these interminable embassies. No doubt the explanation of Hydatius' silence is that he had no information: he did not know why the diplomats had come. Neither Sueves nor Goths are likely to have taken a remote Hispano-Roman bishop into their confidence, nor will they have had any reason to publicize their activities among the Roman population at large in Galicia. Did even the rank and file of the Sueves themselves know at this date what was going on in the councils of their kings? It may be that the Visigothic king was in general trying to put some limit to Suevic plundering expeditions;[13] but if so, he did not succeed.

The policy of King Euric (466–84), who came to the throne as a result of murdering his elder brother, Theoderic II (just as Theoderic II had reached the throne by murdering his eldest brother, Thorismud) was very different in this respect as in others from the policy of his Romanophile predecessor. He reactivated the force of Goths in southern Spain. In 469 they were operating at Merida and in the neighbourhood of Lisbon, and at Astorga in Galicia, and then again in parts of Lusitania.[14] With that year the Chronicle of Hydatius comes to an end; but happily our knowledge of what was going on continues in some degree owing to the survival of an inscription relating to Merida in 483. This inscription, which exists only in a ninth-century copy and which is metrical (after a fashion) tells us that a certain Salla, after equipping Merida, the capital of Lusitania, with splendid walls, repaired the bridge over the river Guadiana, part of which had collapsed, with the aid of the Bishop Zeno.[15] (The bridge at Merida, by the way, was the largest that the Romans ever built in Spain: it was nearly 800 metres in length with 80 arches.)[16] Now, we know this Salla from Hydatius.[17] Theoderic II, shortly before he was murdered in 466, had sent him as an envoy to the Sueves of Remismund. It follows that the man who repaired the walls and the great bridge at Merida was a Goth; and although the inscription ends by giving the year of the Spanish era, DXXI, that is, A.D. 483, Salla also dates his work to the time of King Euric, *nunc tempore potentis Getarum Eurici regis*. It is beyond question, then, that the Goths were occupying Merida in the last year of King Euric's reign, and that a Goth was in command there. In one of his last references to the south Hydatius had remarked that a band of Goths were making for Merida in 469.[18] Perhaps the city fell at that very time. If not, it must certainly have fallen shortly afterwards. And so I conclude that Gothic military occupation of the south of Spain, both of Baetica and of Lusitania, began in 458, that it continued in existence after the period covered by Hydatius, and that it was only brought to a close by the arrival of the Sarracens in 711.[19] But it does not follow that there were extensive settlements of Gothic colonists there at such an early date. The settlements came later.[20]

It was Euric who began the formal conquest of northern Spain. In 469 he initiated a very much more positive policy than that of Theoderic II, but unhappily this is exactly the point at which Hydatius' Chronicle comes to an end. St. Isidore reports a later stage of Euric's operations. He does not give a precise date, but since he goes on to report the fall of Arles and Marseilles to the Goths in 473 we may presume that what he tells us about Spain happened a little before that year. According to the saint, after plundering parts of Lusitania — this no doubt is a reference to the events of 469 which Hydatius, too, has recorded for us[21] — King Euric went on to capture Pamplona and Saragossa, and thus reduced the whole of "upper Spain" (*Hispania superior*) to his sway. He had achieved what the Sueves had never succeeded in doing, though they had made the attempt twice: at one stroke he had conquered Tarraconensis, the only province of the Spanish peninsula that hitherto the barbarians had always failed to occupy. From the great invasion of 409 until now it alone of the Iberian provinces had scarcely been touched by the barbarians. Now, however, between the years 469 and 472 the forces of Euric took it over. But the province did not fall without resistance. The presence of the Goths was by no means welcome to all the Hispano-Romans of that area. The nobility of Tarraconensis resisted them in arms, one of the rare occasions on which the Western nobility organized armed resistance to the invaders. The Goths had to undertake a military campaign to crush the nobles, but crush them they did. The attitude of the lesser citizens is not recorded: they are not said to have fought for or against anybody.[22]

St. Isidore is not a reliable authority when he speaks about the fifth century without the backing of Hydatius. But fortunately the Gallic chronicler of A.D. 511 supports and supplements the saint's remarks in this connexion. This chronicler states that soon after the fall of the Western Emperor Anthemius in July 472 Euric sent his Count Gauterit to take Pamplona, Saragossa, and some neighbouring cities.[23] A little later a Goth called Heldefred and the Vincentius whom we have already met (p. 175 above) went to besiege Tarragona and to take the maritime cities.[24] This, as St. Isidore puts it, meant the fall of "upper Spain" to the kingdom of Toulouse. The one mistake that Isidore makes in this connexion is to represent Euric himself as taking the field in Spain. The truth was that Euric acted through his generals, Gauterit, Heldefred, and Vincentius. The king himself, deeply though he influenced the history of Spain, is not known ever to have visited the peninsula.[25]

Can we define the date of these events? Shortly after his Spanish expedition Vincentius fell fighting in Italy on behalf of Euric; and not long after his death Euric captured Arles and Marseilles, and thus ended for ever the Roman occupation of Gaul. No part of France has ever since been governed by an Italian power. These events took place before the accession of the Eastern Emperor Zeno in October 474. Let us say, then, that Vincentius died in the campaigning season of 473 (though 474 is not out of the question); and so the conquest of "upper Spain" is securely dated to the seasons of 472 and 473. Bury rightly remarked that when Euric died less than a dozen years later, in 484, the Spanish peninsula apart from the Suevian kingdom in the northwest (and, we may add, the wild mountains of the Basques) was entirely under the dominion of the Goths. And that, for what it is worth, was more or less the opinion of Jordanes, who tells us that before Euric died he ruled in his own right, and not as the vassal of the emperor, the whole of the Spanish and Gallic provinces.[26] In the reign of the Western Emperor Anthemius (467–72), however, some persons in Tarragona still recognized Leo I and Anthemius as their rightful rulers and set up a dedication to them in that city. But very soon after Anthemius' death the city and the province of which it was the capital, after holding out against the barbarians for so long, passed from Roman power for ever.[27]

These actions of Euric's armies were purely military operations, and they resulted in the political submission of Tarraconensis. But it would be going beyond the evidence to suppose that the Goths began to settle in Spain in substantial numbers in the time of Euric. We can fairly believe no more than that the garrison troops and some administrators were planted in the peninsula. But things changed towards the end of the century. The Chronicle of Saragossa suggests that something different came about in 494, ten years after Euric was in his grave. According to this chronicle, "the Goths entered Spain" in that year;[28] and the words suggest a considerable Visigothic immigration south of the Pyrenees in 494. In 497 the Goths are said explicitly to have settled in Spain, evidently on an extensive scale: indeed, one student of the period has rather imaginatively called this influx of Goths into Spain an "avalanche."[29] And finally, that same source which speaks of the events of 494 and 497 tells us that in 506 Tortosa (the Roman Dertosa) near the mouth of the Ebro was "entered by the Goths."[30]

From all this it seems to follow clearly enough that the Gothic military conquest of Spain took place in the reigns of Theoderic II and Euric, whereas Gothic settlement in Spain on an extensive scale took place only towards the end of the fifth century and in the first few years of the sixth, that is to say, during the reign of King Alaric II (484–507). So all four Gothic kings, Theoderic I, Theoderic II, Euric, and Alaric II, had distinct and different attitudes towards Spain. Their attitudes ranged from the indulgent neutrality of Theoderic I to the outright aggression and the occupation of southern Spain in the time of Theoderic II, and from the military conquest of the north under Euric to the extensive settlement there in the reign of Alaric II.

The resistance put up vainly by the Roman aristocracy of Tarraconensis around the years 472–73 (p. 191 above) was not the end of Roman opposition to the conquest. There also appeared on the scene in eastern Spain two "tyrants," that is to say, two usurpers. A certain Burdunelus seized power in 496 and was betrayed by his followers and sent to Toulouse, where the Goths put him to a gruesome death. The scene of his activities is not mentioned, but there can be little doubt that it was somewhere in Tarraconensis, perhaps near Saragossa, where lived our authority for the little that is known about him: no other area of Spain is known to have been actively threatened with Gothic settlement at this date. And secondly, we hear of the "tyrant" Peter, who established himself at Tortosa and was put to death by the Goths in 506.[31] The Goths, it seems, were remorseless towards Spanish rebels in this period. Were they remorseless because the rebels were Spanish, or because they were usurpers, or because they had some social significance that is now hidden from us? To these questions there can be no answer. At all events, some remarks about the parallels between Spain and the British tyrants of the years following 410 will be found in *Britannia,* viii (1978), 316 f. The probability is that after the political authority of Rome had vanished representatives of the doomed Hispano-Roman nobility, or of some other social class, seized a futile power in some irregular way — presumably without reference to the remote and helpless emperor — and tried without lasting success to enlist provincial levies, to organize local defences against the invading barbarians, and to prolong the twilight of Roman civilization. Whatever the exact nature of the movement, a very few years saw its beginning and its end.

What we find, then, is that the Goths controlled southern and southwestern Spain since soon after the middle of the fifth century. That is to say, they had garrisons there and presumably could issue orders to the Roman provincial governors and other Roman officials who still survived in the provinces of Baetica and Lusitania. Now since Euric conquered the north of the country, or at any rate the province of Tarraconensis, at the beginning of his reign, it would follow that he had lines of communication between Tarraconensis and his southern dominions in Baetica and Lusitania. In fact, he must have won control of practically the whole of the

Spanish peninsula (apart, of course, from the Suevic kingdom in Galicia and the Basques in their mountains), though the sequence of events in Carthaginiensis is wholly unknown. But Gothic settlement in Spain on a considerable scale began only at the very end of the century and is explicitly attested only for the province of Tarraconensis. Yet there is a tiny piece of evidence which suggests that some Goths may have settled even in Baetica soon after the year 500, for we still possess the sarcophagus of a lady named Hilduarens, doubtless a Gothic woman, who died at Ecija (the Roman Astigi), not far from Cordoba in 504.[32] And in addition we know of the Gothic garrisons in Merida and Seville. But there is reason to think that in the long run fewer Goths settled in Baetica than in any other province of their Spanish kingdom.[33]

It cannot be denied that we have no more than fragments and shreds of evidence. But if we accept the view that the Goths conquered southern Spain only in the middle of the sixth century, our position will be even weaker.[34] In this case we must not only admit that we have no evidence whatever to support any such theory, but—what is worse—we have to ignore or to explain away such scraps of testimony as do exist. In fact, there is not a single hint in any of our sources of information that a conquest of southern Spain took place in the mid-sixth century. At that time we hear of a revolt against the Gothic government—the revolt of Cordoba—which is a very different thing from a conquest and indeed presupposes a conquest.[35]

II. THE CATHOLIC CHURCH

It is strange that Hydatius should give us so little information about the Catholic church in the forty years following 427, the year in which he himself was consecrated as bishop: stranger still that for the last ten years covered by his chronicle he never mentions the church at all, though in those years it was not altogether a church without a history. What he does in general is to provide a number of disconnected pieces of information which do not allow us to write a continuous history of the church in Spain in the mid-fifth century; and indeed some of what he tells us would be all but unintelligible had we not some further information at our disposal to throw light on it. It is certain that what chiefly interested thoughtful Spanish Catholics in that twilight period between the collapse of Roman power and the Visigothic conquest of the Iberian peninsula was the struggle against the dark forces of Priscillianism. Yet Hydatius gives us no systematic account of the progress of that strange controversy.

Here are examples of what he does. Most of the notices in his chronicle referring to the papacy are later intrusions into his text and are not his own work at all.[36] But under the year 447 he mentions that Leo I (440–61) was presiding over the Roman church. It was reasonable for Hydatius to put the pope's *floruit* in this year, the year of his important correspondence with the Spanish bishop Turribius on the problem of Priscillianism. We still possess Leo's letter, which is dated 21 July 447.[37] It is nevertheless peculiar that when the chronicler has occasion to mention the publication of anti-Manichaean documents a couple of years earlier, in 445, he says that the publication was due to "the bishop who was then presiding at Rome."[38] Why not mention Leo's name at that point rather than wait until the entry of 447? Why leave the pope of 445 apparently anonymous? It almost looks as though Hydatius was not certain who was pope in 445, though we might think that if he did not know the name of the current pope he could hardly have written a chronicle at all. Again, at Lugo in 433 Pastor and Syagrius were consecrated as bishops against the will of Agrestius, bishop of Lugo.[39] Hydatius states the fact, but he does not tell us who was heterodox and who was orthodox. In fact, we happen to know that Pastor and Syagrius were Catholics and that they published some writings against Priscillianism, a fact which Hydatius omits to tell us. The chronicler gives no explanation and no hint at the background of the dispute; but since Pastor and Syagrius were Catholics, Agrestius presumably had Priscillianist leanings.[40] Moreover, in 441 Bishop Sabinus was driven from his see of Seville, and Epiphanius was consecrated in his place "by fraud, not justice," according to Hydatius; and Sabinus, who had gone to Gaul, was able to return home to Seville only about twenty years later.[41] Once more the chronicler says nothing of the causes and nature of the dissensions; but he does express disapproval of Epiphanius, a fact which suggests that the new bishop was a Priscillianist, and hence that Sabinus was a Catholic.[42]

A question which we cannot answer concerns the events of 445. In that year some Manichaeans were unmasked in Astorga, and a record of the episcopal enquiry which was held when they were exposed was sent by Hydatius himself and by Turribius, bishop of Astorga (the correspondent of Pope Leo), who had heard the heretics, to Antoninus of Merida, metropolitan of the province of Lusitania. It is not clear why the metropolitan of Lusitania should have been involved in an incident that took place in Galicia.[43] Where was the metropolitan of Braga? The extraordinary fact is that throughout the whole of his chronicle Hydatius never once refers to the metropolitan see of his own province: he neither names nor even hints at the existence of a bishop of Braga. I do not know how to account for this oddity. As for the events of 445, was it the case that in that year the Sueves had suppressed the Catholic bishopric of their capital city, Braga, or at any rate that they had made conditions there so harsh that the metropolitan was no longer able adequately to carry out his duties? Improbable, for a metropolitan of Braga is still found in the year 538 under the Arian rulers, and the first Catholic councils have nothing to say about any such act of suppression or persecution, which would have been out of character with the barbarian kingdoms of Europe. It looks, then, as though the metropolitan of Braga in the year in question, 445, could not be trusted to deal firmly with Manichaeans or Priscillianists. Perhaps he was himself tainted with one or other of these heinous errors. But even if this were so, it is still a mystery why the chronicler mentions none of the other Galician metropolitans: they can hardly have been heretics to a man.

Leo's full disquisition against the Priscillianists (the letter to Turribius which we have already mentioned) was brought in the year 447 to the Spanish bishops by Pervincus, one of Turribius' deacons, and was approved by the bishops of Galicia. But some of them did not approve it in good faith.[44] Evidently, the heresy was still making inroads into the Galician hierarchy, still winning adherents in high places there; and those two bishops, Agrestius and Epiphanius, were not alone in their heretical tendencies. But the reception of Leo's letter has a further significance. It shows not only that communication with Italy was still open at this date but also that the bishops of Galicia were able to meet together in a synod even in the darkest days of Suevian overlordship. There was no ban as yet on their assembling together, for the pagan monarchs were even more tolerant in this respect than some of their Arian successors were to be later on. Here, as throughout the whole of Hydatius' chronicle, there is no trace of a persecution of the Catholic church by the Sueves. Even under the rule of the most ferocious pagan kings, when the chronicler tells of many crimes, he never speaks of the persecution of Catholics. What he does mention is the persecution of Manichaeans and Priscillianists by the Catholics themselves. In the middle of wars and plundering expeditions, the sack of cities and the fall of the Roman Empire Catholics were able to persecute their opponents and neighbours, and they performed this task with relish.

In 448 a Roman from the imperial capital, Pascentius by name, who had been living in Astorga and who now fled from it, was arrested by Antoninus of Merida on a charge of Manichaeism and was expelled from Lusitania, where he had taken refuge.[45] Once again, it was the Catholics who were the persecutors. It would be interesting to know the attitude of the new king, Rechiarius, himself a Catholic. We do not hear that he incited Antoninus or that he aided or abetted him by word or deed. Antoninus' action in expelling Pascentius from Lusitania could have been considered a gross interference with the secular law, but Hydatius reports no reaction on Rechiarius' part. Perhaps the subtleties of Roman law meant little to this crude barbarian.

That is as far as the chronicler takes the story of Priscillianism in his day, and it all amounts to little. The heresy had won adherents on an extensive scale among the Catholic hierarchy, not least in Galicia. A bishop of Lugo and a metropolitan of Seville and perhaps also of Braga were among the heresy's conquests. But to the barbarian kings, even to the Catholic Rechiarius, all these things were matters of indifference.

There exists also some information about the discipline of the church in those dark years towards the end of the period that Hydatius covers. In 463 or 464 Ascanius, metropolitan of Tarragona, and the other bishops of his province met together at a synod.[46] Like the landowners (p. 177 above), the bishops, too, were able to organize and travel to an agreed meeting place. Civilized life had by no means broken wholly down in Tarraconensis in the mid-sixties, though conditions may well have been very different in Galicia at that same date. This synod wrote to Pope Hilary asking for his advice on their "false brother," Silvanus, bishop of Calahorra. Seven or eight years previously Silvanus had consecrated a bishop illegitimately, for the people of the area where the new bishop was to serve had not asked for any such appointment. That is to say, Silvanus had established single-handed a new see (which is never mentioned again). Not only that, but he had also gone on to appoint to a bishopric a priest who belonged to another diocese than his own, the diocese of Saragossa, in spite of the priest's protests. The bishop of Saragossa had accordingly raised the matter at a synod of the bishops of Tarraconensis, for Silvanus had frequently disregarded the reprimands of neighbouring bishops "with the spirit of rebellion" and "with damnable obstinacy."[47] Ascanius now asked the pope what he ought to do about Silvanus and also about those whom Silvanus had consecrated.

It is clear from this letter that the bishops of Tarraconensis held the see of Rome in the most profound respect. They had no hesitation in looking to Rome for guidance. For them the bishop of Rome was beyond all question the vicar of St. Peter, to be feared abjectly, to be loved by all. His authority was undisputed. He would give his instructions without error and without presumption but with the deliberation worthy of a pontiff. This respectful attitude towards the papacy continued so long as the rulers of Spain were heretics. But, surprisingly, in the seventh century when the rulers of Spain were devout Catholics the Spanish bishops revealed a different attitude. They then either ignored Rome altogether or reacted to the approaches of the popes with a truculent arrogance that would have dismayed and shocked Ascanius — and there is no hint in our evidence that the bishops of Tarraconensis were any more respectful in the seventh century than their brethren in the other five provinces of the Gothic kingdom.

A year or so after sending off their letter Ascanius and the other bishops of Tarraconensis wrote again to Rome, and on this occasion their attitude towards canon law was decidedly less orthodox and more simple-hearted. Nundinarius, bishop of Barcelona, had recently died. He had bequeathed such property as he possessed to another cleric, whose name was Irenaeus and whom he had himself appointed as bishop of some subordinate town in his own see, an illegal action which, however, had the consent of his comprovincials. On his deathbed Nundinarius had gone so far as to ask that Irenaeus be appointed as his own successor in the see of Barcelona. All the clergy and populace of Barcelona including the richest and most numerous of the provincials of the neighbourhood, hoped that Irenaeus would indeed be appointed. The bishops had translated Irenaeus, as the dead Nundinarius had wished; and they were now writing to Pope Hilary asking him to confirm what they had done. They ended their letter by remarking with some little surprise that the Pope had not yet replied to their letter about Silvanus. Perhaps that was due, they politely added, to the negligence of their messenger or to the difficulty of the long journey to Rome. They did not suggest that it might equally well be due to the negligence of Hilary himself.[48]

On 19 November 465 a synod of bishops, including some Gauls and Africans, headed by Hilary (whose birthday fell on that day), met together in the church of St. Mary in Rome. And the meeting is of especial interest in that it is the first Roman synod of which we still possess *verbatim* minutes, though the details of those minutes do not concern us now. On 30 December the pope wrote at last to Ascanius and the other bishops of Tarraconensis, acknowledging receipt of both letters, that about Silvanus and that about Irenaeus. His decretal survives.[49] In it he gives strict instructions (i) that no bishop should be consecrated without the knowledge of the metropolitan, Ascanius; (ii) that no one should leave his own church and go to another—the bishops had been wholly wrong to approve of Irenaeus' translation; (iii) that Irenaeus must go back to his original see—if he refused to go he would be demoted from the rank of bishop[50]—and a new bishop must be appointed in a regular fashion from among the local clergy at Barcelona, since a bishopric must never be regarded as descending by hereditary right; (iv) that although the bishops who had been ordained by Silvanus without Ascanius' knowledge ought strictly to be removed from office Hilary agreed that, provided none of them had been married, he would confirm their appointments. He reminded the bishops of Tarraconensis that there must never be two bishops in the one church—for some time Nundinarius and Irenaeus appear to have been bishops in the one church—that no illiterate could be appointed to the episcopacy, or anyone who was physically blemished, or an expenient. (The pope does not explain, and we cannot conjecture, why he felt it necessary to make these last points.) The bishops must not pay so much attention to the requests of the people—such as the recent request of the people of Barcelona—as to abandon the will of God.

This letter was carried to Spain by a subdeacon called Trajan, and the pope does not express in it any fear that the journey might be a dangerous one. In fact, there is no evidence that in this period the journey from Italy to Tarragona was beset by dangers either from the Vandals or from anyone else. At about the same time the pope wrote a stiff rebuke to Ascanius;[51] and it is beyond doubt that Ascanius had acted in a manner that was unusual in a metropolitan bishop.

What emerges from this correspondence is that life in at least the province of Tarraconensis was going ahead as though the old Roman peace was still undisturbed. No doubt the Visigothic invasion of 456–57 had caused untold havoc in the west of the Iberian peninsula, and the western cities were always liable to surprise by the Sueves. No doubt, too, Tarraconensis had been troubled by Basilius and the Bacaudae before 454. But in Tarraconensis in the sixties of the century meetings were held, men travelled, letters were delivered, and ideas were discussed and debated and communicated as though the Sueves and the Vandals and the other barbarians were still far away beyond the Rhine and the Danube, and the tranquillity of Spain was still unbroken. From the letters of the bishops and the pope we could not guess that a spear had ever been thrown in anger or a house burned or a town pillaged or a woman raped south of the Pyrenees. So far as this correspondence goes, life continued in its conventional and commonplace way as it had done since the Roman conquest of Spain had been brought to completion by Caesar Augustus five hundred years before. But would the picture be unchanged if the papal letters had been addressed not to Tarraconensis but to Galicia? And if Trajan had tried to continue his journey so as to end it not at Tarragona but at Braga, would he ever have reached his destination?

III. THE DARK AGE OF GALICIA

After the year 469, the year with which Hydatius closed his chronicle, we have no continuous source of information about events in Spain; and although St. Isidore has something to tell us about the Visigothic part of the country in the sixth century our ignorance of the Suevic kingdom at that period is almost total.

At some date in this obscure time the Sueves managed to expand their kingdom southwards so that it reached the mouth of the River Tagus instead of that of the Douro. And so in the later sixth century, when sources of information become available again, the term "Galicia" refers to a larger province than had been known there in Roman times and during Hydatius' lifetime. That is why the Second Council of Braga, which met in 572, was attended by the bishops of Viseu, Coimbra, Idanha, and Lamego. And these four bishoprics are included in the province of Galicia in the Suevic *Parochiale,* which dates from the period 572–82. Now, when the Visigoths overran the Suevic kingdom in 585 and incorporated it in their own realm, they did not at first change the boundaries of Galicia and Lusitania, but left them as they had become during the dark age of the later fifth and early sixth century. It was only towards the middle of the seventh century that the old frontiers were at last restored. The initiative came from one Orontius, who was metropolitan of Lusitania *c.* 638–53. He persuaded King Reccesuinth (653–72) to restore to Lusitania the dioceses which it had lost to Galicia so many years earlier. The matter was mentioned at the Council of Merida which met in 666, but at that time the decision to revert to the fifth-century definition of "Galicia" already lay in the past: the question only arose because the decision of Reccesuinth had given rise to a dispute between the sees of Idanha (the Roman Igita) and Salamanca.[52] And so we find that this Council of Merida in 666, which was a provincial synod of the bishops of Lusitania, was attended by the bishops of Lisbon (Olisippo), Lamego, Idanho, and Coimbra. On the other hand, the Third Council of Braga, which met in 675 and which was a synod of the bishops of the province of Galicia, was attended by the bishops of Braga, Tuy, Oporto, Astorga, Britonia, Orense, Lugo, and Iria (the modern El Padron), but by no bishop from the dioceses which lay between the lower Douro and the lower Tagus. These sees were now included in the province of Lusitania and no longer in that of Galicia. Indeed, at the Council of Merida the bishop of Idanha, a Goth or a Sueve called Sclua, somewhat aggressively signed himself at the end of the minutes as "Sclua, bishop of the city of Idanha belonging to the province of Merida,"[53] a formula that does not recur among the very numerous Spanish signatory lists. Sclua is an enthusiast and will leave no one in any doubt: he does not belong to Galicia but to Lusitania. It is sad that we do not know whether his fervour was due to local or provincial pride, to a personal whim, to hostility to Sueves, or to some other current of feeling.

In the fifth century, or at any rate in the part of it which Hydatius' chronicle covers, there appear to have been no Suevic settlements in the southern tip of Galicia (in the sixth-century meaning of that term) be-

tween the lower Douro and the lower Tagus. On the contrary, this area
was the victim of their vicious attacks. The Sueves entered Lisbon treacherously in 457 and again in 469.[54] They treacherously entered Coimbra in
465 and three years later destroyed it.[55] (But when we hear of cities being
"destroyed" we must not take the term too seriously, and in fact Coimbra
survived as a bishopric even in the seventh century.) In Coimbra in 465 the
barbarians plundered the "noble family" of a man called Cantaber. It may
not be a coincidence that at the Council of Merida which, as we have seen,
met in the year 666 the bishop of Coimbra was called Cantaber; and it is
not out of the question that the two men were related, that the existence
of this noble family was continuous, and that the Cantabri as an eminent
family had survived all the storms and upsets of at least two centuries.[56]
However that may be, the Sueves harassed the countryside around the
mouth of the Douro in 457, and two years later attacked Oporto.[57] They
did not live in these places at the time when they were plundering them;
and they did not live in the territory of Aquae Flaviae in 460, for in that
year they caused destruction there and carried off Hydatius himself from
it. Beyond question, when these events were taking place, the region between the lower Douro and the lower Tagus was still Roman and still part
of the old Roman province of Lusitania.

Can we find out when approximately they expanded into this southern
area? When did they stop raiding the place and instead begin to settle in
it? The date must fall after 469, when they were still pillaging it—and Hydatius would hardly have avoided making mention of such an annexation,
if he had known of it. But the date may well have fallen before the end of
the century, for after 500 or at any rate 511 (when Theoderic the Great, the
Ostrogothic king of Italy, became regent of Spain), the opportunity for
annexation would hardly have arisen. The Goths would scarcely have tol-
erated Suevic expansion after that time. Let us agree, then, that the Sueves
reached the Tagus in the period 470–510. There is no certain means of nar-
rowing these limits; but it is not out of the question that a letter of Pope
Simplicius to a Bishop Zeno may be relevant to the problem.[58] The Zeno
to whom the letter is addressed is usually assigned to the see of Seville; but
conclusive arguments have now been brought forward to detach him from
that city, and from an inscription we hear of a Zeno who was metropolitan
of Lusitania in the year 483.[59] It would be an unusual coincidence if the
metropolitans of Baetica and Lusitania were both called by the Greek name
Zeno at that one time, and we may safely suppose that the two Zenos are
in fact one and the same person, the bishop of Merida. Now, Pope Simplicius survived until 10 March 483, and he could well have written to Zeno
of Lusitania in or before the last months of his life—perhaps long before,

for we do not know when exactly Zeno was appointed as metropolitan. The letter in question, after complimenting Zeno on his excellent administration of his see, informs him that his position will be strengthened if he is promoted to serve as a papal vicar: "fortified by the energy of this office you would in no wise permit the decrees instituted by the apostles and the boundaries (*terminos*) of the holy fathers to be transcended."[60] At this period the popes appointed papal vicars from time to time in order to deal with important or urgent problems which called for swift and decisive action on the spot and which could not await the long delays of communication with Rome. But this is an unusually vague commission. The vicar's duties are not specified at all except in the matter of the "boundaries"; and it looks as though the pope made the appointment primarily in order to deal with the contraction of the old province of Lusitania.[61] A major question affecting the boundaries of the province appears to have been under urgent consideration. It was a problem of such consequence as to require the attention of a papal vicar; and since the metropolitan was so excellent an administrator and diplomat he was upgraded to the post. It may be that the problem to which Simplicius refers was nothing other than the expansion of the Sueves and the consequent loss to Lusitania of a number of its dioceses, a loss of which the church did not approve but which it could not prevent. The letter was written at latest in March 483; but the news of the crisis in Lusitania will have taken some time to travel to Rome. The pope's decision to appoint a papal vicar in Spain will not have been made precipitately. The expansion of the Sueves, therefore, probably took place well before the year 483. We might think it likely that the barbarians risked such an audacious act when Euric was an old man rather than when he was in his prime; and so we could go on to say that the Sueves expanded about the year 480. But on the other hand it may be that the expansion had taken place several years earlier, in the vicinity of the year 470, when Euric was in his prime but was preoccupied with events elsewhere: certainly the region between the lower Douro and the lower Tagus was at that time under very heavy pressure from the Sueves.

There is much in all this that is hypothetical; but the arguments, such as they are, suggest that the province of Galicia took on its sixth-century area, when the boundary in the south lay on the Tagus and no longer on the Douro, during the reign of King Euric. After the turn of the century the Visigoths or their Ostrogothic overlords were too strong to be harassed or provoked. The Sueves will have remained at peace in the sixth century, whether they liked peace or not. There was nothing to be gained by challenging neighbours who were so much more powerful than themselves and who had already beaten them into the dust in 456. Even when the

Visigothic kingdom of Spain was in a state of chaos and near disintegration during the disastrous reign of King Athanagild (555–68) and extensive areas of it near the Suevic border were in revolt against the government of Toledo the Sueves made no move to expand their kingdom eastwards at the expense of the ill-led and disorganized Goths.[62]

How were the Sueves governed during this dark age, in the years which Hydatius' chronicle does not cover? At one stage in the fifth century it had looked as though Hermeric and his son Rechila and his grandson Rechiarius had managed to found a permanent hereditary dynasty. But in fact after Rechiarius' death the monarchy lapsed for a number of years, and the Sueves reverted to a system of unrelated war leaders. At the time when Hydatius' chronicle ends, then, the monarchy was not firmly established. It had recently been overthrown, and it was not out of the question that it would be abolished again.

It is well known that from the year 469, the year with which Hydatius ended his historical work, until about 560, when St. Martin of Braga was active in Galicia, we do not know even the names of the kings, if kings there were. The only evidence for the very existence of the monarchy in these ninety years is a passage towards the close of St. Isidore's *History of the Sueves* in which, having come to the end of his one and only source of information, the chronicle of Hydatius, he remarks that there followed many Suevic kings, all of whom were Arian heretics until the reign of Theodemir in the 560s.[63] But how did Isidore know that there were many kings in that period if he no longer had any source of information to draw upon? How can we account for the fact that he does not name a single one of these "many" Arian kings? Did he know anything whatever about them? Are we to believe that Isidore did indeed have oral sources of information at his disposal but that he shrank from speaking in detail about Arian monarchs because they were so uncongenial to him? No, for no Catholic author tells us more about uncongenial Gothic and Suevian Arian monarchs than St. Isidore, who wrote a *History of the Goths* and a *History of the Sueves* to say nothing of his *History of the Vandals*.[64] Now, the Sueves appear to have had a king named Veremund in the year 485, though that is disputed, and we cannot discuss Veremund at present. But the fact that Isidore asserts that they had kings is no proof that that was continuously the case: they may well have lived for some of the time without an hereditary monarchy or without any kind of monarchy at all, especially when they were at peace. St. Isidore, we may think, having no sources has told us only what he thought was probable. It may or may not have been fact. But if he is right and such kings existed, it is hardly open to doubt that he is also right on the further assertion that they were Arians.

We have some information about an intriguing event that took place in the period of darkness. This is the arrival of a swarm of Britons in the neighbourhood of Mondoñedo, where they founded a "British Church," *ecclesia Britoniensis* or *Britanniensis.* I have discussed this influx of Britons elsewhere and need not linger over the diocese of Britonia here.[65] Presumably the immigrants were in flight from the Saxon or less probably the Irish invaders of their country.[66] It is improbable that they exterminated the local Hispano-Roman population of the region in which they now settled; and yet it is puzzling that in the one document that refers to the British church there is no reference whatever to the native Roman population around Mondoñedo. Had they been expelled by the invaders from the huge area of the diocese? Had they migrated from it voluntarily? Or were they still pagans who had no parishes that could be included in the *Parochiale* which alone tells us of the bishopric? And was the organization of this British church based on monasteries rather than on parishes, as some have believed? These are only a few of the questions that we cannot answer when we try to discuss the *ecclesia Britoniensis.*

The British invasion of Armorica in the northwest of France seems to have taken place for the most part in two waves. The first of these has been dated to the third quarter of the fifth century, when we hear of numerous Britons in northwestern Gaul. The later fifth century and the first half of the sixth saw immigration from Britain to Armorica on a reduced scale. But in 552 and in 577 the Saxons won the battles of Old Sarum and of Dyrham (six miles north of Bath) respectively, the second of these victories delivering over to them the lower reaches of the river Severn. Accordingly, the third quarter of the sixth century may have brought an even more massive immigration of Britons into Armorica than that of the previous century.[67] Perhaps it is more likely that the British settlement in Spain is to be associated with the later rather than with the earlier flight. We might suppose that in the years 450–70 there was no cause for British fugitives to sail to so remote a district as Galicia, whereas in 550–80 most of the best sites in Brittany had already been occupied, and some of the migrants accordingly decided to try their luck further afield. Thus, too, we could account for the vagueness of the writer of the *Parochiale* when he comes to deal with the British church: the settlement was very recent—it may even have been still in progress when the author of the compilation was writing in 569—and the turmoil was still such that he could gather no precise information beyond a few words about the monastery of a certain Maximus.

In the year 538 communications between Galicia and Rome seem to have been unimpeded. On 1 March of that year Pope Vigilius (537–55) in

Rome wrote a letter to Profuturus, metropolitan bishop of Braga, who had asked his advice on several problems that had arisen in Galicia. The metropolitan's letter has been lost, but we still possess the pope's reply.[68] In it Vigilius remarks on the fact that the Galician Catholics live "in the most outlying parts of the world" (*extremis mundi partibus*), and he compliments Profuturus on his piety. From the decretal as a whole a number of inferences may be drawn about life in the Suevic kingdom during its obscurest age.[69] There is no hint at any repression of the Catholics by the Arian government of the country. Many problems had arisen but not that of persecution. There appears to have been nothing unusual in a Catholic's sending a letter to Italy or in writing to the pope. The Catholics, if we may judge by Vigilius' letter, were free to correspond and to worship as they pleased, free to construct new churches and to dedicate them, free to rebuild those that needed repair. The Catholic hierarchy continued to work unimpeded by the state, and the pope could refer casually to the "other bishops throughout their dioceses."[70] Further, it is clear that this hierarchy was free to comment on beliefs which it regarded as heretical and to defend its dogmas against its opponents. It could speak and act against Priscillianism and Manichaeism, and it need not be doubted that it could act against Arianism itself. In his letter to the pope Profuturus had expressed no need for enlightenment on any tenet of Arian doctrine, as he required a pronouncement on the loathing of the Priscillianists for animal flesh. The reason, no doubt, was that in the Catholic view the theoretical position of the Arians had been exploded generations ago. There was nothing further to be said against them. The errors of Arianism were now clear to all, except the Arians. What Profuturus asks on the subject of Arianism is how to treat Catholics who had joined those heretics and who now wished to return to the fold. If it was in general careerists and time-servers who tended to join the Arians it would be interesting to know what it was that was attracting them back to Catholicism in the year 538. Whatever the reason, the Sueves appear to have put no obstacle in the path of the rebaptized who wished to rejoin the Catholic church.

But before the year 560 or thereabouts something happened which caused the Suevic rulers to change their attitude towards the Catholic church and to modify their tolerance of it. For when Lucretius, metropolitan of Braga, addressed the First Council of Braga on the Kalends of May, 561, he distinctly implied that synods of the Catholic church in Galicia had been banned by the kings and that the ban had only now been lifted.[71] It was certainly the case that in the neighbouring kingdom of the Visigoths the meeting of provincial synods of the Catholic church had been prohibited, probably by King Agila in the years 549–55; and national assemblies embracing all the provinces of the Spanish kingdom had never been permitted by the Visigothic kings.[72] The same became the case now in Galicia, though it had not been so at the time when Pope Leo advised the Spanish bishops to meet in 447. The position in 538, when Vigilius wrote to Profuturus, is unfortunately not clear.

Why were synods banned? It might be argued that Agila had banned synods in the Visigothic kingdom because of the Byzantine landings on the south coast of his realm in 552: he feared that the Catholics of Spain, if adequately organized, would join the invaders or at any rate would assist them, should they break out of Malaga and Cartagena and penetrate northwards into the interior of the Visigothic kingdom. And although it is not easy to imagine a sixth-century synodical meeting of bishops planning a military campaign or an underground movement to support the Byzantines or anybody else, we might continue the argument by supposing that the Catholics among the Hispano-Romans would be regarded by the government as a "fifth column" in the country if the Byzantines should advance from their bridgeheads on the coast into the interior.

Possibly: but even the most pessimistic of Suevian military judges in his moments of deepest gloom would scarcely have expected that the soldiers of East Rome would march from Malaga and Cartagena to the remote mountains of Galicia, destroying Toledo and the Visigothic kingdom on the way. That would indeed have been a despondent forecast. And equally it would have been a wildly fanatical supporter of Byzantium who would have supposed that the Catholics of the Suevic kingdom would have welcomed the East Roman soldiers or that they would have risen in arms to a man in order to assist them. After all, when the Byzantines landed in Cartagena the substantial citizens of that city took flight into the kingdom of ·the heretical Visigoths rather than face the taxes and the grinding misrule of the Catholic officials of Justinian.[73] There was no very obvious reason, then, why the Suevic kings should have banned the synods of the Catholic bishops because the Byzantines had landed in Malaga and Cartagena.

And yet there is no doubt about the existence of the ban. Were the Hispano-Romans threatening a revolt? Was there a potential Athanagild in Galicia contemporary with the real Athanagild in Baetica? If so, history knows nothing of him. Those maritime communications between Frankish Gaul and Galicia that we hear of at a somewhat later date (p. 172 above) — were they threatening the position of Suevic overlordship in Galicia in some way that Gregory of Tours knew nothing about? But they were certainly not threatening the Visigoths, and yet the Visigoths, too, had banned Catholic provincial synods. Clearly, some factor that affected both the kingdoms in the peninsula — the Visigothic kingdom as well as the remote northwest—began to influence both governments alike in the middle of the century; and both alike drew the conclusion that it would be unsafe to allow the Catholic bishops to assemble in any numbers. But what that factor may have been, and whether such meetings would in fact have been dangerous, we cannot tell.

11

Spain and Britain

The history of most of western Europe in the middle and later fifth century can hardly be said to be known. The areas of which we have some detailed knowledge are very much the exceptions—southern Gaul, Italy, and momentarily that part of Austria which lies between the rivers Mur and Danube (for Eugippius' *Life of Severinus* gives us an extraordinarily vivid glimpse of conditions in Noricum late in the century). We sometimes forget that there is a fourth exceptional region: thanks to Hydatius we have a continuous chronicle of events in Spain, or at any rate in northwestern Spain, down to 469. It is strange that what the ancients regarded as one of the remotest parts of the Western Empire should be so well documented (relatively) at a time when northern Gaul and the Rhineland and even romanized Baetica itself are all but beyond our knowledge. It cannot be said that we know very much about Astorga and Lugo in the middle of the fifth century; and yet we know more about them than we know of London and Paris and not much less than we know of Athens and Jerusalem in those same years.

True, we cannot catch a clear glimpse of any individual person who lived in Galicia at that time. We know no Hispano-Roman even to the extent that we know Sidonius Apollinaris in southern Gaul and no barbarian to the extent that we know King Theoderic in Italy. The personality of Hydatius himself hardly exists, and the characters of the various Suevian kings are as obscure to us as the personalities of Vortigern and of Hengist and Horsa (if they ever existed). So far from being able to define differences in the Suevian kings' policies, we do not know even that they had policies. Perhaps they just lashed out blindly from year to year at any place that they suspected would supply them with food, valuables, or money.

The courts of the Visigothic kings of Toulouse and of the Ostrogothic kings of Ravenna were crowded not only with fur-clad barbarians but also with Romans—lawyers, diplomats, officials, advisers, bishops, and so on. But we never hear of Roman lawyers and counsellors at the court of Rechila or of Rechiarius; and the reason doubtless is that these monarchs employed none. They formed their own plans without Roman aid. They were marauders, and, so far as Hydatius knew, they were nothing else. They acted on too low a level to need theoretical discussion or a knowledge of precedent or protocol. Not being federates, they did not need to regulate their land relationships in accordance with Roman law. Having no Latin law-code they needed no Roman lawyers. Their diplomacy was evidently too crude to call for the subtleties of Roman diplomats. For the most part they negotiated with foreign powers through Suevian, not Roman, envoys, though admittedly on one occasion Hermeric negotiated with the imperial court through the bishop Symphosius, and at the end of Hydatius' period (in 469) Remismund sent the Roman Lusidius, a native of Lisbon, with a number of Sueves to negotiate with the emperor.[1]

The result is that, although some Romans could draw vivid pictures of the court of Toulouse, no one could describe the court of Braga. No Roman was sufficiently familiar with it. Information about Theoderic II of Toulouse or about Theoderic the Great of Ravenna was available to civilized Gauls and Italians, but there was no information about Rechila. The outside world learned dimly, if at all, about his raids and outrages, but not of his day-to-day life, his plans, his religion, his relations with his henchmen and with his hard-pressed subjects. And even if any Roman could have written about the daily life of the Suevian kings, as Sidonius wrote about that of Theoderic, he would hardly have wished to do so. He would have had no public. Men were glad to have information about the appearance and daily life of Theoderic II of Toulouse. He was an important monarch in a rich and populous region, who could even set up a Roman emperor, if he chose. There were many Roman noblemen among his advisers and confidants. Even the Burgundian (or Frankish) prince Sigismer was of much interest, and c. 470 Sidonius wrote a lively description of him and his colourful bodyguard to a prominent citizen of Lyons.[2] But no one cared about the personality or the activities of a mountain brigand in Galicia at the world's edge. What went on in those remote and rain-swept uplands interested nobody, except the unfortunates who lived there. We may wonder whether Sidonius himself knew much more than we do about the court of Maldras or of Framtane. It can hardly be doubted that he was very much less interested than we are.

And yet, surprisingly, the Gothic kings were very interested indeed in the activities of the Sueves. Hydatius reports the despatch of endless embassies from Toulouse to Braga and from Braga to Toulouse (and it is significant of his position that he can tell us the purpose of not a single one of them). On two occasions Visigothic women were sent off to marry Suevic kings, a prospect that they may have found less than exhilarating. The reason for this interest of the Visigothic court in Galicia is obscure. Perhaps even at this early date the Goths saw some future for themselves south of the Pyrenees. Why the Vandals should have sent envoys from Africa to Galicia in 458 is a complete mystery. And why they found it worth while to sail up the Atlantic coast in 445 and plunder a place in Galicia it is hardly possible even to guess.[3]

What Hydatius' chronicle gives us is not a picture of a barbarian community which settled inside the Roman empire forcibly, without reaching any agreement with the imperial government. He tells us nothing of the effects which the settlement in a Roman environment brought about on the institutions and customs and ideas of the settlers (apart from a few words expressing the fact of their conversion to Arianism). He tells us nothing of the barbarians' attitudes towards those among whom they settled. What interests him is the fate of the Roman provincials upon whom they preyed in *Gallaecia infelix*, as he sadly calls it (§219). His book is not about barbarians: it is about Romans. He sees the barbarians only from the outside. It is scarcely open to doubt that he knew nothing of their language and that he was acquainted with no one who had mastered Suevic. And so he can say nothing of the barbarians' beliefs and motives and attitudes, what they laughed at, or how they prayed. Of their paganism he is wholly ignorant, and it would never have occurred to him to interest himself in it. Of their conversion to Arianism he states the fact and no more. He is interested to some extent in the man who brought the conversion about and writes some details about him, but of the Sueves' motives and reactions he says not a word and probably knew and cared nothing at all. In fact, his picture of the barbarians is a wholly external one, not at all like Sidonius' picture of Theoderic II. It is significant that while he can give us endless information about what the Sueves did to the Romans, on only two occasions can he tell us what they said (§§231, 247). How he came to hear of these reports we do not know. What is significant is that there are only two such reports in the forty-two years of his bishopric. (He speaks of a report of an embassy of 459 (§197), but on that occasion one of the envoys was a Roman.)

In Gaul the position was different. Sidonius was obliged to share a house with some Burgundians, and so he came to know Burgundians more intimately than he wished to know them. But for him the experience was a fit subject for an amusing poem. He could smile wryly as he recalled how his Burgundian "guests" belched garlic into his face or as he remembered the smell of the rancid butter with which they smeared their hair. But there was little place for a smile in Galician households. Relations there were too deadly for laughter.

We must not make the picture too gloomy or too uniform. Hydatius never complains that the Sueves persecuted the Romans on religious grounds. They did not go out of their way to destroy or pillage the churches or to interfere with the work of the clergy; and in Galicia itself it seems to have been possible even in the darkest days for the clergy to travel to church synods. Indeed, the Catholic clergy were all too free under Suevic rule to persecute their Manichaean opponents, and it is sad to record that the chronicler Hydatius himself played his full part in this unpleasant business.

We have also seen how complex was the reaction of the Roman population to the arrival of the barbarians in Spain (pp. 178 ff. above). By the end of the period that Hydatius deals with some prominent Romans were apparently reconciled to the fact that the Sueves were now the masters of northwestern Spain, that they were likely to remain so, and that the days of Roman rule were gone for ever. They began to accommodate themselves to the new state of affairs. Ospinio and Ascanius supplied information to the Gothic commander Sunieric and a little later performed the same service for the Sueve Frumarius. Later still Lusidius, who had become the political boss of his native city Lisbon, betrayed it to the Sueves, and we hear in one of the last entries in the chronicle that King Remismund sent him together with some Sueves on a diplomatic mission to the emperor.[4] Perhaps these men had much the same attitude as that of Arvandus and Seronatus in contemporary Gaul. They looked forwards to the future, not backwards to a time of Roman domination. They were prepared to throw in their lot with the new order of things, and indeed Lusidius' diplomatic mission travelled to the emperor in the very year in which Arvandus was brought to trial in Rome for his collaboration with Euric.

Although we cannot be said to know any individual from fifth-century Spain, we know enough to see that one of the kings, if only our information were fuller, might well rank as one of the most interesting political characters of the century. This is Rechiarius, who reigned from 448 to 456. It is a startling and unaccountable fact that we find a Catholic barbarian king some forty or fifty years before the baptism of Clovis. We cannot guess at the motives which led to his conversion, for, characteristically, Hydatius gives us not a single detail. Rechiarius' action is not made easier to understand by his marriage to a Visigothic princess, a daughter of Theoderic I, who was undoubtedly an Arian and who is not said by Hydatius to have changed her faith when she married.[5] A Catholic king, married to an Arian queen, ruling over a pagan court and a pagan people, is something of an historical surprise.

Again, Rechiarius was by far the earliest barbarian king to mint coins in his own name (p. 165 above); and it has been pointed out that by his use of the word *ivssv* on these silver coins he is expressing his personal right to mint them. He mints his coins aggressively. The legend is an innovation and "constitutes a revolution in the Roman Empire and confirms . . . the independence of the Sueves vis-à-vis the Empire."[6] Further, Rechiarius' foreign policy differed in two respects from those of the other fifth-century kings of Galicia. He not only made an all-out attack on Tarraconensis, which the other kings had left alone, but also, most strikingly, he is the only Dark Age king of any country who is known to have collaborated with the Bacaudae. I do not know what principle, or set of principles, induces a pagan to become a Catholic, to initiate a dramatic innovation in the history of coinage, and to display an unmatched spirit of bloodthirsty aggression. It will hardly be denied that Rechiarius was a man of some originality; but of his personality and of what made him act as he did, we know nothing at all.

At first sight it might seem that we could get some impression of what life must have been like in the Saxon-dominated districts of Britain by inference from what we know of western Spain. Can England have been very different from what we read in the entries in Hydatius' chronicle—a raid in practically every year, cities surprised and plundered, some towns entered over and over again, a few Romans eventually cooperating with the invaders, the general population inert and helpless? In fact, any such parallel between Spain and England would be a false one.

When the Sueves went out to raid they did so under one or at most two leaders. There were at most two areas of fighting at any one time. It is true that on some occasions Sueves and Romans came to blows when the king or the military leader was not present. We may suppose that brawls between men of the two nationalities or riots of one against the other were not unknown; and in 458 some Roman noblemen were killed in one such outbreak (§196). But in Saxon-dominated England there is no reason to suppose that the fighting was at all so restricted or that there was any central direction of the aggression. In each generation each locality will have had its own leader, more or less aggressive according to circumstances. Indeed, if there had been a fifth-century British chronicler he would have found it far beyond his powers to record each and every advance of the invaders in each and every part of the country.

And the ferocity of the aggression in Britain seems to have outdone anything that happened in Spain. There is no hint in Hydatius that civilized life in any extensive area of Spain had broken utterly down as Gildas says that it had done in northern Britain. Hydatius tells us that Spanish cities were occupied by the invaders, some of them more than once: but he only once (§241) says that any of them was left deserted. The one exception is Coimbra. In 468 this city was surprised in peacetime and plundered. Some houses were destroyed and part of the walls torn down. The inhabitants were taken prisoner or else they dispersed, and the city was left empty. But that was not the end of Coimbra. It was represented by its bishop at the Second Council of Braga in 572, and no doubt the desertion of the site by its occupants was only momentary. Otherwise, we never hear that the population of any Spanish city had to take to the mountains, the forests, and the caves, as happened in Britain, according to Gildas, in the 440s. We never hear that Spaniards were obliged to flee to other parts of their own country when their towns were attacked, much less that they fled overseas. Gildas records that after the failure of their appeal for help to Aëtius in 446 the Britons suffered so severely from starvation that they were reduced to fighting one another for food. No such calamity is recorded from Spain. And yet after a number of years the Britons began to fight back against the invaders in the mountains and woods, presumably ambushing and surprising the marauders.[7] They had already defeated the Saxon invasion of 408, and after the Saxon federates began their war in northern Britain Ambrosius Aurelianus led the Britons for the third time in the century to victory. This ability to round upon the invaders and defeat them seems to have been a peculiarly British phenomenon. Hydatius can record a local, small-scale victory over the Sueves, but to an extensive and successful military revival ending in a general repulse of the barbarians he can record no parallel. There is no Ambrosius Aurelianus in his pages; nor can he tell us of anyone resembling Germanus of Auxerre.

What about the repeated power struggles which Gildas records from Britain? There is no parallel in contemporary Spain, where the imperial government still continued to function and apparently was still recognized by the majority of Hispano-Romans. But of course if we had a reasonably full source of information about conditions in, say, Carthaginiensis in the middle or the last quarter of the century, it is not out of the question that we would hear of the rise and fall of local bullies and despots and "strong" men. Even with our existing sources we hear of two usurpers who established themselves in Tarraconensis at the end of the century.[8] And how did Lusidius come to be the virtual ruler of Lisbon at the end of Hydatius's period?[9]

But if we stand back from the texts of Gildas and Hydatius and take a

wider view of events in Spain and Britain, we shall be able to see fundamental differences between the fates of the two regions. First, we find the
disappearance of the place-names in Britain. The only groups of place-
names that have survived in eastern England (east of a line drawn from the
Yorkshire wolds to the New Forest), are those of some Romano-British
towns, the big rivers like the Trent and the Thames, and some hills and
forests.[10] Otherwise, isolated individual place-names have survived because
isolated enclaves of Britons managed to escape annihilation. But these
were very much the exceptions. In general the names disappeared along
with the people who used them. Nor were the people enslaved, except no
doubt for some of the women and children. Germanic society at this date
had little place for slave labour even in the relatively highly developed
communities just beyond the Roman frontier, for example, among the
fourth-century Visigoths or Ostrogoths. When the Saxons lived on the
continent they were far removed from the great centres of Roman civilization; and at the time of the invasions they are likely to have lived at a
lower rather than a higher stage of economic and social development than
most of the Germanic invaders of the empire, and hence they will have had
less place than, say, the Goths for the enslavement of adult male prisoners.
It follows that the bulk of the British menfolk were either massacred or
driven far away to the west or to countries overseas. That is perhaps why
Gildas has so little to say about the enslavement of the Britons by the Saxons. He does indeed tell us that a number of them surrendered expecting
to be enslaved, and, while some were not disappointed, others were massacred instead.[11] The British women and children could be used as household
slaves, the women in addition as concubines. (Genteel English historians
speak of "intermarriage" and "coexistence" at this stage between Britons
and Saxons: it is not respectable to mention rape.) And so, though there
were some few exceptional localities, we may speak of the extermination
of the Britons, especially in eastern England. In any event, the whole process was carried through with such bestial cruelty that it gave rise, in the
minds of those Britons who survived, to a burning hatred of the Germans
which did not abate as the years and generations went by. Even in the time
of Bede,[12] who noted the fact and deplored it, they were still resolutely opposed to preaching the Christian faith to those whose ancestors had
treated them with such gruesome savagery. The Saxons' atrocities in the
mid-fifth century were still remembered with profound resentment and
without forgiveness after nearly two hundred years. Although the Irish
acted as missionaries throughout England north of the Thames, no Cum-
brian or Welshman, no Cornishman or Breton is known to have made any
effort to save the souls of the Saxons, so fiercely did their hatred still burn.

To all this there is no parallel in Spain. The *Parochiale* gives us about 130 place-names from the province of Galicia, and the names give no support to the view that there was a large-scale alteration of them. The place-names have survived as though the Sueves had never been.[13] Even the villages are still in existence in 569. The western Spanish cities had been taken and taken again; but they, too, survived. The bishoprics of the Suevian period were bishoprics still in the seventh century. At no time did city life become impossible over a considerable area for a considerable time, and few Galician cities will have lain empty and deserted for long because of the Sueves (though some Spanish cities are known to have been desolated before the arrival of the Sueves).[14] We even have some slight reason to believe that the family of the Cantabri survived in Coimbra itself from the fifth century until the seventh.[15] Where Roman and Sueve lived in the one city — and this happened rarely — the experience of Lugo in 460 suggests that they kept themselves rigidly separate and that no effort was made on either side to weld them into one people: but that did not kill the cities in question. In Britain, on the other hand, there is no evidence, and it is in the last degree unlikely, that Roman and Saxon ever shared the one city after 410. Whether the missionary Ajax, who converted the pagan Sueves to Arianism in 464 and the following years, was a Gaul or a Galatian he was certainly some sort of Roman. Yet he brought Christianity, as he saw it, to the Sueves (though if he had been a Galician his missionary fervour might have been somewhat cooler). It must be admitted that the work of Hydatius does not suggest that it ever occurred to the chronicler or to any of his Catholic contemporaries to spread Christianity among their brutish rulers. On the other hand, there is little trace in the chronicle of that ferocious hatred which the British survivors felt for so many generations.

When we read the entries in the chronicle we may well be shocked at the endless list of raids, wars, battles, and the fall of cities. But what we read in Hydatius is only a shadow of what must have happened in Britain. The Sueves did not destroy the Latin language in Galicia: the Saxons destroyed it in Britain. Christianity and the organization of the Catholic Church outlived the Sueves: in eastern Britain they did not survive the Saxons. Lisbon and Astorga and Lugo and the rest are cities still: what are Silchester and Verulamium and Caistor-by-Norwich? In a word, Galicia survived its Germanic invaders: Britain did not. Evil though the Suevian occupation of Galicia may have been — and the chronicle of Hydatius shows it to have been horrifying — the Saxon occupation of Britain was worse by far.

In fact, by the term "the end of Roman Spain" we mean no more than the disappearance of the imperial government's political and military control of the peninsula. And for this disappearance we have a clear *terminus ante quem*. In 461 Theoderic II recalled no less a personage than the Master of the Soldiers himself, Nepotianus by name, and replaced him by a Roman called Arborius (p. 175 f. above). It is inconceivable that a barbarian king could have taken this dramatic step if the emperor still in any way controlled Spain. I conclude that in a political and military sense Roman Spain ended before 461.

But if this is so, we cannot believe that Roman power in Spain was overthrown by the barbarians. It is true that the remote mountains of the northwest had been controlled by the Sueves for half a century and that the western cities of the peninsula were under attack for many years by relatively small bands of Sueves. It is also true that in 458—against no opposition—Theoderic established a garrison in Baetica (p. 189 above). But he will certainly not have buried a large force there, so far away from Toulouse: we cannot believe that this garrison numbered thousands of men —more probably a few hundred would be the correct figure. The Suevic raids and the Visigothic garrison were pinpricks. They did not affect Tarraconensis or the vast areas of Carthaginiensis. What is of capital interest is that the Goths could maintain themselves at all in Baetica, so many hundreds of miles from their base at Toulouse. This fact shows that there was no Roman military opposition of any significance; and indeed we have seen reason to believe that the Roman garrison in Spain had disappeared long before this time (p. 172 above). It was only in the reigns of Euric and Alaric II, that is, in the period 466–507, that the Goths attacked Spain in earnest and settled in it. It is not an exaggeration to say that Roman control of Spain outside Galicia disappeared *before* the barbarian invasions of the greater part of the peninsula seriously began.

Consider again the case of Britain. We can date with extreme precision the end of imperial rule in that island. It ended in 409 as a result of a rebellion on the part of the Britons (or some of them), who expelled the imperial officials and abolished the use of Roman law. We do not hear that the rebels had first to defeat the Roman garrison: so far as our inadequate sources go, there was then no Roman garrison in the island. It would seem that Roman military power had already evaporated. But perhaps the most significant fact about the rebellion is that the Romans, who had suppressed countless revolts in the centuries of their history, could not even begin to suppress this one. And in the following year the emperor admitted as much: he wrote to the British cities and explicitly informed them of this inability. Once again, as in Spain, the disappearance of Roman power antedated the main barbarian invasions. The conquest by the Goths in the one case and by the Saxons in the other had little or nothing to do with the end of imperial rule. And the reasons for this ending of imperial rule cannot be discovered on the basis of the Spanish and British evidence alone.

What the Spanish and the British evidence shows clearly is the difficulty of maintaining that the barbarians "assassinated" the Roman Empire or that "the internal weakness of the empire cannot have been a major factor in its decline."[16]

APPENDIX A:
A NOTE ON ST. ISIDORE'S USE OF HYDATIUS

We are not concerned here with the general problem of Isidore's use of his sources throughout his entire historical corpus. It may be observed, however, that although this is a question that was ably discussed long ago by Hugo Hertzberg,[17] a new and comprehensive study might not be labour lost. But what is of interest at present is the narrower question of how Isidore used the chronicle of Hydatius.

What is the value of Isidore's additions to Hydatius and of his alterations of Hydatius' text? Since we have no alternative accounts by means of which to check the Saint in such passages the answers to these questions must necessarily be somewhat subjective.

In 428, according to Hydatius, 89, the Vandal Gunderic occupied Seville and desecrated a church there. The chronicler does not give the name of this church, no doubt because he did not know it. But Isidore is able to tell us which church it was: it was the church of St. Vincent the Martyr.[18] It would be absurd to doubt him. The memory of the outrage could well have been preserved in Seville, St. Isidore's own city, for two hundred years. The act of desecration was never forgotten; and I have no doubt that Isidore here is either drawing on a valid oral tradition or even perhaps relying on an inscription commemorating the reconstruction of the church after the "vandalism" of 428, or both. Gunderic's crime had always been remembered in the place where he committed it.

In another passage Isidore even seems able to correct Hydatius. The fifth-century chronicler tells us that one daughter of the Emperor Valentinian III was married to Geiseric's son, whose name he gives as Gento. But Isidore, whose source here appears at first sight to be Hydatius alone, changes this and correctly says that the princess was married to Huneric.[19] Evidently then Hydatius was not his sole source after all. Isidore had independent knowledge of the members of the imperial family and of their fate in the fifth century. On this occasion he is right. It follows that in general his account is not to be rejected out of hand on every occasion on which he contradicts the account of Hydatius. He is usually wrong, to be sure, on these occasions, but he is not always wrong. He describes Andevotus as

217

Romanae militiae ducem, and this probably depends on no source, written or oral. But as a guess, it is a lucky one. I cannot see who else Andevotus can have been and am inclined to accept Isidore's version.[20]

On the other hand, the metropolitan is careless in transcribing proper names from his source. King Maldras in Hydatius becomes Masdras in Isidore's histories, though Mommsen has "corrected" the text, blamed the fault on the manuscript tradition, and so saved the credit of the Saint of Seville.[21] Maldras' father, Massilia, as Hydatius, 181, calls him, becomes Massila twice in Isidore;[22] and King Remismund appears to have borne strange names in the Saint's orthography.[23] Again, the Suevic leader Framtane is twice called *frantan* in Isidore;[24] and while the Gothic general, Sunieric, in one version of Isidore's histories remains Sunieric, in another he becomes Sumeric and the like.[25] The Gothic leader, Cyrila, as Hydatius, 192, calls him, is Ceurila in Isidore.[26] The *Auregensium loca* of Hydatius, 202, become the meaningless *Auriensium loca* of Isidore, though Mommsen in a fit of textual generosity has once again stepped in to rescue the Saint.[27]

These are details, but they suggest that Isidore was inclined to read his source too quickly and without adequate care.

He is capable of monstrous mistakes. For instance, he puts Majorian's expedition to Spain and his murder by Ricimer *before* the capture of Rome by Geiseric in 455, though Hydatius, 200, 210, had correctly dated these two events respectively in 460 and 461.[28] It is hard to forgive the Saint for so crass a misunderstanding. Nor is it a detail to say, as one version of Isidore says, that Ajax, the man who converted the Sueves from paganism to Arianism, in fact converted them from Catholicism to Arianism.[29] Isidore was careless enough to be misled by the statement of Hydatius, 232, that Ajax was "the enemy of the Catholic faith and of the Divine Trinity," *hostis catholicae fidei et divinae trinitatis.* Here he is guilty of a major mistake. He was also mystified because, although Rechiarius was a Catholic, his father Rechila died a pagan—and so he inserts the words "as they say," *ut ferunt,* into Hydatius' information, thereby throwing an unnecessary doubt on the fact of Rechila's paganism.[30] Finally, the Saint was evidently puzzled by another word in this passage of his authority. Hydatius describes Ajax as *senior,* a difficult term that appears to mean either "bishop" or "priest"—we do not know which, if either. For whatever reason—perhaps because he, too, could not precisely understand it—Isidore omits the word altogether and puts nothing in its place.

Hydatius gives no hint that the Suevic King Remismund was the son of the earlier King Maldras; but Isidore mentions this relationship twice, and Ludwig Schmidt is inclined to accept that they were in fact father and son.[31] I am sceptical. If the report is true, we must suppose that this piece of information was preserved until the seventh century by Hispano-Romans, for Isidore is not likely to have cross-examined Sueves in order to find out the relationships of one odious Suevic king to another (or for any purpose, for that matter). But Hispano-Romans are unlikely to have been so interested in such a matter of detail as to remember for centuries whether one of their grim oppressors was or was not the father of his successor. And even if some of them did remember it, is it probable that Isidore would have thought of picking out this particular relationship and of cross-questioning Galicians on such a minor point? If Hydatius did not know of any such relationship, it seems all but incredible that Isidore could have found it out or that he would have thought it worth while to take the trouble to find it out. Maldras and Remismund were two successive kings: therefore they must have been father and son. That is how the matter presented itself to Isidore. And so I would reject this relationship out of hand and with it the evidence which Isidore's false conjecture provides for an hereditary monarchy at this date.

The Saint also appears to have precise information about the first of the Suevic kings of Spain, Hermeric. He was king, says Isidore, at the time when the Sueves entered Spain with the Vandals and Alans in 409, and he continued to reign for thirty-two years. Isidore could have learned from Hydatius (122) about the seven years of Hermeric's illness, but he could not have learned from him of the thirty-two years (409–41) of Hermeric's alleged reign. Hydatius does record his abdication in 438 and his death in 441, but says nothing of his accession.[32] The precision of Isidore's information seems at first sight impressive. It appears to suggest that he had access to a reliable source of information about the length of Hermeric's reign, though it would be hard to guess what that source might have been. Hydatius (71) first mentions Hermeric in connection with the events of 419 and gives no hint at the identity of the king of the Sueves between 409, when they entered Spain, and that same year 419, when he knew that their king was Hermeric. The most probable explanation of Isidore's display of knowledge, in my belief, is that it is nothing better than a feeble guess: since no ruler was recorded to have preceded Hermeric in the period 409–19, therefore Hermeric himself must have been the ruler in those years. If anybody else had been king, Hydatius would have mentioned his name. But Hydatius mentions no name: therefore no one else was king.

That is an argument which we are not bound to accept. Bury cautiously omits the name of the Suevic king, alone of the barbarian kings of Spain, in 417–18; and I believe that he was right to do so.[33] We do not know when exactly Hermeric became king of the Sueves. He was certainly king in 419: beyond that we cannot safely go. But this is not the only mistake which the Saint makes in connexion with Hermeric. He goes on to say that Hermeric's son and successor, Rechila, was sent by his father to Baetica where he defeated Andevotus.[34] Now, it is true that Hermeric survived for years after his son had reached the throne; but from this fact Isidore has drawn a false inference. He supposes that, although Hermeric had abdicated, he nevertheless retained some powers over his son, including the power to send him to fight in Baetica. Of this Hydatius says nothing, and it is hardly credible.

The case of the Bacaudae is different. There can be little doubt that Isidore has not made a mistake but—what is much worse—has deliberately suppressed mention of them. Hydatius speaks of them several times. He says (142) that in 449 Rechiarius plundered the region of Saragossa in company with the leader of the Bacaudae, Basilius. St. Isidore, on the other hand, will allow no place to the Bacaudae in his interpretation of history. All reference to the Bacaudae must be suppressed. Hence, according to him, Rechiarius harassed the region of Saragossa "with the help of the Goths." It is a curiosity of the study of the fifth century that no less a scholar than Mommsen himself was inclined to agree with Isidore on this wanton alteration.[35] What makes it particularly odd is that Isidore goes on to omit all reference to the other passages (128, 158) where Hydatius mentions the Bacaudae. This is crude social prejudice on the part of the holy man of Seville.

What are we to say, then, about Isidore's "corrections" and additions to Hydatius' chronicle? He certainly knows which church in his own city of Seville was desecrated by Gunderic: it was the church of St. Vincent the Martyr. He is certainly right in a matter relating to the imperial family where Hydatius was wrong: Valentinian's daughter married Huneric, not Gento. I have guessed that he hit the mark perhaps more by accident than by good judgement in naming the post held by Andevotus: Andevotus was indeed *Romanae militiae dux*.

These points are discouragingly few when set down side by side with his misunderstandings and slips and prejudices, of which even the long list assembled by Hertzberg is not complete. We approach with gloom the question of the value of Isidore's account of what happened after 469, the year with which Hydatius' chronicle comes to an end. For the next eight decades or so the metropolitan had no written source of information bearing on the Sueves and the province of Galicia. In all its history under the Sueves Galicia had but one chronicler. After Hydatius there was to be no second Hydatius. Now, it will hardly be doubted that Isidore knew practically nothing about the period immediately following 469, or, if he did know a few facts, he did not choose to mention them in his anaemic

220

chronicle. I do not wish to imply that it would have been impossible for anyone writing in 625 to find out something, if he had had a mind to do so, about Suevic history in the period 469–560. But a busy metropolitan bishop with no great taste for history may not have cared to spend his time in carrying out historical researches about remote events that had taken place in distant Galicia among those intolerable heretics long ago, events which in his own day had lost all their significance and which nobody had ever bothered to chronicle. He was more interested in eulogizing the Visigoths, who ruled Spain when he was writing, than in elucidating the irrelevant history of one of the lesser peoples whom the Goths had overrun. It was one thing to paraphrase Hydatius. It was a very different thing to do original research and find out the history of a period of eighty years when there was no Hydatius to paraphrase.

But we must not go too far. It would be unfair to Isidore to end without recalling that in dealing with the fourth century it is he alone who tells about the Gothic "confessors" and the "former" Goths who clashed in the time of Fritigern.[36] He alone of our authorities for the late fifth century mentions the law-code of Euric.[37] (But he has nothing to say about the *Breviarium* of Alaric II.) As for the history of the later sixth century in Spain, for which we have the magnificent chronicle of John of Biclarum, it is not John who tells us of Leovigild's revision of the Visigothic law-code, of the conversion to Arianism or Semi-Arianism of the Catholic bishop of Saragossa, or of Leovigild's harsh measures against political rivals at home. All this important information we owe to Isidore alone. Only a Mommsen could dare to blast the reputation of the sage of Seville with the phrase, "homine non erudito, attamen litterato."[38]

APPENDIX B:
SOME RECENT STUDIES OF THE BACAUDAE

The ancient evidence for the history of the Bacaudae has been very usefully collected and discussed by B. Czúth, *Die Quellen der Geschichte der Bagauden,* Acta Antiqua et Archaeologica, tomus ix (Szeged, 1965). For further discussion see E. A. Thompson, "Peasant revolts in late Roman Gaul and Spain," *Past and Present,* ii (1952), 11–23, reprinted with corrections in M. I. Finley (ed.), *Studies in Ancient Society* (London and Boston, 1974), pp. 304–20, and Samuel Szádeczky-Kardoss, P.-W., Supplbd., xi. 346–54, and for St. Isidore on the Bacaudae see above p. 220.

That the Bacaudae attacked the Gallic cities is asserted by Aurelius Victor, *Caes.* xxxix. 17, "pleraeque urbium tentare," and need not be doubted. But it is unfortunate that R. A. B. Mynors in his edition of the *Panegyrici Latini* should have accepted *Bagaudicae* instead of *Batavicae* at *Pan. Lat.* ix (iv). 4. 1: evidently he had not read P. le Gentilhomme, "Le désastre d'Autun en 289," *Revue des Études Anciennes,* xlv (1943), 233–40.

Several scholars, e.g. Reinhart, 45, de Abadal, 41, etc., curiously convert the Basilius of Hydatius (141) into a Roman general who slew the Bacaudae when they piously fled into a church in Tarazona! De Abadal adds the heart-rending detail that the good Bishop Leo died while protecting the poor oppressed peasants from the villainous Romans! On this ludicrous error see S. Szádeczky-Kardoss, "Zur Interpretation zweier Hydatius-Stellen," *Helikon,* i (1961), 148–52, at 149 f., to whose paper a reply ought not to have been published by Laszlo Varady, "Zur Klarstellung der zwei Hydatius-Stellen," ibid., ii (1962), 259–63. Varady makes Basilius "ein gotischer Seigneur" and the federates become "Huns." From this incident in the church at Tarazona I would not infer an especially hostile attitude on the part of the Bacaudae towards the Catholic Church: *contra,* S. Mazzarino, "Si puo parlare di rivoluzione sociale alla fine del mondo antico?," *Settimane,* ix (Spoleto, 1962), 410–25, at 422. Nor can I accept the quixotic opinion of C. Sanchez-Albornoz, ibid., 437 ff., who thinks that the Bacaudae were a national movement of the Basques: whether on this theory we are to regard the Armoricans, too, as Basque nationalists is not clear! There is little of interest in E. Englemann, "Zur Bewegung der Bagauden im römischen Gallien," *apud* H. Kretschmer (ed.), *Vom Mittelalter zur Neuzeit: Festschrift H. Sproemberg,* i (Berlin, 1956), 371–85. For a recent discussion of the Bacaudae in general see Sirago, 376 ff., but his remarks on the Spanish movement (pp. 382 ff.) are wild.

For a well balanced account of the Bacaudae in Gaul see Frank M. Clover, *Flavius Merobaudes: A Translation and Historical Commentary,* Transactions of the American Philosophical Society, lxi, i (Philadelphia, 1971), 46 ff., with good bibliographical material. But nothing new emerges from the discussion of the etymology of *Bacaudae* by Clifford E. Minor, "Bagaudae or Bacaudae?," *Traditio,* xxxi (1975), 318–22. No authentic coins of Aelianus have been identified, but for possible coins of Amandus see P. H. Webb *apud* H. Mattingly and E. A. Sydenham, *The Roman Imperial Coinage,* v, ii (London, 1962), 579, 595.

In R. G. Collingwood and J. N. L. Myres, *Roman Britain and the English Settlements* (Oxford, 1937), pp. 303 f., Collingwood suggested that the Bacaudae were active in Britain as well as in Gaul. I have tried in *Antiquity,* xxx (1956), 163–67, and again in *Britannia,* viii (1977), 303–18, to show that there is in fact all but direct evidence for this in Zosimus, vi. 5. 2 f., who says that in 409 it was in imitation of the Britons that the Armoricans expelled the Roman administration and declared themselves independent of the imperial government. The question which I would put to the doubter is, Who else in the Roman West, other than the persons who made up the Bacaudae, would ever have considered leaving the Roman Empire voluntarily?

APPENDIX C:

HYDATIUS, 247, AND THE FALL OF ASPAR

See Courtois, *Byzantion,* 26 f., on the extreme difficulty of this entry in the chronicle of Hydatius. According to our text of the chronicle, Suevic envoys who had been sent to Italy in 467 returned in 469 with news of the preparations of the Eastern Emperor Leo for his vast expedition against the Vandals in Africa, which in fact sailed in 468. The envoys reported (i) that Ricimer had become the son-in-law of the new Western Emperor Anthemius and also patrician, and (ii) that in the East Aspar had been reduced to the rank of a private citizen (i.e. that he had been cashiered from the army), while his son had been put to death: they had been accused of plotting against the Roman Empire in the interests of the Vandals.

As for the first of these reports, Ricimer had in fact become a patrician on 28 February 457,[39] so that on the face of it there was little need for the ambassadors to report *that.* It was hardly "hot" news. And yet the entry means, "that Ricimer, the son-in-law of Anthemius, was also made a patrician," whereas what we want is "that Ricimer the patrician was also made the son-in-law of Anthemius"; he married Anthemius's daughter Alypia at Rome in 467.[40] I do not believe that we are justified in rejecting the authority of this part of the entry or in altering the text merely because of this confusion. We must rather suppose that Hydatius, living as he did so far from the centre of affairs, had missed the news of Ricimer's elevation and simply had not known about his patriciate. The information had not hitherto reached Galicia. The chronicler assumed, wrongly as we know, that Ricimer was only given the honour now, in 467. Indeed, the Suevic envoys may have misunderstood what they were told in Italy—the matter will not have been of burning interest to them.

The second part of the ambassadors' report is far more serious. Aspar was not merely degraded, as our text puts it: he was treacherously murdered along with his sons, so that in this respect the report is no mean understatement. But what is even more disconcerting is that Aspar's death is securely dated to 471, a couple of years after the close of the period with which the chronicle deals—and very possibly a couple of years after the death of Hydatius himself. Courtois concludes that a later interpolation has found its way into the text of §247.

We must reject that last supposition, for it merely puts the problem a step further back. At what date would a Western (Spanish or maybe even

Gallic) scribe, who knew of this far-away event though not very accurately, have thought it fitting and important to interpolate his information into Hydatius' work? And why did he interpolate it at the end of a passage of indirect speech? Why not tack his information on to the end of the chronicle, in the normal style of continuators, where it would have been chronologically in place?

It is clear that the theory of a later interpolator raises more questions than it solves. Now, there is one fact which we cannot reasonably doubt: it is that Aspar and his sons finally fell and were put to death in 471. Accordingly, the majority of our authorities tell of their murder *after* they have told of the great African expedition of 468. This is true of Procopius, Jordanes, Theophanes, and a number of Byzantine writers as well as the Latin chroniclers, Cassiodorus, Marcellinus Comes, and Victor Tonnennensis.[41] But it is of deep interest to find that Aspar's fall and death are dated *before* the African expedition of 468 by the fifth-century historian Candidus. The work of this writer survives only in Photius' summary; but Photius clearly makes him tell first of Aspar's death and then of the campaign against the Vandals. And that is not all. This is no mere oversight or slip on Photius' part, for in addition to the envoys in Hydatius John Malalas beyond a doubt tells of the events in that same order, while the *Chronicon Paschale* dates the death of Aspar precisely to 467.[42] We thus have two chronologies for Aspar's fall, 467 and 471, both well attested, though the later date is supported by more writers than the earlier.

In any event, it is certainly the case that Aspar's power had drastically declined by 467. Priscus (frag. 35) tells how Leo rejected Aspar's advice to stay neutral in a war between the Sciri and the Goths at this time: the emperor sent help to the Sciri. But that was a trivial detail in comparison with what happened in 468: Aspar's prestige received a public and shattering blow when the emperor gave the high command of the African expedition, not to him, but to Basiliscus. Indeed, this rebuff to Aspar was of such dimensions as to suggest that his power in 468 had all but evaporated, that he was, as the Suevic envoys reported, reduced to civilian status. It is certain, then, that something drastic had happened to Aspar's position in the years immediately preceding 468.

Let us look again at what it was that the Suevian ambassadors reported. I believe that they are not speaking of the final fall of Aspar, who was undeniably murdered in 471. What they reported was Aspar's disgrace and the execution of one of his sons. I believe that our authorities give two different dates because they are talking of two different events. Those who speak of 467 are referring to Aspar's dismissal from his military appointment. Those who speak of 471 are relating his final fall and execution. We must bear in mind the brevity of all these historians' works. Even Procopius, when he deals with the fifth century, gives us only an outline, while the entire work of Candidus (which if it had survived intact would have been of capital value) exists only in a four-page summary by Photius. I suggest that they have all alike telescoped the events. Suppose that Aspar was cashiered and one of his sons executed in 467, and suppose further that Aspar and two other sons were put to death in 471. In this case might not the historians, aiming at brevity, have narrated his fall as if it had happened, not in two stages, but in one? If that is what they did, we would expect that some of them would date the fall to 467, the date of the first major stage in Aspar's disgrace, and others to 471, the date of his murder. And as we have seen, that is precisely what we do find.

But the sceptic might ask: if that is the case, is it not strange that not one of our authorities — and they are very numerous — gives the slightest hint that the events were spread over a number of years? Fortunately, we have at our disposal one author who does indeed distinguish carefully the two stages in the fall of Aspar. This is the writer of the *Vita S. Danielis Stylitae*,[43] a document of which the importance to the historian was first pointed out by the late Professor Norman H. Baynes.[44] From this *Vita* (cap. 55) we learn some facts which none of our other authorities mentions. It turns out that Leo was informed that Aspar's son, Ardaburius, *magister militum per Orientem,* was in a treasonable correspondence with the Persians. The emperor therefore dismissed him from the service and reduced him to the status of a private citizen (*holopaganos*). In the next chapter (56, p. 175) the author of the *Vita* goes on to give his own, rather idiosyncratic account of the African campaign of 468. It is only ten chapters later (66, p. 184 f.) that he mentions the death of Aspar and his sons. Beyond a doubt we have confirmation here of our theory that Aspar's fall was brought about in two stages, one before and one after the African expedition. The first stage took place after the great fire at Constantinople of 2 September 465 and should be placed in 466 or more probably in 467.[45] That the second fell in 471 is not in doubt. But there are still some discrepancies.

(i) In the *Vita* Aspar is described as a member of the senate. That can hardly be doubted: it is confirmed by John Malalas and the *Chronicon Paschale,* who call him *princeps senatus* and patrician.[46] He is a patrician in several other writers, too — Marcellinus Comes, for instance, and Cassiodorus and Jordanes. What we cannot accept is the view that Aspar even retained his rank of *Magister* until his death; but in fact the only passage which might seem to support any such view is Zachariah of Mitylene, *Hist. Eccles.* iii. 12, "In the third year of his [Leo's] reign Aspar the general [*stratelates,* the correct word for the *Magister*] and his sons were killed." This is unsup-

225

ported by any other writer. But Zachariah is simply identifying Aspar (and incidentally writing the "third" instead of the "thirteenth" year of Leo's reign). The *Chronicon Paschale* describes Aspar as *Magister* in 464; thereafter no one of our numerous sources of information apart from Zachariah gives him any military rank. There is no reason why we should not suppose, therefore, that when the Suevic ambassadors reported by Hydatius declared that Aspar had been "demoted to private life," they meant that he had been dismissed from the army command which he had hitherto held. They did not report, and they did not mean, that he had lost his senate membership and his patrician status. It is true that the author of the *Vita* does not say that Aspar was now dismissed from his military appointment, but he does not contradict the Suevic envoys, who did say so.

(ii) According to the author of the *Vita,* the trouble arose because of Ardaburius' intrigues with Persia. According to the ambassadors, father and son alike were intriguing not with Persia but with the Vandals. It may well have been the case that, while the son was preparing to betray East Rome to Persia, as the *Vita* tells us, the father was engaged in the same activity with Carthage, as the ambassadors said. In that case both our authorities would be right. But that was in 466–67. In 471 the emperor's motives for putting them both to death were different. He now found that they were conspiring against his throne. That is not open to doubt. It is the view of Cassiodorus, Procopius, John Malalas, Theophanes, and others, including the author of the *Vita.* As for his motives in 466–67, the fact that Aspar was not appointed to command against Geiseric strongly suggests that the Suevic ambassadors were right to think that he had been communicating with the Vandals and that he had been discovered and cashiered.

(iii) There is only one point, in fact, in which the *Vita* and the ambassadors are irreconcilable. According to the former, Ardaburius was dismissed from the service in 466–67 for his treasonable communications with the Persians and was reduced to civilian status. According to the envoys, Ardaburius (though he is not named) was put to death because of his treasonable relations with the Vandals. In view of the unanimity of all our other sources it seems best to suppose that the envoys or their informants overstated what had happened and that Ardaburius was disgraced but was not put to death. In fact, he is found instigating a revolt in Thrace in 469–70, and it cannot reasonably be doubted that he survived until 471.[47]

I conclude that this entry in the chronicle is the work of Hydatius rather than of a continuator, and that the contents of the entry are wholly credible apart from the statement that one of Aspar's sons was put to death in 467.

APPENDIX D:

MOMMSEN'S EDITION OF THE CHRONICLE OF HYDATIUS

The Photographic Department of the Deutsche Staatsbibliothek in Eastern Berlin has kindly supplied me with a microfilm of the codex Berolinensis Phillipps. 1829, fol. 153–72, which contains by far the best text of the chronicle; and this microfilm I have had enlarged so that it is to a considerable extent, but not entirely, an adequate substitute for the manuscript itself. As we might expect, it shows that Mommsen's edition is superb both in its reporting of the readings of the original hand and of the corrector, and in the layout of the complicated text. The edition is beyond praise, but it would be a mistake to suppose that it is infallible.

It is decidedly open to criticism in its reports of Hydatius' dating by Olympiads. On his p. 6 Mommsen states that each Olympiad normally precedes the regnal year with which it begins. Take an example. Olympiad 297 is placed immediately before the year XV of Arcadius and Honorius. Now, the fifteenth year of these two emperors was 409. To find the date of the Olympiad in terms of the years of the Christian era we may apply the formula supplied by Courtois, *Byzantion* p. 31: $(x-1)4-(776-1)$, where x is the number of the Olympiad. So Olympiad 297 began, sure enough, in 409. But the manuscript is not consistent. Often (Mommsen goes on) the note of the Olympiad is mixed in with the immediately preceding entries in the chronicle, and he cites as examples Ol. 290, 298, 299, and 308. But even so, no note of the Olympiad is put into the imperial year preceding that with which it actually began. Consequently, Mommsen has always placed the Ol. date directly before the appropriate regnal date, irrespective of whether B does so or not. In the critical notes printed underneath the text itself Mommsen says no more of the matter.

The reader would not easily guess, therefore, that B places Ol. 295 opposite to §31 — to be precise, before the words *observanda de ecclesia disciplina.* Nor does Mommsen say that B has the regnal year VI, not where he prints it, but before *statuuntur quaedam* in §31, and the regnal year VII, not facing an empty line, as he shows it, but before the words *in eodem concilio* in that same §31. Mommsen may well be right in disentangling all this, but he ought at least to have pointed out that his own rule (mentioned above) is broken here: B does put the start of the Olympiad before the regnal year with which it began: Ol. 295 is here placed in the year VI (= 400), the sixth year of Arcadius and Honorius, instead of in the year VII (= 401). Moreover, we find, when we compare Mommsen's text with that given by B, that the editor has removed some of the Olympiad datings to considerable distances in the interests of consistency. Thus Ol. 308 is put forward by 27 lines of the printed page, while Ol. 309 is put forward by no fewer than 50 printed lines. In a mediaeval scribe such a transference would be considered to be chaotic, and we should not accept it even when the scribe is Mommsen. The truth is that Hydatius did not set to work with the systematic and Teutonic methods of a Mommsen. To be sure, he *ought* to have put his Olympiad dates immediately before his note of the first imperial year of each Olympiad. But his mind was not as tidy as that of Mommsen. His practice is here and there a little irregular and inconsistent.

We might have expected that all this, and a multitude of similar facts, would have been placed before the reader in any edition of Hydatius that followed Mommsen's. Unhappily, M. Alain Tranoy, *Hydace: Chronique,* Sources chrétiennes, vols. 218–19 (Paris, 1974), has chosen to follow Mommsen with equally little explanation in his critical notes. Thus, in §31, where, as we have seen, Mommsen has made some drastic changes, Tranoy has no critical note at all!

None of Courtois' arguments in his *Byzantion* article is more valuable than that whereby he shows that there is a lacuna in Hydatius' account of the reign of the Western Emperor Severus. Severus came to the throne on 19 November 461. According to Hydatius' dating-procedure, then, which he describes in §26, the year 461 will be reckoned simultaneously as the last year of Majorian and the first of Severus. The years 462, 463, 464, and 465 will be respectively the second, third, fourth, and fifth years of Severus, who died on 14 March 465. But in 466 there was an interregnum in the West, and no emperor sat on the throne of Rome or Ravenna in that year. According to Courtois, Hydatius was therefore obliged to refer to 466 as the sixth year of Severus, for there was no other very obvious way of numbering it. But when we turn to the text of Hydatius we find that that text includes references only to the first (§212), second (§222), and third (§231) years of Severus, and that it says nothing of the fourth, fifth, and the alleged sixth.

Courtois, *Byzantion,* 34–38, concludes that the figure II at §222 and the figure III at §231 are errors for V and VI respectively, and that it is Hydatius' account of this emperor's second, third, and fourth years which has been lost through a lacuna in the text and that it is his account of the fifth and sixth years which has been preserved. What proves the point, Courtois remarks, is that the first year of Olympiad cccxi, which Mommsen prints after §221, is in fact the year 465, i.e. the fifth year of Severus, according to Hydatius' method of numbering—and it is at that point that B has the regnal year II, which on this theory ought to be V, the easiest of slips.

All of this brilliant argument is convincing and is a great gain to Hydatian studies—except in one point. What Courtois did not know, because

Mommsen suppresses the fact, is that the presence of the words "OLYMPI CCCXI" at §221 is a figment of Mommsen's. The manuscript B has no Olympiad dating whatever at that place. The fact is that the scribe of B wrote from "OLYMPI CCCX" at §193 to "OLYMPI CCCXII" at the beginning of §242 (not before §245, where Mommsen prints it) without at first noticing that he had no "OLYMPI CCCXI" in his text at all. But when he noticed his omission he decided to insert "OLYMPI CCCXI," but apparently could not decide where exactly to put it, for he began in the end to write it at §217 "Agrippinus Gallus," etc., but lost confidence and inserted only the letters "OLYMPI" without any numeral after them. The inference is that no "OLYMPI CCCXI" existed in the text which he was copying from, for otherwise in all probability he would *either* not have omitted the date in the first place *or*, if he had done so by an oversight, he would have inserted both the word "OLYMPI" and the numeral at the appropriate place as given by his *Vorlage*. Whether in fact when he noticed the omission he went back to §217 by mere guesswork or whether there was some indication of a lacuna at that point in the manuscript from which he was copying, there is no means of saying. But what appears to be the total omission of an Olympic date from his source is another proof of a lacuna in this part of our text of Hydatius. Unhappily, however, the lacuna includes at least the beginning of A.D. 465, the fifth year of Severus, so that Courtois' argument should be reexamined.[48]

I mention all this in order to show that we have not yet got an authoritative edition of the chronicle, and I hope that some one with more energy than I possess will soon provide us with one. There is one conjectural reading which Mommsen confidently introduced into his text and which our hypothetical new editor will with even greater confidence reject. In §31 Mommsen has changed B's *sectatores* to *insectatores,* so that Symphosius and Dictinius, followers of Priscillian, become assailants of Priscillian. In fact, they had been adherents of his but had later returned to the Catholic belief. There are documents attached to the acts of the First Council of Toledo which bear upon their renunciation of the heresy. Hydatius in §31 refers to these documents, and says that Symphosius, Dictinius, and other bishops of Galicia, who had previously been supporters (*sectatores*) of Priscillianism, now turned on the heresy and condemned it. The reading *insectatores* misses the point that they had formerly been heretics themselves. But as a conjecture, it hardly deserves the silence in which Tranoy passes it over.

12

Barbarian Collaborators and Christians

In one vital respect our knowledge of the barbarian peoples is defective: we are never, or hardly ever, able to penetrate into the minds and attitudes of the peoples whom we are trying to understand. In the earlier centuries of the Roman Empire they were illiterate, or rather "preliterate"; and when they did learn to write (other than in runes) late in the fourth century they composed but few books — and fewer still have survived into the modern world. Who in the Middle Ages would have troubled to copy out and preserve a book written by a heretic in an incomprehensible language — the old, forgotten language of the Goths and the Vandals? We have to be content with the accidental survival of books written when the barbarian kingdoms still existed; and of these there are exceedingly few. In fact, we do not possess a single word written in their native tongue in this period — the fourth, fifth, and sixth centuries — by a Vandal or a Burgundian or a Frank. Even from the Goths, apart from fragments of Bishop Ulfila's translation of the Bible, we have only sixteen pages of a dry, uninformative commentary on St. John's Gospel, together with a few scraps and shreds of Gothic, mostly of an ecclesiastical character, practically all of them written in Italy in the first half of the sixth century.

We happen to possess a short chronicle written in Latin soon after the year 590 by John of Biclarum (an unidentified monastery somewhere in Spain). But if another writer, St. Isidore of Seville, had not chanced to mention that John was a Goth — for a Gothic author was something of an oddity in St. Isidore's eyes — we should never have doubted that he was as Roman as Isidore himself or as his contemporaries, Gregory the Great and Gregory of Tours. John himself never mentions his nationality. He was highly educated in Greek and Latin, and it is by no means certain that he knew Gothic. For him the only matter of significance was that he was a Christian and a Catholic. In this case, then, even when we possess the work of a Goth, the work tells us little or nothing about him *as a Goth*. So far as we can judge from his book, John had been completely absorbed by Roman civilization. To us he is a Goth in name only.[1]

Again, by good luck we still have a history of the Goths, or what passes for a history, written in Latin by a Goth called Jordanes in the middle of the sixth century. As an historian Jordanes is deplorable; but he was a Goth and proud of being a Goth, and so in his history he translated into Latin a few old folk tales or songs, which the Goths of his own day sang to the strains of the harp. From the Vandals and the others we have nothing.

The result is that we have to look at these "barbarians" from the outside. It is difficult not to see them as the Romans saw them; and the Romans had no wish to enter into their minds and to understand their outlook. No doubt there were many Roman exprisoners of war who could speak Germanic and who knew much about their captors; but for an educated Roman nobleman to learn a Germanic language was an event of extreme rarity. The most fervently pro-Gothic of all the early sixth-century Italians, Cyprianus by name, brought up his sons to speak Gothic as well as Latin; but a more characteristic attitude, we may suspect, was revealed by Sidonius Apollinaris when he heard that his friend Syagrius had learned Burgundian. In Syagrius' presence, he says, the barbarian will now be afraid to commit a barbarism in his own language! To Sidonius such an accomplishment as understanding a Germanic language is a joke and a very amusing joke.[2] So we can hardly ever listen to the barbarians as they speak for themselves. Occasionally their words were taken down by Roman observers, as we have seen (pp. 4 ff. above), but very rarely. Before the foundation of their kingdoms, the educated, literate section of the Roman population feared and despised them. The overwhelming majority of the Christian bishops made no effort to propagate the Gospel among them, and there is even a hint in the writings of one bishop—and an Arian at that—that anyone who tried to convert the barbarians might be guilty of nothing less than an impiety.[3] As an old pagan Roman had said—and many a Christian Roman said much the same thing later on—the barbarians had the limbs and voice of man but none of his other qualities. They were submen, quasi men, or they were brutes and animals.[4] The literate Roman of the later Empire saw them as invaders and destroyers: they fought, plundered, burned, raped, and killed—nothing more.

And so History, like the world in which they lived, has been unkind to them. Their attitude towards the outside world, towards natural phenomena and the gods, towards society and their fellow men, their hopes and ambitions, what they laughed at, and how they loved and prayed, cannot now be known, or at best are matters of little more than guesswork. Their songs and their folk traditions were never written down in the original language, and we have only the two or three examples which Jordanes preserved in Latin prose summaries. Even their law-codes, which have survived, are written in Latin, and for the most part were composed by Romans. Occasionally they followed the Roman practice of carving an inscription on the tombstones of their dead relatives; but these inscriptions are written in Latin without exception and, were it not for the Germanic personal names, we should never have guessed that they are the memorials of non-Romans. In spite of the loud volume of criticism and abuse which the Romans raised against them, in spite of the movements of countless armies and many peoples, the barbarians in this sense have passed from history, as it were, in silence.

And yet these same barbarians of the later Roman period provided much of western Europe for some generations with governments that were stable, secure, and by the standards of their time just and fair. So long as the kings were heretical Christians, Arian Christians, all of them (apart from the rulers of Africa) showed a tolerance of their Catholic subjects that was wholly alien to the last Roman emperors of the West and to the later Catholic barbarian kings. The sixth century is not usually regarded as an age of tolerant government; but that is what it was, at any rate in Spain and in its earlier years in Italy and parts of France. In those countries Catholics, Jews, and (within limits) pagans were free to worship as they pleased. The heartless persecutions of the heterodox, which had characterized the Roman Empire from the time of Theodosius the Great, seemed to be things of the past under the first barbarian kings. But with the triumph of Catholicism it was tolerance itself that became a thing of the past.

I. BARBARIANS ADOPT ROMAN WAYS

The subtler ways in which Roman civilization influenced barbarian attitudes and practices both in the period of the early Empire and in that of the later are likely to escape our notice altogether. Did Germanic warriors win much prestige at home from having served abroad with the Roman armies? If so, did this prestige bring them significantly more authority than they would have had if they had not served with the Romans? If there were several soldiers retired from the imperial service in any one community, were the centres of power (in so far as power existed at all) shifted to an appreciable degree? As mercenaries in Roman service they had been subject to Roman law (a fact which some of them found difficult to understand: p. 6 above): did Roman legal ideas and practices make any impression on the native societies when numbers of such men came home? Did Roman ideas of authority and command, of coercive power, of *imperium*, penetrate to any extent into Germany? Again, there may not have been much coming and going between the free Germans beyond the Rhine and those Germanic communities which had been incorporated in the Roman Empire, for the Roman authorities did not welcome random barbarian visitors. But there was *some* degree of intercourse: what then was the effect on opinion beyond the frontier of the news that the subject Germans were enjoying a higher level of material life than was known in the free Germanic settlements? An Alamannic warrior named Mederic, when serving as a hostage in Gaul in the middle of the fourth century, became an adherent of the worship of Serapis. When he returned to Germany he changed the name of his son Agenaric to Serapio. Mederic can hardly have been the only German to become attached to a Roman form of religion.[5] What was the effect (if any) on Germanic religion of the return home of such men as Mederic when they had finished their service in the Empire? Did they modify the character of Germanic paganism to any degree or had their new ideas no substantial influence?

These and similar questions can hardly be answered, but they suggest that it may have been misleading to speak, as I have done on earlier pages, of the "common warriors" and the "rank and file" of the tribesmen, as though the warriors other than the chiefs and the leading men were a homogeneous, undifferentiated mass. In fact, service with the Romans, the acquisition of Roman ideas and tastes, travel abroad for trading and other purposes, and especially the ownership of different numbers of cattle and weapons and Roman imports will have brought about distinctions and differences among the "rank and file" of the population. But we may suspect that no factor caused such intense divisions and such bitter internal hostility as the attitudes of the leading men towards the Roman Empire. From the reign of Augustus to the end of the Western Empire, we may think, no subject divided the Germanic communities more deeply than the question of their relationship with the imperial government. From the days of Segestes and Arminius to those of Eriulf and Fravitta (p. 41 above), from the time of Theoderic II and Euric to that of Eraric and Totila, this was the basic problem in at least Gothic society. The dilemma of the leaders was clearly stated by Athaulf (p. 45 f. above): should we lead our fellow tribesmen or govern them, and should we overthrow the Roman Empire or become part of it? We have seen that these are not two questions but only one and the same question.

The problem existed for much humbler persons than Athaulf. In the year 358 the Caesar Julian was at the height of his success in Gaul. When he came in contact with the Frankish people of the Chamavi he was able to beat them easily enough when they faced him in a pitched battle.[6] But then they broke up into the tiny plundering bands which were customary and indeed necessary for the northern invaders once they had set foot in the provinces.[7] These bands inflicted very extensive damage on the countryside of the Moselle valley, and Julian was at a loss to know how to deal with them. He was saved by Charietto.

Charietto was a barbarian of great physical strength and courage who had begun his career outside the law: he had been a brigand on the Gallic frontier with a few followers but had then drifted into Trier. No doubt, like many another barbarian, he was attracted to the great city by the possibility of picking up a little cash among the throngs of troops, officials, and traders who crowded into the military capital of the Gallic Prefecture. At Trier he noticed the freedom with which the barbarians were plundering the towns and countryside outside the walls; and before Julian arrived in Gaul at the end of 355 Charietto had decided to draw upon the knowledge and skill which he had acquired when he was a brigand, and to assure himself of an income by toadying to the government. Guided by the experience which he had gained in his previous profession as a brigand he went alone into a likely spot deep in the neighbouring forests, and when he located a band of barbarians drinking and sleeping after a successful day's plundering he stole up to them and cut off a few heads, which he brought back to Trier and displayed in the streets of the city. By repeating this performance several times and thereby spreading some demoralization among the raiders of the area he soon found himself at the head of an increasing number of other exbrigands and broken men, who had presumably been none too successful in the practice of their craft in a land from which the barbarians had already extracted the loot. Charietto quickly had a sizable force to follow him. And Charietto, we are told, himself remained the cunningest brigand and the strongest man among them all.[8]

He was now important enough to approach the Caesar himself and explain his tactics. Julian was still puzzled to know how to deal with the elusive night raids of the Chamavi. Perhaps now, certainly on other occasions, he was reduced like Valens in his campaign in Gothia in 367 to the despicable expedient of offering a reward to anyone who could bring in an enemy's head: he legalized murder.[9] But though the barbarians were everywhere at night they vanished during the day, and Julian could find no trace of them. As an historian said of other barbarians in similar circumstances, they were "ghosts rather than men."[10] In fact, as Charietto knew very well, they were hiding in the woods which surrounded the cultivated areas of the region and were living on the food which they gathered on their forays. Julian had no choice but to set one thief to catch another. He gave official status to Charietto and his friends, added a number of Salian

Franks to their band, and worked out a new strategy with his new lieutenant. Charietto and his motley company, who were of course well practised
in all the ways of brigandage, were to locate and attack the Chamavi by
night, while the Caesar would keep up the pressure by day; and these tactics soon brought the Chamavi to surrender.[11] Seven years later Charietto,
now Count of Both Germanies, was killed by the Alamanni when leading
an orthodox type of Roman army detachment. A rapid march had
brought him upon a body of Alamannic warriors, and so long as his troops
fought with arrows and light missiles he was able to hold his own; but
when they came to close quarters and fought with swords the Roman line
was broken by a vigorous Alamannic charge, the troops lost their nerve,
and Charietto fell while trying to hold up the route.[12] His methods had become more conventional as he himself became a conventional Roman
officer.

So Charietto in his relatively humble way supported the Roman establishment and abandoned his fellow countrymen. But he was a minor figure compared with Athaulf and Amalasuntha and others that we know of.
Among the Ostrogoths, for example, we hear of two very prominent officers in the Byzantine army in the time of the Emperor Anastasius: they
were Godidisclus and Bessas, who had not gone to Italy with Theoderic in
488. They were both noblemen.[13] Sisifrid, a Goth who was "exceedingly
loyal to the Romans," rose to be commander in Assisi in 545.[14] Similarly,
an Ostrogothic officer called Gento, who had married a Roman wife from
Epirus, was in command of a Roman force which was preparing to fight
against other Ostrogoths in 479.[15] A certain Sidimund, who is not reported to have been in the military service of East Rome, owned a rich estate near Epidamnus and also received an income from the Emperor.[16] But
even these were small fry in comparison with Theoderic himself, afterwards known as the "Great." When he died in 526 how many of his followers remembered that nearly half a century earlier, in 479, when he had
seized Dyrrhachium and parts of Epirus, he stated in his conversations
with a Roman official called Adamantius that in return for certain services
he wished to be appointed as Master of the Soldiers by the Eastern government and to be "received into Constantinople to take a place in public life
(*politeusonta*) in the Roman manner"?[17] Even in his case, then, his personal
ambition was to detach himself from his fellow Goths, to secure a high
place in Roman society and politics, and presumably to end his days as a
Roman landowner. Although he ought to have known what this sort of
ambition had done to the Visigoths, he can hardly have dreamed of the extent to which it would one day play a part in the destruction of his own
people.

II. BARBARIANS IN THE IMPERIAL ARMY

On the continent of Europe we must picture the Visigoths and the Ostrogoths, as they searched for land on which they could settle permanently, travelling from one province to another in their long wagon trains, which were far from easy to manage in mountainous districts. On one occasion near Lychnidus in Illyricum the East Romans inflicted a stinging defeat on the Ostrogoths, taking more than 5,000 prisoners and capturing 2,000 wagons, some of which they burned while using the rest to transport military supplies.[18] After the battle of Adrianople in 378, where "whole armies disappeared like a shadow," according to a contemporary,[19] the Visigoths were on the move in separate groups throughout the next four decades with few intervals from one province to another, sometimes tramping through the dust beside the great winding train of wagons — which in one group of the invaders numbered as many as 4,000 — sometimes taking their turn to rest upon them; and one of their Roman prisoners survived to write a poem in which he mentions his captivity and the dust and the wagons and the heavy load that he carried.[20] Sometimes the mere approach of such an enormous line of wagons would so scare the citizens of a Roman town that they would abandon their city altogether and leave it empty to fall into the hands of the barbarians: that was how the Ostrogoths took Scampia or Scampis in Macedonia in 479.[21] In a moment of danger the wagons would be drawn up in a circle which the Goths themselves called a *carrago* and which formed a powerful fortification.[22]

But the greatest problem of all was the supply of food. Often enough famine followed by plague would break out among them. This happened, for example, when the Visigoths were attacking the towns in Macedonia.[23] The famine in the cities and the larger villages undoubtedly resulted now as during the third-century raids in pestilence.[24] Indeed, such was the destruction of men, cattle, and livestock of all kinds that even districts not directly affected by the fighting began to suffer from starvation and plague, which, relentless and impartial, would destroy invader and invaded, soldier and civilian, alike.[25] Hence, after Adrianople a number of Visigoths were actually induced to take service in the Roman army, presumably in order to avoid starvation — for even in the third century famine and plague had driven some Goths into service with the imperial forces.[26] Some of their chiefs joined Theodosius for a very different reason (p. 41f. above) and even assisted him to defeat parties of their own kinsmen; but the humbler Visigoths who were obliged to put on Roman uniform did not fail to keep the bulk of their fellows informed of Roman plans and movements. They were constantly "fraternizing" with their kinsmen, they facilitated their movements, they abandoned the Romans without scruple at critical moments, and once they almost enabled their friends to capture the Emperor Theodosius I himself.[27] By their mere presence in the imperial army these men would sometimes overawe and demoralize the Roman troops, but they did not spare the Roman provincials whom they were supposed to defend. Even higher rates of pay and special terms of service could not secure their loyalty; and Theodosius was therefore obliged to transfer some of them to Egypt and doubtless others to other distant provinces.[28] Fravittas did not share the opinions and attitudes of men such as these.

Similar divisions can be traced even among the free Germans living outside the imperial frontier. We are particularly well informed about the Roman wars against the Alamanni (who lived east of the Rhine and south of the Main) in the middle of the fourth century. Even when an Alamannic warrior joined the Roman army his loyalty to his paymasters was by no means in all cases to be relied upon. During Constantius' campaign of 354 the Romans could have crossed the Rhine and inflicted severe damage on the enemy, had not the Alamanni mysteriously made their appearance opposite the precise spot where the emperor had secretly decided to ford the river. Nothing could be proved, but information was believed to have leaked out; and strong suspicion fell on three high officers in the Roman army, all three of them Alamanni.[29] Again, Valentinian I promoted one of the tribal nobility of the Bucinobantes named Hortarius to a command in his army, only to find out not long after that Hortarius was contriving to send back information to the rest of the Bucinobantes, with whom Valentinian was then at war. The emperor brought home to him the benefits of Roman civilization by torturing him until he confessed his "treachery" and by then burning him alive.[30] It was not only barbarians who gave away military secrets to the enemy. The Caesar Julian was dangerously besieged in Sens for a month because "deserters" had revealed to the enemy how few were the regiments that he had with him in the town.[31] In the great campaign of 357 the Alamanni were fired to heights of confidence when a deserter told them that Julian's army consisted of no more than 13,000 men. Indeed, deserters appear even to have reported the Caesar's tactical dispositions during the battle itself.[32] We do not, however, know the nationality of the deserters in these two cases.

Yet it is hard to believe that the Romans would have recruited and promoted barbarians on such a scale as they are known to have done if the danger of treachery had been extreme; and what is remarkable about the detailed narrative of Ammianus Marcellinus is not the frequency of such acts of treachery but their rarity.

On the other hand, some of the Alamanni assisted the Romans. When

Julian penetrated ten miles across the Rhine in 357, he was warned of what might have been a disastrous ambush "by the report of a deserter"; and when Valentinian decided to assassinate or kidnap Macrianus, chief (*rex*) of the Bucinobantes, deserters told him where he could take his victim off his guard.[33] The Alamannic leader Gundomad opposed his followers' desire to join in the campaign against the Romans in 357 because of his friendship for the enemy; and he was quickly assassinated. His brother Vadomarius, too, it seems, had been none too anxious to fight against the Romans and had only been compelled to take part in the conflict by his *plebs*: at any rate, that was the excuse that he gave, and it is not an excuse that he is likely to have invented, for it reflects discredit on his influence and renown.[34] He afterwards made his peace with the Romans and rose to become military commander (*dux*) of the Roman province of Phoenicia. Later still he helped to besiege Nicaea for Valens in the struggle with the usurper Procopius, and we last hear of him in 371 as cogeneral with one Traianus fighting against the Persians in Mesopotamia.[35]

There is no point in multiplying examples.[36] In fact, wherever we have first-rate sources of information, such as Tacitus or Ammianus or Procopius, we find among the more advanced of the barbarian peoples—whether inside or outside the frontier, whether the Ostrogoths or the Visigoths or the Alamanni—a section of the local nobility which is attracted to Rome and which would have had little inclination to disagree with the famous change of heart of which Athaulf spoke (p. 45 above). And there is small room for doubt that the main reason of many of them for inclining to such a point of view was not only to advance their own material interests but also, in a society which knew as little of coercive power as did the Achaeans of Homer, to impose their will upon their followers. Athaulf could not impose "laws" on his men any more than Agamemnon could impose "laws" on Achilles and the Myrmidons. But Athaulf had a resource which was not open to Agamemnon: he could become part of a developed and powerful state in which the concept of "law," which was unknown to the Achaeans, had been established in writing for a thousand years. Athaulf could therefore join in upholding, and becoming part of, that Roman world in which he could employ coercive power over against his followers. Other barbarians may have had no grander ambition than to exchange a dismal hut east of the Rhine or north of the Danube or of the Black Sea for the comforts of life in a villa near Constantinople (as Eraric and others wished) or near Epidamnus (like the Ostrogoth Sidimund). Yet others would have been glad to live their lives, as Charietto did, as well paid officers in the imperial army.

So, as the long wagon trains of the Goths wound their way westwards, the men who tramped beside them had other topics to discuss besides land on which they could settle or the supply of food or of women or of slaves. They could also discuss their attitude towards the Roman Empire and—the same question in a different form—their attitude towards their own leaders.

Of one thing these men could be fairly sure as they marched on their interminable journeys: although it was likely enough that the imperial armies would try to intercept and even destroy them, it was all but certain that the peasants of the countryside, like the townsfolk, would leave them alone and risk no interference with their progress. The apathy of the citizens of the provinces is well known but not easy to account for. We have seen (p. 102 above) that traders, sailors, slaves, and others helped Belisarius to defend Rome during the great siege of 536–37, though they were helped to do so by his offer of payment for their services. In 544 during the siege of Edessa by the Persian king Roman soldiers in the city launched an attack on the besiegers, and 'rustics and some of the *demos*' joined them in the assault.[37] It frequently happened in Justinian's reign that the steppe nomads would invade Thrace and Illyricum, where the emperor forbade the imperial forces to attack them: he wanted to use the nomads as allies against the Goths or some other enemy. Accordingly, it often happened that the farmers of the invaded districts would attack these "Huns" as they fell back towards the Danube since their women and children had in many cases been taken prisoner and were about to be enslaved. The farmers often scored victories in these encounters, rescued their relatives, and made off with the nomads' horses into the bargain.[38] We have seen an occasion in Spain where the occupants of a fort—though they were civilians—attacked and killed a number of the Sueves (p. 178 f. above). We have seen how some of the Noricans were persuaded by Severinus to attack and defeat a party of the barbarians (p. 130 above). In 443 the citizens of Asemus in Moesia defeated a band of Huns.[39] But we have to scour the ancient sources to find even a handful of cases where the countryfolk resisted actively the invaders of the places where they lived. Once again, the exceptional case is Britain, where the provincials, or a substantial number of them, attacked and defeated the invaders on three occasions during the fifth century—in 409, soon after 446, and in the days of the mysterious Ambrosius Aurelianus. But how are we to explain the general lack of resistance? It would be superficial to say that the citizens could not fight because Roman law had forbidden them to carry arms. If men have to defend their homes and even their lives, they will find arms quickly enough. *Furor arma ministrat.* Perhaps a truer judgement is given by Zosimus. Recording the destruction of Sparta by the Visigoths in 396, he makes this comment:

"Even Sparta herself was swept away in the common destruction of Hellas. She was no longer fortified by arms or by warriors owing to the exploitation (*pleonexia*) of the Romans, but had been given up to rulers who were traitors and who eagerly served the pleasure of the conquerors [i.e. the Romans] in everything that led to our common ruin."[40] The calamities of one of the most famous places of the ancient world were due to causes far more profound than a mere passing raid of the Visigoths. Roman rule had not deprived the provincials of weapons. It had robbed them of their morale and their will to survive.

III. CONVERSION OF BARBARIANS

Between the conversion of Constantine in 312 and the accession of Justinian in 527 the Catholic Church is not known to have sent missionaries beyond the imperial frontier so as to convert the pagan barbarians who lived there. Ulfila went to the Goths beyond the lower Danube to serve as bishop to those Christians who were already living in Gothia.[41] Palladius was sent by the pope to Ireland in 431 to minister to "the Scots who believe in Christ."[42] And we know of no emperor in this period who believed that a common religion might be a political link between two states. But that was not wholly true of the heretics. The Arian Visigothic king, Theoderic II, sent Ajax among the Sueves of Galicia in Spain, and he converted these barbarians from paganism to Arianism (p. 215 above). It would not be easy to find a Catholic parallel in the fourth, fifth, or early sixth century.

There has been endless discussion of the conversion of the Germanic peoples to Christianity. The truth seems to be that before the disappearance of the Western Empire in 476 none of the Germans, except the Rugi, was converted to Christianity while still living outside the imperial frontier; and after they had made their way into the provinces none of them except the Anglo-Saxons remained pagan for more than a generation or two.[43] But what of the conversion of the nomads?

About the year 400 one or two Roman prelates took some interest in the nomads. John Chrysostom, patriarch of Constantinople, about that date sent some missionaries "to the nomadic Scyths encamped along the Danube," though not necessarily outside the frontier.[44] But the historian who mentions the fact cannot claim that these missionaries managed to convert any of the nomads to Christianity. One difficulty was the language problem. The number of Romans who knew the Hun language was small. Even in the middle of the fifth century, of all the non-Hun characters who crowd the pages of Priscus of Panium only two or three could speak Hunnish. One had been a war prisoner among the Huns. Another was an official interpreter. A third had originally been a war prisoner but had later settled down among the Huns.[45]

Theotimus was bishop of Tomi (Constantsa on the coast of the Black Sea) at this same time. We are told that the Huns along the Danube were impressed by his merits and used to call him "God of the Romans," for they had had experience of miraculous deeds performed by him. It was said that one day, as he was skirting barbarian country, he and his companions saw a band of Huns riding towards them. The bishop's companions lamented that they were about to be killed; but Theotimus simply dismounted from his horse and began to pray. The barbarians rode past: they could not see him or his companions for the good reason that they had all been made invisible! It was a custom of the bishop to entertain Huns and to present them with "gifts," thus changing them from their bestial character to gentler ways. Since he could entertain so lavishly, one of the Huns assumed that the bishop was a rich man, and so he plotted to take him prisoner. He tried to lasso the bishop (for the Huns, like all self-respecting cowboys, were good with the lasso); but when he raised his arm to throw the rope he could not lower it again—his arm had become fixed and paralysed. At the request of his companions Theotimus prayed to God, and only then was the Hun's arm freed from its invisible bonds.[46]

Now, our authority for these matters is not able to vouch for the truth of his stories about how the bishop and his friends were rendered invisible and how the Hun's lasso-arm became petrified. He tells these tales as "reports," no more. Nor does he give the slightest hint that Theotimus converted a single nomad to Christianity. But what is even more striking is the fact that he gives no indication whatever that Theotimus ever even tried to convert the heathen. So far as he knows, it never entered the bishop's head that he might win a nomadic soul for the Church. Whatever purpose may have brought him to the edge of the steppe, it was not an ambition to save barbarians from the Fire Everlasting.

In this indifference to the spiritual welfare of the barbarians Theotimus seems to have been characteristic of the fourth- and fifth-century clerics. We know that in the fifth century individual barbarians, who had enlisted in the imperial armies, might be converted to Christianity; and war prisoners might win over some of their captors. But such converts were few.[47] And whether examples were known from among nomadic mercenaries is not recorded. An exceptional area in this connexion was Arabia.

Towards the end of the reign of the Persian king Isdegerdes, *c.* 420, there was a sharp persecution of the Christians in Persia. Many of the victims of the persecution fled, or tried to flee, for refuge to the Roman provinces. Now, the Saracen chief Aspebet, who was a pagan, disapproved of the persecution and did not prevent a number of Christians from escaping. He was denounced to Isdegerdes and himself took refuge in the Roman Empire. The imperial authorities made him paramount chief of the Arab tribes in that area. Then the holy man Euthymius healed his son of a paralysis, and so Aspebet and all his followers accepted Catholic Christianity. He took on the baptismal name Peter, and before the year 431 he was consecrated as bishop of the Saracens by Juvenal of Jerusalem.[48] From Bedouin sheikh to Catholic bishop was a rarely trodden path. Somewhat later in the fifth century, *c.* 473, in the reign of the Emperor Leo I, an Arab chief called Amorcesus abandoned the Persians, established himself as paramount chief among the Saracens of his area, and seized the Roman island of Iotabe in the Red Sea. He expelled the Roman customs officers and enriched himself with the Roman customs dues. He tried to come to terms with the Romans and wanted to be recognized as paramount sheikh over the Arabs in the neighbourhood of Petra. Leo summoned him to Constantinople, entertained him at his table, even allowing him to sit among the patricians. In return he became a Christian! In this case, however, it is noteworthy that there were already Christians in his tribe, for Amorcesus opened his negotiations with Leo through "Peter, bishop of his tribe." If there was a bishop there, evidently the number of Christians in the community was not small.[49]

With Justinian we enter a new period. He believed that a people which accepted the Catholic faith would be likely to act as the allies of the Catholic Empire. He made this point explicitly to the Franks as early as 536, when he formulated the doctrine that Franks and Byzantines ought to cooperate because of their identical religion.[50] He also proposed to the Ethiopians and the Homerites that they should join with East Rome against Persia "because of their identity of belief."[51] Procopius goes so far as to represent the Lombards as appealing to Justinian for an alliance against the Gepids on the ground that he and they are alike Catholics whereas the Gepids are Arians.[52]

Another new phenomenon in the sixth century is the arrival in Constantinople of individual barbarians, or of groups of barbarians, asking of their own accord to be baptized. A certain Gretes, king of the Germanic Heruls, came to the capital with his retinue and twelve kinsmen and asked to become a Christian. They were all welcomed by Justinian and were baptized. What must have given particular pleasure to the emperor was that as they returned joyfully to their own country, they promised to be his allies whenever he wished to call upon them for assistance. But in this case the initiative came, not from Justinian, but from the barbarians.[53] The outcome of the conversion was not always so happy as that of Gretes the

Herul. A certain Grod or Gordas, king of the Huns near the Crimean city of Bosporus, went to Constantinople and was baptized. Justinian sent him back with many gifts to the Crimea to guard the Roman possessions there, especially the city of Bosporus. Grod's people, of course, were pagans and worshipped idols. Grod proceeded — somewhat prematurely, as it turned out — to melt down the idols, which were made of silver and electrum; and he sold them for cash in Bosporus. This rather tactless action infuriated the pagan priests, who murdered Grod and made his brother Mugel king in his place. This was one of the relatively few cases where a barbarian ruler was converted and his people did not follow his example. It shows that the conversion of the king did not inevitably entail the conversion of the people at large.[54]

An aged presbyter called Julian from the diocese of the Monophysite patriarch of Alexandria "conceived an earnest spiritual desire to christianize the wandering people who dwell on the eastern borders of the Thebais beyond Egypt, and who are not only not subject to the authority of the Roman Empire, but even receive a subsidy on condition that they do not enter or pillage Egypt."[55] This Julian was a Monophysite heretic and, although the empress Theodora supported him, Justinian was annoyed by his mission and sent out Catholic missionaries of his own to the Nobadae. But the successful mission was Julian's: he converted the king and princes of the Nobadae and even instructed them in the "errors" of the Council of Chalcedon. Julian's successor in these remote parts was a certain Longinus, he travelled beyond the Nobadae to the Alodaei, who were supposed to be Ethiopians, for "when the people of the Alodaei heard of the conversion of the Nobadae, their king sent to the king of the Nobadae, requesting him to permit the bishop, who had taught and baptized them, to come and instruct them in like manner."[56]

Here we have some phenomena which could hardly be paralleled from the fourth and fifth centuries. First, a Christian cleric decided on his own initiative to go outside the imperial frontier for no other purpose than to spread the gospel among a pagan people there. Again, the ruler of a pagan people living far beyond the frontier actually summoned the missionary to his presence with the explicit purpose of being instructed in the faith. It is lamentable that we know nothing of the motives which led the king of the Alodaei to take this almost unparalleled step. He was certainly not aiming at winning the friendship of Justinian, for the emperor had strongly opposed the expedition of Longinus. Indeed, he had contrived to delay the start of Longinus's mission for three years.[57] Julian had reinforced the strength of his theological arguments by giving the king of the Nobadae "rich gifts," but Longinus is not reported to have used this style of persuasion.

When Longinus reached the Nobadae he ordained a native clergy, taught them the order of divine service, and also built them a church. But the reign of Justinian saw another missionary among the northern nomads, and a very interesting one he was. His name was Kardutsat, "bishop of the country of Arran."[58] He went with seven other priests from Albania into Hun territory to comfort the Roman captives who languished there. He stayed there "for a week of years" and made many converts among the Huns (perhaps the Sabiri). In connexion with this mission we are told one fact of great interest: he and his companions translated some books (of the Bible?) into the Hun language. Our authority gives no hint that it was Kardutsat himself who provided these Huns with a written language; and there is certainly no evidence that they had had one before this time. Indeed, in the middle of the sixth century Procopius turns aside from his narrative to emphasize that the Huns in general were absolutely illiterate.[59] Who was it that first devised an alphabet for this group and wrote down their language? We do not know: perhaps it was Kardutsat and his seven friends, perhaps some forgotten hero of a somewhat earlier day. In any event the reading public that may have existed among them must have been exceedingly small; and it probably consisted only of a tiny handful of the converted.

Kardutsat's mission was not fruitless. His achievement so impressed another Armenian bishop, whose name was apparently Maku, that he, too, with some other priests went out to the Huns "after two more weeks of years." Zachariah of Mitylene, our authority for Maku, goes on to say that "he built a brick church and planted plants and sowed various kinds of seeds and did signs and baptized many." What was the fate of his and Kardutsat's converts? We know no more of that than we do of the result of Maku's interesting experiment in raising pastoral nomads up to a settled, agricultural way of life. He certainly saw one essential of the problem of converting the nomads to Christianity. Few Byzantine churchmen would have been able—I say nothing of whether they would have been willing— to endure the hardships of nomadic life on the open steppe. Yet the task of conversion would be infinitely harder if the Huns were not exposed to the continuous influence of a missionary permanently resident among them. Maku, therefore, tried to divorce them from their nomadism and to group them around a church which he intended to be the centre of a community. In this community they could live without the necessity of travelling ceaselessly from pasture to pasture, following the green grass, as the nomads were compelled to do. If our authorities were better we might hear of other efforts to convert the nomads; but few of them would have deserved success better than Maku with his economic insight or than that unknown scholar who first wrote down the language of the "Huns."

The mid-sixth century, then, brought a number of new phenomena. Hitherto individuals had been converted when serving in the Roman army; but now entire groups were converted when they joined the imperial forces. Individuals and even companies of individuals travelled from the wilds of *barbaria* to Constantinople with the precise and avowed aim of being baptized. The Christianized barbarian undertakes to be the political ally of the Romans. On the southern frontier and also on the edge of the steppe priests, though rarely Catholic priests, are inspired to go outside the frontier of their own accord and to spread the Gospel there. The emperors begin to believe that a common religion would mean a common foreign policy, though the belief did not often turn out to be justified. To the Franks and the Byzantines their own material interests were very much more important than the fact that they both called themselves Catholics. Land, plunder, and power were of more immediate interest than the nature of the Trinity.

IV. ST. PATRICK

Tacitus was neither the first nor the last Roman author to draw attention to the military possibilities of the wine trade with the Germans. "If you should indulge their intemperance," writes the senator, "by supplying as much as they crave, they will be conquered as easily by their vices as by arms." He mentions that a cohort of them was destroyed by a trick of the citizens of Cologne, who gave them a splendid feast with plenty of wine, and when the Germans fell asleep they shut the doors of the building in which they lay and set it on fire.[60] What was an interesting speculation in Tacitus' day had become something more concrete late in the fourth century. "So the barbarians, too, have wine," writes St. Ambrose, "the Romans gladly indulge them with it so that they may be dissolved into drunkenness and, thus weakened, may be conquered as a result of their own inebriety."[61] Since the bishop expresses no distaste at this procedure there is no reason to think that he disapproved of it. It does not seem to have weighed with him that the course of action which he was recommending was contrary to the law. The sale of wine abroad was now illegal. The saint wrote these words after 386, that is, not many years after the emperors in the period 370–75 had banned the export of wine and oil to the barbarians (p. 10 above). The emperors did so for a purely economic or military reason and certainly not for a moral one. But whether economic, military, or moral Ambrose thought nothing of it.

St. Ambrose also has an elevating word of advice for moneylenders, traders, and others in their dealings with non-Romans. Commenting on the text Deuteronomy, xxiii. 19–20, "Thou shalt not lend upon usury to thy brother. . . . Unto a stranger thou mayest lend upon usury. . . . ", he writes the following choice passage: "Who was a 'stranger' in those days if not the Amalekite, if not the Amorite—that is, enemies? Exact usury among them, he says. The man whom you rightly long to kill, the man against whom it is just to take up arms—from him usury is taken legitimately. With your twelve per cent you can quickly avenge yourself on him whom you cannot easily conquer in war. Lend upon interest to him whom it is no crime to kill. The man who asks for interest fights, though without iron. He who exacts usury from the foe avenges himself upon the enemy, though without the sword. So, where there is the right of war, there also is the right of usury." Observe that the saint accepts trade with the enemy without question, and also that he assumes that these barbarians are living in circumstances where usury can be exacted from them even when they may not be wholly eager to pay it.[62] He does not give us his comment on the delicately worded law issued about the year 374 by which the Romans were *legally bound to steal* any gold which they found in the possession of those whom the Romans called "barbarians."[63]

Fortunately, there were Christians of a different stamp from St. Ambrose, the clerical bully of Milan. One such was a Briton called Patrick. St. Patrick was not a perfect character. Like most Britons, he had no sense of humour. He deeply resented the criticisms which were made of his career as bishop by British clerics, who thought that he was unfitted for his post. Indeed, towards the end of his life he developed something of a chip on his shoulder. Apart from what he tells us in the two little books that he has left us, we know several things about him. He flourished in the first half of the fifth century, he was not the first bishop to be sent to Ireland, and he was sent there to minister to the Christians who were already living there —the decision to convert the pagan Irish was his own.[64] He is the only writer to leave us books written outside the northern frontier of the Western Empire, and he is the first missionary to describe his life as an evangelist.

A mediaeval writer advises a friend of his who proposed to go out as a missionary to take with him a large train of attendants and fellow workers and to make a great display of food, clothing, and so on. The heathen will be impressed if they see wealth and will allow themselves to be converted. The missionary must be sure to take none of their goods. If they offer him anything, he must give them back more than he receives so that they will know that he had not come among them for gain.[65] St. Patrick had thought of all these things centuries earlier. He started by giving presents to the chief of the tribe in which he wished to work, but the nature of these presents he does not specify. He would also pay the local chief's sons and induce them, if he could, to travel about with him so as to ensure in some measure his personal safety.[66] He expects the readers of his *Confession* to know how much he had spent in bribing "those who administer justice through all the regions" which he was in the habit of visiting. The sum expended on these alone was "the price of fifteen men"; and at the time of writing he is still prepared to pay and pay again.[67] Now, the price of an unskilled slave in contemporary Gaul was some twenty-five or thirty *solidi*, so that if the price in Ireland was at all comparable—though it would not have been reckoned in *solidi* there—it would follow that Patrick had disbursed the equivalent of more than six pounds of gold in bribing the judges. If he means not the price of fifteen unskilled slaves but the ransom price of fifteen freemen, then the total sum might be considerably larger. The conduct of a foreign mission, it seems, was a matter requiring considerable financial backing. Patrick says nothing of the sources of his income. If his funds came from Britain, then there was no need to mention their source in his *Confession,* which is addressed primarily to Britons who would be familiar with the facts already; and the matter was irrelevant to the theme of his shorter work, the *Epistle to the Soldiers of Coroticus.* It is not easy to believe that his source of supply was the contributions of his converts and of the Christians who were already living in Ireland when he arrived there some time after the year 431.

In spite of his bribery of the chiefs the Patrician documents show only too clearly that the missionary's life was a dangerous one. If he made some converts among one people, a gang of ruffians from elsewhere might well descend upon them, butcher most of the men and carry off the women and children to sell them as slaves in some distant slave market. This is what happened to some of Patrick's neophytes who became the victims of the "warriors" of the nominally Christian and nominally Roman Coroticus.[68] And even without the interference of external forces there were perils enough. Patrick constantly expected to be defrauded or killed or enslaved, and indeed slavery seems to have been a common misfortune among his subordinate priests.[69] Even when the chiefs accepted the bribes they might still arrest the missionary and his companions, and then the danger of death was not far away. On one such occasion a chief seized Patrick and his friends and wished to kill them. He kept them in chains for a couple of weeks and robbed them of their goods; and they were set free and their property was restored only because of certain "near friends whom we had provided beforehand," a tantalizing but discreet phrase.[70] (I am not sure why he felt it necessary to be so discreet in this passage of the *Confession*: the friends whom he had provided beforehand and who could influence the chief were presumably Irishmen, and it is hardly likely that hostile Irishmen were likely to read the *Confession*.) Indeed, Patrick himself was often enslaved but always managed to escape.[71] His work called for extreme tact. It was essential to keep faith with the tribesmen and their leaders: a false step might start a persecution. "God knows, I defrauded none of them," he writes, "nor do I think of doing so, for God's sake and his Church's, in case I should raise a persecution against them and against us all, and in case the name of the Lord should be blasphemed on account of me."[72] Again, the numerous little gifts which Patrick's converts would offer to him and lay upon the altar for him he consistently refused to accept in spite of the pain which his seeming churlishness would cause; for only so were the "infidels" likely to admit him to the people, and only so could he avoid leaving an opening for defamation and disparagement. And although he won "thousands" of converts and ordained numbers of clergy he boasts that from not one of them did he receive the price of a shoe.[73] Patrick found that the converts themselves put up with many hardships and reproaches and persecutions from their kindreds.[74] But hardest of all was the lot of the slave women who were converted: they would defy the fury and "terrors" of their owners so as to join the forbidden sect.

Humourless though he is and far from even-tempered, Patrick is perhaps better known to us than any other figure of the migration period. Carried off as a slave to Ireland when he was only sixteen years of age he was unable to complete his education. Therefore the tricks of the rhetoricians and the fancy vocabulary of the *littérateurs* of his time are far beyond his powers. He has no choice but to write straight from his heart, and he does so with a passionate sincerity and an utter conviction of the righteousness of his cause that compel our admiration and respect. St. Ambrose's ideal (p. 245 f. above) of the drunken heathen gripped in the clutches of the moneylenders is not one that would have appealed to St. Patrick. When he was a slave still in his teens he guarded his owner's sheep on a mountainside in Connaught in snow, frost, rain, and loneliness. Little can he have dreamed at that time that one day his fame would be scarcely less than that of Constantine the Great.

Ulfila in the fourth century and Patrick in the fifth were unique in going out to convert the heathen to Christianity. It has to be confessed that a full history of the barbarian invasions of the Roman Empire would contain but few references to the Catholic Church. To Christians of those centuries doctrinal differences were more important that the fall of cities or the enslavement of peoples.

Appendix
Abbreviations
Notes
Index

Appendix:
The Visigoths in Aquitaine: Why?

I offer no excuse for returning to the problem of the settlement of the Visigoths on the western coast of France. That settlement was in fact the foundation of the kingdom of Toulouse, and it conditioned the history of southern and central France for the following ninety years. The importance of the question is not in doubt.

Unfortunately, in 1961 discussion of the matter was thrown into confusion by some ill-judged pages of J. M. Wallace-Hadrill, *The Long-Haired Kings* (London, 1962), 26 ff., a paper reprinted from the *Bulletin of the John Rylands Library*, xliv (1961). He can point to no flaw in the argument as set out in chapter two above; and even he does not suggest that the theory is improbable in itself or that the Roman government is unlikely to have defended the great estates of Aquitaine in this way. His technique is to argue that while the Armorican theory (as I may call it) "has its attractions," yet it is only one possibility out of many. There were numerous other enemies against whom the Roman authorities may have been taking precautions when they carried through the settlement of Aquitaine. Everything is conjecture. The Armorican theory is only one out of many. He reaches the scintillating conclusion that "we do not know why the Visigoths were settled in Aquitaine."

At first sight this procedure seems innocent enough. It is only when we look at his alternative suggestions and find that they are all wildly improbable and that one of them is wholly unintelligible that we may wonder what Wallace-Hadrill's reasons are for being so anxious to get rid of the Armoricans. The merit of the Armorican theory is that it accounts for all the known facts — that is not in dispute. It explains the date, the site, and the nature of the settlement. Wallace-Hadrill's alternatives account for none of these. It cannot be said of any of them that they have their attractions.

He points out, apparently as some kind of parallel, that when the Alamanni moved into Alsace in 455, the senators of Lyons at once permitted the Burgundian federates in Savoy to expand towards them so as to counter the possibility of an Alamannic thrust in their direction. The Burgundians were invited into the

251

Rhone valley so as to block a foreign enemy, the Alamanni. All, no doubt, quite possible. But what foreign enemy threatened Aquitaine in 418? Even the most pessimistic landowners of that region in their moments of suicidal depression can hardly have persuaded themselves that the Alamanni or the Franks were likely to drive westwards from the other side of the Rhine, cross the whole of France, reach the Atlantic coast, and occupy the great estates of Aquitaine. It looks, therefore, as if we must identify some other foreign aggressors. It is a small matter that E. James believes that there is hardly a problem ("there was a wealth of enemies to choose from"), for by an unfortunate oversight he has forgotten to share these riches with the rest of us, and so the identity of this wealth of enemies is obscure.[1] Wallace-Hadrill suggests as one possibility that the treaty with the Visigoths in 418 was "a measure designed to keep Saxon and Frankish sea-pirates at bay." It is this improbable suggestion that has bedevilled much of the discussion. We know that the rich landowners surrendered one third of the arable of their estates voluntarily and without a word of protest, so far as any of our authorities knows, with the result that a horde of unpleasant barbarians settled on their lands and in some cases even shared their houses. It is beyond argument that Aquitanian (or any other) estate-owners would have made so drastic a sacrifice only if an immediate and monstrous threat were seen to be menacing them. They would have surrendered so much of their land (we may think) only if the alternative had been to lose it all, and only if this alternative had been clear to every one of them. Such a sacrifice as they voluntarily made was a measure of desperation, almost of panic. If it was caused by fear of the activities of Saxon and Frankish pirates, then the pirates' threat must have been acute and must have been seen to be acute by them all. In other words, we have no alternative but to suppose that in the years immediately preceding 418 the pirates would each summer come swarming up the shores of Aquitanica Secunda in irresistible numbers, that raids were probably being replaced by settlements, that the barbarian pirates were beginning to overwinter on land, and that it was obvious, and obvious beyond all cavil, that the complete loss of the province was only a matter of time, and of a short time. On such a supposition as this, and on no other, could we explain the actions of the landowners if they were due to the raids of Saxon and Frankish sea-pirates.

Let us turn first, then, to the literary sources for the opening years of the fifth century to see what they have to tell us about these catastrophic raids. It comes as something of a surprise—I use the language of a moderate man—to find that they never even mention them! By good fortune we have the poem of Rutilius Namatianus in which he describes his journey from Rome to his native Gaul in 417: of sea raids on Gaul he knows nothing. For Salvian, a priest of Marseilles writing in 440–41, the Saxons were a fierce and chaste nation (as he thought) but they were as remote as the Franks and the Huns.[2] In order to suggest the existence of Saxon raids on Gaul before 418, Wallace-Hadrill feebly tells us that in 463 Saxons were active in Angers. These, we are told, were Saxon pirates.[3] About 478 Sidonius Apollinaris tells us definitely of Saxon pirates operating off the west coast of France, though not, it would seem, in massive numbers and certainly not threatening to settle on the Aquitanian estates or to overwinter on land.[4] In a poem included in a letter written in 476 or a little later Sidonius indicates that Saxon pirates had been sighted off Bordeaux.[5] I would suggest with some confidence that what the Saxons did, and what Sidonius wrote, in the 470s are unlikely to have influenced what Constantius did in 418.

Wallace-Hadrill next tries his luck with archaeology and the *litus Saxonicum*, the defended coast of southeastern Britain and of part of France. For the present purpose the vital question is, What part of the French coast was defended against Saxon raiders? "Notably the Garonne," we are told, "and the Dordogne with their tributaries, and to some extent the Charente also."[6] If these rivers were indeed fortified against Saxon raiders, and if forts constructed on them were part of the Saxon Shore defences, then the thesis of Wallace-Hadrill would take on some degree of credibility—provided, of course, that the chronology of these defences was appropriate. However, the facts are very different. The Charente, the Dordogne, and even the Garonne are alike unknown to the Saxon Shore. The recent study of the Saxon Shore by an archaeologist, Stephen Johnson,[7] shows that the forts were built in the decade 276–85, a fact which proves that in the third quarter of the third century there were massive Saxon raids on the southeast of Britain and on the relevant part of Gaul: otherwise the imperial government would not have incurred the expense of such large constructions nor would it have locked up so many of its armed forces in the defence of these forts. But what is the "relevant part" of Gaul? It appears that the Continental defences began at the mouth of the Rhine and extended southwestwards along the French coast to the mouth of the Seine. Indeed, it is not altogether certain that they reached so far as the Seine, for the westernmost fort, Grannona, cannot be identified and is only placed at the Seine's mouth by conjecture.[8] This is a long, long way from the Garonne, the Dordogne, and the Charente!

So literature and archaeology alike, so far from supporting the theory that the settlement of 418 was due to the Romans' need of a defence force to beat off Saxon sea-raiders, seem if anything to contradict it. If we would understand the circumstances which led to the foundation of the kingdom of Toulouse, we must first rid our minds of those elusive Saxons scampering up the beaches of Vendée and Charente-Maritime and threatening the large estates of Aquitaine. Nor is there any reason to suppose that the settlement was directed against attack from the rivers. You can best beat off a river-borne attack if you occupy both banks of the river in question. But the Visigoths are not said to have been planted south of the Garonne or north of the Loire. And how do these theories account for the date 418?

But we are now told that, after all, the choice does not lie between the Saxons and the Bacaudae,[9] and, to be sure, that is true enough, seeing that the Saxons do not come into the question at all. What the Romans were trying to do (we are now told) was to draw off the Goths from Spain and to pin them down in a "manageable" area of Gaul. That is to say, the Roman government withdrew the Goths from Spain, where they were fighting valiantly and successfully in the imperial interest. They had already destroyed the savage Alans as well as the Siling Vandals and were in process of dealing with the Asding Vandals. Why not allow them to finish off the Asdings? And in what sense were the Goths more "manageable" in Aquitaine than they would have been in Spain or on the Rhine, where they could have fended off the Franks or the Alamanni? After all, if you want to pin down a burglar, you do not pin him down in a bank. Aquitaine is the wrong place for pinning. And what of the landowners of Aquitaine? Did they surrender their land without a murmur because of these hare-brained military theories? Were they glad to share their estates with barbarians so as to stop the Goths from winning victories for Rome south of the Pyrenees? How did Constantius convince them that the Goths, if they could be brought on to the Aquitanian estates, would be in some mysterious way "manageable"? Did it not occur to the estate-owners that if the Goths had to be "pinned down" and "managed" in Aquitaine, their estates might well become a battlefield? Only estate-owners of an unusual kind are willing to see their estates fought over, backwards and forwards, by contending armies. If this was indeed Constantius' plan for managing the Visigoths, one might have expected a murmur of protest from the landowners. No such murmur is audible in our sources of information.

But now it turns out that Constantius probably had a good reason for his otherwise unaccountable action: Aquitanica Secunda "was probably overdue for a little rough treatment." I find this remark unintelligible and so cannot comment on it.

It is clear, then, that none of Wallace-Hadrill's suggestions account for the date of the settlement. They do not explain the site of the settlement: on his various theories, why not place the Visigoths between the Pyrenees and the Garonne? They do not account for the nature of the settlement. This speculation concludes with the assertion that "if . . . there was a danger against which the Goths could defend Gallo-Roman interests this cannot be identified." Not so. In all probability the danger lay north of the Loire.

It is a relief to turn from Wallace-Hadrill's "arguments" (as they might perhaps be called) to the thoughtful paper of Bernard S. Bachrach,[10] who wisely completes his paper without even mentioning the Saxon and Frankish sea-pirates. He suggests that the aim of Constantius was twofold. In 418 the Visigoths had already wiped out the Alans and the Siling Vandals in Spain and were now about to give similar treatment to the Asding Vandals. If these, too, were heavily defeated, Spain would lie at the mercy of the Visigoths. Second, the weakened Asdings might be put to good use by the Romans on some future occasion. Bachrach concludes that the recall of the Visigoths from Spain in 418 was designed to prevent the destruction of the Asdings.

It cannot be denied that this hypothesis may be correct. The reason why I reject it is that it accounts only for part of the evidence. It accounts for the date of the withdrawal of the Visigoths from Spain. Had they been allowed to remain in Spain for another year or two, they might well have finished off the Vandals and would thus have had the entire Iberian peninsula at their feet. What the hypothesis does not account for is the settlement in Aquitaine. Why were the Visigoths not planted, for example, somewhere on the left bank of the Rhine? And why the curious form of the settlement, whereby the Goths could not defend their own interests without at the same time defending the interests of their Roman "hosts"? And why the absence of complaint by the estate-owners? A theory which accounts for *all* the facts, as the Armorican theory does, is undoubtedly preferable to one which accounts for only some of them. But it is something to account even for one of them. Wallace-Hadrill cannot account for any of them.

Abbreviations

I. ANCIENT AUTHORITIES

AASS: *Acta Sanctorum*

Agathias: Agathias, *Histories*, ed. L. Dindorf, *Historici Graeci Minores*, vol. ii (Leipzig, 1871)

Amm. Marc.: Ammianus Marcellinus, ed. C. U. Clark, 2 vols. (Berlin, 1910, 1915)

Anthol. Lat.: *Anthologia Latina*, ed. A. Riese, 2 vols. (Leipzig, 1894, 1926)

Augustine, *Ep.*: Augustine, *Epistulae* in *CSEL*, vols. 34, 44, 57

Caesar, *BG*: Julius Caesar, *Bellum Gallicum*, ed. R. du Pontet (Oxford, 1900)

Cassiodorus, *Var.*: Cassiodorus, *Variae* MGH (AA), vol. xii

Chron. Min.: *Chronica Minora*, ed. T. Mommsen, MGH (AA), vols. ix, x, xii (but often referred to as i, ii, and iii). This work includes the *Chronica Caesaraugustana* (*Chron. Caesaraug.*), the *Chronicle of A.D. 452* (*Chron. Gall. a. CCCCLII*), the *Chronicle of 511* (*Chron. a. DXI*), as well as the *Fasti Vindobonenses Priores*, and the Chronicles of Hydatius, Isidore, and Marius of Aventicum

CIL: *Corpus Inscriptionum Latinarum*, vols. i–xvi (Berlin, 1861 ff.)

Claudian: Poems, ed. with transl. M. Platnauer (London, 1922)

Cod. Euric.: *Codicis Euriciani Fragmenta*, MGH (Leges), vol. i, 1, 3–32, a volume which also includes the Laws of the Visigoths

Cod. Justin.: Law Code of the Emperor Justinian (527–65), ed. R. Schoell and W. Kroll, 3 vols. (Berlin, 1895), including the *Digest* in vol. i

Cod. Theodos.: Law Code of the Emperor Theodosius II published in 438, ed. Mommsen and Meyer (Berlin, 1905)

Coll. Avell.: *Epistulae Imperatorum Pontificum aliorum Avellana quae dicitur collectio* in *CSEL*, vol. xxxv

Cons. Italica: *Consularia Italica* in *Chron. Min.*, vol. i

CSEL: *Corpus Scriptorum Ecclesiasticorum Latinorum*

Cyril of Scythopolis: ed. E. Schwartz (Leipzig, 1939)

Dio Cassius: *Historia Romana*, ed. U. P. Boissevain (Berlin, 1895)

Ennodius: ed. G. Hartel (Vienna, 1882)

Eugippius, *Vita Sev.*: *Vita S. Severini*, ed. P. Knoell, *CSEL*, vol. ix (Vienna, 1886); and by H. Sauppe, MGH (AA), vol. i, 1–30 (Berlin, 1879), but the best edition is that of R. Noll (Berlin, 1963) with German translation and notes

Eunapius: Historical fragments, ed. L. Dindorf, *Historici Graeci Minores* (Leipzig, 1870)

***Expositio*:** *Expositio Totius Mundi et Gentium*, ed. J. Rougé (Paris, 1966)

***FIR*:** *Fontes Iuris Romanae Ante-Iustinianae*, ed. S. Riccobono and others, 3 vols. (Florence, 1940–43)

Fredegarius: the relevant parts of his Chronicle are ed. with transl. J. M. Wallace-Hadrill, *The Fourth Book of the Chronicle of Fredegar* (London, 1960)

Gildas, *de Excidio Britanniae*: MGH (AA), vol. xiii, 15–85; also ed. H. Williams, 2 parts (London, 1899)

Greg. Tur., *HF*: Gregory of Tours, *Historia Francorum*, ed. B. Krusch and W. Levison, MGH *Scr. rer. Merov.*, vol. i, part i (Hannover, 1951)

Herodian, *Hist.*: *Histories*, ed. L. Mendelssohn (Leipzig, 1883)

Hilarus (Pope Hilary), *Ep.*: *Epistles*, ed. A. Thiel, *Epistulae Romanorum Pontificum* (Braunsberg, 1867), 127–70

Hydatius: *Chronicle*, MGH (AA), vol. xi, 13–36, and ed. A. Tranoy, *Hydace: chronique*, Sources chrétiennes, vol. 218 (Paris, 1974)

***ILS*:** *Inscriptiones Latinae Selectae*, ed. H. Dessau, 3 vols. (reprinted Berlin, 1954)

Isidore, *Etym.*: Isidore, *Etymologiae*, ed. W. Lindsay (Oxford, 1911)

Isidore, *Hist. Goth.*, *Hist. Vand.*, *Hist. Sueb.*: Histories of the Goths, Vandals, Sueves, MGH (AA), vol. xi, 267 ff.

Jerome, *Epp.*: *CSEL*, vols. liv–vi

Jo. Biclar.: John of Biclarum, *Chronicle*, MGH (AA), vol. xi, 211–20

John of Antioch: fragments of the *Histories* in C. Müller, *Fragmenta Historicorum Graecorum* (*FHG*), vol. iv, 538 ff., vol. v, 27 ff.

John of Ephesus: transl. R. Payne Smith (Oxford, 1860)

Jordanes, *Get.* and *Rom.*: Jordanes, *Gothic* and *Roman History*, MGH (AA), vol. v

***Legg Burg.*:** *Leges Burgundionum*, MGH (*Leges*), vol. i, 2, 36 ff

***Legg Visig.*:** *Leges Visigothorum*, MGH (*Leges*), vol. i

Libanius: ed. R. Foerster (Leipzig, 1903–22)

***Liber Pontificalis*:** MGH (*Gest. Pont. Rom.*)

Malalas: John Malalas, *Chronographia*, ed. L. Dindorf (Bonn, 1831)

Malchus: ed. L. Dindorf, *Historici Graeci Minores*, vol. i (Leipzig, 1870)

Marcellinus and Marcellinus Auct.: *Chronicle*, MGH (AA), vol. xi, 60–104

Marius Aventic.: Marius of Aventicum (Avenches in Switzerland), *Chronicle*, MGH (AA), vol. xi, 225–39

Merobaudes: ed. F. M. Clover, *Transactions of the American Philosophical Society*, new series, vol. 61, part i (Philadelphia, 1971)

Notitia Dignitatum: ed. O. Seeck (Berlin, 1876)

Olympiodorus of Thebes: ed. L. Dindorf. See Malchus

Orientius: *Commonitorium*, ed. R. Ellis, *Poetae Christiani Minores* (Vienna, 1888), 205–43. The volume also contains Paulinus of Pella, *Eucharisticon*, 289–314

Orosius, *Hist.*: *Historia adversus Paganos*, ed. C. Zangemeister (Leipzig, 1882)

Panegyrici Latini: ed. E. Galletier (Paris, 1949ff.)

Patrick, Saint: ed. L. Bieler, 2 vols. (Dublin, 1952)

Paulinus, *Euch.*: See Orientius

Paulus Diaconus, *Hist. Langob.*: *Historia Langobardorum*, ed. G. Waitz (Hannover, 1876)

Peter the Patrician: ed. L. Dindorf. See Malchus

Philostorgius: *Historia Ecclesiastica*, ed. J. Bidez (Berlin, 1913)

Priscus: Fragments, ed. L. Dindorf. See Malchus

Procopius, *BG, BP, BV, Anecd.*: Procopius, *Bellum Gothicum, Bellum Persicum, Bellum Vandalicum, Anecdota*, ed. J. Haury (Leipzig, 1905ff.)

Prosper: *Chronicle* with *Additamenta*, MGH (AA), vol. ix, 385ff.

Prudentius: ed. M. Lavarenne (Paris, 1943ff.)

RIB: *The Roman Inscriptions of Britain*, ed. R. G. Collingwood and R. P. Wright (Oxford, 1965)

Rutilius Namatianus: ed. J. Vessereau and F. Préchac (Paris, 1961)

Salvian, *De. Gub. Dei*: *De Gubernatione Dei*, MGH (AA), vol. i

Sidonius, *carm.*: Sidonius Apollinaris, *carmina*, ed. W. B. Anderson, 2 vols. (London, 1936, 1965)

Simplicius, Pope, *Ep.*: ed. A. Thiel, *Epistulae Romanorum Pontificum* (Braunsberg, 1867)

Socrates, *Hist. Eccles.*: *Historia Ecclesiastica*, ed. R. Hussey, 3 vols. (Oxford, 1853)

Sozomen: *Historia Ecclesiastica*, ed. J. Bidez and G. C. Hansen (Berlin, 1960)

Strabo: *Geographia* (Leipzig, 1884)

Suidas (or *Suda*): *Lexicon*, ed. A. Adler (Leipzig, 1928)

Synesius: *Letters*, ed. Migne, *Patrologia Graeca* (= *PG*), lxvi, 1321ff.; other works ed. N. Terzaghi (Rome, 1944)

Tacitus, *A, G, H*: *Annals*, ed. C. D. Fisher (Oxford, 1906); *Germania*, ed. R. M. Ogilvie and I. Richmond (Oxford, 1967), and R. Much (Heidelberg, 1967): *Histories*, ed. C. D. Fisher (Oxford, 1910)

Themistius: *Orationes*, ed. H. Schenkl, G. Downey, and A. F. Norman (Leipzig, 1956)

Theodoret: *Historia Ecclesiastica*, ed. L. Parmentier (Berlin, 1911)

Theophanes: *Chronographia*, ed. C. de Boor (Leipzig, 1883)

Theophylactus Simocatta: *Histories*, ed. C. de Boor (Leipzig, 1887)

Velleius Paterculus: the relevant parts of his History are ed. A. J. Woodman (Cambridge, England, 1977)

Victor Tonnennensis: *Chronicle*, MGH (AA), vol. xi, 184–206
Victor Vitensis: *Historia Persecutionis*, *CSEL* vol. vii (Vienna, 1881), ed. M. Petschenig
Vitas Patrum Emeretensium: ed. J. N. Garvin (Washington, D.C., 1946)
Zachariah of Mitylene: *Chronicle*, transl. F. J. Hamilton and E. W. Brooks (London, 1899)
Zonaras: *Epitome Historiarum*, ed. L. Dindorf (Leipzig, 1868)
Zosimus: *Histories*, ed. L. Mendelssohn (Leipzig, 1887)

II. MODERN WORKS

Bury: J. B. Bury, *History of the Later Roman Empire*, 2 vols. (London, 1923)
Chron. Min.: *Chronica Minora*, ed. T. Mommsen, MGH (AA), vols. ix, xi, xii, often referred to as *Chron. Min.*, vols. i, ii, iii respectively
Courtois, *Byzantion*: Christian Courtois, "Auteurs et scribes: remarques sur la chronique d'Hydace," *Byzantion*, xxi (1951), 23–54
Courtois, *Vandales*: Christian Courtois, *Les Vandales et l'Afrique* (Paris, 1955)
Dahn: F. Dahn, *Die Könige der Germanen*, vol. vi (Leipzig, 1885)
David: P. David, *Études historiques sur la Galice et le Portugal du VIe au XIIe siècle* (Lisbon and Paris, 1947)
Gibert: R. Gibert, "El reino visigodo y el particularismo español," *Settimane di studio del centro italiano a Spoleto*, iii (1956), 537–83
Jones: A. H. M. Jones, *The Later Roman Empire, 284–602: A Social, Economic, and Administrative Survey*, 3 vols. (Oxford, 1964)
JRS: *Journal of Roman Studies*
Maenchen-Helfen: J. Otto Maenchen-Helfen, *The World of the Huns* (Los Angeles, 1973)
Mansi: J. D. Mansi, *Sacrorum Conciliorum nova et amplissima collectio* (Paris, 1759–98)
MGH: *Monumenta Germaniae Historica*; (AA): *Auctores Antiquissimi*, 15 vols. (Hannover and Leipzig, 1877–1919). Reprint 1961. MGH *Leges*, vol. i, ed. K. Zeumer. MGH *Gest. Pont. Rom.: Gesta Pontificum Romanorum*, 1 vol. MGH *Scr. rer. Merov.: Scriptores rerum merovingicarum*, 7 vols.
Migne, *PG*: J. P. Migne, *Patrologia Graeca*, 162 volumes (Paris, 1857–1912)
Migne, *PL*: J. P. Migne, *Patrologia Latina*, 221 volumes (Paris, 1844–64)
Mommsen, *Ges. Schr.*: T. Mommsen, *Gesammelte Schriften*, 8 vols. (Berlin, 1905–13)
P.-W.: Pauly and Wissowa, *Realencyclopädie der classischen Altertumswissenschaft* (Stuttgart, 1893ff.)
Reinhart: Wilhelm Reinart, *Historia general del reino hispanico de los Suevos* (Madrid, 1952)
Schäferdiek: K. Schäferdiek, *Die Kirche in den Reichen der Westgoten und Suewen* (Berlin, 1967)

Schmidt, *Ostgermanen*: L. Schmidt, *Geschichte der deutschen Stämme; die Ostgermanen* (Munich, 1941)

Schmidt, *Wandalen*: L. Schmidt, *Geschichte der Wandalen* (Munich, 1942)

Schmidt, *Westgermanen*: L. Schmidt, *Geschichte der deutschen Stämme: die Westgermanen* (rept. Munich, 1970)

Seeck, *Untergang*: O. Seeck, *Geschichte des Untergangs der antiken Welt*, 6 vols. (Stuttgart, 1910ff.)

Stein: E. Stein, *Histoire du Bas-empire*, 2 vols. (Paris, 1949, 1959)

Thompson, *EG*: E. A. Thompson, *The Early Germans* (Oxford, 1965)

Thompson, *GS*: E. A. Thompson, *Goths in Spain* (Oxford, 1969)

Thompson, *VTU*: E. A. Thompson, *The Visigoths in the Time of Ulfila* (Oxford, 1966)

Tranoy: A. Tranoy, *Hydace: chronique*, Sources chrétiennes, no. 218 (Paris, 1974)

Vives: J. Vives, *Inscripciones cristianas de la España romana y visigoda* (Barcelona, 1942)

Wallace-Hadrill, *Barbarian West*: J. M. Wallace-Hadrill, *The Barbarian West, 400–1000* (London, 1967)

Wallace-Hadrill, *Kings*: J. M. Wallace-Hadrill, *The Long-Haired Kings* (London, 1962)

Notes

CHAPTER 1:
INTRODUCTION: ECONOMIC WARFARE

1 Velleius Paterculus, ii. 107.

2 Tacitus, *H* iv. 63; Jordanes, *Get.* 143.

3 Procopius, *BG* viii. 19. 14 ff.

4 Idem, *BV* iii. 12. 8 ff. Observe that in the narrative the murdered man is one of the "friends" of the other two, whereas in Belisarius' speech he is their kinsman, which is unlikely in view of *BG* vi. 14. 4. Cf. Agathias, *Hist.* ii. 7, for a somewhat similar case.

5 Caesar, *BG* vi. 1. 3; Tacitus, *H* v. 25. The very same argument was put forward by the eunuch Narses in 552: Procopius, *BG* viii. 29. 6, cf. vi. 28. 17.

6 Herodian, *Hist.* iii. 4. 8 f. For a later date note John of Ephesus, vi. 2; Procopius, *Anecd.* xxv. 25.

7 Theophylact. Simocatta, ii. 16.

8 Dio Cassius, lxvii. 7. 4; lxviii. 6. 1; 9. 3 and 5; cf. Peter the Patrician, frag. 5.

9 Caesar, *BG* ii. 29. 4; 30 f; 33.

10 Ibid., i. 13. 2 (bridge-building); ii. 12. 5 (siege-engines which the Gauls had never seen or heard of before); iv. 25. 1 f. (warships); vii. 29. 2 (siege warfare); A. Hirtius, *BG* viii. 43. 4 f.

11 Tacitus, *H* iv. 30.

12 Socrates, *Hist. Eccles.* vii. 18. 4; M. P. Charlesworth *apud* P. R. Coleman-Norton, *Studies in Roman Economic and Social History* (Princeton, 1951), 131–43. Note the Roman silk workers who are forced to emigrate to Persia: Procopius, *Anecd.* xxv. 25.

13 Zonaras, xii. 1. (For a different account see John of Ephesus, vi. 24); Priscus of Panium, frag. 8, p. 303. 23, ed. Dindorf.

14 Herodian, iv. 10. 4; Libanius, *Or.* lix. 66 ff. From Procopius, *BP* ii. 29. 1, it would seem that these Persians could make siege-engines.

15 *RIB* 1280-81; cf. I. A. Richmond, "Excavations at High Rochester and Risingham, 1935," *Archaeologia Aeliana,* ser. 4, vol. xiii (1936): 170–98, at 180 ff.; idem, "Roman Britain and Roman Military Antiquities," *Proceedings of the*

British Academy, xli (1955), 297–315, at 308 ff.; D. Baatz, *Bonner Jahrbücher,* clxvi (1966), 194–207.

16 *Digest,* xxxix. 4. 11 (Paul); xlviii. 4. 1–4 (Scaevola). There are some remarks on this topic by G. Vismara, "Limitazioni al commercio internazionale nell' impero romano e nella communita cristiana medioevale," *Scritti in onore di C. Ferrini* (Milan, 1947), i, 443–70.

17 *Cod. Justin.* iv. 41. 1; 63. 2. I owe the point to Vismara, art. cit., 445 ff.

18 *Cod. Theod.* vii. 16. 3; *Cod. Justin.* xii. 44 (45). 1.

19 *Cod. Theod.* ix. 40. 24; but we happen to hear that in the reign of Valerian "Scythians" used boats on the Black Sea and on at least one occasion they forced prisoners to row for them: Zosimus, i. 32–34.

20 So Maenchen-Helfen, *The World of the Huns,* 75. Certainly, the Goths were no seamen: see Norman H. Baynes, *Byzantine Studies and Other Essays* (London, 1955), 220 f.

21 *Cod. Justin.* iv. 41. 2. Contrast Procopius, *BG* viii. 15. 20.

22 Ibid.; Procopius, *BP* i. 19. 25 f.; *Anecd.* xxv. 4.

23 *Expositio,* xxii.

24 Dio Cassius, lxiii. 3; Menander Protector, frag. 9, p. 8. 21 ff., ed. Dindorf.

25 Tacitus, *G* xli. 1–2, with Much ad loc.

26 Tacitus, *H* iv. 64–5; Dio Cassius, lxxi. 15; Thompson, *VTU* 14 ff.

27 Dio Cassius, lxxi. 11. 3; lxxii. 19. 2.

28 *Expositio,* lvii.

29 Peter the Patrician, frag. 14; Themistius, *Or.* x. 135 CD, with *Hermes,* lxxxiv (1956), 376 f.; *ILS* 775; W. Schleiermacher, "Nundinenses," *Germania,* xxxii (1954), 326–28. But Roman and Persian traders are restricted in Menander Protector, frag. 11, p. 21. 22 ff. (A.D. 562), so as to facilitate the collection of customs dues.

30 *Cod. Justin.* iv. 63. 4.

31 Augustine, *Ep.* xlvi.

32 See Thompson, *EG,* pp. 140 ff.

33 Tacitus, loc. cit.; Dio Cassius, lxxi. 11. 3; Themistius, x. 161. 30 ff.; Zosimus, iv. 30. 4; *Cod. Justin.* iv. 63. 4.

34 Priscus of Panium, pp. 287. 3 ff., 345. 27, ed. Dindorf.

35 Amm. Marc., xxxi. 3 ff.; Eunapius, frag. 42, p. 237, ed. Dindorf.

36 Orientius, *Commonitorium* ii, 184.

37 Jordanes, *Get.* 266; John of Antioch, frag. 214. 4 and 6.

38 Jordanes, *Get.* 264 "pacem et annua solemnia"; cf. Procopius, *BG* vii. 34. 6 and 10.

39 Ibid., 270 f. Cf. 264 "maluerunt a Romano regno terras petere quam cum discrimine suo invadere alienas."

40 Priscus, frag. 28.

41 Jordanes, *Get.* 272; Priscus, loc. cit., for the size of the subsidy; Prosper, s.a. 459 (i. 492).

42 Priscus, frag. 39.

43 Jordanes, *Get.* 273–76; John of Antioch, frag. 206 *fin.* (for the Goths in Pannonia). For a vivid picture of the chaotic life on and beyond the imperial frontier after the collapse of Attila's empire see Jordanes, *Get.* 272–79.

44 Jordanes, *Get.* 277–79.

45 Ibid., 283.

46 Malchus of Philadelphia, frag. 2, p. 387. 20, Dindorf.

CHAPTER 2:
THE SETTLEMENT OF THE BARBARIANS
IN SOUTHERN GAUL

1 *Chron. Min.* i. 469 s.a. 419 "Constantius patricius pacem firmat cum Wallia data ei ad inhabitandum secunda Aquitanica et quibusdam civitatibus confinium provinciarum," ii. 19. s.a. 418, "Gothi intermisso certamine quod agebant per Constantium ad Gallias revocati sedes in Aquitanica a Tolosa usque ad Oceanum acceperunt." The treaty is discussed by G. Kaufmann, "Ueber das Foederatverhältniss des tolosanischen Reichs zu Rom," *Forschungen zur deutschen Geschichte,* vi (1866), 433–76, at 441–44.

2 Salvian, vii. 7 ff.

3 *Vita S. Orientii* iii (*AASS* i. May, 63). There are some inconsistencies in the extant accounts of the war of 439, but they are not sufficient to warrant us in denying the value of this *Vita. Contra,* C. Lecrivain, *Annales du Midi,* iii (1891), 257 f., A. Molinier, *Les sources de l'histoire de France,* i (Paris, 1901), 48. Even P. Courcelle, *Revue des Etudes Anciennes,* xlix (1947), 169–77, who (unnecessarily, in my view) doubts the value of the *Vita* as a whole, allows (ibid., 177 n. 1) that the episode about Litorius does not depend on any extant source and that it has some historical value. Why he should suppose (ibid.) that Salvian used a "source" for his account of Litorius' campaign in 439 is more than I can say.

4 *Chron. Min.* ii. 19 s.a. 418, "per Ligerem fluvium."

5 The suggestions put forward by place-name scholars, e.g. Gamillscheg, should be treated with reserve, as these scholars appear to have used faulty methods in reaching their conclusions: see F. Lot, "Que nous apprennent sur le peuplement germanique de la France les récents travaux de toponymic?" *Compte rendus de l'Academie des Inscriptions et Belles-Lettres* (1945), 289–98.

6 W. Reinhart, "Sobre el asentamiento de los Visigodos en la Peninsula," *Archivo español de Arqueologia,* xviii (1945), 124–39; J. Werner, *Germania,* xxviii (1944–50), 279–81. It is a pity that Reinhart does not give a bibliography to the illuminating map which he publishes, ibid., 137.

7 *Chron. Min.* i. 600 s.a. 443 "Sapaudia Burgundionum reliquiis datur cum indigenis dividenda."

8 For bibliography and discussion see P. E. Martin, "Le Problème de la Sapaudia," *Zeitschrift für schweizerische Geschichte,* xviii (1933), 183–205; F. Lot, "Les limites de la Sapaudia," *Revue savoisienne,* lxvii (1935), 146–56. But the equation Ebrudunum = Yverdon should not be lightly rejected: see D. van

Berchem, "Ebrudunum-Yverdon, station d'une flotille militaire au Bas-empire," *Zeitschrift für schweizerische Geschichte,* xvii (1937), 83–94.

9 *Chron. Min.* i. 305 s.a. 457 "post cuius [= Rechiarius, who died in December 456] caedem Gundiocus rex Burgundionum cum gente et omni praesidio annuente sibi Theodorico ac Gothis intra Galliam ad habitandum ingressus societate et amicitia Gothorum functus," ii. 232 s.a. 456, "eo anno Burgundiones partem Galliae occupaverunt terrasque cum Gallis senatoribus diviserunt."

10 Fredegarius, ii. 46.

11 *Legg. Burg.* liv. i. a law which cannot have been issued by any other king than Gundobad: E. T. Gaupp, *Die germanischen Ansiedlungen und Landtheilungen* (Breslau, 1844), 320 f.

12 H. Zeiss, "Studien zu den Grabfunden aus dem Burgundenreich an der Rhone," *Sitzungsberichte der bayerischen Akademie der Wissenschaften, philosophisch-historische Klasse* (1938), vii, 9 ff. The finds listed by him are not all certainly Burgundian.

13 *Chron. Min.* i. 660 s.a. 442 "Alani, quibus terrae Galliae ulterioris cum incolis dividendae a patricio Aetio traditae fuerant, resistentes armis subigunt et expulsis dominis terrae possessionem vi adipiscuntur," ibid., s.a. 440, "deserta Valentinae urbis rura Alanis, quibus Sambida praeerat, partienda traduntur." These two groups must not be confused: W. Levison, *Neues Archiv,* xxix (1904), 136 f. Orleans is mentioned in connection with the former group by Jordanes, *Get.* xxxvii. 194.

14 For a full discussion with bibliography see F. Lot, "Du régime de l'hospitalité," *Revue belge de philologie et d'histoire,* vii (1928), 975–1011.

15 Amm. Marc., xxvii. 5. 4–7; Zosimus, iv. 10–11; cf. Eunapius, frag. 37 *fin.;* Fiebiger-Schmidt, *Inschriftensammlung,* no. 167. The fact that Themistius says nothing of the battle does not outweigh the fact that Ammianus *does* mention it; for Themistius, ἅτε εἰρήνης ὢν ἐραστής (*Or.* xvi. 206 C), more than once omits reference to military operations which another orator might have lingered over.

16 Amm. Marc., xxvii. 5. 7 "aderant post diversos triennii casus finiendi belli materiae tempestivae: prima quod ex principis diuturna permansione metus augebatur hostilis; dein quod conmerciis vetitis ultima necessariorum inopia barbari stringebantur."

17 Orosius, vii. 43. i "interdicto praecipue atque intercluso omni commeatu navium et peregrinorum usu commerciorum." It would be of the utmost interest to know how the prohibition of overseas trade forced the Visigoths to leave Narbonne and go to Spain. What foreign commodities did they need so desperately?

18 Olympiodorus, frag. 29. The name *truli* in this fragment is discussed by M. Vasmer, "Ein vandalischer Name der Goten," *Studia Neophilologica,* xv (1942–43), 132–34.

19 Olympiodorus, frag. 31; Orosius, vii. 43. 12 f.; *Chron. Min.* i. 468 s.a. 416, ii. 19 s.a. 416; Jordanes, *Get.* xxxii. 165 (who says nothing of the famine). There is a discussion of the treaty of 416 in Kaufmann, art. cit., 436–440.

20 Orosius, loc. cit.

21 On the date of the *de Gub. Dei* see A. Haemmerle, *Studia Salviana,* Diss. Erlangen, 1893, 14 f., A. Schaefer, *Römer und Germanen bei Salvian* (Breslau, 1930), 38 f.

22 *Legg. Visig.* x. i. 16. Theodoric II is shown taxing the Romans in his kingdom in *Vita S. Viviani,* iv (*MGH Scr. rer. Merov.* iii, 96). Attention was drawn to this *Vita* by C. Lécrivain, "Un épisode inconnu de l'histoire des Wisigoths," *Annales du Midi,* i (1899), 47–51, but he wrongly took the Theodoric in question to be Theodoric I. The value of the *Vita* has been defended successfully, in my opinion, by F. Lot, "La *Vita Viviani* et la domination visigothique en Aquitaine," *Mélanges Paul Fournier* (Paris, 1929), 467–77, and Lot's position has not, I think, been upset by Courcelle, art. cit.

23 *Legg. Burg.* liv. 2; Sidonius, *carm.* xii; *Ep.* viii. 3. 2; Baehrens, *Poetae Latini Minores* iv, 363, a poem of which an English translation will be found in the unsigned article, "Ulfilas, the Apostle of the Goths," *Edinburgh Review,* cxlvi (Oct. 1877), 361–95, at 362. This article was written by Thomas Hodgkin, and apart from some lectures on Claudian it was his first contribution to the study of Italy and her invaders: see Louise Creighton, *Life and Letters of T. Hodgkin* (London, 1917), 419 ff., cf. 102 f.

24 For an excellent estimate of Aëtius' career, see E. Stein, *Geschichte des spätrömischen Reiches,* i (Vienna, 1928), 501–17, where note that his military capacity is not called in question.

25 H. Delbrück, *Geschichte der Kriegskunst*[3], ii (Berlin, 1921), 339–41, 347; A. Coville, *Recherches sur l'histoire de Lyon du Vme siècle au IXme siècle* (Paris, 1928), 190; Lot, art. cit., 989–93, etc. There is a fair measure of agreement on this point.

26 *Legg. Burg.* li. i. et saep. It is hoped to discuss elsewhere the Burgundian laws relating to the inheritance of the *sortes.*

27 Eunapius, frag. 43, which cannot refer to the time of Valens.

28 Salvian, vii. 8.

29 Amm. Marc., xiv. 10. 2; cf. xvii. 8. 1.

30 So C. Jullian, "Notes Gallo-romaines," *Revue des Études Anciennes,* xxii (1920), 275 f.; Coville, op. cit., 115–17.

31 Rutilius Namatianus, i. 213–16; Zosimus, vi. 5. 3; *Querolus,* pp. 16 f., ed. Peiper; cf. *Past and Present,* ii (1952), 11–23.

32 Zosimus, loc. cit.

33 Rutilius, loc. cit.

34 Constantius, *Vita Germani* xxviii, cf. xl. The defeat of Tibatto was completed before 446; Merobaudes, *Paneg.* ii. 13. Aëtius' wars against the Armoricans are also mentioned in John of Antioch, frag. 201, 3.

35 Bibliography and discussion in Coville, op. cit., 115–17, who believes, however, that the military strength of the Burgundians was far greater after 437 than it appears to have been in fact.

36 H. Nesselhauf, "Die spätrömische Verwaltung der gallisch-germanischen Länder," *Abhandlungen der preussichen Akademie der Wissenschaften,*

philosophisch-historische Klasse (1938), ii, 73, holds this view, but his arguments are far from convincing. So, too, G. J. Wais, *Die Alamannen* (Berlin, 1943), 111 ff. Contrast P. E. Martin, "La fin de la domination romaine en Suisse et l'occupation germanique," *Bulletin de la société d'histoire et d'archéologie de Genève*, vi (1935), 3–30; R. Heuberger, "Das ostgotische Rätien," *Klio*, xxx (1937), 77–109, at 83–93; L. Schmidt, "Zur Geschichte der alamannischen Besiedlung der Schweiz," *Zeitschrift für schweizerische Geschichte*, xviii (1938), 369–79; F. Staehelin, *Die Schweiz in römischer Zeit*[3] (Basel, 1948), 321 ff.; R. Laur-Belart, "The Late *Limes* from Basel to the Lake of Constance," *apud* E. Birley (ed)., *The Congress of Roman Frontier Studies, 1949* (Durham, 1952), 55–67, at 66; R. Fellmann, *Historia*, iv (1955), 214 ff.

37 Laur-Belart, art. cit., 64 f.

38 Sidonius, *carm.* vii. 373–75; Staehelin, op. cit., 321 ff.

39 Sidonius, *carm.* v. 373 ff.; Staehelin, loc. cit.

40 Salvian, iv. 68.

41 *Chron. Min.* i. 660 s.a. 439 "pacatis motibus Galliarum Aetius ad Italiam regreditur."

42 The Alans crushed the landowners in 442, and it is commonly assumed, e.g. by Stein, op. cit., i, 492, that they did so when actually being planted there. But it would not be inconsistent with our source, quoted on p. 266 n. 13 above, to suppose that they had been settled there for some time and that it was only now that trouble broke out.

43 *Chron. Min.* i. s.a. 436 "Gallia ulterior Tibattonem principem rebellionis secuta a Romana societate discessit, a quo tracto initio omnia paene Galliarum servitia in Bacaudam conspiravere."

44 Staehelin, op. cit., 266; L. Blondel, "L'enceinte romain de Genève," *Genava*, ii (1924), 109–29, at 127.

45 Zosimus, vi. 2. 3–5.

46 Flavius Merobaudes, who defeated a Bacaudic revolt in Spain in 443 (*Chron. Min.* ii. 24 s.a. 443), also fought a campaign in the Alps before the year 435; *ILS* 2950 "inter arma litteris militabat et in Alpibus acuebat eloquium." Who were his opponents *in Alpibus*?

47 *Chron. Min.* ii. 22 s.a. 430; Sidonius, *carm.* vii. 233 f.

CHAPTER 3:
VISIGOTHS FROM FRITIGERN TO EURIC

1 See p. 26 above.

2 Mommsen, *Ges. Schr.* vi. 229, esp. n. 3.

3 Eunapius, frag. 60; cf. Claudian, *BG* 81 f.

4 Amm. Marc., xxxi. 12. 9 where *condiciones rei Romanae profuturas* does not merely mean "terms of peace that would be satisfactory to the Romans."

5 Ibid., 14 *suo misit arbitrio* presumably means that he sent the envoys without consulting his council and without their instructions.

6 "Ohne Zweifel waren diese Vorschläge ernst gemeint," says Seeck, *Untergang*, v. 118, who observes ibid., 471, "eine so treffliche Quelle Ammian für

alles ist, was im Römerlager vor sich ging, konnte er doch über die Pläne und Befehle des feindlichen Feldherrn nur mangelhaft unterrichtet sein."

7 For what follows see Eunapius, frag. 60; cf. Zosimus, iv. 56. The first sentence of this extract from Eunapius, which is ungrammatical, was hastily composed by the excerptors of Constantine VII, and gives the erroneous impression that the Visigoths in question first crossed into the Empire in the early years of Theodosius I.

8 *Chron. Min.* iii. 526: add John of Antioch, frag. 190 *fin.* (Flavianus). The marriage with Roman permission is remarkable: Mommsen, *Ges. Schr.* vi, 168.

9 Zosimus, iv. 40; cf. Libanius, *Or.* xix. 22, xx. 14.

10 Zosimus, iv. 34. 4 f.; Themistius, *Or.* xv. 190 CD; Orosius, vii. 34. 7; *Consul. Constantin.* 381 (i. 243); Prosper, 1177 (i. 461); Jordanes, *Get.* xxviii. 142 f., who vividly describes Athanaric's reactions on seeing the great city. (In citing the Chronicles I add in parentheses a reference to the volume and page of Mommsen's *Chronica Minora*).

11 Zosimus, iv. 25. 2 f.; Gregory of Nazianzus, *Ep.* 136, cf. 137 (Migne, *PG* xxxvii. 232 f.), dating from the first half of 382, where he is called *Modarius.*

12 Amm. Marc., xxxi. 3. 5; Sozomen, viii. 4. 1.

13 Eunapius, frag. 60 *init.,* who is the source of Zosimus, iv. 56. 1.

14 Ibid., 30. 1.

15 He was unable to use them against Magnus Maximus: ibid., 45. 3. For a vivid picture of their disruptive activities in his rear see ibid., 48. 1.

16 The word *Gruthungus* in Claudian, *In Eutrop.* ii. 196 is poor authority for making Tribigild an Ostrogoth, though the men whom he commanded at Nacoleia were Ostrogoths. That he was Gainas' kinsman is explicitly stated by Socrates, vi. 6. 5, and Sozomen, viii. 4. 2.

17 Socrates, vi. 6. 3 and 6; cf. 13; Sozomen, viii. 4. 1. For Gainas' complex motives for rebelling see Zosimus, v. 13. 1. Tribigild was depressed by what he considered to be his poverty and by lack of "gifts" from Eutropius: Claudian, *In Eutrop.* ii. 178–80, 189–92.

18 Zosimus, v. 13. 4; cf. 14. 1; Eunapius, frag. 75, Synesius, *De Regno* passim; cf. Claudian, *In Eutrop.* ii. 222 *bella dabunt socios.*

19 Socrates, vi. 6. 5; Zosimus, v. 13. 2; John of Antioch, frag. 190.

20 Zosimus, v. 22. 1 f.

21 Ibid., 22. 3.

22 Eunapius, frag. 80; Zosimus, v. 20. 1; Suda, s.v. Φράβιθος.

23 Claudian, *BG* 80–82; Prudentius, *In Symm.* ii. 696–9.

24 Zosimus, v. 40. 2, 48. 2.

25 Ibid., vi. 9. 3, 12. 2; Olympiodorus, frag. 13.

26 Jordanes, *Get.* xxx. 152; cf. e.g. Themistius, *Or.* xvi. 211 CD.

27 Zosimus, v. 48. 3–4, 49. 1, 50. 3; Sozomen, ix. 7. 2–6. For the year 395 see Zosimus, v. 5. 4.

28 Socrates, vii. 10. 3.

29 Cf. Orosius, vii. 37. 2.

30 Claudian, *vi cons. Hon.* 213 f., 236 f.

31 Ibid., 250–3; *BG* 88 f.
32 Claudian, loc. cit., is shown to be an exaggeration by idem, *vi cons. Hon.* 284.
33 Olympiodorus, frag. 16; Sozomen, ix. 14. 2 ff.; *Addit. ad Prosp. Haun.* 411 (i. 300); Prosper, 1243 (i. 466).
34 H. St. L. B. Moss, *The Birth of the Middle Ages* (Oxford, 1935), 45.
35 With this trace of matrilineal inheritance of the chieftainship cf. the case of the queen Gaatha in H. Delehaye, *Analecta Bollandiana,* xxxi (1912), 279. So, too, Theodoric I appears to have been married to a daughter of Alaric: W. Ensslin, P.-W.v.A, 1736 (1934). In later times Visigothic kings sometimes married their predecessors' widows (e.g. Jo. Biclar., s.a. 569 [ii. 212]; Greg. Tur., *HF* v. 38), though this was expressly forbidden in 683 by XIII Toledo 5 (Mansi, xi. 1067 f.) and again in 691 by the third Council of Saragossa, canon 5 (Mansi, xii. 45), which obliged all kings' widows to enter nunneries. For an Ostrogothic parallel to such a marriage see Procopius, *BG* v. 11. 27 (though this marriage did not achieve its aim: ibid., vi. 10. 11, 28. 26). Note also ibid., vii. 39. 14 f. For a Suevic parallel see Jo. Biclar., s.a. 584 (ii. 216), Greg. Tur., *HF* vi. 43 *fin.,* and for a Lombard parallel see Marius Aventic., s.a. 572 (ii. 238). Add these references to those collected by H. M. Chadwick, *The Origin of the English Nation* (Cambridge, 1907), 311 ff.
36 Olympiodorus, frag. 24.
37 Orosius, vii. 43. 5–6.
38 Thompson, *VTU,* 46 ff.
39 Isidore, *Hist. Goth.* 35 = ii. 281 (who is wrong, however, to make this state of affairs last until the reign of Euric), Jordanes, *Get.* xi. 69; cf. H. Brunner, *Deutsche Rechtsgeschichte²* (Leipzig, 1906), i, 150 n. 2; K. Zeumer, *Neues Archiv,* xxiii (1898), 424–26, 438 ff.; K. F. Stroheker, *Eurich, König der Westgoten* (Stuttgart, 1937), 98 n. 29. The change from unwritten to written laws among the Ostrogoths when they settled in Italy is indicated by the Ostrogothic ambassadors in Procopius, *BG* vi. 6. 17.
40 Thompson, *VTU,* 46 ff.
41 Olympiodorus, frag. 24, Jordanes, *Get.* xxxi. 160. Athaulf married Placidia *after* changing his attitude towards the Empire. She did not originate his new policy, but she encouraged him to carry it out: Orosius, vii. 40. 2, 43. 7.
42 References to Visigoths who bore Roman names are collected in *Hermathena,* xc (1957), 57 f. Add the Dubius in Olympiodorus, frag. 26. None of these persons were Arian Christians.
43 On the chronology see Bury, i, 199 n. 4. The essential passages are Orosius, vii. 43. 3 and 8. On Spanish events Orosius, even though he gives the motive only as a rumour, is a better authority than Jordanes, *Get.* xxxi. 163; Philostorgius, xii. 4; and even Olympiodorus, frag. 26, all of whom give different accounts of the motives which inspired the assassination. Observe that Orosius is not contradicted by our other Spanish authority, Hydatius, 60 (ii. 19).
44 Olympiodorus, frag. 26.
45 Ibid.; Jordanes, *Get.* xxxi. 163; Prosper, 1257 (i. 467).

46 Isidore, *Hist. Goth.* 20 (ii. 276). Cf. Olympiodorus and Orosius, loc. cit.

47 Orosius, vii. 43. 10.

48 Ibid., 10–12; Prosper, 1259 (i. 468).

49 Orosius, vii. 43. 13–5; Hydatius, 63 ff. (ii. 19).

50 Thompson, *VTU,* 51 ff.

51 Towards the end of their revolt in A.D. 70 the Batavians had realized this: Tacitus, *H* v. 25 "nec posse ab una natione totius orbis servitium depelli, quid profectum caede et incendiis legionum nisi ut plures validioresque accirentur? . . . sin populum Romanum armis vocent, quotam partem generis humani Batavos esse?" etc., cf. *A* ii. 25. 5, xv. 13. 5, and the words which Claudian puts into the mouth of Alaric, *vi cons. Hon.* 294 "omnibus oppeterem fama maiore perustis." For a Persian view of the hopelessness of invading the Roman Empire see Procopius, *BP* ii. 21. 14.

52 See pp. 31 ff. above; "Peasant Revolt in Late Roman Gaul and Spain" *apud* M. I. Finley, *Studies in Ancient Society* (London, 1974), 304–20. For the aims of the Bacaudae see ibid., 316–18. It may be that on rare occasions their leaders would reach an agreement with the barbarians who had been established in the Empire to oppose them. That may be the story behind the following entries in Hydatius' chronicle: 113, "Suevi cum parte plebis Callaeciae, cui adversabantur, pacis iura confirmant" in 438; 141, "Basilius . . . congregatis Bacaudis in ecclesia Tyriassione foederatos occidit" in 449; 142, "Rechiarius [the Suevic king] . . . Caesaraugustanam regionem cum Basilio . . . depraedatur" in that same year. It would be interesting to know whether these unidentified *foederati* had been posted in Tyriasso to protect the town from the Bacaudae. (Observe how Isidore, *Hist. Goth.* 87 (ii. 301), though his source in Hydatius, 142, suppresses mention of the Bacaudae and substitutes Goths for them.) In 457 troops of Theodoric I, who was then operating in Spain, treacherously attacked "Asturica, quam iam praedones ipsius sub specie Romanae ordinationis intraverant," Hydatius, 186 (ii. 30). What does *ipsius* mean there? For possible cooperation between the Visigothic *foederati* in Aquitaine and the Bacaudae of Armorica see some obscure lines of Merobaudes, *Paneg.* ii. 14 f., where the poet, speaking of Armorica, says:

> et quamvis Geticis sulcum confundat aratris
> barbara vicinae refugit consortia gentis.

Why do the Armoricans use Gothic ploughs?

53 For the details of *hospitalitas* see F. Lot, *Revue belge de philologie et d'histoire,* vii (1928), 975–1011. Where exactly they lived in Aquitanica II is unknown, and the suggestions based on alleged placename evidence that have been put forward by E. Gamillscheg, *Romania Germanica* (Berlin and Leipzig, 1934), i, 300 ff., should be read with caution: see F. Lot, *Comptes rendus de l'Académie des Inscriptions* (1945), 289–98; M. Broens, *Annales du Midi,* lxviii (1956), 17–38. The widely held view that the Burgundians originally received one half of each estate and that the laws which suggest that they received two thirds refer to a later readjustment of the system was shown to be untenable

by G. Kaufmann, *Forschungen zur deutschen Geschichte,* x (1870), 377 ff. The view that there was no division of the land itself but only of the products or the income thereof was disproved by J. Havet, *Revue historique,* vi (1878), 91 ff.

54 Sidonius, *carm.* xii; *Legg. Burg.* xxxviii. 4–5. L. Schmidt, *Geschichte der deutschen Stämme: Die Ostgermanen* (Munich, 1934), 173, says that this is due to the division of the estate among heirs; but the Burgundian law in question refers to the estate as being owned by one person (*ipsius*) and certainly does not suggest an estate which had been divided between a father and his sons; cf. H. Delbrück, *Geschichte d. Kriegskunst* (Berlin, 1921), 354; Lot, art. cit., 996 f.

55 Cf. e.g. *Legg. Visig.* v. 3. 4. The Burgundian inheritance laws, which deal mainly with the inheritance of the *sortes,* make this conclusion certain for Savoy.

56 *Legg. Burg.* liv. 2. A Burgundian clan is mentioned in the fourth century in *ILS* 2813. Some at least of the Lombards who settled in Italy in 568 did so in *farae*: Paul. Diacon., *Hist. Langob.* ii. 9; cf. Marius Aventic., s.a. 569 (ii. 238).

57 Delbrück, op. cit., ii. 342 ff.; Lot, art. cit., 994 f.

58 This relationship may be referred to in *Legg. Visig.* x. 1. 11 ff.

59 So Lot, art. cit., 997.

60 *Legg. Visig.* v. 3. 4.

61 *Legg. Burg.* lv. 5, cf. i. 3 and 4, xxxviii. 6, liv. 1; *Extrav.* ii. 14; *Cod. Euric.* 305; *Legg. Visig.* x. 1. 8, etc. Note Leovigild's treatment of a *locum fisci* in *Vitas SS. Patrum Emertensium,* iii. 9.

62 Salvian, v. 21 f., 28, et al.; Paulinus, *Euch.* 306 f., 500 ff. St. Orientius' sympathies lay with the Visigoths in the war of 439: *Vita S. Orientii* iii (*AASS* i. May, 63), on which see p. 265 n. 3 above. For "freedom" see also Eunapius, frag. 50; Zosimus, vi. 5. 3; Orosius, vii. 41. 7; *Querolus,* pp. 16 f., ed. Peiper.

63 Prosper, 1290 (i. 471); cf. *Chron. Gall.* 102 (i. 658); Mommsen, *Ges. Schr.* iv, 535.

64 At any rate, the Romans then gave hostages to Theodoric: Sidonius, *carm.* vii. 214 ff. It is not necessary to take 430 as a rigid *terminus ante quem* for this event.

65 There seems to have been trouble in Spain, too, about this time: Merobaudes, *Paneg.* i. frag. ii A. 23 (p. 9, ed. Vollmer) "triumphum, qui consiliis tuis intra Hispanias [. . ."

66 Prosper, 1338 (i. 477). It is often mistakenly held that the *foedus* of 418 was not renewed in 439, though the opposite is explicitly stated by Sidonius, *carm.* vii. 308, and Jordanes, *Get.* xxxiv. 177, xxxvi. 186. The error is due to a misunderstanding of the objectives of Attila's campaign in Gaul in 451. The Huns were aiming in the first instance at the Visigoths, and the Romans were only involved in the war at the last moment: see E. A. Thompson, *Attila and the Huns* (Oxford, 1948), 130 ff. In 451, then, Avitus' task was not to induce the Visigoths to renew the *foedus* of 418 and to help Aëtius, but sim-

ply to induce them to make a joint resistance to Attila. The power of the Visigoths in 439 is exaggerated and that of the Romans understated by Sidonius, *carm.* vii. 297 ff.; and Salvian, vii. 34.

67 Hydatius, 92 (ii. 21).

68 Still less did the Visigoths wish to "escape" from Aquitaine, despite H. Pirenne, *Mohammed and Charlemagne* (London, 1939), 27 n. 2.

69 For their names see Jordanes, *Get.* xxxvi. 190.

70 Ibid., 215 f.; *Addit. ad Prosp. Haun.* 451 *fin.* (i. 302); Greg. Tur., *HF* ii. 7 *fin.*

71 *Addit. ad Prosp. Haun.* 453 (i. 302 *fin.*)

72 P. 25 above.

73 *Chron. Gall. a. DXI* 621 (i. 663).

74 Prosper, 1371 (i. 483); *Addit. ad Prosp. Haun.* 453 (i. 302); *Chron. Gall a DXI* (i. 663); Hydatius, 156 (ii. 27); Isidore, *Hist. Goth.* 30 (ii. 279). Isidore is of less value than the earlier authors, and we cannot press his words and assume that Thorismud's internal rule was felt to be oppressive. See also Jordanes, *Get.* xliii. 228 (who does not mention any motive); Greg. Tur., *HF* ii. 7 *fin.*

75 Hydatius, 158 (ii. 27) "ex auctoritate Romana."

76 Idem, 217 (ii. 33).

77 Idem, 218 (ii. 33); Marius Aventic., 463 (ii. 232); cf. *Chron. Gall. a. DXI* 638 (i. 664). Priscus of Panium, frag. 30 *init.* The battle has been studied by A. Loyen, *Bulletin de la société archéologique et historique de l'Orléanais,* xxii (1935), 501–7, who places it between Orléans and either Saint-Hilaire or Olivet.

78 Sidonius, *carm.* vii. 495–99.

79 Idem, *carm.* xxiii. 70 f.; cf. Hydatius, 170 (ii. 28).

80 Sidonius, *Ep.* vii. 6. 4, cf. vi. 6. 1. Even in Euric's reign there seem to have been conspiracies against the king, and foreign enemies may have been invited into the kingdom: see K. Zeumer, n. on *Legg. Visig.* ii. 1. 8, and in *Neues Archiv,* xxiv (1899), 59–61. The Burgundians never denounced the *foedus* of 443, and their kings continued to show respect for the Eastern Emperor after the Western Emperors disappeared in 476.

CHAPTER 4:
A.D. 476 AND AFTER

1 Priscus, frag. 8. On the site of Attila's headquarters see R. Browning, "Where Was Attila's Camp?" *Journal of Hellenic Studies,* lxxiii (1953), 143–45 = idem, *Studies on Byzantine History, Literature and Education* (London, 1977), cap. ii.

2 Maenchen-Helfen, *The World of the Huns,* 388 n. 104, and Schmidt, *Ostgermanen,* 98 n. 3, deny the identity of the Hun Edeco with Odoacer's father, but it would be odd if two prominent barbarians who were exact contemporaries bore this same unusual Hun name. See R. L. Reynolds and R. S. Lopez, "Odoacer: German or Hun?" *American Historical Review,* lii (1947), 36–53, at 48, who think that the name Edeco, which is not otherwise found among early Germanic peoples, is probably Ural-Altaic. But if "Odoacer" should

turn out to be a Germanic name, we could infer no more than that his mother was Germanic. (Incidentally, Reynolds' reference to Menander, frag. 69, should be ignored. On the names of Odoacer's son see p. 71 above). Jordanes, *Rom.* 344, makes Odoacer a Rugian, which would seem to be contradicted by Eugippius, *Vita Sev.* vi. 5 ff., as well as by Jordanes himself in *Get.* 242, where he is *Torcilingorum rex*. The views of John of Antioch, frag. 209. 1, that he was a Scirian, and of the *Consularia Italica,* 487. 1 (i. 313), that he was king of the Heruls, and of Theophanes, *Chron.* 119. 22, de Boor, that he was a Goth, are all alike mere guesses.

3 For Odoacer's age see John of Antioch, frag. 214 *a* (*FHG* v, 29): he was sixty years of age when Theoderic murdered him in 493.

4 Bury, i, 40.

5 Jordanes, *Get.* 277 f.

6 Ennodius, *Vita Epif.* 358.

7 Anon. Vales., 38, cf. Jordanes, *Rom.* 344; idem, *Get.* 242.

8 Procopius, *BG* v. 1. 4 ff. There is little to be learned from the workings of the Devil on the soldiers of Romulus: Ennodius, *Vita Epif.* 95, "spe novarum rerum perditorum animos inquietat."

9 Reynolds and Lopez, art. cit., 38 f.

10 Jordanes, *Rom.* 344, *Get.* 242.

11 Bury, i, 406. According to Stein, i, 398, the troops rebelled because Orestes was no longer able to pay them. In that case why did they think that Odoacer would be able to pay them?

12 Cassiodorus, *Var.* ii. 16. 5, cf. Ennodius, *Ep.* ix. 23. Little is known about the settlement on the land of Odoacer's men, but for the settlement of the Ostrogoths see esp. V. Bierbrauer, "Zur ostgotischen Geschichte in Italien," *Studi medievali,* ser. 3, vol. xiv (1973), 1–37, at 10 ff.

13 Mommsen, *Ges. Schr.* vi, 444 f. Note his remark on p. 478, "It is not far from Stilicho to Odoacer and Theoderic." Cf., too, W. Ensslin, *Theoderich der Grosse* ² (Munich, 1959), 160, 194 f. A. H. M. Jones argued his case in "The Constitutional Position of Odoacer and Theoderic," *JRS,* lii (1962), 126–30, with whom contrast Bury, i, 406, "he had no idea of detaching Italy from the Empire." The works of Jones and of J. P. C. Kent (p. 275 n. 16 below) are unknown to Herwig Wolfram, "Intitulatio I: Königs- und Fürstentitel bis zum Ende des 8. Jahrhunderts," *Mitteilungen des Instituts für österreichische Geschichtsforschung,* Ergänzungsbd. xxi (Graz, 1967), which is unhelpful on the constitutional position of Odoacer and Theoderic. A new argument has been put forward by M. McCormick, "Odoacer, Emperor Zeno, and the Rugian Victory Legation," *Byzantion,* xlvii (1977), 212–22, who shows (p. 219) on the basis of John of Antioch, frag. 214. 7 that in sending to Zeno some of the booty from his Rugian campaign "Odoacer was attempting to accentuate his actual or would-be position as a loyal imperial subordinate . . . Zeno, in turn, implicitly recognized Odoacer's position by expressing his satisfaction on this victory."

14 Malchus, frag. 10. The excerptors of Constantine VII frequently botch the initial sentence of their extracts; and, with Müller and Dindorf in their editions, and Mommsen, *Ges. Schr.* vi, 383, I have no doubt that they have done so here in introducing Romulus instead of Odoacer as the person who obliged the senate to send an embassy to Zeno. It is clear from the rest of the fragment that Romulus has already disappeared from the scene. Hence it seems that Bury, i, 407, and Stein, ii, 46, are wrong to say that the deputation came to Constantinople in the name of Romulus.

15 Malchus, loc. cit., but there is no evidence for the view of Stein, ii, 46, that Zeno appointed Odoacer as *Magister militum praesentalis* to a restored Nepos, or for the opinion of Ensslin, "Zu den Grundlagen von Odoakers Herrschaft," *Serta Hoffilleriana* (Zagreb, 1940), 383, that Odoacer exercised his power by virtue of being a patrician.

16 J. P. C. Kent, "Julius Nepos and the Fall of the Western Empire," *Corolla Memoriae Erich Swoboda Dedicata,* Römische Forschungen in Niederösterreich, Bd. 5 (Graz-Köln, 1966), 146–50.

17 The Western names are cited by the chronicler Marcellinus, the *Chronicon Paschale,* etc., but not by Victor Tonnennensis in Africa; and we are told that not a single papyrus document from Egypt, dating from the decade 481–90, ever mentions the consul of the West: so A. Chastagnol, *Le sénat romain sous le règne d'Odoacre* (Bonn, 1966), 55 n. 123. For Mommsen's view see *Ges. Schr.* vi, 373 f., 382 f., 385.

18 J. O. Tjäder, *Die nichtliterarischen lateinischen Papyri Italiens* (Lund, 1955), 288 ff. = *FIR*² iii, 309 f.; Mommsen's edn. of Cassiodorus, MGH (AA), xii, 445; *ILS* 8955 "salvo d.n. Zenone et domno Odovacre." For the papal documents which are equally inconclusive though they sometimes use the word *rex* see Ensslin, art. cit. (in n. 15 above), 384.

19 Chastagnol., op. cit., 42, with plate xxxii, 2–3.

20 So Wolfgang Hahn, *Moneta Imperii Byzantini,* i: *Osterreichische Akad. d. Wissenschaften: phil. hist. Klasse,* Denkschriften, Bd. 109 (Vienna, 1973), 77. I regret that I have not access to L. Brunetti, *Opus Monetale Cigoi* (Bologna, 1966), which Hahn cites. For the older view see F. F. Krause, *Die Münzen Odovacars und des Ostgotenreiches in Italien* (Halle, 1928), 42 ff.

21 Cassiodorus, *Chron.* 1303 (ii. 159).

22 So Mommsen, *Ges. Schr.* vi, 378 f.

23 Jordanes, *Get.* 242, 291; Theophanes, p. 199. Full references in Assunta Nagl, P.-W. xvii, 1889. We cannot attach much weight to Victor Vitensis, *Hist. Persec.* i. 4. 14 "Odouacro Italiae regi."

24 Jordanes, *Get.* 295 "Gothorum Romanorumque regnator"; Marcellinus, s.a. 477 (ii. 91) "Odoacer rex"; *Fasti Vind. Priores,* 622 (i. 310), "a rege Odovacre," etc.

25 Jones, art. cit., 126. Speaking in his own person about Odoacer in the context of the war with Theoderic, Procopius refers to his rule as a *tyrannis* and to himself as a *tyrannos, BG* v. 1. 7 f., 11, cf. vi. 6. 15, but it would be rash to

infer much from this. It suits the Ostrogoths in *BG,* loc. cit., to refer to him as a dictator (*autokrator*) and a usurper (*tyrannos*).

26 Eugippius, *Vita Sev.* praef. 8. See Bierbrauer, art. cit. (on p. 274 n. 12 above), 8, 21.

27 Stein, ii, 41 f.

28 Marcellinus, s.a. 477 (ii. 91); *Fasti Vind. Priores,* 622 (i. 310); Jordanes, *Get.* 243; Auct. Haun., s.a. 477 (i. 311).

29 Mommsen, *Ges. Schr.* vi, 383, cf. Procopius, *BG* vi. 6. 17 ff.

30 John of Antioch, frag. 214 *a* (*FHG* v, 29). Ensslin, art. cit. (on p. 275 n. 15 above), 88, doubts John here but gives no reason for his doubt.

31 Hahn, op. cit., 79. For the older view see Kraus, op. cit., 56, 58; Stein, ii, 48; Chastagnol, op. cit., 53. Apparently none of Thela's coins survive, if he minted any: Kraus, op. cit., 204 f., but Hahn, op. cit., does not even discuss the point.

32 John of Antioch, loc. cit.

33 Mommsen, *Ges. Schr.* vi, 444 n. 3, and Stein, ii, 48, overlooked the vital fact that Odoacer only appointed *magistri militum* when he was at war with the emperor.

34 Anon. Vales., 49, which is not contradicted by anything in Jordanes, *Rom.* 348, *Get.* 290 ff.

35 So Jones, 127.

36 Stein, ii, 40, is reduced to the extraordinary expedient of inventing an otherwise unheard-of office, the *magisterium militum per Italiam,* to describe Theoderic's position in 489.

37 Anon. Vales., 57.

38 This is approximately the position of Ensslin, op. cit. (on p. 275 n. 13 above), 74 f.

39 Mommsen, *Ges. Schr.* vi, 479.

40 *BG* vi. 6. 17, 20, supported by Malalas, p. 384 *init.*

41 On this matter see the masterly pages of Mommsen, *Ges. Schr.* vi, 459–65.

42 Cassiodorus, *Var.* iv. 16.

43 So Bury, ii, 159 n. 4.

44 Cassiodorus, *Var.* viii. 1. 5. In *CIL* v. 6418 he is *d.n. Atalaricus rex gloriosissimus.* On his quarter-siliquae he inscribes his own name in full with the title *rex*: Hahn, op. cit., 87.

45 Jones, art. cit., 127; Procopius, *BG* vi. 6. 14 ff.

46 *BG* v. 1. 25 f.; 3. 12; 6. 19.

47 *BG* vi. 6. 17.

48 *BG* vi. 6. 23.

49 *BV* iii. 14. 5; *BG* v. 3. 12. For *kratos* over the Italians see also vii. 1. 26; 2. 5. Procopius also uses the term of the emperors' rule over Italy: *BG* v. 1. 2; 3. 12; 6. 19.

50 *BG* v. 6. 19.

51 *BG* v. 1. 29.

52 *BG* v. 11. 5, cf. *BP* ii. 2. 1, 4. In *BP* ii. 4. 13 Procopius, speaking in his own

person, says that Belisarius overthrew "Wittigis *basileus* of the Goths and Italians." I believe that he is here simply reproducing ironically the claim of Wittigis's envoys to Persia which he has reported in 2. 4.

53 *BG* vi. 30. 17, 26. Wittigis wore the purple: *BG* v. 29. 5. Ildibad and Eraric did not mint coins: Hahn, op. cit., 78. Theodahad's one claim to fame (apart from his murder of Amalasuntha) is that he put his own portrait on his *folles,* the first time that an Ostrogothic king had done so, leaving aside a medallion of Theoderic's: Hahn, op. cit., 90.

54 *BG* vi. 29. 18–26.

55 *BG* vi. 30. 26.

56 *BG* v. 6. 2 ff.; viii. 24. 4; cf. vii. 37. 6.

57 Hahn, op. cit., 88.

58 *BG* viii. 35. 31.

59 *ILS* 827.

60 *ILS* 125, of which the beginning has been restored by A. Bartoli, "Lavori nella sede del senato romano al tempo di Teoderico," *Bulletino della commissione archeologica comunale di Roma,* lxxiii (1949–50), 77–88. The opening words are: "salvis dominis nostris Anastasio perpetuo Augusto et gloriosissimo ac triumfali viro Theoderico," etc.

CHAPTER 5:
BYZANTINE CONQUEST OF ITALY:
MILITARY PROBLEMS

1 Bury, ii, 182 n. 1, shows that the Anio is meant, not the Tiber.

2 Procopius, *BG* v. 18. 42.

3 Ibid., v. 27. 27. There is a superficial discussion of the problem in H. Wolfram, *Geschichte der Goten* (Munich, 1979), 377 f.

4 It must be conceded that the matter is raised by B. Rubin, *Prokopios von Kaisereia* (Stuttgart, 1954), 172 — an offprint of his absurdly long article on Procopius in P.-W. Here is what he says: "Durch den späten Zeitpunkt dieser Erkenntnis (erste Feindberührung) ist die Nachricht fast so unglaublich wie P.'s Bericht über seine Rekognoszierung in Syrakus. Sollte Belisar nicht längst über die Gefechtsweise der Goten Bescheid gewusst haben?" Either the answer to that question is "No," or Procopius is a wildly overrated historian.

5 Procopius, *BV* iii. 14. 1. See the quotation from B. Rubin in the previous footnote. On his col. 137 he is equally contemptuous of Procopius.

6 Procopius, *BV* iii. 20. 5 f., 16.

7 Ibid., iii. 4. 3 ff.

8 Ibid., iii. 14. 10.

9 So Bury, ii, 129.

10 Procopius, *BV* iii. 10. 29 ff.

11 Ibid., iii. 11. 22.

12 Ibid., iii. 14. 10.

13 Ibid., iv. 8. 12.

14 Read, for example, ibid., iii. 8. 27 f., where he assumes total ignorance in his readers about the Vandals' methods of warfare.

15 Knud Hannestad, "Les forces militaires d'après la guerre gothique de Procope," *Classica et Mediaevalia,* xxi (1960), 136–83, at 162, puts Wittigis' field force at about 20,000 to 25,000 men, but thinks that with the garrison forces of north Italy and Dalmatia they may have amounted to a little more than 30,000 when the war broke out. See also J. L. Teall, "The Barbarians in Justinian's Armies," *Speculum,* xl (1965), 294–322, at 302. These are important studies, but H. Wolfram, *Geschichte der Goten* (Munich, 1979), 374 ff. should be read with caution.

16 Procopius, *BG* v. 27. 3 ff.

17 Ibid., 15 ff.

18 Ibid.

19 F. F. Kraus, *Die Münzen Odovacars und des Ostgotenreiches in Italien* (Halle, 1928), 183. The latest study is that of Hahn, *Moneta Imperii Byzantini,* i: Österreichische Akad. d. Wissenschaften: phil. hist. Klasse, Denkschriften, Bd. 109 (Vienna, 1973), pp. 85, 88, 90 f. When Rome and Ravenna were both lost Totila was obliged to open a new mint at Ticinum but used the Roman mint in 549–52.

20 Cassiodorus, *Var.* vii. 18 f., cf. i. 40.

21 Procopius, *BG* v. 22. 4; 23. 9; vi. 5. 14; vii. 4. 21, but in v. 16. 11 in one of his moments of wild propaganda for Belisarius the historian says that "most" of Wittigis' army had breastplates! This contradicts everything that he tells us elsewhere.

22 Idem, *BP* i. 1. 15. But Hannestad, art. cit., 154, thinks that the Byzantine numbers in Italy were very low in the decade preceding 552, amounting on the average perhaps to 10,000 men. On the defensive armour of Justinian's cavalrymen see J. F. Haldon, "Some Aspects of Byzantine Military Technology From the Sixth to the Tenth Centuries," *Byzantine and Modern Greek Studies,* i (1975), 11–47, at 18 ff.

23 Procopius, *BG* vii. 4. 31; 13. 3; 15. 7 f.

24 Ibid., vii. 5. 13 ff.

25 Ibid., vii. 26. 15 ff.; 28. 13 ff.

26 Ibid., vii. 35. 28; viii. 34. 25.

27 Ibid., v. 21. 3 f. I disagree with the high estimate of the ability of the Goths at siege warfare put forward by Hannestad, art. cit., 176 f. P. Goessler, "Zur Belagerungskunst der Germanen," *Klio,* xxxv (1942), 103–14, goes much too far.

28 Procopius, *BG* v. 22. 1 ff.

29 Ibid., vi. 12.

30 Ibid., v. 23. 17, 23 f., though contrast 24. 4, a passage which taken with ibid. 18 suggests that the engines *did* go into action.

31 The Goths placed wooden towers on the bridge over the river Draco (modern Sarno) and they had *ballistae* there, too: *BG* viii. 35. 9, but, in spite of Bury, ii, 273, they never went into action. For other Gothic *ballistae* see Agathias, *Hist.* i. 9, p. 154, ed. Dindorf.

32 Procopius, *BG* v. 22. 19, 22; vi. 9. 12; 13. 11 and 14. For a city almost taken in this way by the Persians, see *BG* viii. 14. 11.

33 Ibid., vii. 24.

34 Ibid., vii. 35. 2; cf. *Anecd.* v. 17.

35 Procopius, *BG* vii. 6. 1 f.

36 Ibid., vii. 10. 5; 13. 11; 16. 3; 25. 1 f.; 30. 5 (cf. 20); 37. 23; 39. 5; viii. 23. 3; 25. 24. On the cannibalistic landladies of Rimini see ibid., vi. 20. 27; cf. vii. 16. 3.

37 Ibid., vii. 11. 32; 25. 7; Marcellinus Auct., s.a. 539. 3 (ii. 106) says of Milan, "muros diruunt." Note Jordanes, *Rom.* 379, "omniumque urbium munimenta distruens."

38 Procopius, *BG* vii. 8. 10, and note Marcellinus Auct., s.a. 543. 1 (ii. 107), "Totila devastat Campaniam urbesque muratas evertens," etc.

39 Procopius, *BG* vii. 23. 3; viii. 33. 9; Beneventum, vii. 6. 1; 25. 11. On the surrender of Spoletium note *Anecd.* v. 6 f.

40 Idem, *BG* vii. 24. 32 f.

41 Idem, vii. 16. 22 f.; 37. 3; viii. 22. 3; Marcellinus Auct., s.a. 547.

42 Procopius, *BG* vii. 22. 6 f.; 24. 3; cf. 22. 19; Marcellinus Auct., s.a. 547 (ii. 108), "quadraginta aut amplius dies Roma ita fuit desolata ut nemo ibi hominum nisi bestiae morerentur."

43 Procopius, *BG* vii. 25. 8.

44 Ibid., vii. 6. 1, cf. 8. 10; 11. 32.

45 Ibid., vii. 24. 27.

46 Ibid., vii. 25. 11; 8. 10 f.; 37. 11.

47 But there seems to be some evidence in *BG* viii. 32. 8 for Gothic cavalry fighting with other weapons than spears, i.e., presumably with bows.

48 Ibid., vii. 40. 32; viii. 24. 10.

49 Cassiodorus, *Var.* v. 16. 2; 18. 2 f.; 20. 1; cf. iv. 15. 1. For Gothic unfamiliarity with the sea in earlier times see Norman H. Baynes, *Byzantine Studies and Other Essays* (London, 1955), 218–21. But Bury, ii, 232 supposes that there are Gothic warships in *BG* vii. 7. 6.

50 Procopius, *BG* vii. 6. 24; 13. 6; 35. 24; 37. 5. Salona in 536: *BG* v. 16. 10, 16 f.

51 Note Gothic control of the sea near Naples in 552: *BG* vii. 35. 12 f., explained by vii. 13. 6. For the value to the Byzantines of their control of the sea note especially *BG* v. 7. 30; vi. 7. 17; 12. 17; 24. 14; 28. 6.

52 *BG* viii. 23. 10 and 14.

53 *BG* viii. 23. 42. Observe that "long before" the sailing of the 300 ships Totila had sent these forty-seven ships to help attack Ancona: viii. 23. 2. Rubin, op. cit., 243 *fin.*, explains this judgement by supposing that the historian is doing his best for Belisarius by extolling John, son of Valerianus. I see no shred of likelihood in this farfetched proposal.

54 Procopius, *BG* viii. 24. 31 ff. Rubin, op. cit., 244. 5, again reads far more into the text than can be found there. Procopius (we are told) says that the morale of the Goths in Sicily was low, not because it was low, but in order to show that the war was almost decided before the intervention of Narses!

55 Procopius, *BG* viii. 23. 10. Procopius has the phrase again in v. 2. 11; 4. 13; and often, so that the point can hardly be pressed.

56 Ibid., viii. 26. 2.

57 Ibid., viii. 24. 3.

58 Ibid., viii. 26. 4.

59 Ibid., viii. 24. 4 f.

60 On the site of the battle see Hans N. Roisl, "Die Schlacht bei den Busta Gallorum," *apud* F. Altheim, *Geschichte der Hunnen* v (Berlin, 1962), 363–77, with bibliography in the footnotes. See also the same scholar in P.-W. Supplbd. xiv, 749–58, s.v. "Tadinae," and 799–809, s.v. "Totila."

61 Procopius, *BG* viii. 30. 1; Hannestad, art. cit., 153, 173 f. Stein, ii, 600, puts the Byzantine army at hardly less than 30,000 men. Elsewhere Procopius constantly remarks that the Goths were superior in numbers: see *BG* v. 16. 6; vi. 13. 10; 16. 11; 17. 12; 18. 6 and 14; 29. 33; vii. 4. 1 f.; 10. 4; 11. 26; 38; 21. 7; 26. 20; 28. 10; 37. 22. But things have changed in viii. 30. 1 and 17; 32. 14. When the fortunes of the Goths were very low in 541, Totila (then their new leader) had 5,000 men to engage 12,000 Byzantines: *BG* vii. 3. 4; 4. 1 f., and 12.

62 For estimates of Narses see Stein, ii, 356 ff.; A. Lippold, P.-W. Supplbd., xii, 870–889.

63 Procopius, *BG* viii. 32. 6 f.; Hannestad, art. cit., 178, writes: "déjà à la bataille d'Andrinople l'attaque en choc de la cavalerie puissamment cuirassée des Goths avait décidé le résultat du combat," and Totila now wished to repeat the process. In my opinion, (i) Adrianople was a victory of Gothic infantrymen over Roman infantrymen — see *EG* 118; and (ii) neither at Adrianople nor at Busta Gallorum were the Goths in general "puissamment cuirassée."

64 Procopius, *BG* viii. 32. 15.

65 Ibid., viii. 32. 20.

66 Note Procopius, *Anecd.* iv. 39 and 43.

67 Idem, vii. 35. 1; *Anecd.* v. 1 ff.

68 On Totila see Bury, ii, 268 f.; Stein, ii, 568 ff.; and Assunta Nagl, P.-W. vi.A, 1828–38.

69 Procopius, *BG* vi. 21. 39; Marcellinus Auct., s.a. 539. 3 (ii. 106). It might be interesting to know why Wolfram, op. cit. (in n. 3 above), 426, omits reference to this outrage.

70 Procopius, *BG* vi. 21. 6, cf. 7. 38.

71 Bury, ii, 204.

72 Procopius, *BG* vii. 10. 19. For a similar thought see *Anecd.* i. 6.

73 Procopius, *BG* vi. 21. 41. For some other Gothic outrages see Bury, ii, 271. Something not very pleasant seems to lie behind Marcellinus Auct., s.a. 545. 1 (ii. 107), "Totila Firmum et Asculum sub iuramento ingressus est: milite Romano cum rebus suis dimisso crudelitatem suam in Romanos exercuit eosque omnes nudat et necat."

74 V. Bierbrauer, "Zur ostgotischen Geschichte in Italien," *Studi medievali,* ser. 3, vol. xiv (1973), 1–37. at 22 ff.

CHAPTER 6:
BYZANTINE CONQUEST OF ITALY:
PUBLIC OPINION

1 Priscus, frag. 39, p. 348. 8 ff., ed. Dindorf.

2 For a brief account of the settlement on the land see W. Ensslin, *Theoderich der Grosse*[2] (Munich, 1959), 91 f., with references.

3 Procopius, *BG* i. 12. 48 f.; Cassiodorus, *Var.* v. 16. 4. Five *solidi*: Ensslin, op. cit., 190.

4 On *civilitas* see Ensslin, op. cit., 217–20. The concept, of course, is not confined to racial matters.

5 Cassiodorus, *Var.* v. 26 "ut ab armatis custodiatur civilitas."

6 Ibid., ii. 8; iv. 36.

7 See, e.g., ibid., vii. 3. 2 f.

8 Ibid., viii. 3.

9 Ibid., i. 24. 1.

10 Procopius, *BG* v. 2. 3–17. See Bury, ii, 179 n. 1. Gibbon, *Decline and Fall*, cap. xli, vol. iv, 302, ed. Bury.

11 Procopius, *BG* v. 2. 26, though it is not easy to see how he could have found this out: it is not a matter which the queen would have publicized.

12 Procopius, *BG* v. 3. 12, 28.

13 Bury, ii, 163 n. 1.

14 H. W. Garrod, *Classical Quarterly,* iv (1910), 265 f., published two poems about Theodahad and his cliff-top villa at Lake Bolsena.

15 Procopius, *BG* v. 3. 4, 18; 6. 30. On his learning see, too, Cassiodorus, *Var.* x. 3. 4 f.; xi. 13. 4. For some points of interest in his coinage note Kraus, 138 ff.

16 Procopius, *BG* v. 6. 19.

17 Ibid., v. 8. 3; Marcellinus Auct., s.a. 536. 1 (ii. 104); Jordanes, *Rom.* 370; *Get.* 308–9.

18 Cassiodorus, *Var.* x. 31.

19 Procopius, *BG* vi. 13. 3.

20 Ibid., viii. 33. 9 ff.

21 Ibid., vi. 29. 18 ff.; 29. 26; 30. 26, where *basileus* of the Goths and the Italians can only mean "emperor": see p. 74 above.

22 Ibid., vi. 29. 17.

23 Jordanes, *Get.* 313; Marcellinus, s.a. 540. 2, 5 (ii. 106); Procopius, *BP* ii. 14. 10. On the immorality of Belisarius's behaviour on this occasion see Bury, ii, 214. For one of the nobles see Procopius, *BG* viii. 25. 11 f.

24 The Vandal king Gelimer after his capture was not made a patrician because he refused to abandon his Arianism: Procopius, *BV* iv. 9. 14. After the capitulation of 540 we occasionally hear of groups of Goths serving with the Byzantine army. In 545, for example, Assisi was defended for the Empire by a Goth called Sisifrid, who was "exceedingly loyal to the Romans": *BG* vii. 12. 12, 14. Note, too, ibid., vii. 11. 1. There is a Gothic commander serving Justinian in viii. 25. 11. For Goths fighting the Persians on the eastern frontier see Procopius, *BP* ii. 18. 24 f., cf. 21. 4. Arian Goths are still fighting for the

Byzantines on the eastern frontier in 578 and a little later under the Emperor
Tiberius II: they were present at Constantinople with their wives and children: John of Ephesus, iii. 13, 26.

25 Procopius, *BG* vii. 2. 17, cf. 4. 12. Bury, ii, 228, suggests that the Goths accepted Eraric "presumably because there was none among themselves on
whose fitness for the throne they could agree." This guess is very doubtful in
view of the abilities of future Gothic leaders.

26 Procopius, *BG* vi. 29. 17 f., cf. 30. 9. It is not easy to see from what class of
Ostrogoth the clergy were recruited. And what of the man who wrote the
Codex Argenteus?

27 The Sisigis who surrenders in Procopius, *BG* vi. 28. 28–35 is a nobleman.
The deserters ibid., vi. 20. 4 and 24. 17 may well have been Roman inhabitants of Urbs Vetus (Orvieto) and Auximum (Osimo) respectively. There is
no question of "desertion" in the action of the defenders of Auximum in
joining the imperial forces after their surrender. They had held out to astonishing lengths during the siege and famine: *BG* vi. 28. 32–4. For a Goth
called Goar who was taken prisoner in Wittigis' reign and afterwards served
Justinian unreliably, eventually deserting to the Lombards, see *BG* viii. 27.
5 ff. The Gothic commander at Tarentum, Ragnaris by name, opened negotiations with the local Byzantine general with a view to surrendering, but he
later changed his mind: *BG* viii. 26. 4; 34. 9 ff. (Ragnaris in fact appears to
have been a Hun: see Averil Cameron, *Agathias* [Oxford, 1970], 42 f.) There
are few parallels to *BG* vii. 18. 3.

28 They are outnumbered in Procopius, *BG* v. 27. 23, owing to bad tactics on
Wittigis' part. Contrast ibid., 24.

29 Procopius, *BG* vi. 26. 1–15, 24, 29.

30 Ibid., v. 7. 36; 15. 1; Marcellinus, s.a. 538 (Batza). In the case of Dalmatia it
is not easy to see the difference between Gothic "settlers" and troops serving
in the army in the normal way: *BG* v. 7. 36.

31 Ibid., viii. 35. 13.

32 Ibid., vii. 2. 7–9.

33 Ibid., v. 17. 7; 18. 7, cf. 19. 22; 20. 7 (perhaps referring to civilian deserters).

34 Ibid., v. 25. 15–17.

35 Ibid., v. 28. 4.

36 Ibid., vi. 1. 30, cf. vii. 19. 4. Note the very different attitude of the Moors to
Gezon in *BV* iv. 20. 12 ff.

37 Procopius, *BG* vi. 6. 3. Little significance can be attached to an isolated incident such as the action of some of the Heruls serving with Belisarius who in
a fit of pique sold slaves and livestock to the Goths at a handsome profit to
themselves: *BG* vi. 22. 6.

38 Ibid., vii. 1. 25 *neotera pragmata.*

39 Ibid., vi. 6. 6 f.; vii. 1. 33; 9. 1 ff.; 10. 10; 12. 2; 26. 6; 36. 26; *Anecd.* xxii.
7 and 20.

40 Procopius, *BG* vii. 5. 19.

41 Ibid., vii. 12. 8.

42 Ibid., vii. 12. 3. For an explanation see *Anecd.* iv. 39.

43 Procopius, *BG* vii. 11. 10.

44 Ibid., vii. 11. 13 f.

45 Ibid., vii. 11. 27 ff.

46 Ibid., vii. 15. 7. But note how Belisarius turned this phenomenon of desertion to his own advantage, ibid., vii. 19. 4; 23. 1 ff.

47 Procopius, *BG* vii. 23. 3. On Spoleto see also *Anecd.* v. 6 f., where we hear
why a certain Herodian betrayed it to Totila.

48 Procopius, *BG* vii. 18. 28.

49 Ibid., vii. 26. 10, 14.

50 Ibid., vii. 30. 8.

51 Ibid., vii. 35. 23 f., cf. viii. 23. 1.

52 Ibid., viii. 31. 12; 32. 20. For other Roman deserters see vii. 23. 9, 40. 20.

53 Ibid., viii. 33. 10.

54 Ibid., vii. 20. 1 ff.; 36. 7. On the eastern frontier desertion to the Persians is
much less often reported, but see Procopius, *BP* ii. 7. 37, where the cause is
lack of pay.

55 Idem, *BG* viii. 26. 6.

56 Ibid., v. 8. 13, 15.

57 Ibid., 15, 18.

58 Ibid., v. 8. 27; *BV* iii. 16. 9; 20. 20; Cassiodorus, *Var.* xi. 13. 5 (Rome
speaks), "si Libya meruit per te recipere libertatem, crudele est me amittere
quam visa sum possidere." Bury, ii, 128, writes that "Gelimer's Roman subjects longed for restoration to the Empire and would do all they could to assist the invaders": but he cites no evidence for this opinion. He is right to say
(ii, 126 n. 2) that "the war was also welcomed by the eastern traders residing
at Carthage, who saw in the reunion of Africa with the Empire advantage to
their commercial interests."

59 Procopius, *BG* v. 8. 7–11.

60 Ibid., 17, cf. v. 9. 8.

61 Ibid., v. 8. 19 f.

62 Ibid., 21. Observe that the overseas traders in Carthage were suspect in the
eyes of the Vandals, who thought that they had incited Justinian to invade
Africa: *BV* iii. 20. 5 f.

63 *BG* v. 8. 22, 29 ff., 34.

64 Ibid., 41; cf. v. 10. 24–26.

65 Ibid., v. 8. 34.

66 Ibid., v. 9. 1.

67 Ibid., v. 10. 35.

68 Ibid., v. 10. 29, 34. Contrast Jordanes, *Rom.* 370 f.; *Liber Pontificalis,* 60.

69 Ibid., 97. 3, p. 290, ed. Duchesne, "quia noluerunt cives Neapolitani aperire
ei."

70 Ibid., Jordanes, *Rom.* 370; Marcellinus Auct., s.a. 536. 3 (ii. 104).

71 Procopius, *BG* v. 14. 4; vii. 7. 12.

72 Ibid., v. 11. 23.

73 Ibid., v. 14. 13.

74 Ibid., 16; cf. 20. 5.

75 Ibid., v. 20. 7; 24. 14.

76 Ibid., v. 26. 1; 28. 1. But this feeling did not last: vi. 3. 14.

77 Ibid., v. 20. 5; 28. 18; 29. 26; cf. v. 25. 11. There were senators and rich men inside Rome during much of the two sieges: *BG* v. 20. 7; vi. 3. 9 f.; vii. 1. 21; 17. 10; 19. 14; 20. 27; 21. 12 ff.; 36. 29. Pope Silverius himself together with some senators were suspected of treachery, and Belisarius exiled them: Procopius, *BG* v. 25. 13 f.; Marcellinus Auct., s.a. 537. 1 (ii. 105). On Silverius see also Procopius, *Anecd.* i. 14 and 27. A Roman senator and patrician called Clementinus handed over to the Goths a fort near Naples: *BG* vii. 26. 13.

78 Ibid., v. 25. 2, 11. Observe that in Ariminum in 538–39 it was the *demos* who opposed the continuance of the resistance to the Gothic besiegers: ibid., vi. 16. 15.

79 Ibid., v. 16. 3.

80 Ibid., vi. 10. 5 f.

81 Ibid., vi. 7. 35, cf. 38. For the tragic result see vi. 12. 26 ff., 21. 1 ff.

82 Ibid., vii. 4. 5 ff.

83 Ibid., v. 8. 1 f.

84 Ibid., v. 15. 3. The Calabrians need persuasion in vii. 18. 17, cf. v. 24. 14. Note how they receive kid-glove treatment in vii. 18. 17. I cannot find evidence to support the view of Stein, ii, 346, that "les romains de la province de *Lucania et Bruttii* l'accueillirent en libérateur." Certainly, the Romans of the Salona region were not well disposed to the Goths: Procopius, *BG* v. 7. 10, 36.

85 Ibid., v. 4. 6, 28. Amalasuntha's popularity: v. 2. 3 f., 4. 28 f.

86 Ibid., vii. 6. 5.

87 Ibid., vi. 7. 35; 10. 5 f., vii. 18. 21.

88 Ibid., vi. 17. 1 ff.

89 Ibid., vii. 22. 1 ff., 20. There is no evidence for what Stein, ii, 579, calls "l'aversion que les paysans éprouvaient pour les barbares mécréants."

90 Procopius, *BG* vii. 13. 1; 22. 20.

91 Ibid., vi. 20. 2.

92 Ibid., vii. 16. 14 f., 25. Stein, ii, 570, is wrong to say that Totila brought about "l'affranchissement en masse des esclaves." Yet so many slaves escaped and married free persons that Justinian felt himself obliged to legislate about them when the war was over: Justinian, *Novellae* Appendix vii. 15.

93 Procopius, *BG* v. 20. 14.

94 Ibid., v. 18. 40.

95 Ibid., v. 20. 11.

96 Ibid., vi. 6. 15 ff.

97 Ibid., vii. 4. 16; cf. vii. 9. 10; 21. 12 ff.

98 Ibid., vi. 6. 15 ff. Justinian unfairly states to the Frankish kings that the Ostrogoths had indeed taken Italy by force: ibid., v. 5. 8.

99 Ibid., vii. 6. 4; 20. 29 f.
100 Ibid., vii. 7. 16; 30. 21 f.; 31. 21; 36. 25; 37. 14. In vii. 36. 25 ff., Procopius
analyses the reaction of the troops. At first they all opted to go back to Byzantium, but then because of (i) shame at their defeat, (ii) fear of ambush after
surrender, and (iii) disgust at not having been paid for so long, all remained
with the Gothic army apart from two men who had wives and children from
whom they could not bear to be parted. In one curious case we hear of Roman soldiers fighting "unwillingly" for the Goths: vii. 39. 22. The reference
may be to troops who had chosen the second of these alternatives.
101 Ibid., vii. 8. 1 ff. For a somewhat similar incident, where the Avars showed
mercy to the citizens of Sirmium, see John of Ephesus, vi. 32.
102 Procopius, BG vii. 35. 9.
103 Ibid., vii. 21. 6 f.
104 Ibid., v. 11. 26; 26. 1. For another massacre of senators see viii. 34. 3 ff.
105 Ibid., vi. 21. 39; cf. Bury, ii, 204.
106 Ibid., vii. 20. 23.
107 See Stein, ii, 581 n.
108 Procopius, BG vii. 15. 14. Note also vii. 19. 34 for another example of vin-
dictiveness; cf. vii. 6. 26. For an example of obscene cruelty see vii. 30. 21.
109 Ibid., vi. 18. 14; 28. 17.
110 So Bury, ii, 178.
111 Procopius, BG v. 7. 30; vi. 7. 17 f.; 12. 17; 24. 14; 28. 6; cf. vii. 15. 9 ff.; 18.
11; etc. But in spite of Bury, ii, 236, it is not certain that there are any ships
in Procopius, BG vii. 15. 1 f.
112 Ibid., vii. 9. 4.
113 Ibid., viii. 31. 18 ff.
114 Ibid., viii. 35. 24 ff.
115 Agathias, i. 20 (p. 172. 20 ff., ed. Dindorf), cf. 174. 13.

CHAPTER 7:
THE END OF NORICUM

1 J. B. Bury, The Life of St. Patrick (London, 1905); D. A. Binchy, "St. Patrick
and His Biographers: Ancient and Modern," Studia Hibernica, ii (1962), 7–
173; R. P. C. Hanson, St. Patrick: His Origins and Career (Oxford, 1969).
2 F. Lotter, Severinus von Noricum: Legende und historische Wirklichkeit, Mono-
graphien zur Geschichte des Mittelalters, Bd. 12 (Stuttgart, 1976), 201 ff.,
followed by Gerhard Wirth, "Anmerkungen zur Vita des Severin von Noricum," Quaderni Catanesi di Studi Classici e Medievali, i, i (1979), 217–66, at
224 n. 16.
3 For an astonishing series of conjectures relating to Severinus's earlier career
see Lotter, op. cit., 218 ff., 241 ff., 246 ff., 251, et al. Even Wirth, art. cit.,
who follows Lotter in much, wilts here and there, e.g. on his p. 265. For a
criticism see F. Prinz, "Zur Vita Severini," Deutsches Archiv, xxv (1969),
531–36. Those who collect wierd and wonderful theories will not waste their

time if they also read F. Kaphan, *Zwischen Antike und Mittelalter* (Munich, n.d.), 119 ff., where the brigands known as the Scamarae become Severinus' underground intelligence network!

4 See Lotter, op. cit., 67 f., and the critical note in R. Noll, *Eugippius: Das Leben des heiligen Severin,* lateinisch und deutsch (Berlin, 1963). The Latin quoted in the text means: "At the time of the death of Attila, king of the Huns, both provinces of Pannonia and all other places adjacent to the Danube were in confusion and uncertainty, *and as the first act great struggles broke out among his sons about gaining control of the kingdom. These men, puffed up with the disease of despotism, thought their father's death an occasion for crime on their part.* At that date, then, Severinus, coming from the East, was staying in the little town called Asturis."

5 So E. Vetter *apud* Noll, op. cit., 35.

6 Jordanes, *Get.* 259–63 on the Nedao but with no exact indication of date.

7 The chronicler Victor Tonnennensis, s.a. 453. 2 (*Chron. Min.* ii. 185), for what it is worth, dates the battle to 453. Bury, i, 296, Stein, i, 336, and W. Ensslin, *Theoderich der Grosse*[2] (Munich, 1959), 9, date the Nedao to 454 precisely; and Maenchen-Helfen, *The World of the Huns,* 145–47, shows that the battle cannot have been fought later than the summer of 455.

8 In this chapter the figures in brackets refer to the chapter and section of Eugippius's *Vita.*

9 *Cons. Italica,* 577 (*Chron. Min.* i. 304); but Mommsen makes it clear there that there is something wrong with the text, so that the argument is hardly worth pursuing.

10 Isidore, *Etym.* xi. 2. 4. On the meaning of the word see the *Thesaurus Linguae Latinae* i, 797. 61 ff.; cf. 1126. 29 ff.

11 John of Antioch, frag. 214 *a* (*FHG* v, 29).

12 Jordanes, *Get.* 282 ff.; cf. Schmidt, *Ostgermanen* 277; Stein, i, 356. On the date and site of the Ostrogothic settlement in Pannonia see W. Ensslin, "Die Ostgoten in Pannonien," *Byzantinisch-neugriechische Jahrbücher,* vi (1927–28), 146–59.

13 *Contra,* Lotter, op. cit., 166, 207 ff., 253.

14 I am not concerned in this paper with the identification of the ancient place names. For a discussion in English see Johanna Haberl *apud* C. and S. Hawkes, *Greeks, Celts, and Romans, Archaeology into History* (London, 1973), 97–149. Miss Haberl has since written *Wien-Favianis und Vindobona* (Leiden, 1976). For archaeological notes in English on these cities see H. Vetters *apud* M. W. Barley, *European Towns, Their Archaeology and Early History* (London and New York, 1977), 261–90. The survival of the place-name Batavis-Passau no more proves continuity of urban life than does the survival of Londinium-London.

15 So, correctly, Geza Alföldy, *Noricum* (London, 1974), 216.

16 The *foedus* which the citizens of Tiburnia struck with the Ostrogoths (xvii. 4) is of quite a different character. It was simply a peace treaty which ended a war. It did not entail settling federates in Tiburnia. Schmidt, op. cit., 120, and Stein, 397, suppose that several Norican towns had admitted federates, Comagenis being only one of them. There is no hint of this in Eugippius.

17 *Cod. Theod.* vi. 8 "de metatis."

18 Wirth, art. cit. (in n. 2 above), 232, thinks it "possible" that the troops were hired by the townspeople but does not see the implications of this "possibility." Bieler *apud* L. Bieler and L. Krestan, *Eugippius: The Life of St. Severin,* The Fathers of the Church, vol. 55 (Washington, 1965), Index, p. 124, s.v. "Comagenis," says on the basis of i. 3 f., that the town was "held by barbarians under treaty." That is a misunderstanding of the words.

19 See *Cod. Justin.* ix. 8. 5; *Digest,* xlviii. 4. 3, etc.

20 So the *Vita* xxxiii. But Schmidt, op. cit., 120, takes the federates to be Rugi, while E. Norden, *Alt-Germanien* (Leipzig and Berlin, 1934), 75 n. 1, suggests very tentatively that they may have been Ostrogoths.

21 Bieler, op. cit., 59, translates the phrase "their hostile neighbours," which is correct. But Noll, op. cit. (in n. 4 above), 61, has "Feinden aus der Nachbarschaft," which seems to introduce a third party in addition to the citizens of Comagenis and the federates. The same misunderstanding has led Lotter, 211, into serious difficulties, and he is even less convincing when he discusses the same incident on his pp. 136 f., 156 f.

22 *De Excidio,* xxiii.

23 There is no reason to follow Lotter, op. cit., 33 (cf. 166, 270, 107), in thinking that Avitianus was a "bewaffneter Gefolgsmann des Rugierfürsten Ferderuch." Eugippius gives no hint that Avitianus was a member of any *comitatus* or that he had any permanent relationship with Ferderuchus. L. Varady, *Das letzte Jahrhundert Pannoniens (376–476),* (Amsterdam, 1969), 348 f., supposes that Feletheus and after him Ferderuchus held Roman military ranks and in Favianis commanded Roman military units. Varady's work was damagingly criticized by J. Harmatta, "The Last Century of Pannonia," *Acta Antiqua Acad. Scient. Hungaricae,* xviii (1970), 361–69.

24 I do not know why Lotter, op. cit., 193, wants to give Severinus a detachment of troops to lead on this occasion.

25 Eugippius' *Epistle* to Paschasius, 8, with Noll ad loc.

26 Hydatius, 93, 95 (*Chron. Min.* ii. 22); Sidonius, *carm.* vii. 233.

27 A possible parallel is the revolt of the *hostes Pannonii* of Jerome, *Ep.* 123. 16. For various theories about these see Varady, op. cit., 218 ff.

28 Priscus, p. 310 f., ed. Dindorf, with Varady, op. cit., 319 f.

29 On them see Schmidt, op. cit., 117–28. On the attitude of Eugippius and Severinus towards the barbarians see M. van Uytfanghe, "La Bible dans la 'Vie de saint Severin' d'Eugippius," *Latomus,* xxxiii (1974), 324–52, at 337 ff. I doubt if Sidonius, *carm.* v. 476, can be taken as evidence that Majorian included a Rugian contingent in his forces. The poet has simply thrown in the name of every northern people that he could think of.

30 Procopius, *BG* vii. 2. 1.

31 *Vita* v. 1. It does not follow that the Ostrogoths had occupied Noricum Mediterraneum at this time: *contra,* Schmidt, op. cit., 120, though they seem to have controlled access to it.

32 The Class I manuscripts have *turba latrocinantium barbarorum,* and Noll rightly rejects *barbarorum,* which does not appear in the Class II manuscripts. But in his note ad loc. (p. 125) Noll speaks of the Rugi suffering "unter den Räu-

bereien eines anderen germanischen Stammes, dessen Name leider nicht gennant ist." But these brigands were not barbarians, a fact which puzzled the scribes of Class I and led them to convert them into barbarians. Schmidt, loc. cit., and Lotter, op. cit., 202, keeping *barbarorum,* think that the *latrones* were Ostrogoths from Pannonia. But if they had been Goths, why did not Eugippius say so?

33 I cannot agree with Wirth, art. cit. (in n. 2 above), 256, that Flaccitheus simply wanted to launch a plundering foray on Italy rather than to emigrate with his entire people. In fact, there was a substantial number of Rugi serving in the Imperial army in Italy in 476; Jordanes, *Get.* 291; Ennodius, *Vita Epif.* 118 (p. 99); 119 (p. 99). When they had gone there and why they had left their fellow countrymen, we do not know.

34 Procopius, *BG* vii. 2. 1 and 18; Marcellinus Comes, s.a. 541. 2; 542. 2 (ii. 106 f.)

35 Procopius, *BG* vii. 21. 3. This was also the rule among the Visigoths: see *Legg. Visig.* iii. 1.1.

36 Ennodius, *Vita Epif.* p. 361. 25 "qui parere regibus vix dignantur."

37 *Vita* iv. 12 *ecclesiae hostes haeretici*: viii. 1, et al.

38 Op. cit., 121.

39 See B. Saria, *Völker und Kulturen Südosteuropas,* Schriften der Südosteuropa-Gesellschaft, Bd. 1 (Munich, 1959), 17–31, with good bibliographical material in the footnotes. On the life of the Church in Severinus's time, and especially on the celebration of the Mass in the evening, see K. Gamber, "Die Severins-Vita als Quelle für das gottesdienstliche Leben in Norikum während des 5 Jh.," *Römische Quartalschrift für christliche Altertumskunde u. Kirchengeschichte,* lxv (1970), 145–57, though see also Bieler, op. cit., 41.

40 See esp. xxxi. 3. According to Lotter, op. cit., 193, 204, they were on even friendlier terms than we might have guessed. Thus, when Severinus prophesied a barbarian raid, he was doing nothing miraculous: the barbarian leaders had tipped him off beforehand! Nor did the saint predict (in v. 2) the departure of the Goths from Pannonia *c.* 472: the Goths had let him into the secret in advance!

41 See the remarks of J. Zeiller, *Les origines chrétiennes dans les provinces danubiennes* (Paris, 1918), 563.

42 Zeiller, op. cit., 541, thinks that Gibuldus was probably an Arian. There is no hint in Eugippius that this was so. Christianity is not known among the Alamanni before 500.

43 H. Jänichen *apud* J. Hoops, *Reallexikon der germanischen Altertumskunde*[2], (Berlin, 1973), i, 140, infers an 'Einkönigtum,' but the alternatives mentioned above are also possible.

44 There is no justification for the statement of H. Baldermann, "Die Vita Severini des Eugippius (II Teil)," *Wiener Studien,* lxxvii (1964), 162–73, at 171, "Die Rugierkönigin, eine eifernde Arianerin, verfolgt die Provinzialen, weil sie katholisch sind." Lotter, op. cit., 191, also speaks of forceable conversion to Arianism.

45 See respectively Bieler, op. cit., 24, and Zeiller, op. cit., 562.

46 *Vita* xlix. 1–3. The pagan Hunumund murdered a priest in the baptistery of a church: xxii. 4.

47 The Vandals under Gunderic desecrated the church of St. Vincent the martyr in Seville in 428: Hydatius, 89 (ii. 21); Isidore, *Hist. Vand.* 73 (ii. 296). See p. 217 below.

48 *Vita* xi. There is evidence of considerable Christian violence against the pagan shrines, statues, etc., late in the fourth century in Noricum: see Alföldy, op. cit. (in n. 15 above), 210 f., but not in the time of Severinus.

49 Lotter, op. cit., 194 n. 61, is inclined to think that the forty guards were soldiers of the *numerus* at Batavis mentioned in xx. 1. The phrase *viros oppidi* does not suggest soldiers.

50 For other references to this precaution see Thompson, *EG,* 141 n. 3. Add Procopius, *BG* v. 14. 17.

51 Note xxii. 4 "Hunumundus paucis barbaris comitatus," etc. Contrast xxv. 3 "Alamannorum copiosissima multitudo," which failed, however, to capture any of the *castella*—the term is a relative one. Their characteristic weapons apparently were the bow and the sword (xxxi. 5), but *tela* in Jordanes, *Get.* 26. Were they mounted or infantrymen? In addition to the royal family there were optimates among them (xxxiii. 1).

52 Cf. xxvii. 1 "mansores oppidi Quintanensis, creberrimis Alamannorum incursionibus iam defessi, sedes proprias relinquentes in Batavis oppidum migraverunt," though admittedly this is the only passage where Eugippius makes the point explicitly. I do not exactly understand xvii. 2 "quamvis ex duro barbarorum imperio famis angustias sustinerent." On the other hand, the severe famine at Favianis reported in iii. 1 is not said to have been caused by raiding.

53 *Vita* xxxi. 5 "ne tanti exercitus compulsione vastentur potius quam migrentur." I refer to this action of Severinus as a "failure." If the citizens were prepared to make a fight of it, his action was not far removed from treachery.

54 Procopius, *BG* vi. 14. 9 and 24.

CHAPTER 8:
HYDATIUS AND THE INVASION OF SPAIN

1 Hydatius, 65, 108[a], 191. Our text of Hydatius dates Augustine's death to 436 instead of 430. The entire entry is missing from B; and Courtois, *Byzantion,* 25, 27, believes that it is an interpolation. No doubt. But would it not be surprising if Hydatius gave less space in §.53 to that preeminent Saint than he gave to Paulinus of Nola in §.81 or to St. Jerome in §.59? Observe that the refutation of Donatism is the chief merit of St. Augustine in the eyes of Hydatius. That the Saint had combated Priscillianism as well is a fact that Hydatius does not mention. Did he know of it?

2 Courtois, *Byzantion,* 51 n.6. I have accepted his revised chronology. There is little of interest in Casimiro Torres Rodríguez, "Hidacio, el primer cronista español," *Rivista de archivos, bibliotecas, y museos,* lxii (1956), 755–94, or in V. A. Sirago, *Galla Placidia e la trasformazione politica dell' Occidente,* Université de Louvain: recueil de travaux d'histoire et de philologie, sér. 4, fasc. 25 (Louvain, 1961), 15 f.

3 *CIL* ii. 2517.
4 Strabo, iii. 1. 2; 3.5 and 7 f. Note St. Fructuosus of Braga writing to Braulio (Braulio, *Ep.* 43; Migne, *PL* lxxx. 691) "nos longe positos et occidentis tenebrosa plaga depressos."
5 Hydatius, 40.
6 Idem, 215, though Mommsen, ad loc., without any very obvious reason thinks that *Isauriae* is corrupt; Greg. Tur., *HF* iv. 40. For some remarks on Hydatius and Jerome, see F. Giunta, "Idazio ed i barbari," *Anuario de estudios medievales,* i (1964), 491–94.
7 Hydatius, *praef.* 6 f., 130; Leo, *Ep.* 15 §.17 (Migne, *PL* liv. 692).
8 Idem, 96. What did his visit to Aëtius achieve? Aëtius sent the Count Censorius to the Sueves in the following year, 432: idem, 98. The long delay was apparently due to Aëtius' preoccupation with the Franks; but it was only after Censorius' return to the Court that Hermeric made peace with the Galicians, and then only because a bishop, or a number of bishops, had intervened: idem, 100. Censorius may have taken part in the negotiations, but it is not certain that he achieved anything of value. Aëtius could hardly have done less.
9 Hydatius, 201.
10 We can hardly accept his statement on p. 13. 5 f., Mommsen, "quae secuntur ab anno primo Theodosii Augusti, ut comperi, et descripsi," for he was not yet born in the first year of Theodosius I. Again, how do we account for his statement in 175, "regnum destructum et finitum est Suevorum," referring to the year 456? Only two years later, in 458, the Goths and the Vandals alike found it worth their while to send envoys to the Sueves: Hydatius, 192. Even Isidore, *Hist. Goth.* 32 (ii. 280), is obliged to insert a *paene,* and goes on to say that when Maldras was appointed King, "regnum reparatur Suevorum." It looks as if Hydatius wrote 175 soon after the Battle of the Campus Paramus in 456, was convinced that Suevic power was broken and forgot to revise the entry when the Sueves partially recovered their strength. There are some interesting remarks in Tranoy, i, 51.
11 Hydatius, 109, 145, 151, respectively.
12 *Chron. Min.* ii. 7.
13 Hydatius, 56.
14 Idem, 150 *memorantur.*
15 Idem, 170, 188, 190, 208, 219. See also Giunta, art. cit.
16 Hydatius, 156 *spirans hostilia.*
17 Idem, 183.
18 Idem, 174, 186; "pro-Roman," 170.
19 Orosius, *Hist.* vii. 40. 8.
20 Hydatius, 218; cf. Priscus of Panium, frag. 30, i. 339 f.
21 Hydatius, 128.
22 S. Oost, "Aëtius and Majorian," *Classical Philology,* lix (1964), 23–29.
23 Hydatius, 34, with Seeck, P.-W. ix. 41.
24 Hydatius, 43: contrast 48 f.

25 Idem, 95, 110, followed by Fredegarius, ii. 51.

26 Hydatius, 92, with E. A. Freeman, *Western Europe in the Fifth Century* (London, 1904), 276 n.

27 Sidonius, *Ep.* viii. 5, and perhaps ix. 12; C. E. Stevens, *Sidonius Apollinaris and his Age* (Oxford, 1934), p. 65 n. 1.

28 Hydatius, 138. On Pascentius see P. Brown, "The Diffusion of Manichaeism in the Roman Empire," *Journal of Roman Studies,* lix (1969), 92–103, esp. 101, who does not doubt that it was his Manichaeism which brought Pascentius from Rome to Astorga.

29 For an admirer of Aëtius (if that is what he was, and I do not believe it) Hydatius gives a surprising amount of information about Aëtius' opponent Sebastian: see 99, 104, 129, 132, 144.

30 Idem, 153 f., 160, 162.

31 Idem, 145.

32 Leo, *Ep.* 102 ad fin. (Migne, *PL* liv. 988), "quae volumus per curam dilectionis vestrae etiam ad fratres nostros Hispaniae episcopos pervenire: ut quod Deus operatus est nulli possit esse incognitum." In 454 Leo addressed a letter "to the bishops of the Gauls and the Spains" on the problem of the date of Easter in 455, and it is unfortunate that we do not know whether in this case, too, the Pope's information went from Gaul to Spain rather than directly to the Spanish bishops.

33 Hydatius, 231.

34 On the reception of Chalcedon in the West see G. Bardy, "La répercussion des controverses christologiques en Occident entre la concile de Chalcédoine et la mort de l'Empereur Anastase (451–518)," *apud* A. Grillmeier and H. Bacht (editors), *Das Konzil von Chalkedon,* ii (Würzburg, 1954), 771–89.

35 Hydatius, 115, 118.

36 Idem, 120 (Sicily), 167 (Rome), 144 (Sebastian), 192 (Vandal ambassadors).

37 Marcellinus, s.a. 455 (ii. 86), and other references cited by Seeck, P.-W. vi, p. 926, and Courtois, *Vandales,* 196.

38 Hydatius, 167, "ut mala fama dispergit."

39 Note "ut aliquorum relatio habuit . . . dictus est," ibid., 89.

40 Idem, 62^b.

41 Avitus' letter is printed in Migne, *PL* xli. 805 ff. He writes, "sed impeditum est desiderium meum [to return home to Galicia], per totas iam Hispanias hoste diffuso." On Avitus of Braga see A. Lambert, *Dict. d'hist. et de géogr. ecclés.,* v. 1201.

42 Severus of Majorca, *Epistola de Iudaeis* (Migne, *PL* xx. 735, cf. 742).

43 Hydatius, 127.

44 Idem, 106.

45 Idem, 109.

46 Idem, 238, 247.

47 Idem, 106. This entry is discussed by Casimiro Torres, "Peregrinos de Oriente a Galicia en el siglo V," *Cuadernos de estudios gallegos,* 11 (1957), 53–64.

48 Hydatius, 106.

49 Idem, 177, "orientalium naves Hispalim venientes per Marciani exercitum caes[os Laz]as nuntiant." The MS. B has simply *caesas*. Mommsen's conjecture is based, I suppose, on Priscus of Panium, frag. 25. Tranoy accepts Mommsen's conjecture without comment.

50 Hydatius, 109.

51 Idem, 146 f., 184, 157, respectively.

52 Idem, 215. This entry relates to the year 461, but the great earthquake which shattered Antioch in this period occurred on the night of Saturday, 13 September 458: see Glanville Downey, "The Calendar Reform at Antioch in the Fifth Century," *Byzantion,* xv (1940–41), 39–48, and E. Honigmann, "The Calendar Change at Antioch and the Earthquake of 458 A.D.," ibid., xvii (1944–45), 336–39, neither of whom discusses the problem of Hydatius, 215. Why does he give so late a date for the earthquake? There is evidence for a second earthquake at Antioch in 459 (Downey, art. cit., 42 f.; Honigmann, art. cit., 338), but none, so far as I know, for any such disaster there in 461. I take it that Hydatius only learned of the event several years after it had occurred and was misinformed about the date. That would be another piece of evidence for the difficulty and delay of communication between the East and the far West in the middle of the fifth century; but observe that Hydatius is the only Western writer who has any knowledge of *any* earthquake at Antioch in this period.

53 J. N. Hillgarth, "Visigothic Spain and Early Christian Ireland," *Proceedings of the Royal Irish Academy,* vol. 62, Section C, no. 6. 167–94.

54 Pope Simplicius, *Ep.* 21 (pp. 213 f., Thiel), "Plurimorum relatu comperimus," etc.

55 Pope Hilary, *Ep.* 14, §.1 (p. 157, Thiel).

56 Idem, *Ep.* pp. 13 ff. (pp. 155 ff., Thiel).

57 Pope Felix II, *Ep.* 5 (p. 242, Thiel).

58 Thus, the well-known theory of Norman H. Baynes, *Byzantine Studies and Other Essays* (London, 1955), 315 f., that it was the Vandal fleet which broke the unity of the Mediterranean world, is not supported by the evidence from Spain.

59 Bury, i, 295; cf. Prosper, 1367 (i. 482); Jordanes, *Get.* 42. 223.

60 Hydatius, 154.

61 Seeck, P.-W. i, 703, s.v. Aetios (5). The passage of Hydatius is misunderstood by Maenchen-Helfen, *The World of the Huns,* 138.

62 The contentious passage is in Jerome, *Ep.* 123. 15 (written in 409), "quicquid inter Alpes et Pyrenaeum est, quod Oceano Rhenoque concluditur, Quadus, Vandalus, Sarmata, Halani, Gypedes, Heruli, Saxones, Burgundiones, Alamanni, et—o lugenda res publica—hostes Pannonii vastaverunt." Observe that Orosius, *Hist.* vii. 40. 3, also points out that the Vandals, Alans, and Sueves crossed the Rhine in 406 "multaeque cum his aliae [gentes]."

These chapters on Spain deal at some length with the Sueves. These people were eventually converted to Catholicism, and for a view of the evidence for this conversion the reader may care to look at a paper in Edward James (editor), *Visigothic Spain: New Approaches* (Oxford, 1980), 77–92.

63 This *non sequitur* is accepted even in the thoughtful, though unconvincing, paper of E. Schwarz, "Der Quaden- und Wandalenzug nach Spanien," *Sudeta,* iii (1927), 1–12, followed by P. Goessler, P.-W. xxiv, 1. p. 645, cf. Tranoy, ii, 35. Dahn, 546 n.2, wisely refrains from speculation on Suevic history before 406. The student of Suevic history will learn little from Otto Wendel, "Das Suebenreich auf der Pyrenäen Halbinsel," *Zeitschrift für deutsche Geisteswissenschaft,* v (1942–43), 306–13, or from W. Reinhart, "Los Suevos en tiempo de su invasion de Hispania," *Archivo español de Arqueología,* v (1942–43), 131–44, or from L. Vazquez de Parga, "La obra historica de San Isidoro," *apud* M. C. Diaz y Diaz (editor), *Isidoriana* (Leon, 1961), 99–105.

64 Jordanes, *Get.* 277–79.

65 *Origo Gentis Langobardorum,* 4; Paulus Diaconus, *Hist. Langob.* i. 21; ii. 26.

66 Swaffham, etc.: E. Ekwall, "Tribal Names in English Place Names," *Namn och Bygd,* 41 (1953), 129–77, at 150 f.; cf. J. N. L. Myres, *Anglo-Saxon Pottery and the Settlement of England* (Oxford, 1969), 72 f. I owe the first of these references to Professor K. C. Cameron, University of Nottingham, Honorary Director, English Place-Name Society. There is a stimulating paper on the earlier history of the Sueves by R. L. Reynolds, "Reconsideration of the History of the Sueves," *Revue belge de philologie et d'histoire,* xxxv (1957), 19–47, who makes it clear that there is no valid evidence for identifying the Sueves with the Quadi: in fact, the relevant authors carefully distinguish between them. But I do not follow him in rejecting, as he is inclined to do, the traditional opinion that the Sueves crossed the Rhine in 406, that they ravaged Gaul at the same time as the Vandals and Alans in 406–9, and that they entered Spain in the autumn of 409. Reynolds, followed by Schäferdiek, 105, ingeniously argues that they may have reached Galicia by sea. Hydatius, 42, can hardly be wrong on such a point; and we cannot disregard the explicit statement of the Spaniard Orosius, *Hist.* vii. 38. 3, 40. 3, who was in Spain in 409.

67 Dahn, 546 n. 1, cf. F. Miltner, P.-W. viii. A i. 307. Freeman, op. cit., p. 134, supposes that some crossed the mountains on 28 September, and others on 13 October, which again is not what Hydatius says.

68 So Courtois, *Vandales,* 50 f., cf. Tranoy, i, 25.

69 Jerome, *Ep.* 123. 15, "ipsae Hispaniae iam iamque periturae cotidie contremescunt recordantes inruptionis Cymbricae," etc.

70 *Chron. Min.* ii. 3. The only evidence, if it can be called such, is the explicit statement by Procopius, *BV* iii. 3. 2, that Honorius allowed the Asding Vandal leader, Godegisel, to settle in Spain: we need confirmation of Procopius when he speaks of the fifth century, but note Olympiodorus, frag. 16, where we hear of federates who must be the *Honoriaci,* not the invaders of 409.

71 Bury, i, 204.

72 Stein, i, 263; Reinhart, 65; Schmidt, *Wandalen,* 22; Schäferdiek, 105; cf. Dahn, 546, 563, who dates the alleged *foedus* to 417.

73 The correct conclusion is reached by Gibert, 557 ff.; Tranoy, i, 35 ff.

74 Hydatius, 249. According to Reinhart, 52, they lived between Lusitania and Astorga; but we can be more precise. In this passage the Aunonenses seem fairly clearly to be contrasted with Lusitania and also with the Galician city of Astorga. The inference is that they did not live in Lusitania, but were situated in Galicia at some place other than Astorga (since the province of Carthaginiensis hardly comes into the question). The view of Schmidt, *Westgermanen* i, 212 n.2, that Aunona lay in Lusitania is accordingly contradicted implicitly by Hydatius' words. There is little likelihood in the view of Gibert, 566, that Aunona could well have been a place subject to the Visigoths, for the Visigoths ruled none of Galicia before 585. What clinches the matter, I believe, is that in the *Parochiale* of Suevic Galicia we find a *pagus* called *Aunone* in the diocese of Tuy: see the edition of this document in David, 43, or *Corpus Christianorum, series Latina,* vol. 175, p. 419. It is hardly open to doubt that this is the place to which Hydatius is referring, for there will hardly have been two places with this same name in Galicia. As for the year 460, when Rechimund ravaged localities of the Auregenses and of Lugo (Hydatius, 202), the implication seems undoubtedly to be that the Auregenses lived in Galicia. For different opinions about its precise location see Reinhart, 50, n.35. Schmidt, *Westgermanen* i, 211 n.1, seems to be right in believing that *Auregenses* means the inhabitants of Orense.

75 Hydatius, 49; Orosius, *Hist.* vii. 40. 10, "habita sorte et distributa usque ad nunc [A.D. 417] possessione."

76 For this untenable view see Reinhart, 35, 65 f. The author of *Chron. Gall. a. DXI* 557 (i. 655), whose source here is Hydatius, saw in this passage a reference only to the casting of lots for the provinces of Spain and no reference whatever to the *hospites*. Both he and Hydatius give no hint at the existence of a *foedus* or at the *sortes* of the *hospites*; and Seeck, *Untergang* vi, 61, rightly follows them.

77 Schmidt, *Westgermanen* i, 22.

78 So Gibert, 558, rightly. He also points out on 559 that the word *servituti* in Hydatius, 49, will not describe the relations of the provincials with any federates who were in their country, but it does describe the relations of the conquered provincials with their barbarian conquerors.

79 Hydatius, 74, where the Asdings leave Galicia and go to Baetica.

80 From Orosius, *Hist.* vii. 43. 14, Stein, i, 263, infers that all the barbarians in Spain tried to induce the Emperor Honorius to conclude a *foedus* and so to recognize in law their possession of the lands which they had seized. I would hesitate to draw this or any other conclusion about the barbarians from that passage of Orosius. There is also much to disagree with in J. Straub, *Historia,* i (1950), pp. 75 f.

81 Hydatius, 68.

82 Idem, 71.

83 Orosius, *Hist.* vii. 41. 2.

84 Hydatius, 77.

85 Idem, 71, 74.

86 Idem, 86, 89.

87 E. A. Thompson, "Christianity and the Northern Barbarians," *apud* A. D. Momigliano, *The Conflict Between Paganism and Christianity in the Fourth Century* (Oxford, 1963), 69 ff. Orosius, *Hist.* vii. 41. 8, goes too far in implying that the conversion of the Vandals and Sueves (to say nothing of the Burgundians) took place before 417, when he was writing. His implication may be true of the Vandals, but not for the Sueves.

88 Hydatius, 71, with Reinhart, 38, and especially Tranoy, ad. loc.

89 See the references in Courtois, *Vandales,* 55 n.1.

90 Hydatius, 71, 74. Whatever the meaning of the words "aliquantis Bracara in exitu suo occisis" in the latter entry (74), there is one meaning that they cannot bear: they cannot mean that a number of Vandals were killed in Braga, though that is how the words are taken by Schmidt, *Wandalen,* 26; and even Bury, i, 208, is ambiguous; but see now Tranoy's translation, which may be right.

91 Isidore, *Hist. Sueb.* 92 (ii. 303), gives the kingdom a life of 177 years. He is counting from 409, when the Sueves first entered Spain, until 585, when the Visigothic King Leovigild subjugated them.

92 Ibid., 85 (ii. 300), "Gallici autem in parte provinciae regno suo utebantur."

93 Hydatius, 74; but see n. 91 above.

94 Idem, 186, 249.

95 Idem, 199, 201.

96 Idem, 199.

97 Salvian, *De Gub. Dei* vii, 27 f.

98 The figure of 25,000 is accepted by J. Lacarra, *Settimane,* vi (Spoleto, 1959), 324; but Reinhart, 32 f., thinks that the Sueves may have numbered 30,000 to 35,000 persons, with some 8,000 or 9,000 warriors. That the Sueves were few in number is accepted by Reynolds, art. cit., 33, who points out that "the whole lot of them stood siege in the northern mountains from the Vandals": Hydatius, 71. Note Wallace-Hadrill, *Barbarian West,* 118, who thinks that "30,000 might not be a bad guess." It seems to be agreed among modern students of the question then, that 25,000 to 35,000 is approximately the number of the Sueves in Spain; and this would give them some 8,000 to 10,000 warriors at the most.

99 *Notitia Dignitatum,* Oc. xlii. 34 and 44; *Année épigraphique* (1951), 267. There is a photograph of this inscription in Courtois, *Vandales,* Plate V. For the name Ermengon, cf. Vives, 188, found on a sarcophagus at Pontevedre, dating from 624.

100 Procopius, *BG* vii. 34. 42 f.; Jerome, *Chron.* s.a. 373.

101 Amm. Marc., xvi. 12. 19, "indicavit per triduum et trinoctium flumen transisse Germanos"; 26, "armatorumque milia triginta et quinque," a figure of which the veracity is sometimes (unnecessarily) doubted.

102 Pliny, *Nat. Hist.* iii. 28.

103 F. Mateu y Llopis, "Hallazgos monetarios (vi)," *Ampurias,* xiii (1951), 203–55, at 231 f. (who wrongly ascribes the *solidus* of Constantine III to Constantine the Great); J. Lafaurie, "La chronologie des monnaies de Constantin III et de Constant II," *Revue numismatique,* ser. 5, vol. 15 (1953), 37–65. It is possible that there is another reference to the invasion of 409 in the following lines from the Spanish Anthology:

> glorificat nostra pax quos contemserat hostis,
> et onor est potior his quam concussio leti,
> nos dedimus sedem istis cum laude perenni,
> vos traite famulos in regni sorte futuri.

See O. Fiebiger and L. Schmidt, *Inschriftensammlung zur Geschichte der Ostgermanen,* Kais. Akademie d. Wissenschaften in Wien: phil.-hist. Klasse, Denkschriften, 60 Bd. 3 Abh. (Vienna, 1917), No. 32.

104 Hydatius, 49.

CHAPTER 9:
THE SUEVIC KINGDOM OF GALICIA

1 Hydatius, 86. For a different view see J. L. M. de Lepper, *De Rebus Gestis Bonifatii* (Brada, 1941), 82 f.

2 Hydatius, 119; cf. Isidore, *Hist. Sueb.* 85 *fin.* (ii. 300). I do not think that E. A. Freeman, *Western Europe in the Fifth Century* (London, 1904), 236, is quite right when he says that, as a result of the Vandal capture of Seville in 425 (Hydatius, 86), "Seville now passed away from the Roman power for ever." There must have been some kind of imperial rule there in 425–41.

3 Hydatius, 123.

4 Idem, 86.

5 *Chron. Caesaraug.* s.a. 460 (ii. 222).

6 Hydatius, 123 (cf. 139), 137.

7 Idem, 123.

8 Jordanes, *Get.* 229 f., which may be no more than good guesswork.

9 Hydatius, 142.

10 Isidore, *Hist. Sueb.* 87 (ii. 301), who mentions only the first Suevic attack on Tarraconensis and seems to know nothing of the second. On the condition of Tarragona see Orosius, vii. 22. 8.

11 Hydatius, 170, 172; Jordanes, loc. cit.

12 Jordanes, *Get.* 231; cf. Hydatius, 186, *variae nationis.* Dahn, 550, is far-fetched, I believe, when he suggests that if Rechiarius had once gained control of Spain he would have become a threat to Toulouse: hence Theoderic's attack. How often has an army from Spain invaded France? The words *in campo Paramo* are not in Hydatius. They are preserved only in the *Chron. Caesaraug.* s.a. 458 (ii. 222).

13 Sidonius Apollinaris, *Ep.* viii. 12, with C. E. Stevens, *Sidonius Apollinaris and His Age* (Oxford, 1933), 66 f.

14 Isidore, *Hist. Goth.* 31 (ii. 279).

15 Hydatius, 173, 175; *Chron. Caesaraug.*, loc. cit.; Auct. Prosp. Haun. s.a. 457 (i. 305); but Jordanes, *Get.* 232, is wrong here as elsewhere (p. 168 above). He has a story that Rechiarius embarked on a ship on the "Tyrrhenian Sea" but was driven back by a storm and so was captured by the Goths. This tale should be rejected in view of Hydatius' statement that the king fled to Oporto, not the Mediterranean Sea, which must have been far beyond his reach. The term "Tyrrhenian Sea" is used of the whole western Mediterranean right down to the Straits of Gibraltar: see e.g. Orosius, i. 2. 7, cf. 69.

16 Hydatius, 174.

17 So Dahn, 548.

18 Hydatius, 188, 193, 240, 249, respectively.

19 Reinhart, 135 f., who there modifies the doubts about the authenticity of these coins which he had expressed in "El reino hispanico de los suevos y sus monedos," *Archivo español de Arqueologia*, xv (1942), 308–28, at 326 f. Few will follow A. Solari, "Intorno a Richiario capostipite della dinastia suebica," *Rivista di filologia*, N. S. xv (1937), 46–47, who thinks that the coin dates from before 409 and that the Rechiarius in question was Hermeric's otherwise unknown father.

20 Hydatius, 71, 74. On the Nervasian Mountains see Courtois, *Vandales*, 55 n.1.

21 Hydatius, 91, 96, 100, cf. 114.

22 Idem, 137.

23 See pp. 39 ff. above.

24 Dahn, 547, cf. 561, ingeniously suggests that Heremigarius may have been king simultaneously with Hermeric: they would have been an example of that dual leadership which was common among the early Germans and which we find among the Sueves, too. However, there is no hint in Hydatius that Heremigarius was a king, for the F version of Hydatius, 90, carries no weight.

25 Hydatius, 90.

26 Idem, 181, "Suevi . . . Maldras sibi regem constituunt"; cf. Dahn, 568 f.

27 Hydatius, loc. cit.

28 Idem, 188, "pars Framtano, pars Maldras regem appellant."

29 Idem, 188 f. Schmidt, *Westgermanen* i, 210, thinks that they did fuse, but there is no evidence for that opinion. On Isidore, *Hist. Sueb.* 88 (ii. 28), see H. Hertzberg, *Die Historien und die Chroniken des Isidorus von Sevilla, Erster Teil: Die Historien,* Inaugural-Dissertation (Göttingen, 1874), 58. Hereafter cited as Hertzberg, *Historien.* For the second part of Hertzberg's useful work see *Forschungen zur deutschen Geschichte,* xv (1875), 289–360.

30 Hydatius, 193.

31 Jordanes, *Get.* 277.

32 Hydatius, 195, 198.

33 Idem, 201, 207.

34 Idem, 203.

35 Surprisingly, Schmidt, *Westgermanen* i, 210 n.4, and Schäferdieck, 109 n.14,

believe that Rechimund and Remismund were one and the same person: but see Tranoy, ii, 119 f.

36 Hydatius, 223, 226.

37 Bede, *Hist.* iv. 12. Cf. Paulus Diac., *Hist. Langob.* ii. 32.

38 Hydatius, 180, 187.

39 Jordanes, *Get.* 233 f.

40 Yet see Seeck, P.-W. i, 1129 f., and *Untergang* vi, 343: he identifies Aioulf with the Agiulf of Hydatius, 139, who had Censorius strangled at Seville in 448, which is not impossible. Jordanes' story is also accepted by Dahn, loc. cit., Reinhart, 47 f.; Stein, i, 373 (who says that Agiulf fell before a Visigothic army: contrast Hydatius, 187); Schmidt, *Westgermanen* i, 209 n.6, who doubts the equation of Aioulf with Agiulf.

41 Thompson, *EG,* 96.

42 Jo. Biclar. s.a. 585 (ii. 217), *thesaurum.*

43 Isidore, *Hist. Goth.* 45 (ii. 285). Early in the seventh century King Sisebut used his *thesaurus* to ransom war prisoners: ibid., 61 (ii. 291). For Amalaric's *thesaurus* see Greg. Tur., *HF* iii. 10. W. Reinhart, *Mitteilungen der bayerischen numismatischen Gesellschaft* (1937), 151–89, argues that certain *solidi* which bear the mintmark N or NR were minted at Norba Carsarina. This town is the modern Caceres, which is nowhere near Galicia, so that the coins can hardly be Suevic.

44 Little can be learned about the kings' advisers and servants from Martin of Braga, *Formula Vitae Honestae,* 1 237. 15, ed. Barlow.

45 Hydatius, 199. Tranoy, *Contra,* i, 46; ii, 112 f.

46 Isidore, *Etym.* xiv. 5. 21.

47 Hydatius, 102, 194, 202.

48 Idem, 179, 214[a]. Cf. *CIL* ii. 4215 *conventus Bracaraugustanus.*

49 Hydatius, 201.

50 Idem, 249 f. Cf. *CIL* ii. 4072 *conventus Asturicensis.* On these *conventus* or assise circuits see Kornemann, P.-W. iv. 1174–79, and especially E. Albertini, *Les divisions administratives de l'Espagne romaine* (Paris, 1923). A new effort to study them has been made by Dulce Estefania, "Notas para la delimitacion de los conventos juridicos en Hispania," *Zephyrus,* ix (1958), 51–57. For the earlier Roman background see G. P. Burton, *JRS,* lxv (1975), 92–106.

51 Sidonius, *carm.* ii. 361 f.; Vives, 502–3, of A.D. 624, "Protheus fecit Thuresmude, uxori sue. obiit ipsa sub die viii kl. Ianuar. era DCLXXII," found at Mogadouro near the River Douro, south of Braganca.

52 Procopius, *BG* vii. 2. 3.

53 See his Plates II and III, facing pp. 110, 116, respectively.

54 Thompson, *GS,* 64.

55 David, 79, or *Corpus Christianorum, series Latina,* vol. 175, 415.

56 Jordanes, *Get.* 261.

57 Olympiodorus of Thebes, frag. 30.

58 Hydatius, 142 *per dolum,* 186 *dolis et periuriis instructi.*

59 Idem, 188.

60 Idem, 229 *dolose,* cf. 241.

61 Idem, 246. I do not see why Dahn, 555, and Schmidt, *Westgermanen* i, 212, think that Lusidius was commanding the town in the name of the Gothic king. Observe the remarkable reading of the shorter (P) text of Isidore, *Hist. Sueb.* 90 (ii. 302), "cives vero qui illic praeerant custodiendos tradidit Lusidio": the city council handed over the city to Lusidius to protect! In *The Goths in Spain,* 333 f., I ought to have mentioned the partial destruction of the walls of Coimbra by the Sueves.

62 Hydatius, 201, 121.

63 Idem, 142, 202, 249–50.

64 Idem, 119, 123.

65 Idem, 186, 206.

66 But de Lepper, op. cit., 81 f., holds that Seville fell once only.

67 Hydatius, 86, 89. I do not know the evidence for the statement of J. M. Lacarra, *Settimane di Spoleto* vi (1959), 328, that the Roman cities of Veleia and Juliobriga disappeared in this period. He says that Leon yielded its importance to Astorga and played no role in these struggles. Not so: Astorga was in Galicia and Leon in Tarraconensis, which was rarely troubled by the Sueves. Archaeology, according to Lacarra, shows some forts to have been wiped out in the second half of the fifth century, though they had been flourishing in the first half. Is it possible to interpret fifth-century evidence so nicely?

68 Hydatius, 224; Gregory of Tours, *De Virtutibus S. Martini* i. 11 (144–46). This text of the *Vita S. Fructuosi* was published by M. Diaz y Diaz, "A proposito de la *Vita Fructuosi,*" *Cuadernos de Estudios Gallegos,* viii (1953), 155–78, at 178.

69 Hydatius, 74. But Greg. Tur., *HF* ii. 2, has a story of how the Sueves suggested to the Vandals that the dispute should be settled by single combat: the Vandals agreed and withdrew when the Suevic champion won the duel. In this unlikely version the Romans played no part. For the Roman garrison in Spain see Jones, i, 197.

70 Hydatius, 77; *Chron. Gall. a. CCCCLII,* 107. s.a. 431 (i. 658), which gives the figure of "about 20,000"; Prosper, 1208 (i. 469). On Castinus' rank see Bury, i. 209 n.1. But de Lepper, op. cit., 83, makes the interesting suggestion that *Chron. Gall.,* loc. cit., refers to a second battle fought before the departure of the Vandals in 429. According to his view, the Roman government fought so desperately because its aim was to keep the Mediterranean ports of Spain from falling into barbarian hands.

71 Hydatius, 114; Isidore, *Hist. Sueb.* 85 (ii. 300), "Andevotum Romanae militiae ducem." Seeck, P.-W. i. 2124, oddly describes him as a mere "reicher Bandenführer in Baetica."

72 Hydatius, 125, 128, 134.

73 Idem, 134.

74 Idem, 155.

75 Zosimus, vi. 5. 1.

76 Hydatius, 200; Priscus of Panium, frag. 27, etc.
77 So L. Vassili, "La strategia di Maggoriano nella spedizione gallico-vandalica," *Rivista di filologia,* N.S. xiv (1936), 296–99, who supposes that the Vandals, the Visigoths, and the Sueves had formed a *bloc* in 458: cf. Hydatius, 192, who unfortunately does not explain the purpose of the embassies which he mentions—perhaps he did not know it. Vassili's suggestion cannot stand, for Gothic forces accompanied Nepotian and harassed the Sueves: the Visigoths had entered no *bloc* with the other barbarians.
78 Hydatius, 201. The phrase *habitantes Dictyni* has defied interpretation: where was the place? See Tranoy, ad loc. Is the reference to Sueves or Hispano-Romans? I would guess, to the former.
79 Hydatius, 213, cf. 230.
80 Hilarus, *Ep.* 14 §.1 (p. 157, Thiel), "dux provinciae nostrae."
81 *Chron. Gall. a. DXI,* 652 (i. 665), *dux Hispaniarum*; ibid., 653 (i. 665), "Vincentius . . . quasi magister militum."
82 Hydatius, 199.
83 Idem, 113.
84 Idem, 239, 249.
85 Idem, 96, 100.
86 Hilarus, *Ep.* 16 *init.* (pp. 165 f., Thiel).
87 On Varea see A. Schulten, P.-W. viii A. 373.
88 On Tritium see idem, P.-W. vii A. 1, 244.
89 Hilarus, *Ep.* 13 §.2, "episcopus Calagurae in ultima parte nostrae provinciae constitutus."
90 Orosius, vii. 40. 5, "adversus tyrannum et barbaros."
91 Ibid., 5–10; cf. Zosimus, v. 43. 2, vi. 1. 1, 5; Sozomen, ix. 11. 4. On this incident see Courtois, *Vandales,* 52 n. 3; K. F. Stroheker, *Germanentum und Spätantike* (Zürich, 1965), 73. Note also Freeman, op. cit., 70–78.
92 Why Palencia? The only answer that I have found to this question is that of C. E. Stevens, *Athenaeum,* xxxv (1957), 327 ff., "as a reward for successful operations against [Honorius' relatives] they were permitted to pillage their estates," and ibid., n. 83, he argues that Cauca, the birthplace of Theodosius I, is close enough to the *campi Palentini* of Orosius, vii. 40. 8, to allow this inference. In fact Coca is some 100 kilometres by road from Palencia, but I can think of nothing better. Hydatius, 2, makes an unexpected mistake when he describes Cauca as a Galician *civitas*: in fact, it lay in Carthaginiensis.
93 Hydatius, 91, 171, 186. Note Fergus Miller, *JRS,* lix (1969), 28 f., who, however, does not discuss the evidence of Hydatius. Reinhart, 48, says that the *Coviacense castrum* is the castle of Coyanza on the River Esla, today Valencia de Don Juan, three miles from Palencia; and this opinion was held even in the eighteenth century. Hübner, P.-W. iv. 1679, wisely observes that the site is wholly unknown, being mentioned only in this one passage of Hydatius, who gives no hint even at its approximate position. This point was not taken by W. Ensslin, P.-W. xiv. 1. 858 f., s.v. "Maldras."

94 Hydatius, 100. I have sometimes wondered whether in the phrase *sub interventu episcopali* Hydatius is not referring self-effacingly to himself. If so, then on one occasion he did play the positive part of a Severinus.

95 Hydatius, 101.

96 Orosius, iii. 20; Avitus, Migne, *PL* xli. 805 ff.

97 Possidius, *Vita S. Augustini* xxx. 5 = Augustine, *Ep.* 228 §. 5 (*CSEL* 57. 488). Severus Maioricensis, *Epistola de Iudaeis* (Migne, *PL* xx. 739), "duo quidam primarii Iudaeorum, Meletius Theodori frater et Innocentius, qui Hispaniarum cladem nuper effugiens," etc.

98 Hydatius, 131. Reinhart, 43, cites the view that this place was situated a short distance from Tuy. This is correct. The *Parochiale* lists a place called *Turonium* among the parishes of Tuy: David, 43, or *Corpus Christianorum, series Latina,* vol. 175, p. 419. A Vandal embassy reached the Sueves in 438 and later returned to Africa (Hydatius, 192); but in this case we do not know the route by which they travelled.

99 Procopius, *BG* vi. 15. 27 ff.

100 Hydatius, 171; A. Schulten, P.-W. viii A. i, 373.

101 Hydatius, 194.

102 Orosius, vii. 41. 7.

103 Salvian, *De Gub. Dei* v. 23.

104 Hydatius, 200 f., cf. 207 "contra votum et ordinationem supra dictorum delatorum."

105 Idem, 137.

106 See M. I. Finley (ed.), *Studies in Ancient Society* (London, 1974), 304–20.

107 Hydatius, 125, 128. The evidence bearing on the site of Aracelli is discussed by Hübner, P.-W. ii, 366. The view of Jones, op. cit. (in n. 69 above), that the three Masters were in fact *Comites Hispaniarum* who had been upgraded to the rank of *Magister* seems to multiply hypotheses unnecessarily.

108 Hydatius, 134 "succedentibus cum rege suo illic Suevis."

109 Idem, 141.

110 Idem, 142.

111 Idem, 158, "per Fredericum Theuderici regis fratrem Bacaudae Terraconenses caeduntur ex auctoritate Romana." The adjective *Terraconenses* here does not imply, in my opinion, that there were other Bacaudae in other parts of Spain.

112 Jo. Biclar., s. aa. 572, 577 (ii. 213, 215).

113 See Finley, loc. cit.

114 Hydatius, 179. Recent literature on the Bacaudae is cited on p. 221 below.

CHAPTER 10:
THE GOTHIC KINGDOM
AND THE DARK AGE OF SPAIN

1 Isidore, *Hist. Sueb.* 87 (ii. 301). According to the text of B, Hydatius uses a curious variety of names, or at any rate of spellings, for the Visigothic kings. He calls Theoderic I by three different names: *Theodoricus* (70), *Theodoris*

(142), and *Theodorus* (140, 150). Theoderic II appears as *Theodericus, Theodoricus, Theudericus, Theudoricus*. It is unfortunate that Hydatius is not a little more explicit in §97: "Vetto, qui de Gothis dolose ad Gallaeciam venerat, sine aliquo effectu redit ad Gothos." What is the meaning of *dolose?* Whom did he propose to betray? Did he hope to make himself king of the Sueves in 431?

2 Hydatius, 77, 134.

3 Idem, 140, 142.

4 Idem, 192.

5 Bury, i, 327.

6 Thompson, *GS,* 291.

7 Hydatius, 193.

8 Idem, 201, 206, 212, 250.

9 Idem, 186, 192 f.

10 Idem, 205, 208.

11 Idem, 219 f., 226, 230.

12 Idem, 233, 237.

13 Cf. Hydatius, 233, referring to A.D. 466.

14 Idem, 245 f., 250.

15 Vives, 363; J. Vives, "Die Inschrift an der Brücke von Merida und der Bischof Zenon," *Römische Quartalschrift für christliche Altertumskunde,* xlvi (1938), 57–61, who removes the inscription from the reign of King Erwig (680–87) and puts it securely in that of King Euric (466–84). A text will also be found in E. Diehl, *Inscriptiones Latinae Christianae Veteres* (reprinted Berlin, 1961), 777.

16 So Vives, art. cit., 57 n. 1.

17 Hydatius, 237.

18 Idem, 245.

19 Seeck, *Untergang* vi, 334, rightly saw that from 456–57 the Visigothic occupation of southern Spain was continuous until the Arabs arrived in 711. So, too, Reinhart, 48.

20 I do not know the reasons of R. de Abadal, *Del reino de Tolosa al Reino de Toledo* (Madrid, 1960), 43, for suggesting that there began *c.* 462 extensive settlements of Goths in the Castilian Meseta and elsewhere. Our sources know nothing of such early settlements there.

21 Hydatius, 245, 246, 249 f.

22 Isidore, *Hist. Goth.* 34 (ii. 281).

23 *Chron. Gall. a DXI* 651 (i. 664), "Gauterit comes Gothorum Hispanias per Pampilonem, Caesaraugustam, et vicinas urbes obtinuit."

24 Ibid., 652. De Abadal, op. cit., 44, takes the passages of Isidore and the Chronicle of 511 to refer to two different campaigns. But we can hardly think that Pamplona and Saragossa fell *twice* to the Goths.

25 But in this error Isidore is followed even by C. E. Stevens, *Sidonius Apollinaris and his Age* (Oxford, 1934), p. 152.

26 Jordanes, *Get.* 244; Bury, i, 344. So also Stevens, op. cit., 139 f.; Stein, i, 393. But the Goths never subjugated the Basques.

27 *ILS* 815, "b. f. s. dd. nn. Leonis et Antemi Augg." Hübner is there said to have proposed "bonum factum, saluti" for the beginning of this inscription.

28 *Chron. Min.* ii. 222, "Gotthi in Hispanias ingressi sunt." De Abadal, op. cit., 45, remarks that these words cannot mean the entry of a Gothic army and some officials, for these had long been in the peninsula. They must refer, he rightly says, to a large group of the Gothic population.

29 *Chron. Min.,* loc. cit., s.a. 497, "Gotthi intra Hispanias sedes acceperunt"; cf. de Abadal, op. cit., 46, who points out that this is the very expression used by Hydatius, 69, when referring to the establishment of the Goths in Aquitaine in 418: "Gothi . . . sedes in Aquitanica . . . acceperunt."

30 *Chron. Caesaraug.* s.a. 506 (ii. 222), "his cons. Dertosa a Gotthis ingressa est." De Abadal, op. cit., 60, asks whether this means that the Goths arrived at Tortosa for the first time in 506 or whether they now recovered it after a revolt.

31 *Chron. Caesaraug.* s. aa. 496, 506 (ii. 222). I assume with Schmidt, *Ostgermanen,* 497, and de Abadal, 45 f., that Burdunelus was a Roman rather than a Gothic rebel.

32 Vives, 149 f., "Hilduarens famula Dei vixit annos plus minus xxxviii. recessit in pace d. idibus Mar. era δxlii."

33 Thompson, *GS,* 291.

34 This is the opinion of de Abadal, op. cit., 64, cf. Wallace-Hadrill, *Barbarian West,* 117.

35 Thompson, *GS,* Index s.v "Cordoba."

36 Courtois, *Byzantion,* 42 ff.

37 Hydatius, 135; Migne, *PL* liv. 677 ff.

38 Hydatius, 133, "per episcopum Romae tunc praesidentem."

39 Idem, 102.

40 G. Morin, "Pastor et Syagrius: deux écrivains perdus du Ve siècle," *Revue bénédictine,* x (1893), 385–94; xii (1895), 388; xix (1902), 237–42. See especially Henry Chadwick, *Priscillian of Avila* (Oxford, 1976), 217 ff.

41 Hydatius, 124, 192^a.

42 Note G. Morin, "Le commentaire inédit de l'évêque latin Epiphanius sur les Evangiles," *Revue bénédictine,* xxiv (1907), 336–59. Dahn, 563, cf. Schäferdiek, 112 f., thinks that it was probably Suevic influence that expelled Sabinus and replaced him by Epiphanius.

43 Hydatius, 130.

44 Idem, 133, 135.

45 Idem, 138.

46 Hilarus, *Ep.* 13 § 3 (Thiel, p. 156), *fraternitate collecta;* cf. *Ep.* 17 § 1, *concilii.* On the relations of Ascanius with the papacy there is an unfruitful study by P. Angel Custodio Vega, "El primado romano y la iglesia española en los siete primeros siglos," *La Ciudad de Dios,* cliv (1942), 237–84, at 240–4.

47 Hilarus, *Ep.* 13 (Thiel, pp. 155–57).

48 Idem, *Ep.* 13 (pp. 157 f.) Observe the great number of variants for *Barcinonensium* which Thiel reports on his p. 157 n. 4, cf. 165 n. 3, 167 n. 12. Was Nundinarius really bishop of Barcelona or of some other see?

49 *Ep.* 16 (Thiel, pp. 165–69).

50 Ibid., § 6.

51 Ibid., *Ep.* 17. On the episodes of Silvanus and Irenaeus see Custodio, art. cit., 240–44, who suggests (243 n. 3) that the basic reason why Hilary was so harsh towards Irenaeus and yet so lenient to Silvanus is that strong representations on behalf of the latter had been made by the landowners of the seven places listed on p. 177 above. Hilary's words are (*Ep.* 16 § 1, p. 166 *init.,* Thiel), "honoratorum et possessorum Turassonensium," etc. — there follow the place-names — "cum subscriptionibus diversorum litteras nobis constat ingestas, per quas id, quod de Silvano querela vestra deprompserat, excusabant."

52 For the best text see J. Vives, *Concilios Visigoticos e Hispano-Romanos* (Madrid-Barcelona, 1963), 331 (canon 8 of the Council of Merida).

53 Vives, op. cit., 343, "ego Sclua Igiditanae civitatis ecclesiae episcopus pertinens ad metropolim Emeretensem," etc.

54 Hydatius, 188, 246.

55 Idem, 229, 241.

56 Idem, 229. David, 80, points out that the parish called *Cantabriano* in the diocese of Lamego was established on a great estate and belonged to the family of Cantabri. He supposes that our Cantaber was a member of that family.

57 Hydatius, 190, 195.

58 Simplicius, *Ep.* 21 (p. 213 f., Thiel). Thiel describes the addressee as Zeno of Seville, but see his p. 9 and the paper of Vives cited on p. 302 n. 15.

59 Vives, *Inscripciones,* 363.

60 *Ep.* 21 (p. 214, Thiel), "cuius vigore munitus, apostolicae institutionis decreta vel sanctorum terminos patrum nullo modo transcendi permittas." Zeno also received an extant letter from Pope Felix II (*Ep.* 5, p. 242, Thiel), who held office from 483 to 492.

61 For other Spanish examples of papal vicars see Pope Simplicius, *Ep.* 16 (pp. 728 ff., Thiel), Hormisdas, *Epp.* 24. 142 (pp. 787 f., 979 ff., Thiel).

62 Thompson, *GS,* 62.

63 Isidore, *Hist. Sueb.* 90 (ii. 302).

64 Dahn, 556; Schmidt, *Westgermanen* i, 213; and others. I agree here with Schäferdiek, 116 n. 39.

65 In addition to David's discussion see S. Ruiz, *Dict. d'histoire et de géographie écclesiastique,* x. 767, s.v. 'Britonia'; Nora K. Chadwick, "The Colonization of Brittany from Celtic Britain." *Proceedings of the British Academy,* li (1965), 235–99, at 284; E. A. Thompson, "Britonia," in M. W. Barley and R. P. C. Hanson, *Christianity in Britain, 300–700* (Leicester, 1968), 201–5; but there is nothing of interest in J. Orlandis, "Las congregaciones monasticas en la tradicion suevo-gotica," *Anuario de estudios medievales,* i (1964), 97–119, at 105 ff.

66 The view that the Britons who colonized Brittany were in flight from the Irish rather than from the Saxons is revived by Mrs. Chadwick, art. cit., but it was rendered unnecessary by the observations of K. Jackson, *Language and History in Early Britain* (Edinburgh, 1953), 13 f., 25 ff.

67 Jackson, op. cit., 11 ff.
68 It is conveniently printed as Appendix 2 in Claude W. Barlow, *Martini epis-copi Bracarensis Opera Omnia* (New Haven, 1950), 290–3.
69 Schmidt, *Westgermanen* 561.
70 In § 3, "in aestimatione tuae fraternitatis aliorumque pontificum per suas dioceses."
71 Barlow, 105. 7 ff.
72 Thompson, *GS*, 36, 328.
73 Leander of Seville, *Regula* 21 (Migne, *PL* lxxii. 892).

CHAPTER 11:
SPAIN AND BRITAIN

1 Hydatius, 101, 251. It is not clear whether Palogorius, a nobleman of Gali-cia, had gone to Theoderic II of Toulouse as an envoy of Remismund or on a private mission: idem, 219.
2 Sidonius, *Ep.* iv. 20.
3 Hydatius, 131, 192; cf. F. M. Clover, "Geiseric and Attila," *Historia,* xxii (1973), 107 n. 13.
4 Hydatius, 251.
5 Idem, 140. On the conversion of the Sueves to Catholicism see p. 292 n. 62 above.
6 X. Barral i Altet, *La circulation des monnaies suèves et visigothiques* (Munich, 1976), pp. 24 f., cf. 49, 51 f.
7 Gildas, *De Excidio* xx "tum primum inimicis per multos annos praedas in terra agentibus strages dabant," where note the imperfect: there were several massacres.
8 *Chron. Caesaraug.* s.aa. 496, 497, 506; cf. *Britannia,* viii (1977), 316 f.
9 Hydatius, 246 "cive suo, qui illic praeerat, . . . Lucidio."
10 K. Jackson, *Language and History in Early Britain* (Edinburgh, 1953), cap. vi. Margaret Gelling, *Signposts to the Past* (London, 1978), p. 88, remarks that "the survival of pre-English place-names . . . proves that there was a period of coexistence by Welsh and English speakers." She does not tell us who in her opinion coexisted on the British side. How would she describe the "coex-istence" of the Romans and the Sueves in Galicia? Mass slavery in early Saxon society is incredible.
11 *De Excidio* 25.
12 *Hist. Eccles.* ii. 20 (p. 125, Plummer).
13 Curiously enough, there is a place called *Francos* in the diocese of Idanha: on it see David, pp. 75 ff.
14 Ilerda: Ausonius, *Epist.* xxix. 58; Tarragona: Aur. Victor, *Caes.* xxxiii. 3; Orosius, vii. 22. 8.
15 See p. 201 above, where by an oversight I omitted to mention the place called *Cantabriano* which the *Parochiale* gives as one of the parishes of Lamecum: on it see David, p. 80.
16 These are the famous theses respectively of A. Piganiol, *L'empire chrétien (325–395)* (Paris, 1947), 422; and Jones, ii, 1068.

17 Hertzberg's work is cited on p. 297 n. 29 above.

18 Hertzberg, *Historien,* 55; Isidore, *Hist. Wand.* 73 (ii. 296).

19 Hydatius, 216; Isidore, op. cit., 77 (ii. 298). On this difficult matter see Courtois, *Vandales,* 396 f. Hydatius, 162, *Valentiniani filiam,* appears to be in some doubt as to which daughter of Valentinian was married to Palladius, son of Petronius Maximus. Does he mean Placidia or Eudocia, or was he uncertain which of the two enjoyed this questionable privilege? For a discussion of the problem see F. M. Clover, *Flavius Merobaudes: A Translation and Historical Commentary,* Transactions of the American Philosophical Society, new series, lxi, pt. i (1971), 25 f.

20 *Hist. Suev.* 85 (ii. 300).

21 *Hist. Goth.* 32 (ii. 280); *Hist. Sueb.* 88 (ii. 301).

22 Ibid.

23 See Mommsen's critical note on p. 280. 30. On the whole subject see Hertzberg, *Historien,* 36 ff., who cites many slips of Isidore's. It must be remembered, of course, that Hertzberg wrote before Mommsen's edition of the chronicles had appeared.

24 *Hist. Sueb.* 88 (ii. 301). Contrast Hydatius, 188 f.

25 Isidore, *Hist. Goth.* 33 (ii. 280).

26 Ibid.

27 Idem, *Hist. Sueb.* 89 (ii. 302).

28 *Hist. Vand.* 76 f. (ii. 297 f.).

29 *Hist. Sueb.* 90 (ii. 302), "cuius seductione Suevi a fide Catholica recedentes in Arrianum dogma declinant."

30 Ibid. 86 (ii. 301), "Emerita sub cultu, ut ferunt, gentilitatis vitam finivit." All that Hydatius, 137, says is "Rechila . . . Emerita gentilis moritur."

31 Isidore, *Hist. Goth.* 33 (ii. 280); and the short version of *Hist. Sueb.* 89 (ii. 302); Schmidt, *Westgermanen* i, 210 n. 5; Hertzberg, *Historien,* 58.

32 Hydatius, 114; Isidore, *Hist. Sueb.* 85 (ii. 300). Observe, however, that the shorter version of Isidore gives fourteen years as the length of Hermeric's reign, for the MS P reads *quattuordecim.* In point of fact this may be correct, though, if so, the figure is likely to be a lucky guess.

33 Bury, i, 203.

34 Hydatius, 114. Note the Latin of the shorter version of Isidore, *Hist. Sueb.* 85 (ii. 300), "hic iubente patre ab eo missus."

35 Isidore, *Hist. Sueb.* 87 (ii. 301). Mommsen on Hydatius, 142 (ii. 25), *cum Basilio,* writes "'cum auxilio Gothorum,' Isidorus, recte ut videtur."

36 E. A. Thompson, *VTU,* 103 f.; Isidore, *Hist. Goth.* 10 (ii. 271 f.)

37 Ibid. 35.

38 *Chron. Min.* ii. 254. Cf. the very unfavourable judgement by Hertzberg, *Historien,* 64, 75, whose work impressed Mommsen, loc. cit., as a "commentarium acutum et utilem hodie."

39 Mommsen, *Chron. Min.* i. 305, 582; cf. *Classical Review,* lx (1946), 106.

40 John of Antioch, frag. 209. 1; Sidonius Apollinaris, *carm.* ii. 484–6; *Ep.* i. 5. 10.

41 Procopius, *BV* iii. 6. 27; Jordanes, *Rom.* 338; Theophanes, a.m. 5963; Cassiodorus, *Chron.* s.a. 471 (ii. 158); Marcellinus Comes, s.a. 471 (ii. 90); Victor Tonnennensis, s.a. 471 (ii. 188).

42 John Malalas, p. 371 f., Bonn, *Chronicon Paschale*, p. 596, Bonn.

43 Edited by H. Delehaye, *Analecta Bollandiana*, xxxii (1913), 121–229, at 173 f.

44 Norman H. Baynes, "*The Vita S. Danielis Stylitae*," *English Historical Review*, xl (1925), 397–402.

45 So Baynes, art. cit., 399. On the relations of Aspar and Leo see also E. W. Brooks, "The Emperor Zenon and the Isaurians," ibid., viii (1893), 209–38, at 210–15.

46 John Malalas and *Chronicon Paschale*, loc. cit.

47 John of Antioch, frag. 206. 2.

48 Tranoy, facing p. 88, publishes a photograph of §§219–229 as given by B. The reader will search the photograph in vain for that "Olympi CCCXI" which Tranoy explicitly ascribes to B on his p. 170.

CHAPTER 12:
BARBARIAN COLLABORATORS AND CHRISTIANS

1 Text in *Chron. Min.* ii. 211–20; cf. Isidore, *de vir. illustr.* 62.

2 Sidonius, *Ep.* v. 5; Cassiodorus, *Var.* v. 40. The author of the little poem beginning "inter eils goticum," etc. must also have known at least a little Gothic: *Anth. Lat.* 285. But many a Goth could speak Latin: see e.g. Procopius, *BG* vi. 1. 14 f., 26. 3; 6. 14 ff.; for written Gothic vi. 24. 3.

3 *Opus Imperfectum in Matthaeum*, Homily xli (Migne, *PG* lvi. 824).

4 Velleius Paterculus, ii. 117. 3; cf. Prudentius, *c. Symm.* ii. 816–9; Jordanes, *Get.* 122 "quasi hominum genus," etc.

5 Amm. Marc., xvi. 12. 25.

6 Ibid., xvii. 8. 5.

7 See Thompson, *EG*, 140 ff.

8 Zosimus, iii. 6. 4; 7. 1–3; Eunapius, frag. 11; cf. Amm. Marc., xvii. 10. 5; xxvii. 1.

9 Libanius, *Or.* xviii. 45, 73; Socrates, *Hist. Eccles.* iii. 1. 27; Dio Cassius, lxxii. 14. 1, cite other examples of this unpleasant practice.

10 Zosimus, iv. 48. 2.

11 Zosimus, iii. 7. 3–7; Eunapius, loc. cit.; Peter the Patrician, frag. 18; cf. Julian, *Ep. ad Athen.* 280 B.

12 Amm. Marc., xxvii. 1. For the name Charietto see also Greg. Tur., *HF* ii. 9.

13 Procopius, *BP* i. 8. 3.

14 Idem, *BG* vii. 12. 12.

15 Malchus, frag. 18, p. 419. 5, ed. Dindorf.

16 Ibid., p. 411 f.

17 Idem, frag. 18, p. 417. 11 f. For other examples of barbarians from various parts of the world who joined the Romans see D. Hoffmann, "Wadomar, Bacurius und Hariulf," *Museum Helveticum*, xxxv (1978), 307–15.

18 Malchus, frag. 18, p. 418, ed. Dindorf; Marcellinus, s.a. 479 (ii. 91 f.)

19 Themistius, *Or.* xvi. 206 D.

20 Zosimus, iv. 25. 3, cf. Amm. Marc., xxxi. 8. 1; Claudian, *cons. Stil.* i. 94; *Carmen de Providentia Dei* 57 f. (Migne, *PL* li. 618), the author of which puts into the mouth of an imaginary critic the lines: "tu quoque pulvereus plaustra inter et arma Getarum / carpebas duram, non sine fasce, viam."

21 Malchus, frag. 18, p. 413. 10 (though admittedly he does not say explicitly that the inhabitants left because of the approach of the barbarians); Zosimus, i. 35. 1, etc.

22 Claudian, *in Rufin.* ii. 127–29. For the *carrago* see the *Thesaurus Ling. Lat.,* s.v.

23 Ambrose, *Ep.* xv. 7 (Migne, *PL* xvi. 957), cf. Amm. Marc., xxxi. 8. 4. There is a discussion in *EG,* 140 ff.

24 Zosimus, i. 26. 2, and for Gaul idem, i. 67. 1.

25 Ambrose, *Exposit. in Lucam* x. 10 (Migne, *PL* xv. 1806 f.), written in 378: "quae omnium fames, lues pariter boum atque hominum ceterique pecoris, ut etiam qui bellum non pertulimus debellatis tamen nos pares fecerit pestilentia." Plague broke out among the Visigoths in Arcadia in 397: Claudian, *iv cons. Hon.* 467; Ambrose, *Ep.* xv. 5 and 7 (Migne, *PL* xvi. 956 f.); cf. Orosius, vii. 40. 10. As for Britain see M. Todd, "*Famosa pestis* and Britain in the Fifth Century," *Britannia,* viii (1977), 319–25.

26 Zosimus, iv. 30–1, 33, repeatedly refers to these men as "deserters," using the same term which Strabo, vii. 292, had long ago used of the Cheruscan Segestes. For the third century see Zosimus, i. 45. 1, 46. 2.

27 Idem, iv. 31. 2 ff., 33. 3; cf. 45. 3, 48. 1 ff.

28 Idem, iv. 31. 1; 40. 2 f.; 7. Egypt: iv. 30. 2 ff.

29 Amm. Marc., xiv. 10. 7 f.

30 Idem, xxix. 4. 7; cf. xxvii. 2. 9.

31 Idem, xvi. 4. 1. C. J. Simpson, "Where Was *Senonae?*," *Latomus,* xxxiii (1974), 940–2, ingeniously suggests that *Senones* in Ammianus here was not Sens but the village now known as Senon in the Dép. Meuse. But would Ammianus have expected his readers to know this place?

32 Amm. Marc., xvi. 12. 2; Libanius, *Or.* xviii. 54.

33 Amm. Marc., xvii. 1. 8; xxix. 4. 2.

34 Idem, xvi. 12. 17.

35 Idem, xxi. 3. 5; xxvi. 8. 2 "Vadomario . . . ex duce et rege Alamannorum"; xxix. 1. 2. There is a fantastic judgement on Vadomarius by P. Goessler, P.-W. (Zw. R.), 2071 *fin.*

36 For some interesting cases see Hoffmann, art. cit.

37 Procopius, *BP* ii. 27. 23, cf. 35.

38 Idem, *Anecd.* xxi. 26–8.

39 Priscus, frag. 5. Note also Amm. Marc., xxxi. 6. 2; Sozomen, ix. 11. 4; Zosimus, v. 15. 5, vi. 4. 3; Orosius, xii. 40. 6 ff.

40 Zosimus, v. 6. 5.

41 Philostorgius, ii. 5.

42 Prosper, 1307 (i. 473).

43 I have set out my views on this matter in A. D. Momigliano, *The Conflict Between Paganism and Christianity in the Fourth Century* (Oxford, 1963), 56–78. For a full bibliography with discussion see K. Schäferdiek, *Reallexikon f. Antike und Christentum,* x (1977), 492–548, s.v. "Germanenmission."

44 Theodoret, *Hist. Eccles.* v. 31, cf. v. 37. 4.

45 Rusticius in Priscus, pp. 294. 32; 318. 26, as well as Bigilans and the merchant of Viminacium with whom Priscus conversed in Attila's camp. For the languages used in Attila's camp see P. Scardigli, *Die Goten: Sprache und Kultur* (Munich, 1973), 87–94, with whose conclusions I am not wholly in agreement, though that is not to deny the great interest of his work.

46 Sozomen, vii. 26. 6–8.

47 Pseudo-Prosper, *De Invoc. Omnium Gentium* ii. 33 (Migne, *PL* li, 717 f.)

48 Cyril of Scythopolis, *Vita Euthymi* x, xv.

49 Malchus of Philadelphia, frag. 1.

50 Procopius, *BG* v. 5. 9.

51 Idem, *BP* i. 20. 9.

52 Idem, *BG* vii. 34. 24. For the conversion of the Tzanni in 526 see idem, *BP* i. 15. 25, and note that Procopius, *BP* ii. 29. 15, describes the Abasgi as "Christians and friends of the Romans from of old."

53 Malalas, 427 f.; Theophanes, a.m. 6020 (p. 174 f., de Boor); Procopius, *BG* vi. 14. 33 f.

54 Malalas, 431 f.; Theophanes, a.m. 6020 (p. 175 f.) See also Malalas, p. 438.

55 John of Ephesus, iv. 6, transl. Payne Smith.

56 Idem, iv. 49.

57 Idem, iv. 8.

58 Zachariah of Mitylene, pp. 329, 330. He wrote this part of his work, xii. 7, in 555 (cf. Hamilton and Brooks, Introd. to their translation, p. 5), and he dates Kardutsat's visit to the Huns to "about twenty years ago and more," i.e. 535 or a little earlier.

59 Procopius, *BG* viii. 19. 3.

60 Tacitus, *G* xxiii. 2, translated by Anderson; cf. Seneca, *Ep.* lxxxiii. 22. Cologne: Tacitus, *H* iv. 79. It is not a waste of time to look at e.g. A. Grenfell Price, *White Settlers and Native Peoples* (Melbourne, 1950), Index, s.v. "Liquor."

61 *De Helia et ieunio,* liv.

62 *De Tobia,* xv. 51. There is a discussion of trade between the invaders and the Romans, especially the slave-trade, in *Florilegium,* ii (1980), 71–88.

63 *Cod. Justin.* iv. 63. 2 "non solum aurum barbaris minime praebeatur, sed etiam si apud eos inventum fuerit, subtili auferatur ingenio."

64 R. P. C. Hanson, "The Date of St. Patrick," *Bulletin of the John Rylands Library,* lxi (1978), 60–77. According to Prosper, cited in n. 75 above, Palladius was the first bishop to be sent to the Scots.

65 See Ebbo, *Vita Ottonis ep. Babenbergensis* ii. 2 (MGH Scriptores xii).

66 Patrick, *Conf.* 51 f.

67 Ibid., 53, reading *iudicabant,* not *indicabant.*

68 *Ep. ad Corot.* passim.

69 *Conf.* 52, 55.

70 Ibid.

71 Ibid., 35, cf. 37.

72 Ibid., 48.

73 Ibid., 37 f., 49–51.

74 Ibid., 42. I have little doubt that the opposition came from *pagan* parents: *contra,* J.B. Bury, *The Life of St Patrick* (London, 1905), 172.

APPENDIX

1 *The Merovingian Archaeology of South-West Gaul,* BAR Supplementary Series 25 (i), 1977, 6.

2 Salvian, *De Gub. Dei* iv. 67, 81; vii. 64.

3 Greg. Tur., *HF* ii. 18.

4 Sidonius, *Ep.* viii. 6. 13 ff. I take the date 478 from K. Stroheker, *Der senatorische Adel im Spätantiken Gallien* (Tübingen, 1948), 194, no. 253.

5 Sidonius, *Ep.* viii. 9. 5, lines 21 ff.

6 Wallace-Hadrill, *Kings,* 29.

7 *The Roman Forts of the Saxon Shore* (London, 1976). The book has been criticized: see Philip Bartholomew, *Britannia,* x (1979), 367–70. But the criticisms hardly bear on the points under discussion.

8 Johnson, 92 f. For the various conjectures about Grannona see D. A. White, *Litus Saxonicum* (Madison, Wisconsin, 1961), 59. See both these passages for the wholly unsupported theory that *Blabia* is Blaye on the Garonne estuary. As White points out, the first equation depends on the alteration of *Carronensium* to *Garonensium* in *Not. Dign.* 37. 15 *fin.* He also remarks that *Blabia* could also be Blavet in Brittany.

9 Wallace-Hadrill, loc. cit.

10 "Another Look at the Barbarian Settlement in Southern Gaul," *Traditio,* xxv (1969), 354–58.

Index

Note: b. = bishop; e. = east; k. = king; r. = river; R. = Roman(s); RE. = Roman Empire; s. = son; w. = west.

Abasgi, 309 n. 52

Abydus, 6

Achaeans, 238

Acherontia, 87

Admantius, 235

Adrianople, Battle of, 17, 38, 39–40, 45, 236, 280 n. 63

Aegidius, 141, 172

Aëtius, consul, 454, 151

Aëtius, patrician, 23, 66; resettles Burgundians, 24, 26, 27, 29, 32, 33, 51; settles Alans at Orleans, 25, 34; and at Valence, 25, 34, 35, 36; sympathetic to landowners, 26, 27, 28; sends Huns against Burgundians, 26, 33; sends Alans against Armoricans, 32, 185; motives of, 32–34; treaty with Theoderic, 34; crushes Noricans, 35, 124, 142; success of, 37; Litorius and, 53–54; at Catalaunian Plains, 54; advises Thorismud, 54; repels Huns from Italy, 54; ruler of Italy, 65; consul for third time, 120; meets Hydatius, 140, 165, 179, 290 n. 8; praised by Merobaudes, 141; relations with Majorian, 141; Hydatius' attitude to, 142; rivalry with Boniface and Sebastian, 143; murder of, 143, 163; crushes Anaolsus, 143, 166; Britain and, 213; mentioned, 70, 119

Africa: Vandals in, 17, 65, 79, 161, 165; Visigothic attempt to enter, 26, 48; under barbarian rule, 100; Aëtius and, 142; Hydatius on, 145; Sebastian in, 145; Orosius in, 146; Leo's expedition against, 147, 148, 224; communications with Spain, 150; and with Gaul, 172

Agenaric, 233

Agila, Visigothic king (549–55), 169, 205–6

Agrestius, b. of Lugo, 195, 196

Agriwulf. See Aioulf

Aioulf, 168–69

Ajax, Arian missionary, 215, 218, 240

Alamanni, 29, 30, 32, 36, 37; raid Alsace and Bellinzona, 33; 'drunken', 34; pagan, 126; Gibuldus king of, 126–27; raid Quintanis, 129; defeated at Batavis, 130; possible raids on Noricum, 131; mentioned by Eugippius, 132; defeat Charietto, 235; divisions among, 237–38; in Alsace, 251; weapons of, 289 n. 51

Alans, non-Germanic nomads, 3; enter Africa, 17; cross Rhine in 406, 17, 130; at Orleans, 25, 27, 32, 54; Goar king of, 25, 32, 36, 185; Sambida king of, 25, 34, 35; at Valence, 25, 34, 36; attacked by Huns about 370, 27; decimated in Spain, 30, 156, 186, 189, 253; invade Gaul, 31; attacked at Orleans, 54; invade Spain in 409, 146, 153, 178; allotted two provinces in Spain, 155; numbers of, 159

Alaric, Suevic leader, 167

Alaric I, Visigothic leader, 26; captures Rome in 410, 43; policy of, 43, 46; battles of, 44; R. influence on, 44; succeeded by Athaulf, 44

Alaric II, Visigothic king (484–507), 193, 216, 221

Albania (in the Caucasus), 244

Alexander the logothete, 99

Alexandria, 137, 139, 141, 144

Alicante, Bay of, 174, 181

Aligern, 109

Alodaei, 243

Alps, 24, 29, 34, 35; Cottian Alps, 93, 97

Alsace, 32, 33, 36, 251

Alypia, 223

Amalaric, Visigothic king (511–31), 298 n. 43

Amalasuntha, daughter of Theoderic the Great, 93; betrays Goths, 74, 95, 235; opposes racism, 93; regent for son Athalaric, 93; difficulties in ruling, 93–94; negotiates with Justinian, 94, 96; murdered by Theodahad, 95; dislikes barbarism, 96, 97; popularity of, 103

Ambrosius, friend of Severinus, 63

Ambrosius, St. Ambrose, 245–46

Ambrosius Aurelianus, 213, 239

Ammianus Marcellinus, historian, 25, 237, 238; on Fritigern at Adrianople, 39–40

Amorcesus, Arab chief, 242

Anaolsus, Visigothic marauder, 53, 143, 165

Anastasius, emperor (491–518), 72, 73, 76, 235

Ancona, 87, 279 n. 53

Andevotus, 173, 174, 182, 217–18, 220

Angers, 252

Anio r., 77, 277 n. 1

Anthemius, emperor (467–72), 147, 176, 191, 192, 223; father of Alypia, 223

Antioch, 139, 148, 292 n. 52

Antiochus, merchant at Naples, 101

Antoninus, b. of Merida, 195, 196

Apulia, 103

Aquae Flaviae, 139, 140, 167; *conventus* of, 170; betrayed, 171, 181, 201

Aquitanica I, R. province in Gaul, 159

Aquitanica II, Aquitania, Aquitaine, R. province in w. Gaul, 23, 25; Visigoths settled in, 26, 27, 32, 35, 50, 119; landowners of, 27, 252; riches of, 29, 30, 50; supplies grain to Rhine army, 29, 30; strategical importance of, 30, 31; not threatened by Saxons, 30, 252–54; menaced by Armoricans, 31, 254; influenced other barbarians, 64, 251–55

Arabia, 41, 147, 241–42

Aracelli, 183

Arborius, 175, 216

Arcadiopolis, 18

Ardaburius, s. of Aspar, 225, 226

Ardaric, 70

Arianism, Arian Christianity, 43, 63, 70, 96, 103, 105; Rugi converted to, 125; of Giso, 127; Vandals converted to, 157; Suevic, 203, 205, 210, 215, 240; tolerance of, 232; Gepids and, 242

Arigern, 73

Ariminum. *See* Rimini

Arles, 26, 32, 191, 192; Anaolsus near, 53, 143, 165; Visigoths menace, 54

Armenia, 244

Arminius, 233

Armorica, Armoricans, 31, 50, 52; suppressed by Exuperantius, 31; led by Tibatto, 32; sealed off, 36, 251–55; revolt of, 124; invaded by Britons, 204

Arran, 244

Artaxata, Armenian city, 14, 15

Arvandus, 211

Arzugis, African town, 14

Ascanius, b. of Tarragona, 197–98, 199

Ascanius, R. renegade, 171, 181, 211

Asclepiades, b. of Crimea, 11

Asclepiodotus, a Neapolitan, 101

Asculum, 280 n. 73

Asdings, section of Vandals, 153, 155–56, 157, 254; besiege Sueves, 157, 171; numbers of, 159; leave Galicia, 160; cross to Africa, 161; defeat Romans, 173

Asemus, 239

Asia, unrest in, 42

Aspar, fall of, 223–26

Aspebet, 241–42

Assisi, 235, 281 n. 24

Asterius, 173

Astigi (modern Ecija), 194

Astorga, 179, 208; Turribius of, 140, 143; sacked by Visigoths, 141, 178; Pascentius of, 143; inhabited by Sueves, 171, and by Goths, 171; ravaged, 172; Visigoths at, 190; Manichaeans in, 195, 196; b. of, 200; survival of, 215

Asturia, population of, 159

Asturis, place in Noricum, 115, 116, 117; Severinus appears in, 133; taken by barbarians, 118, 128, 132

Asturius, 173, 174, 182–84

Athalaric, Ostrogothic king (526–34): succeeds Theoderic, 73; constitutional position of, 74; R. education of, 93–94; death of, 94; his quaestor Fidelius, 102

Athanagild, Visigothic k. (555–68), 203, 206

Athanaric, Visigothic chieftain, 46; in Constantinople, 5, 41; defeated by Huns, 16; death of, 41; in Wallachia, 61

Athaulf, Visigothic chieftain, 26; capitulates to R., 26; tries to cross to Africa, 26; his accommodation with the R., 40, 45–47, 49, 233, 235, 238; marries Placidia, 41, 46; succeeds Alaric, 44; his son Theodosius, 47; death of, 47, 54–55; his plans realized, 52; driven into Spain, 156

Athens, 208

Attalus, Alaric's puppet emperor, 44

Attila, Hun leader: dies in 453, 3, 114, 115; his lieutenant Onegesius, 9; sons of, 15, 61, 115; aftermath of death of, 18, 115, 116; fights at Catalaunian Plains, 54, 189; Ostrogoths subject to, 92; visited by Priscus, 124; in Italy, 143, 151; attacks Eastern RE., 148; meets Pope Leo, 151

Atuatuci, a people of Gaul, 8

Augsburg, 12

Augustine, Saint (354–430): correspondent of, 14; death of, 137, 145; on bishops of Spain, 179–80; Hydatius on, 289 n. 1

Aunonenses, 154, 176, 294 n. 74

Auregensium loca, 218, 294 n. 74

Aurelian, emperor (270–75), 85

Auxerre, 32, 133; 179, 213

Auximum (modern Osimo), 97, 99, 104, 282 n. 27

Avars, steppe nomads, 7, 9, 255 n. 101; envoys of in Constantinople, 11

Avitianus, last R. soldier in Noricum, 122, 287 n. 23

Avitus, emperor (455–56), 24, 56, 141, 163, 189, 272 n. 66

Avitus of Braga, 145–46, 148, 179

Bacaudae, rebellious peasants of Gaul and Spain, 31, 34, 36; in Alps, 35; fight Romans in Gaul, 53; attacked by Visigoths, 55–56, 189; in Spain, 56, 144, 183–87, 271 n. 52; interrupt communications, 150; Sueves and, 184; attack cities, 184, 221; confined to Tarraconensis, 185, 199; collaborate with Rechiarius, 212; Isidore omits reference to, 220; literature on, 221–23; in Britain, 222

Baduila, alternative name of Totila, 81, 98

Baetica, R. province in southern Spain, 30, 208; Merobaudes born in, 141; allotted to Silings, 155; Vandals in, 157; conquered by Sueves, 162, 182, 187, 220; Visigothic campaigns in, 163; Rs. defeated in, 173; harassed by Rs., 173, 184; Heruls make for, 181; Bacaudae not reported in, 185; Visigothic army in, 189, 191,

216; Visigothic control of, 193; Visigothic settlement in, 194

Balconius, b. of Braga, 145–46

Balearic Islands, 146, 161

ballistae, Roman artillery, 7–8; use of confined to legionaries, 10; at Rome, 80; Ostrogoths try to use, 83–84, 278 n. 31; not used by barbarians in Spain, 172

Barbaria, noble lady, 64

Barcelona, 26, 198, 199

Basel, 32

basileus, Greek term for R. 'emperor,' 74, 75

Basiliscus, 148, 224

Basilius, consul of 480, 68

Basilius, leader of Bacaudae (184–85), 199, 220; misunderstandings of, 222

Basques, 143, 144, 150; attacked by Rechiarius, 163, 177; neighbours of Vardulli, 180; not conquered by Visigoths, 192, 194; Bacaudae and, 222

Batavians, 7, 8–9

Batavis. See Passau

Bede, 168, 214

belagines, Gothic customary usages, 46

Belisarius, Justinian's leading officer: punishes barbarian soldiers, 6; voyages to Africa, 6, 79; dialogue with Ostrogoths, 73; on Odoacer and Theoderic, 74; on Zeno's motives, 74; offered Western throne by Ostrogoths, 74, 95; enters Rome, 77; first battle against Ostrogoths, 77; ill-instructed on enemy, 79; in Sicily, 79; begins defence of Rome, 80; successes to 540, 81; transferred to East, 81; repels Wittigis' siege-engines, 83; repels Totila at Rome, 84; failures in 544–49, 88–89, 107; reports destruction of Milan to Justinian, 90; defeats Wittigis, 95; in 540 returns to Constantinople, 96, 99; fears treachery, 98; in Italy, 535–40, 98; cannot halt desertion, 99; addresses Neapolitans, 100; defence of Rome, 102, 239; on reasons for Ostrogothic defeat, 107; reoccupies Rome, 107; exploits desertion, 283 n. 46; exiles pope Silverius, 284 n. 77. See also Procopius, historian

Bellinzona, 33

Beneventum, 84, 279 n. 39

Besançon, 33

Bessas, 235

Bethlehem, 139, 140

Bigilans, 309 n. 45

Bilbao, 180

Bizye, 18

Blabia, 310 n. 8

Black Sea, 15, 147, 241

Boethius, widow of, 106

Bohemia, 12

Boiotro, 122, 123, 126

Bolia r., battle on, 19, 63, 167

Bologna, 99

Boniface, 143

Bonosus, barbarian monk, 131

Bordeaux, 47, 253

Bosphorus, 11

Bosporus, Crimean city, 243

Bostra, 13

Bows and Arrows, 11

Bracara Augusta, modern Braga, 139, 199; sacked by Visigoths, 141; Martin of, 144; Avitus of, 145; Balconius of, 145–46; allotted to Sueves, 155; Sueves slain in, 157; inhabited by Sueves, 157, 160; their capital, 158; population of, 159; falls to Goths, 164, 168; *conventus* of, 170; Fructuosus of, 172; brigands at, 186; metropolitan of unmentioned, 195; Third Council of, 200; Second Council of, 200, 213; First Council of, 205; Lucretius of, 205; Profuturus of, 205; embassies to, 210

Brachila, 70

Braga. *See* Bracara Augusta

Breastplates, 11, 81

Bremenium. *See* High Rochester

Britain: panic in, 17; revolt in, 50, 124; after 410, 119; federates in, 120; Aëtius and, 142; Germanus in, 179; Heruls avoid, 181; compared with Spain, 193, 212–15; rebellion of 409, 216; Bacaudae in, 222; St. Patrick a native of, 246; Saxons and, 253

Britonia, 200, 204

Britons: flee to Spain, 204; invade Armorica, 204; refuse to preach to Saxons, 214, 215; defeat barbarians, 239

Bronze, 11

Bruttium, 82, 103

Bucinobantes, 237, 238

Burdunelus, 193

Burgos, 23, 177

Burgundians, Germanic people: in Savoy, 23, 26, 27, 32, 33, 153; kingdom overthrown in 534, 24; defeated by Huns in 437, 26, 29; inheritance laws of, 28, 272 nn. 54, 55; settled on Rhine by Honorius, 29; Aëtius' motives in settlement of Savoy, 32–33, 36, 37; clans of (*faramanni*), 51; fight Rs. in 436–37, 53; receive women of Milan, 89; destruction of at Worms, 142; some remain e. of Rhine, 152; fight in Visigothic army, 163; k.s Gundioc and Chilperic, 163; Sigismer, 209; Sidonius' knowledge of, 210–11; repel Alamanni, 251

Buri, barbarian people, 11

Busas, Roman renegade, 7

Busta Gallorum, battle at: 88, 91, 100, 108; site of, 280 n. 60

Byzantium, Byzantine, capital of e. Roman Empire, 92–109 *passim*; cavalry of, 78, 80, 88; traders in Africa, 79; cavalry armour and weapons, 82; defeated by Totila, 82; stand siege, 85; in Centumcellae, 86; archers at Busta Gallorum, 88; high morale of in 552, 88; development of warfare, 90; high rate of desertion among, 98–100; attitude of Italians towards, 102–4; control sea, 107–8, 279 n. 51; invade Spain, 206; Franks and, 242, 245; numbers in Italy, 278 n. 22

Caceres, 298 n. 43

Caedwalla, 168

Caesar, Julius: on R. power, 7; defeats the Atuatuci, 8; use of traders' reports, 15; mentioned, 8, 90

Caesar Augustus, 7, 45, 101, 199, 233

Caesarea, in Palestine, 139

Caesena, 84

Calabria, 103, 284 n. 84

Calahorra, 177, 197

Calatayud, 23, 30

Callinicus, 14, 15

Campania, 64, 100, 279 n. 38

Campus Paramus, battle of, 163, 164, 168, 189, 290 n. 10

Candidianus, 46

Candidus, historian, 224, 225

Cannibalism, 84, 279 n. 36

Cantaber of Coimbra, 201, 215, 304 n. 56

Cantabria, 170, 180

Cantabrianum, 304 n. 56

Caracalla, emperor (211–17), 9, 10

Caratacus, 89

carrago, 236

Cartagena, 144, 150, 184, 206; occupied by Vandals, not by Sueves, 162, 172; Majorian in, 174, 175

Carthage: traders in, 79, 283 n. 58, 62; surprised by Vandals, 145

Carthaginiensis, R. province of eastern Spain, 177; allotted to Alans, 155; conquered by Sueves, 162, 182, 187; harassed by Romans, 173, 184; Bacaudae not reported in, 185; conquered by Visigoths, 194, 216; our ignorance of, 213

Cascantum (modern Cascante), 177

Cassiodorus, high official in Ostrogothic Italy, 68, 73, 95; on fall of Aspar, 224, 225, 226

Castinus, 156, 173, 188

Catalaunian Plains, battle of, 54, 141, 189

Cauca (modern Coca), 178, 300 n. 92

Caucasus Mountains, 147

Cavalry: Byzantine and Ostrogothic, 77–78; Ostrogothic, 86

Celtiberia, 170

Censorius, 290 n. 8, 298 n. 40

Centumcellae (modern Civita Vecchia), 85

Cenwahl, 168

Chalcedon, Council of, 144, 145, 148, 243

Chamavi, early Germanic people, 233, 234

Champanges, 35

Charietto, a brigand, 234–35, 238

Chersonese. *See* Crimea

Cherusci, early Germanic people, 42

Chilperic, Burgundian k., 163

Chronicon Paschale, 224, 225, 226

Cimbri, early Germanic people, 8

civilitas, 92

Clementinus, 284 n. 77

Clovis, Frankish k. (481–511), 23, 211

Clusium, 95

Coalla, 160

Coccas, 100

Coimbra, 170, 171, 200, 201, 213, 215; walls of, 299 n. 61

Cologne, 5, 12, 245

Comagenis, 116; barbarians in, 118, 120, 128; barbarians fail to capture, 132

Comes, plural *comites,* member of a Germanic retinue, 51

Commercium, 13

Commodus, emperor (180–92), 11

Connaught, westernmost province of Ireland, 248

consors, plural *consortes,* part owners of estates subject to billeting, 27, 31, 32, 51, 52; not in Galicia, 154. *See hospites, hospitalitas*

Constantine the Great, emperor (306–37), 7, 240; exports iron to Persia, 10; empire of, 101; fame of, 248

Constantine III, emperor (407–11), 35, 160

Constantinople, capital of e. RE: Athanaric in, 5; foreign envoys in, 11; punished by Theodosius, 41; Gainas and, 42–43; Huns visit, 61; Italy ruled from, 65; Nepos' envoys in, 66; Odoacer's envoys in, 66; Ostrogothic attitude to, 97; Flavian of, 141, 144, 146; Nestorius expelled from, 146; communications with Spain, 149–50; fire at, 225

Constantius II, emperor (337–61), 237

Constantius, patrician, later emperor (421): settles Visigoths in Aquitaine, 23, 27, 30, 119, 250; blockades Visigoths in Gaul and Spain, 26, 38; sympathetic to landowners, 28; motives of, 30, 31; success of, 37, 38; drives Visigoths from Gaul, 47

conventus, judicial district, 170

Cordoba, 169, 194

Corfu, 86

Coroticus, 247

Corsica, 86, 87, 88, 90

Coviacense castrum, 178, 300 n. 93

Crimea, 11, 243

Croton, 87

Cucullis, 128

Cueva, 160

Cumae, 105, 109

Cumbria, 214

Curials, town councillors, 28

Cyprianus, 231

Cyprus, 129

Cyril of Alexandria, 141, 144, 147

Cyrila, 189, 216, 218

Dacia, approximately modern Rumania, 7, 13, 16. *See* Gothia

Dalmatia: Nepos exiled in, 63, 66; Ostrogoths willing to evacuate, 75; coast of, 86; lost by Theodahad, 95; Goths in, 97, 282 n. 30; Sueves in, 167

Danube r.: bridge over, 9; Regensburg on, 12;

Danube r. (*continued*)
  barbarian boats banned on, 13; frontier on breached, 15, 16; Visigoths driven over, 38; Visigothic oath sworn at, 39–41, 43, 47, 49; traffic across, 122–23; Sueves on, 171
Daras, 14
Decebalus, Dacian k., 7–8
Denmark, 159, 180
Dertosa (modern Tortosa), 192, 193, 303 n. 30
Dictinius, 229
Diocletian, emperor (284–305), 13
Domitian, emperor (81–96), 7–8
Dordogne r., 253
Douro r., 163, 170, 200, 201
Draco r. (modern Sarno), 278 n. 31
dromon, a type of warship, 86
Dubius, 270 n. 42
Dyrham, 204
Dyrrhachium, 235

East Rome. *See* Constantinople
Ebremud, Evermud, or Ebrimus, 95
Ebro r., 23, 30, 143; valley of invaded by Sueves, 162; Bacaudae in, 184, 185, 186, 189
Ecija. *See* Astigi
Edeco, father of Odoacer, 61, 62, 273 n. 2; father of Hunoulf, 63; disappearance of, 63; leads Sciri, 63
Edessa, Syrian city now Urfa, 11, 239
Egypt, 42, 139, 237, 243
Elbe r., 3, 7
Embargo on export of strategic goods, 10, 11; on trade with Visigoths, 25, 26
Ennodius, b. of Pavia (473/4–521), 132
Ephesus, Council of, 147
Epidamnus, 235, 238
Epiphanius, b. of Seville, 195, 196
Epirus, 235
Eraric, Rugian k. of Ostrogoths, 96, 98, 125, 233, 238, 282 n. 25; coins and, 277 n. 53
Eriulf, 41, 48, 233; killed by Fravittas, 41, 45, 47
Ermanaric, Ostrogothic chief, 16
Ermengon, 159, 295 n. 99
Esla r., 163
Ethiopians, 242
Etna, Mount, 79
Eudocia, 306 n. 19
Eudoxia, 145

Eugenius, usurping emperor (392–94), 39
Eugippius, biographer of St. Severinus, 113–33 *passim*; biography, 63, 113, 208; value of, 113; modern disparagement of, 113–14; on Severinus' date of death, 117; on his military actions, 130; on the Huns, 132
Euphronius of Autun, 141
Euric, Visigothic k. (466–84), 56, 71, 176, 177, 201, 216, 233; policy towards Spain, 190–91, 193; not in Spain in person, 191–92; law code of, 221; conspiracies against, 273 n. 80
Euthymius, 242
Eutyches, heretic, 144
Exuperantius suppresses Armoricans, 31–32

Fanus (modern Fano), 84, 85
faramanni, Burgundian clansmen, 51
Faventia, 82, 105
Favianis: cell of St. Severinus, 63, 116, 117, 128; fleet based at, 118; pays tribute to Rugi, 121; troops in, 121, 131; Giso near, 121, 123, 127; Ferderuchus near, 123; never taken by barbarians, 128, 132; Feletheus in, 131
federates, *foederati,* 25, 32, 39, 42, 53, 188; Alan, 54, 185; Ostrogoths wish to be, 75; in Comagenis, 119, 120, 128, 287 n. 20; in Britain, 120; Sueves not federates, 153–4, 170, 209; in Tyriasso, 271 n. 52
Feletheus, also called Feva, s. of Flaccitheus, Rugian k., 122, 123, 126, 130–31, 287 n. 23; donates Favianis to Ferderuchus, 132
Felix, pope (483–92), 149
Ferderuchus, brother of Feletheus, 122, 123, 126, 287 n. 23; receives Favianis, 132
Fidelius, 102
Firmum, 280 n. 73
Flaccitheus, Rugian k., father of Feletheus, 124, 126, 288 n. 33
Flavian of Constantinople, 141, 144, 146
fleet, Ostrogothic, 86, 87, 98
Florence, 82
Florus, Valerius, 76
Framtane, Suevic leader, 166, 209; Isidore on, 218
Franks, 29, 30; Germanic agriculturalists, 3; defeat Visigoths, 23; destroy kingdom of Toulouse, 56; Totila negotiates with, 86; warfare of, 90; opinion of on Aligern, 109; fight in Visigothic army, 163; Sigismer, 209; Chamavi, 233; Salian, 234–5; Justinian and, 242,

245, 284 n. 98; no menace to Aquitaine, 251; pirates, 252

Fravittas, Visigothic leader: murders Eriulf, 41, 45; sides with Rs., 41, 233, 237; role of, 42, 43, 45; defeats Gainas, 43; defeats R. rebels, 43

Frederic, 54, 56, 185

Fritigern, at Adrianople, 39–40, 45, 48, 55, 221

Fronto, 174

Fructuosus of Braga, 172

Frumarius, Suevic leader (460–64), 167, 171, 181, 211

Gainas, Visigothic defector to the Rs., 41, 42; ambitions of, 42, 43, 269 n. 17; Arian, 43; defeated by Fravittas, 43; killed by Huns, 43

Gallaecia (modern Galicia), 138, 177; Bracara capital of, 139; remoteness of, 139, 205, 208; Sueves in, 140; communications with Gaul, 143, 172; communications with Tarraconensis, 144; Vandal ambassadors in, 145; communications with Mediterranean, 146, 148, 149–50, 196, 206; isolation of, 150; settled by Sueves, 153; nature of Suevic settlement in, 154; raided by Sueves, 154; partly occupied by Sueves, 157; fate of under Suevic rule, 160, 182; Aioulf in, 168; R. administration in, 169; overrun by Leovigild, 172; R. attack on, 175; plebs of, 176, 178, 182; repulse Herul sea raiders, 178; bishops' attitude to Manichees in, 179; Visigoths in, 190; freedom in, 196; bishops of, 196, 197; Dark Age of, 199; frontiers of extended, 200; Britons in, 204; communications with Rome, 204–5

Garonne r., 23, 30, 50, 253

Gaul, Gauls: impressed by R. resources, 8; ravaged by barbarians in 406–9, 17, 153; Alans in, 25; defence of against barbarians, 29; invaded by Vandals, Alans, Sueves, 31, 152; unrest in, 34, 37; Bacaudae in, 35, 36, 55–56; Visigoths in, 38, 253; communications with Spain, 143, 144, 172, 206; Suevic ambassadors in, 144; bishops of, 145; scale of invasion of 406, 159; communications with Africa, 172

Gauterit, 191

Geiseric, Vandal k. (429–77), 65, 71; measures against Catholics, 145; said to have been a Catholic, 145; takes Rome, 163, 218; attacks Heremigarius, 166; father of Gento and Huneric, 217

Gelasius, pope (492–96), 64

Gelimer, Vandal k. (530–34), 79, 281 n. 24

Gento, an Ostrogoth, 235

Gento, s. of Geiseric, 217, 220

Gepids, a Germanic people, 18, 19, 242

Germania Prima, R. province on Rhine, 27, 29, 36

Germans: agriculturalists, 3; attitude to Cologne, 5; absence of State organization among, 6; importance of kindred among, 6; no cities of, 6, 131; underestimate R. power, 6–7; victory of in Teutoberg Forest, 7; impressed by R. techniques, 8; traders of, 12; weak in siege warfare, 82; exact tribute, 132; donate towns, 132; monarchy among, 166; dual chieftainship among, 167; use of slaves, 214; R. attitude towards, 231–2; R. influence on, 232–3; conversion of, 240; wine and, 245

Germanus, Arabian priest, 147

Germanus, b. of Auxerre, 32, 133, 179, 213

Gezon, 282 n. 36

Gibuldus, Alamannic k., 126–7, 288 n. 42

Gildas, Visigothic defector, 113, 213, 214

Ginzo de Limia, Hydatius' birthplace, 139

Giso, Rugian queen, 121, 123, 126, 127

Goar, Alan k., 25, 32, 35, 36, 185

Goar, an Ostrogoth, 282 n. 27

Godegisil, Vandal leader, 293 n. 7

Godidisclus, 235

Gold: export of from RE forbidden, 10; theft of, 246

Gordas. See Grod

Gothia = Dacia when occupied by the Visigoths (c. 275–376), 25, 45, 234, 240

Gothic 'confessors,' 221

Gothic language, 230, 231

Grado, 160

Grannona, 253

Gregory of Tours, 139, 172, 206, 230

Gregory I, the Great, pope (590–604), 230

Gretes, 242

Grod or Gordas, Hun k., 243

Guadalajara, modern Spanish province, 23

Guadalquivir r., 173

Guadiana r., 190

Gunderic, 217, 220

Gundioc, Burgundian k., 163

Gundobad, Burgundian k., (c. 480–516), 24, 28

Gundobad, patrician, 66
Gundomad, 238

habitantes Dictyni, 300 n. 78
Heldefred, 191
helepolis, a type of Roman ballista, 7
Hellespont, 11
Heremigarius, 166, 297 n. 24
Hermeric, Suevic k., 154, 165; father of Rechila, 165, 166, 220; repulsed, 178; makes peace, 179, 290 n. 8; uses Symphosius, 179, 209; Isidore on, 219–20; length of reign, 306 n. 32
Hermione, 80
Hermunduri, Germanic people, 12
Herodian betrays Spoleto, 283 n. 47
Heruls, Germanic people: in Italy, 64, 72; in Noricum, 129; exact tribute from Lombards, 132; mentioned by Eugippius, 132; some live near Denmark, 159, 180, others near Belgrade, 159; raid Lugo from sea, 178, 180; avoid Britain, 181; make for Baetica, 181; Gretes of, 242; trade with Goths, 282 n. 37
Hesbaye, 8
High Rochester, 10
Hilary, pope (461–68), 175, 177, 197–98
Hilduarens, 194
Hippo Regius, 159
Homer, 238
Homerites, 242
Honoriaci, 178
Honorius, emperor (395–423), 29, 154, 178
Horses, export of forbidden, 10
Hortarius, 237
hospes, plural hospites, 'guests' = billeted soldiers, 25, 27, 32, 64, but not in Galicia, 154
hospitalitas, 'billeting,' 25, 27, 28, 51, 55; in Italy, 64, 65, 69; Theoderic on, 65
Huneric, Vandal k. (477–84), 217, 220
Hunimund, 167
Hunoulf, son of Edeco, 63
Huns, non-Germanic pastoralists, 3; not pirates, 11; barred from R. towns, 15; arrival of in Europe, 16; defeat of Ostrogoths and Visigoths, 16; defeat Burgundians, 26, 33–34, 142; attack Alans, 27; press upon Danube frontier, 29; drive Visigoths across Danube, 38, 41; commanded by Litorius, 53; invade Italy, 54; chaos after their fall, 63; move Ostrogoths,

63; an individual, 98; horrifying treatment of Naples, 101; subject Rugi, 125; almost unmentioned by Eugippius, 132; survivors of, 133; attacked by peasants, 239; language of, 240–41; on Danube, 241; Grod, 243. After 453 the term 'Hun' became a generic name for a pastoral nomad, 3, 239
Hunumund, 128, 288 n. 46
Hydatius, chronicler, 17, 137–60; on date of invasion of Spain, 153; on Suevic settlement in Galicia, 154–55; method as chronicler, 161; defective knowledge of e. Spain, 162; horrified by Visigothic atrocities, 164; meets Aëtius, 140, 165, 290 n. 8; unfamiliar with Suevic intrigues, 167; kidnapped, 167, 201; on Aioulf, 168; on conventus, 170; difficulties of, 172; never negotiated with barbarians, 179; on Ospinio and Ascanius, 181; on Visigoths in Baetica, 189; on embassies to Sueves, 190; on Salla, 190; on the Catholic Church, 194–5; investigates Manichaeism, 195; personality of, 208; value of, 208; character of chronicle of, 210; his knowledge of Suevi, 210; on Suevic Arianism, 210; does not accuse Suevi of persecution, 211; hounds heretics, 211; on Rechiarius, 211; on fate of Spanish cities, 213; conversion and, 215; errs on Huneric, 217; used by Isidore, 217–21; on Rechiarius' Catholicism, 218; on Hermeric, 219–20; on Bacaudae, 220; on Ricimer, 223; on fall of Aspar, 223–26; dating by Olympiads, 227, 228; Mommsen's edition of, 227–29; on St. Augustine, 289 n. 1; omits to revise, 290 n. 10; on Antioch, 292 n. 52

Iazyges, barbarian people, 13
Idanha (Igita), 200
Ildibad, Ostrogothic k. (540), 74, 277 n. 53
Illyricum: Master of Soldiers in, 63; Goths in, 236; invaded by nomads, 239
India, reputation of Romans in, 9
Ingenuus, 46
Ingomar, 159
Iotabe, 242
Ioviaco, place in Noricum, 129, 132
Ireland, 149, 240, 246–48
Irenaeus, 198–99
Iria (El Padron), 200
Irish, 147; invade Britain, 204; missionaries of,

214; converted to Christianity, 246–48; Britons flee from, 304 n. 66

Iron, export banned, 10, 11

Isauria, mountainous part of e. Asia Minor, 43, 100, 139

Isdegerdes, Persian k., 241–42

Isidore of Seville, 117, 172, 221; on Sueves in Galicia, 157; on *conventus*, 170; on Andevotus, 173, 217–18; confuses Theoderic I with Theoderic II, 188; on Euric, 191; on sixth century, 199, 220–21; on sixth-century Sueves, 203; on sack of Seville, 217; use of Hydatius by, 217–21; on Ajax, 218; on Maldras and other Suevic leaders, 218; on Hermeric, 219; suppresses reference to Bacaudae, 220; merits of, 221; on John of Biclarum, 230

Italy, 33; Visigoths in, 38; invaded by Huns, 54; *hospitalitas* in, 64; subject to Zeno, 66–67, 72; Zeno sends Ostrogoths to, 71; subject to e. Emperor, 75; attitude of towards Byzantines, 102–4; peasants of, 104; attitude of criticized by Goths, 104–6; fails to support Ostrogoths, 108; reasons for support of Byzantium, 109; Attila in, 143; communications with Spain, 143, 144, 149, 150, 199, 205; invaded by Lombards, 152

Jerome, Saint, 139, 140, 141; death of, 146; letter to Ageruchia, 152

Jerusalem, 139, 145, 146, 147, 208, 242

Jews: in Naples, 101; well treated by Arian k., 101, 232; a Jew of Spain, 180

John, s. of Valerian, 279 n. 53

John, usurping emperor (423–25), 53

John of Antioch, historian, 71

John of Biclarum, chronicler, 221, 230

John Chrysostom, b. of Constantinople, 240

John of Jerusalem, 146

John Malalas, historian, 224, 225, 226

Jordanes, historian, 44, 162; on Danubian Sueves, 167; on Aioulf, 168–69; on Suevic warfare, 171; on Euric, 192; on Aspar's fall, 224, 225; a Goth, 231; on Gothic songs, 232

Julian, a Monophysite, 243

Julian Caesar (355–61), 233–34, 237, 238

Julius Nepos. *See* Nepos

Justin I, emperor (518–27), 73

Justinian, emperor (527–65), 75, 240; addressed by nomad chief, 5; bans export of weapons, 11; overthrows Vandals, 17; Amalasuntha betrays Goths to, 74; begins reconquest of Italy, 75; traders and, 79; ambition to destroy Ostrogoths, 87; destruction of Milan reported to, 89–90; negotiates with Amalasuntha, 94; and with Theodahad, 94; pretext for attacking Italy, 95; his treatment of Wittigis, 96; negotiates with Eraric, 96; contrasted with Totila, 108; officials of in Spain, 206; uses nomads, 239; Franks and, 242; on political value of Catholicism, 242; husband of Theodora, 243; on Ostrogothic occupation of Italy, 284 n. 98

Justinian, general of Constantine III, 35

Juvenal of Jerusalem, 146, 242

Kardutsat, b. of Arran, 244

Lactarius, Mount, 75, 109

Lamego, 200, 304 n. 56

Langres, 33

Lauriacum (Lorch), 118; not stormed by barbarians, 128, 129, 130, 131; evacuated, 132

Lazi (people living south of Caucasus), 147, 150

Leo, b. of Tarrazona, 184, 222

Leo I, emperor (457–74): refuses trade with Huns, 15; expedition of against Africa, 147, 148, 223; in Hydatius, 148; Spain and, 192; rejects Aspar's advice, 224; Ardaburius and, 225; Amorcesus and, 242

Leo I, the Great, pope (440–61), 140, 143; communicates with Galicia, 144, 145; meets Attila, 151; Hydatius and, 195; Priscillianism and, 196; advises holding a synod, 206

Leon, 143, 177, 299 n. 67

Leovigild, Visigothic k. (568–86), 169, 170, 172, 185; lawcode of, 221

Lerida, 162, 163, 171, 189; Bacaudae at, 184, 185

Libius Severus, emperor (461–65), 56, 144, 228

Liburnia, 97

Liguria, 96, 103

Lisbon (Olisippo), 167, 171, 190, 200; Sueves enter, 201; survival of, 215

Litorius, 23, 53

litus Saxonicum, southeast coastline of Britain fortified against Saxon raiders, 253

Livila, 71

Logroño, 177

Loire r., 23, 30

Lombards, 132; invade Italy, 152; Vacho k. of, 152; Justinian and, 242; *farae* of, 272 n. 56; Goth deserts to, 282 n. 27

London, 208

Longinus, Monophysite heretic, 243, 244

Lucania, mountainous region of south Italy: Totila in, 82; attitude of, 103, 104

Lucretius, b. of Braga, 205

Lucullus, castle of, 64

Lugdunensis II, R. province in Gaul, 24, 159

Lugo, 205; inhabited by Sueves, 158, 159, 160; Roman *rector* in, 169; *conventus* of, 170; ravaged, 172, 175; raided from sea, 178, 180, 181; bishops of, 195, 196, 200; life in, 215

Lusidius, 171, 181, 209, 211, 213

Lusitania, R. province in southwest Spain, 30; allotted to Alans, 155; conquered by Sueves, 162, 182, 187; Suevic raids on, 164, 166, 167, 182; Visigoths in, 168, 190–91; Bacaudae not reported in, 185; Visigothic control of, 193; metropolitan of, 195, 200; extent of, 200–201

Lychnidus, 236

Lyon(s), 33, 160, 209, 251

Macedonia, 236

Macrianus, 238

Madrid, 23

Magnus Maximus, usurping emperor (383–88), 269 n. 15

Magona in Minorca, 146

Main r., 14

Mainz, 17

Majorian, emperor (457–61), 174, 187, 287 n. 29; alleged association with Severinus, 114; supported by Aegidius, 141; relations with Aëtius, 141; defeated in Spain, 150, 176, 178; at Saragossa, 162, 175; campaign of, 174; his fleet betrayed, 181; Isidore on, 218; in Hydatius' chronicle, 228

Maku, Armenian b., 244

Malaga, 150, 184, 206

Maldras, Suevic leader (456–60), 166, 290 n. 10; murder of, 167; captures Lisbon, 171; Sidonius and, 209; Isidore and, 218; alleged relationship with Remismund, 218–19

Mamertinus, tribune later b., 116, 121

Manichaeans, 140, 143, 179, 195, 196, 205; persecuted by Catholics, 211

Mansuetus, 174

Marcellinus, chronicler, 142, 145, 224, 225

Marcian, emperor (451–57): on export of weapons, 11, 15; bans trade with Huns, 15; settles Ostrogoths in Pannonia, 18; defeats Lazi, 147; in Hydatius' chronicle, 148; sends troops against Huns, 151

Marcomanni, Germanic people, 12, 13

Marcus Aurelius, emperor (161–80), 7, 13

Markets: Huns barred from, 15; north of Danube, 122–23, 126

Martin, b. of Braga, 144, 203

Massilia (modern Marseilles), 191, 192

Massilia, father of Maldras, 166, 218

Matasuntha, sister of Athalaric, 96

Matrilineal inheritance, 270 n. 35

Mauretania, 161

Maximian, b. of Constantinople, 146

Maximus, monastery of in Britonia, 204

Maximus, usurping emperor (410–11), 153

Mederic, 233

Merida, capital of Lusitania: communications of with Italy, 149; occupied by Sueves before 439, 162, 164, 172, 182; Heremigarius near, 166; Visigoths at, 190, 194; Antoninus of, 195, 196; Council of, 200, 201

Merobaudes: native of Baetica, 141; praised by Hydatius, 141; general, 173, 174, 183–84

Mertola, 171

Messina, Straits of, 86, 95

Meuse r., 8

Milan: walls of demolished by Wittigis, 84; destruction of, 89, 106; b. of, 103; St. Ambrose of, 245–46

Minorca, 146, 180

Modares, Visigothic renegade, 41

Moesia, R. province south of lower Danube, 29, 38, 42, 239

Mondoñedo, 204

Moors, 80, 98, 100, 282 n. 36

Moselle r., 234

Mucellium (modern Mugello), 82

Mugel, Hun chieftain, 243

Mugello. *See* Mucellium

Munderic, Visigothic renegade, 41

Mur r., 208

Muslims, 56

Myrmidons, 238

Nacoleia, 269 n. 16

Naissus (modern Nish), 61

Najera, 177

Naples, 64; bay of, 65; walls of, 84; Totila captures, 85; lost by Theodahad, 95; public opinion divided at, 100; calamitous treatment of, 102, 103; capitulates to Totila, 106; Gothic navy at, 279 n. 51

Narbonensis, R. province in southern Gaul, 23, 26

Narbonne, 45, 46, 56

Narnia, 103

Narses, Byzantine general: on R. power, 7; Armenian eunuch commands at Busta Gallorum, 88; on desertion, 100; Procopius on, 279 n. 54; estimates of, 280 n. 62

Navy. See fleet

Nedao, unidentified r., battle at, 115, 116, 133, 286 n. 67

Nepos, Julius, emperor (473–80): deposed by Orestes, 62, 66; exiled in Dalmatia, 63, 66; probably nominated Basilius as consul, 65; Odoacer and, 66–67; numismatic evidence on, 67; murdered, 75

Nepotian, 175, 216

Nervasian Mountains (unidentified), 157, 165, 171, 173

Nestorius, heresiarch, 146, 147

New Forest, 214

Nicaea, Council of, 90, 238

Nisibis (modern Nusaybin in Mesopotamia), 11, 13, 14, 15

Nobadae (in the modern Sudan), 243–44

Nomads, non-Germanic, 3; include Alans and Huns, 3; in Belisarius' army, 6; Avars, 7, 27; supply cavalry to Byzantines, 78; used by Justinian, 239; conversion of to Christianity, 240–44

Noricum, 113–33 passim; revolt in, 35, 124; Favianis in, 63; Primenius flees to, 70; Ripense defined, 113; Tiburnia in, 117; Mediterraneum, 117, 122, 287 n. 31; disappearance of R. administration from, 118, 119, 133; low morale of citizens in, 121; castella of, 122; population Christian, 126, 128; paganism in, 126, 128, 289 n. 48; defence of cities in, 129; no barbarian settlers in, 131; resistance of, 178

Notitia Dignitatum, list of high R. officers of state dating from c. 400, 118

Novempopulana, R. province of Gaul between Garonne and Pyrenees, 23, 30

Numbers, 80; at Busta Gallorum, 88; in Noricum, 128, 129–30; slain, 141; of Burgundians killed by Huns, 142; of Asdings, 155; of invaders in 406, 159; of R. troops in Spain, 172–73; of R. losses in Spain, 173, 174; of Gothic forces, 278 n. 15, 280 n. 61, 282 n. 28; of Sueves, 295 n. 98

Nundinarius, b. of Barcelona, 198, 199

Ocla. See Thela

Odoacer, first barbarian k. of Italy (476–91), 19; son of Edeco, 61, 273 n. 2; goes to Italy, 63; in R. army, 63; recalls Ambrosius, 63; visits St. Severinus, 63, 117, 122; revolt of, 64, 65; constitutional position of, 65 ff.; relations with Nepos, 66–67; undefined position of, 66–69, 73; whether a patrician, 67, 71; numismatic evidence on, 67; position after Nepos' death, 67; describes his own position, 68; forged coins of, 68; his position in practice, 69; peaceful rule of, 69; Catholic Church and, 70; champion of R. senate, 70; Germanic followers dissatisfied by, 70; indebtedness of Italy to, 70–71; actions after 489, 71; appoints Master of Soldiers, 71; coinage of, 71; father of Thela, 71; murdered by Theoderic, aged 60, 71, 105, 117, 274 n. 3; never independent of Constantinople, 71, 96; Eugippius refers to as rex, 117; did not rule Noricum, 123

Oil, export banned, 10

Old Sarum, 204

Onegesius, a Hun, 9

Oporto, 164, 168, 200, 201

oppidum, 'settlement,' 6

optimates, leading men, tribal nobility: of Visigoths, 38; detach themselves from followers, 39–42, 47, 51–52; policy of, 57

Orbigo r. (Urbicus), 163, 164

Orense, 172, 200

Orestes, father of Romulus, 61; rebels, 62; patrician, 62, 71; ruler of West, 63; refuses demand for hospitalitas, 64; death of, 64, 65, 70, 123, 274 n. 11; ruler of Italy, 65

Orientius, b. of Auch, 23, 179, 272 n. 65

Orleans: Alans at, 25, 32, 35, 54, 266 n. 13; battle at in 463, 56

Orontius, metropolitan of Lusitania, 200

Orosius, historian, 172; travels from Jerusalem, 146, 148; on Suevic settlement in Galicia, 154–56; flees from Spain, 179–80; on R. renegades, 181–82

Orvieto. See Urbs Vetus

Ospinio, 171, 181, 211

Ostrogoths, Germanic agriculturalists, 3; empire in Ukraine destroyed by Huns, 16, 17, 63; allies of Huns, 18; fragmentation of by Huns, 18; subsidized by Rome, 18; settled by Marcian in Pannonia, 18, 286 n. 12; starvation among, 19, 92; moved by Huns, 63; victory at r. Bolia, 63; sent to Italy by Zeno, 71, 75, 105; Belisarius' dialogue with, 73; offer to crown Belisarius, 74, 95; willing to abandon Sicily, 75; wish to remain in RE, 75; archers of, infantry of, 78; cavalry of, 78, 279 n. 47; casualties of, 80; deficient in armour, 81, 278 n. 21, 280 n. 63; besiege Rome, 82–83, 99; destroy city walls, 84–85; desire pitched battles, 85, 89; destroy Tibur, 89; destroy Milan, 89, 105; distribution of in Italy, 90; ignorant of Byzantine warfare, 90; ignorant of Frankish warfare, 90; standard of living in Italy, 92; subjects of the Huns, 92; hostility of to Italians, 92–93, 105, 106; delight in warfare, 93; panic among in 538, 95; treachery of nobility of, 96, 282 n. 27; absence of desertion among, 97; attitudes of in 537, 97; garrison of in Naples, 102; liberal treatment of Italians, 105; not supported by Italians, 108; leave Pannonia, 117, 131; Rugi and, 124; fail to take Tiburnia, 128, 130; fight Sueves on Danube, 152; some remain north of Danube, 152; slavery among, 214; fight Sciri, 224; take Scampia, 236; wagon trains of, 236; numbers of warriors of, 278 n. 15, 280 n. 61, 282 n. 28

Ostrys, Ostrogoth in R. service, 19

Otricoli, 141

Oviedo, 160

Palencia, 23, 30, 141, 172, 178

Palestine. See Caesarea

Palladius, b. in Ireland, 240

Palladius Caesar, 143, 306 n. 19

Palmyra, caravan city, 13

Palogorius, 305 n. 1

Pamplona, 176, 191

Pannonia, R. province south of middle Danube, 13, 118; Ostrogoths in, 18, 124, 126; Orestes born in, 61; r. Bolia in, 63; *hostes Pannonii,* 287 n. 27, 292 n. 62

Paris, 208

Parochiale of Galicia, 200, 204, 215, 294 n. 74, 301 n. 98

Pascentius, 143, 196, 291 n. 28

Passau (Batavis), 113, 117, 286 n. 14; troops in, 121; Gibuldus in, 126; falls to barbarians, 128, 132; survives attacks, 129; citizens' victory at, 130; a priest of, 133

Pastor, Neopolitan, 101

Pastor, Spanish b., 195

Paterculus. See Velleius

Patrician, 62; nature of, 66; Odoacer, 66; Eraric tries to become, 96; Wittigis, 96; Orestes, 123; Felix, 143; Ricimer, 223; Aspar, 225. See also Aëtius, Constantius, Gundobad

Patrick, Saint, 113, 147, 246–48

Pavia, 64, 65, 96, 99

Persian Empire, 238; resources inferior to R., 7, 9, 11; Caracalla and, 9; spices and textiles of, 9; war of against R. in 422, 9; imports iron, 10; merchants of, 10, 14; R. traders in, 15; Ostrogothic embassy to, 74, 107; Wittigis lives near, 96; Ardaburius and, 225, 226; besiege Edessa, 239; Christians in, 241; Isdegerdes k. of, 241; Goths fight against, 281 n. 24; R. troops rarely desert to, 283 n. 54

Perugia, 84, 100, 103

Pervincus, 143, 149, 196

Peter, Arab b., 242

Peter, Spanish usurper, 193

Petra, Arabian city, 242

Petra, Italian city, 84

Petronius Maximus, emperor (455), 143, 163

Phoenicia, 238

Photius, 224, 225

Picenum, 93, 104

Pierius, R. noble, 68

Pisaurum (Pesaro), 84, 85

Pitzas, 97–98

Placentia (Piacenza), 84

Placidia, 26, 46, 47, 270 n. 41, 306 n. 19

Plato, 94, 95, 96

Pliny the Elder, 159

Po r., 29, 92

Portucale, 170–71

Portus, the harbour of Rome, 82, 100, 107

Prayllius, b. of Jerusalem (415/6–21), 146

Primenius, R. noble, 70, 123

Priscillian, Priscillianism, 140, 143, 194–97, 205, 229, 289 n. 1

Priscus of Panium, historian, 124, 224, 240

Proclus, b. of Constantinople (434–47), 146

Procopius, historian, 99, 238; on Belisarius' punishment of barbarian troops, 6; on embargo on export of arms, 11; on deposition of Romulus Augustulus, 64; reports Gothic claims, 70–71, 72–73; on constitutional position of barbarian k.s, 73–74, 75; on Theoderic, 74; on Teias, 75; describes Belisarius' first battle in Italy, 77, 79, 277 n. 4; sent to Syracuse, 79; studies Belisarius, 79; estimates of enemy casualties, 80; on Vandal warfare, 80, 278 n. 14; on Ostrogothic defensive armour, 81; on Ostrogothic desire for pitched battles, 85; on Totila and walls of Rome, 85; on low Gothic morale, 87; describes seafight at Sinigaglia, 87, 91; incomplete knowledge of Totila's strategy, 87, 88, 90–91; on Busta Gallorum, 88, 91; on Milan, 89; will not describe Gothic cruelty at Tibur, 89; on Ostrogothic fleet commander, 98; on Belisarius, 99, 107, 279 n. 53; on public opinion at Naples, 101; on the disaster at Naples, 102; on public opinion at Rome, 102; on Picenum, 104; expounds Ostrogothic opinion, 104–5; reports Belisarius on reasons for Gothic defeat, 107; describes Totila at Busta Gallorum, 108; on unpaid troops, 123; on Rugi, 125; on exaction of tribute by barbarians, 132; on fall of Aspar, 224, 225, 226; on Lombards, 242; on illiteracy of Huns, 244; on Odoacer, 275 n. 25; on Wittigis, 276 n. 52; on attitude of R. troops, 285 n. 100

Procopius, usurper, 238

Procula, 132

Profuturus, b. of Braga, 205

Promotus, 124

Prosper of Aquitaine, chronicler, 115, 144

Prudentius, Christian poet, 172, 178

Pulcheria, empress, 148

Pyrenees Mountains, 143; crossed by barbarians, 17, 23; date of crossing, 153; Majorian retreats across, 175; opened treacherously, 178

Quadi, Germanic people, not identical with Sueves, 152, 293 n. 66; lived in Austria and Slovakia, 152; mentioned, 13

Quintanis, town of Noricum, 129; evacuated, not captured, 132

Raetia, R. province in the Alps, 12

Ragnaris, 282 n. 27

Ravenna, 160, 209; besieged by Alaric, 44; revolt at in 475, 62; Wittigis' capital, 77; lost by Os-

trogoths, 81; Byzantines march from in 552, 88; Goths withdraw to, 97; senators massacred at, 102, 106; Felix lynched at, 143

Rebaptism, 127, 205

Recceswinth, Visigothic k. (653–72), 200

Rechiarius, Suevic k. (448–56), 162, 163, 169, 209; death of, 164, 166; coin of, 165, 212; marriage of, 170, 211; captures Lerida, 171; not approached by Hydatius, 179; acts with Bacaudae, 184–85, 212, 220; marries daughter of Theoderic I, 189; attitude to persecution, 196–97; a Catholic, 211; his wife an Arian, 211; character of, 211–12; attacks Tarraconensis, 212; Isidore on, 218

Rechila, s. of Hermeric, 209, 220; father of Rechiarius, 165; takes Merida and Seville, 172; not approached by Hydatius, 179; defeats Andevotus, 182; our ignorance of, 209; Isidore on, 218

Rechimund, Suevic leader, 167

Recimund, 100

Recopolis, 170

rector, 'provincial governor,' 169, 176

Red Sea, 11, 242

Regensburg, 12

Reichenstein, 35

Remismund, Suevic k., 167–68; called Rimismund by Jordanes, 168; marriage of, 170; Theoderic II and, 190; employs Lusidius, 209, 211; Isidore on, 218; alleged relationship with Maldras, 218–19

Retinue, comitatus, 5, 38, 51, 53, 166

rex, barbarian k., 74

Rhegium, 103

Ricimer, patrician, 66, 70, 170, 218

Rimini (Ariminum): besieged by Wittigis, 83; invites Byzantines, 103; cannibalism at, 279 n. 36; demos in, 284 n. 78; mentioned, 88

Rome, 160; captured by Visigoths in 410, 17, 38, 43; plunder of, 46; Colosseum in, 68; entered by Belisarius, 77; defended by Belisarius, 80; Totila at, 82; besieged by Wittigis, 82–83, 98, 99; walls of, 84, 85; uninhabited, 85; twice betrayed, 100, 106; intimidated by fate of Naples, 102; public opinion at in 536, 102; massacre at halted by Totila, 106; trade with Rugi, 122–23; communications with Spain, 149; taken by Vandals, 163; loses control of Spain, 165; R. administration of Galicia, 169, 176; defeated by Asdings in Spain, 173, and by

Rome (*continued*)
    Sueves, 173; last success in Spain, 173; defen-
    sive strategy of, 174; attack barbarians, 178;
    lose Spain, 178, 216; resist Euric, 191; aims of
    in Spain, 193; respected by Spanish bishops,
    197–98; Church of St. Mary in, 198; synod of
    in 465, 198; collaboration with Sueves, 211;
    Geiseric in 145, 218; attitude of towards bar-
    barians, 231
Romulus, father-in-law of Orestes, 61
Romulus Augustulus, emperor (475–76), 56;
    son of Orestes, 61; elevated in 475, 62; inef-
    fective, 63; deposed, 64, 65, 75; insignia of,
    66; not mentioned by Eugippius, 117; alleged
    embassy of to Zeno, 275 n. 14
Rossano. *See* Ruscianum
Roxolani, barbarian people, 13
Rugi, Rugians, Germanic agriculturalists, 3;
    fragmentation of by Huns, 18; near Constan-
    tinople, 18; defeated by Ostrogoths, 19; in
    Italy, 69, 72, 288 n. 33; provide k. for Ostro-
    goths, 96, 125; sick boy of, 116, 122; live
    north of Comagenis, 120; take tribute from
    Favianis, 121; traffic between RE and, 122;
    plundered by brigands, 124; try to go to Italy,
    124, 125, 131; description of, 124–28; con-
    verted to Christianity, 125, 240; Procopius on
    marriage rule of, 125, 170; did not live in
    towns, 131; exact tribute, 131; move to Italy,
    132; anti-R. sentiments, 165; monarchy of,
    165–66
Rumania. *See* Dacia
Ruscianum, 82
Rusticiana, widow of Boethius, 106
Rusticius, 309 n. 45
Rutilius Namatianus, poet, 252

Sabaria, 116
Sabas, Visigothic saint, 48
Sabinus, b. of Seville, 195
Sabiri, nomadic people, 244
Salarian Bridge, 77; Gate, 105
Salla, 190
Salona, 86
Salt, export of banned, 10
Salvian, priest of Marseilles, 23; silent on Bur-
    gundians, 27, 33, 36; on riches of Aquitaine,
    29; on Alamanni, 34, 36; on Bacaudae, 34,
    181, 182; on unrest in Gaul, 34, 187; on weak-
    ness of Vandals, 158; on Saxons, 252

Sambida, Alan k., 25, 34, 35
Samnium, 93, 97
Saragossa, 162, 163, 172, 176, 187; Aracelli near,
    183; Bacaudae at, 185; falls to Euric, 191;
    chronicler of, 192, 193; diocese of, 197; hereti-
    cal bishop of, 221
Sardinia: Vandal attack on, 79; Ostrogothic at-
    tack on, 82, 86, 87, 88, 90
Sarmatians, nomadic people, 14
Sarracens, 191, 241
Sarus, Visigothic freebooter, 35, 44, 45
Savoy (Sapaudia), 24; landowners of, 27, 251;
    Burgundians planted in, 26, 32, 33, 35, 36,
    37, 51, 119; strategic importance of, 29, 32;
    unrest in, 35, 36; influenced other barbarians,
    64
Saxons, Germanic agriculturalists, 3; unimpor-
    tance of sea raids on Gaul, 30; in Britain, 120,
    152, 204; use of slaves, 214; pagans, 240; pi-
    rates, 252; Britons flee from, 304 n. 66. *See*
    West Saxons
Scallabis, 172, 189
Scamarae, barbarian brigands, 121, 123, 285 n. 3
Scampia, 236
Schleswig, 152
Sciri, Germanic agriculturalists, 19; led by Edeco,
    63; in Italy, 64; fight Goths, 224
Sclua, b. of Idanha, 200
Scots, i.e. Irish, 240
Scyths = Scythians = steppe nomads. *See* Nomads
Sea warfare. *See* Warfare at sea
Sebastian, 143, 145, 291 n. 29
Segestes, 42, 233
Segovia, modern Spanish province, 23, 178
Seligenstadt, 14
Sena Gallica (Sinigaglia), sea battle of, 87, 91
Senators: at Rome, 102, 284 n. 77, 285 n. 104;
    wives of captured, 105, 106
Sens, 237
Septimius Severus, emperor (193–211), 7
Serapio, 233
Serapis, 233
Seronatus, 211
Severinus, Saint, 113–33 *passim*; rescues Ambro-
    sius, 63; visited by Odoacer, 63; study of, 113–
    14; alleged to have been consul, 114; date of
    death of, 118; receives appeals for help, 121,
    122; dies in 482, 122; ransoms R. prisoners,
    122; crosses Danube, 123; on deathbed, 123,
    126; Flaccitheus and, 124; does not convert

barbarians, 125–26; consulted by Rugian monarchs, 126; organizes Noricans, 130, 179; relations with Feletheus, 130–31; greatest failure
of, 131; character of, 133; unique achievement
of, 133. *See also* Eugippius

Severn r., 204

Severus, Libius. *See* Libius

Seville: Eastern traders in, 147, 148; communications with Italy, 149–50; taken by Sueves, 162,
164, 172; taken by Vandals, 172, 217; Visigoths in, 194; Sabinus of, 195, 197; Church of
St. Vincent in, 217, 220; end of R. rule in, 296
n. 2. *See also* Isidore

Shields, export of forbidden, 11

Shipbuilding, 11

Sicily: Ostrogoths wish to abandon, 75; Belisarius in, 79; Totila makes for, 86; Ostrogoths
surrender in, 87; lost by Theodahad, 95; under Gothic rule, 100; Geiseric in, 145

Sidimund, 235, 238

Sidonius Apollinaris, man of letters and b.: letters of to Spaniards, 143; friend of Trygetius,
163; our knowledge of, 208; on Sigismer, 209;
knowledge of Suevi, 209; on Theoderic II,
209, 210; knowledge of Burgundians, 210–11;
on Germanic languages, 231; on Saxon pirates, 252–53

Siege warfare, 82–86, 90, 171

Sigeric, 44, 47, 49, 54

Sigismer, 209

Silchester, 215

Siling Vandals, 30, 155, 156; numbers of, 159;
annihilated, 186, 189, 253–54

Silva Candida, 107

Silvanus, b. of Calahorra, 197

Simplicius, pope (468–83), 149, 201–2

Singillio r., 173

Sirmium, 285 n. 101

Sisebut, Visigothic k. (612–21), 298 n. 43

Sisifrid, 235, 281 n. 24

Sisigis, 282 n. 27

Slaves: trade in, 14, 125, 309 n. 62; attitude of,
104; captured from Rugi, 125, and by Rugi,
126, 127; German use of, 214; price of, 247;
escape, 284 n. 92; among Saxons, 305

Slavs, Totila negotiates with, 86

Smuggling, 9, 10; by sea, 11

Soria, modern Spanish province, 23

sors, 'allotment,' 154

Spain: invaded in 409, 17, 142, 146, 219; Visigoths in, in 416–18, 26, 30, 31, 48, 146; Visigoths capitulate in, 38; Aëtius and, 142; communications with Gaul, 143; communications
with Italy, 143, 144, 149, 199, and with the
East, 146–48; trade of, 148, 150; invaded by
Visigoths in 456, 158; population of, 159;
scale of invasion of 409, 159; no longer ruled
by Rome, 178, 216; sea-raiders of, 180; settlements of Visigoths in, in fifth century, 193,
216; Spanish b.s respect for see of Rome,
197–98; Theoderic the Great regent of, 201;
Byzantine occupation of, 206; comparison
with Britain, 212–15

Sparta, 239–40

Spoletium (modern Spoleto), 84, 100, 103, 279
n. 39, 283 n. 47

Stephanus, citizen of Naples, 101

Stilicho, 44

Strabo, geographer, 139, 149

Strategic and tactical goods, export of forbidden,
10, 11

Subsidies paid by the R.s to barbarians, 18; to
Visigoths, 25, 26, 38; to Nobadae, 243

Sueves, Suebi, Suevi, Germanic agriculturalists,
3; remain in Spain, 17; cross Rhine in 406, 17,
130; raid Ostrogoths, 19; invade Gaul, 31; in
Galicia, 140; ambassadors of in Gaul, 144; interrupt communications, 144, 150; invade
Spain in 409, 146, 153; before crossing Rhine,
152; fight Ostrogoths on Danube, 152; invade
Britain, 152; not identical with Quadi, 152;
date of crossing Pyrenees, 153; defeated by
Visigoths in 456, 154; nature of settlement,
154–55; slain in Braga, 157; theirs the first
barbarian kingdom, 157; besieged by Vandals,
157, 165, 171; massacre R.s in Lugo, 158;
mostly settled around Braga, 158; unmentioned by Salvian, 158; numbers of, 159;
raided by Heruls, 159; some accompany Vandals to Africa, 159; foundation of kingdom,
160; before 439 occupy Merida, 162; situation
of in 456, 162; take Seville in 441, 162; conquer Baetica and Carthaginiensis, 162, 182;
heavily defeated by Visigoths, 163, 186; character of kingdom of, 164, 211; monarchy
among, 165–66, 169, 203, 219; division of,
166–67; Aioulf and, 168; "treasure" of, 169;
marriage law of, 170; new town of, 170–71;
capture cities, 171; warfare of, 171; defeat Vitus, 173; R. attack on, 175; Bacaudae and,

Sueves (*continued*)
184; once only defeat Visigoths, 188; Visigothic embassies to, 190, 210; attitude to Catholic Church, 196, 205; extend kingdom, 200–202; enter Lisbon and Coimbra, 201; harass Oporto, 201; at peace in sixth century, 202; expand their kingdom, 202; Arianism of, 203, 205, 240; impose ban on Catholic synods, 205–7; barbarism of, 209

Sunieric, 175, 189, 211; Isidore on, 218

Swaefe, 152

Swaffham, 152

Swavesey, 152

Switzerland, 32–33, 36, 37

Swords, export of banned, 11

Syagrius, friend of Sidonius, 231

Syagrius, Spanish b., 195

Symmachus, consul of 485, 68

Symphosius, 179, 209, 229

Syracuse, Procopius in, 79

Syria, 139

Tacitus, historian, 166, 238, 245

Tadinum, 88

Tagus r., 23, 200, 201

Tarazona, 177, 184, 185, 189, 222

Tarentum, 87, 282 n. 27

Tarraconensis, R. province in northeastern Spain, 143; Bacaudae in, 56, 183–86; communications with Galicia, 144, and with Italy, 144, 146, 149; not allotted to barbarians, 155; escapes conquest by Sueves, 162, 183; raided by Sueves, 161–62, 163; bishops of, 175, 197–99; lost to R.s, 176, 177–78; freedom in, 177, 197; landowners of, 177–78; Visigoths conquer, 191, 193, 216; settlements of Visigoths in, 194; peaceful life of, 199

Tarragona, 144, 146, 149–50, 199; ruinous state of, 162; besieged, 191; lost to Rome, 192; Ascanius of, 197

Tarvisium (Treviso), 98

Teias, last Ostrogothic k. (552), 75, 100, 109

Tencteri, early Germanic people, 12, 13, 14, 15

Terentianus, 149

tertia, one third of a R. estate, 65

Teutoberg Forest, battle in, 7

Thames r., 214

Thebais, 243

Thela, also called Ocla, s. of Odoacer, 71, 276 n. 31

Theodahad, Ostrogothic k. (534–36), Theoderic's sister's s., 74; war aims of, 75; character of, 94; poems addressed to, 94; negotiates with Justinian, 94, 95; deposed and killed, 95; murders Amalasuntha, 95; appealed to by Neapolitans, 101; unpopularity of, 103; coins of, 277 n. 53

Theodemir, Suevic k., 203

Theoderic, Theodoric I, Visigothic k. (418–51), 28; treaty of with Aëtius, 34; career of, 53; father of Thorismud, 54; death of, 54, 189; uses Orientius, 179; policy towards Spain, 188, 193; daughter marries Rechiarius, 189; wife of, 270 n. 35

Theoderic, Theodoric II, Visigothic k. (452–66), 54–56, 233; sacks Spanish cities, 141, 158, 168, 189; related to Rechiarius, 162; defeats Sueves, 163; recognizes Remismund, 167–68; makes R. appointments, 175, 176, 216; confused with Theoderic I by Isidore, 188; attitude of to Spain, 189, 193; murdered, 190; Salla and, 190; our knowledge of, 209; Ajax and, 240

Theoderic, Theodoric, the Great, Ostrogothic k. in Italy (493–526): on *hospitalitas,* 65; indebtedness to Odoacer, 70–71; never appointed Master of Soldiers, 71; sent to Italy by Zeno, 71, 72, 75, 90; patrician, 72; k. of barbarians, 72, 74; takes over Odoacer's powers, 72, 74, 96; limitations on power of, 72–73; negotiates with emperor Anastasius, 73; Belisarius on, 74; popularity among Italians, 74; Procopius on, 74; termed *rex,* 74; wrongly called 'Augustus,' 76; founds a navy, 86; opposes racism, 92–93, 105, 106; delight in warfare, 93; father of Amalasuntha, 93; succeeded by her son Athalaric, 93; statues of destroyed, 106; murders Odoacer, 117; regent of Spain, 201; our knowledge of, 208; wishes for accommodation with Byzantines, 235

Theodora, empress, wife of Justinian, 243

Theodosius, s. of Athaulf and Placidia, 47

Theodosius I, emperor (379–95): settles Visigoths on lower Danube, 29, 39; after Adrianople, 40; splits Visigoths, 41, 44, 45, 48; born in Spain, 178; intolerance of, 232; barbarian troops of, 237

Theodosius II, emperor (408–50), 148

Theophanes, historian, 224, 226

Theophilus, b. of Alexandria, 137, 147

Theotimus, b. of Constantsa (Tomi), 241

Thorismud, Visigothic k. (451–53): son of Theoderic I, 54–55, 56, 189; disliked by Hydatius, 141

Thrace, 43, 226, 239

Thuringians, Germanic agriculturalists, 129, 131, 132

Tibatto, Armorican leader, 32, 35, 267 n. 34

Tiber r., 277 n. 1

Tiberius, later emperor, 3–4, 64

Tiberius II, emperor (578–82), 9, 281 n. 24

Tibur (modern Tivoli), 84, 89, 107

Tiburnia, capital of Noricum Mediterraneum, 117, 128, 130, 132, 286 n. 16

Toledo, 23, 30, 203, 206; First Council of, 229

tolleno, military engine, 8–9

Tomi (modern Constantsa), 241

Tortosa. *See* Dertosa

Totila, Ostrogothic k. (541–52), 233; war aims of, 75; coinage of, 75, 81, 278 n. 19; successes of, 81; also called Baduila, 81, 98; appointed king, 81, 98; strategy of, 82, 86, 90; captures Caesena, Petra, Beneventum, 84; fails to storm Rome, 84; storms Perugia, 84; destroys city walls, 84, 85; policy of blockade, 84, 90; seeks pitched battles, 85, 89, 90; at Centumcellae, 85–86; makes for Sicily, 86; negotiates with Slavs (perhaps) and Franks, 86; warships of, 86, 279 n. 53; depressed by sea fight at Sinigaglia, 87; death of, 88; fights battle of Busta Gallorum, 88; estimate of, 89, 107; planned treachery at Tarvisium, 98; Byzantine desertions to, 99; treatment of prisoners, 99, 106; Rome betrayed to, 100, 106; succeeded by Teias, 100, 109; Italian peasantry and, 104; slaves and, 104, 284 n. 92; on attitude of Italians, 105; halts massacre at Rome, 106; humane treatment of Naples, 106; protects Rusticiana, 106; cruelties of, 107; dances at Busta Gallorum, 108; numbers of men of, 280 n. 61; Spoleto betrayed to, 283 n. 47

Toulouse (Tolosa), 175, 178, 216; Visigothic capital, 23, 34, 44, 176, 208; threatened by Litorius, 53; Thorismud at, 54; Franks destroy kingdom of, 56

Tours. *See* Gregory of Tours

Traders, barbarian, 12, 14; Roman, in Persia, 15, 264 n. 29; in Carthage, 79, 283 nn. 58, 62; as sources of information, 90, 147, 148, cf. 172; St. Ambrose on, 245

Trajan, emperor (98–117), 8

Trajan, general, 238

Trajan, subdeacon, 199

Transylvania, Transylvanian Alps, 16, 25, 41

Trent r., 214

Tribigild, 42, 43, 269 nn. 16, 17

Trier, 234

Tritium (Tricio), 177

Trygetius, 163

Tudela, 177

Tudera, 95

Tufa, 71

Tuluin, 73

Turcilingi, 64, 69

Turonium, 180

Turribius, b. of Astorga, 140, 143, 195, 196

Tuscany, 94, 95

Tuy, 200, 294 n. 74, 301 n. 98

Tyriasso, 271 n. 52

Tyrrhenian Sea, 297 n. 15

Tzanni, 309 n. 52

Ubii, early Germanic people, 5

Ukraine, Ostrogothic empire in, 16, 63

Ulfila, apostle of the Goths, 26, 240, 248

Ulfila, R. officer, 44, 45

Uraias, 106

Urbicus r. (Orbigo), 163

Urbs Vetus (Orvieto), 282 n. 27

Vacho, 152

Vadomarius, 238

Valence (Valentia), 25, 34, 35, 36

Valens, emperor (364–78), and trade with barbarians, 13; admits Visigoths to RE., 16; at war with Visigoths, 25, 234; at battle of Adrianople, 39–40, 45; usurper Procopius and, 238

Valentinian I, emperor (364–75), 24, 123, 237, 238

Valentinian III, emperor (425–55), 65, 143, 163

Valentinus, b. of Silva Candida, 107

Valerian, emperor (253–59), 264 n. 19

Valerianus, 279 n. 53

Valerius Florus, 76

Vandals, Germanic agriculturalists: overthrown by Justinian, 17; cross Rhine in 406, 17, 130; enter Africa, 17, 154; fight Visigoths in Spain, 26; invade Gaul, 31; 'cowardly,' 33; attack on Sardinia, 79; Belisarius' ignorance of, 79; traders and, 79; unaware of Byzantine approach, 79; in Africa, 79, 165; ambassadors in Galicia, 145; surprise Carthage, 145; invade Spain in 409, 146, 153, 178; Leo's campaign against, 148, 223, 225; fleets of in Mediterranean, 150; some remain north of Danube, 152; converted to Christianity, 157; in Baetica, 157; weakness of, 158; numbers of, 159; capture Rome, 163; Majorian's campaign against, 174; attitude of towards Spain, 180, 210; pirates of attack Turonium, 180, 210; Aspar intrigues with, 226; attitude to R., 283 n. 58

Vardulli, 10, 180

Varega (Vareia), 177

Velleius Paterculus, historian, 3, 231

Vendée, 253

Venetia, 96

Venice, 98

Vercingetorix, 89

Veremund, Suevic k., 203

Verona, 44, 96, 99; attitude of to Byzantines, 103

Verulamium, 215

Vetto, 301 n. 1

Victor Tonnennensis, chronicler, 224

Vienna, 113

Vienne, 32

Vigilius, pope (537–55), 106, 107, 204–5, 206

Viminacium, 309 n. 45

Vincentius, 149, 175, 176, 191–92

Vindelicia, 35

Virgil, 56

viri illustres, the highest grade of the R. nobility, 73

Virovesca (modern Briviesca), 177

Viseu, 200

Visigoths, Germanic agriculturalists, 3; defeated by Valens, 13; trade of with RE., 13; allowed by Valens to cross Danube, 16; driven from Gothia by Huns, 16, 17, 38; capture Rome in 410, 17; nobility of collaborate with R.s, 17, 38–57 *passim;* settled in Gaul, 23–37 *passim,* and 44, 48, 50, 153; at war with Valens, 25;

dependence on R. trade, 25; in Wallachia, 25; blockaded in Gaul and Spain in 416, 26; capitulate to R.s in 416, 26, 48; fight Vandals in Spain, 26, 48, 146, 154, 156, 253; wanderings in years 376–418, 26, 48–49; settled on lower Danube, 29; association with R. peasantry, 31; optimates of, 38, 40, 47, 48; their oath in 376, 39–41, 43, 47, 48; driven from Gaul by Constantius, 47; clans of, 51; success of policy, 53–54; attack Bacaudae in 453, 55–56, 185, 189; independence of kingdom of, 56; support Libius Severus, 56; in Spain, 73, 142, 253; fight in western Spain, 137, 158, 186, 199; not generally criticized by Hydatius, 141; sack Spanish cities, 141; some remain north of Danube, 152; severely defeat Sueves, 163; atrocities of in Spain, 164; gain control of Spain, 165; federates in Spain, 184; betray Castinus, 188; occupy Baetica, 189; garrison Merida, 190; settlement of in Spain, 192, 194; overthrow Suevic kingdom, 200; ban Catholic synods, 205–7; negotiate with Suevi, 209; slavery among, 214; destroy Sparta, 239

Vita S. Danielis, 225

Vitus, 173, 174, 182, 184; Visigoths with, 188

Walamer, 18

Wallachia. *See* Dacia, Gothia

Wallia, Visigothic leader, 26, 30, 47–48; tries to cross to Africa, 48; fights in Spain, 48, 146, 154, 156, 161; death of, 52–53

Warfare at sea, 86–87, 91, 98; Byzantine superiority in, 106–7; Goths and, 279 nn. 51, 53

Warni, 168–69

Weapons. *See ballistae,* Bows and Arrows, Breastplates, Shields, Swords, *tolleno*

West Saxons, 168

Whetstones, export of forbidden, 10

Wine, 5; export of forbidden, 10, 245; political use of, 245

Wittigis, Ostrogothic k. (536–40): embassy of to Persia, 74; marches against Belisarius, 77; attacks Rome, 80, 98, 102; fails to see significance of mounted archers, 80, 86, 90; deposed, 81; and siege warfare, 82; besieges Rome, 82–83, and Rimini, 83; tries to use *ballistae,* 83; tactic of, 84; demolishes city walls, 84, 85; his warships, 86; appointed k., 95; character of,

95; defeated by Belisarius, 95; abandons Arianism, 96; patrician, 96; receives an estate, 96; massacres senators at Ravenna, 102, 106; on Gothic treatment of Italians, 105; estimate of, 107; Procopius on, 276 n. 52; numbers of army of, 278 n. 15, 282 n. 28

Worms, capital of Burgundian kingdom on Rhine, 26, 142

Yorkshire, 214

Zachariah of Mitylene, historian, 225–26, 244

Zeno, b. of Merida, 149, 190, 201–2

Zeno, emperor (474–91): sends Ostrogoths to Italy, 19, 71; Odoacer and, 65, 73; Nepos and, 66; ruler of Italy, 66; ambiguous treatment of Odoacer, 67, 274 n. 13; Theoderic and, 72; Belisarius on, 74; dilemma of, 75; accession of, 192; embassy of Odoacer to, 275 n. 14

Zosimus, historian, 124, 174; on destruction of Sparta, 239–40

JACKET DESIGNED BY ANN BOYLE
COMPOSED BY METRICOMP, GRUNDY CENTER, IOWA
MANUFACTURED BY INTER-COLLEGIATE PRESS, INC.,
SHAWNEE MISSION, KANSAS
TEXT AND DISPLAY LINES ARE SET IN BEMBO

Library of Congress Cataloging in Publication Data
Thompson, E. A.
Romans and barbarians.
Includes bibliographical references and index.
1. Rome—History—Germanic invasions, 3d-6th
centuries. I. Title.
DG504.T46   945'.01   81-50828
ISBN 0-299-08700-X   AACR2